Also in the Variorum Collected Studies Series

DAVID ARMITAGE
Greater Britain, 1516–1776: Essays in Atlantic History

G. V. SCAMMELL
Seafaring, Sailors and Trade, 1450–1750:
Studies in British and European Maritime and Imperial History

RICHARD W. UNGER
Ships and Shipping in the North Sea and Atlantic, 1400–1800

MICHAEL NORTH
From the North Sea to the Baltic:
Essays in Commercial, Monetary and Agrarian History, 1500–1800

URSULA LAMB
Cosmographers and Pilots of the Spanish Maritime Empire

S. ARASARATNAM
Maritime Trade, Society and European Influence in Southern Asia, 1600–1800

ASHIN DAS GUPTA
Merchants of Maritime India, 1500–1800

JACK MORRELL
Science, Culture and Politics in Britain, 1750–1870

FRANÇOIS CROUZET
Britain, France and International Commerce: From Louis XIV to Victoria

A. W. SKEMPTON
Civil Engineers and Engineering in Britain, 1600–1830

DAVID L. COWEN
Pharmacopoeias and Related Literature in Britain and America, 1618–1847

DAVID B. QUINN
European Approaches to North America, 1450–1640

JACOB M. PRICE
The Atlantic Frontier of the Thirteen American Colonies and States:
Essays in Eighteenth-Century Commercial and Social History

VARIORUM COLLECTED STUDIES SERIES

Britain, Canada and the North Pacific

Barry M. Gough

Barry M. Gough

Britain, Canada and the North Pacific

Maritime Enterprise and Dominion, 1778–1914

Published in the Variorum Collected Studies Series by

Ashgate Publishing Limited
Gower House, Croft Road,
Aldershot, Hampshire GU11 3HR
Great Britain

Ashgate Publishing Company
Suite 420, 101 Cherry Street,
Burlington, Vermont 05401–5600
USA

Ashgate website: http://www.ashgate.com

ISBN 0–86078–939–X

British Library Cataloguing-in-Publication Data
Gough, Barry M. (Barry Morton), 1938–
  Britain, Canada and the North Pacific: Maritime Enterprise and Dominion,
  1778–1914. – (Variorum Collected Studies Series: CS786)
  1. Great Britain. Royal Navy – Pacific Ocean – History – 19th Century.
  2. Sea-power – Great Britain – History. 3. Pacific Area – Commerce – History –
  19th Century. 4. Pacific Area – Commerce – History – 18th Century.
  5. Pacific Area – Economic Conditions – 19th Century. 6. Pacific Area – Economic
  Conditions – 18th Century. 7. Pacific Area – Discovery and Exploration
  8. Canada – History. I. Title
  382'. 091823

US Library of Congress Cataloging-in-Publication Data
Gough, Barry M.
  Britain, Canada, and the North Pacific : Maritime Enterprise and Dominion,
  1778–1914 / Barry M. Gough.
       p.   cm. – (Variorum Collected Studies Series: CS786).
  Includes index.
  1. Northwest, Pacific – History. 2. Northwest Coast of North America – History.
  3. Canada – History – 1763–1867. 4. Canada – History – 1867–1914. 5. Latin
  America – History – 19th Century. 6. Great Britain – Colonies – America –
  History. 7. Fur trade – Northwest, Pacific – History. 8. Great Britain – Commerce
  – History. 9. Canada – Commerce – History. 10. Great Britain. Royal Navy –
  History. I. Title. II. Collected Studies: CS786.
  F880.G68 2004
  979.5–dc22   2004047618

The paper used in this publication meets the minimum requirements of the
  American National Standard for Information Sciences – Permanence of
  Paper for Printed Library Materials, ANSI Z39.48–1984. ∞ TM

Printed and bound in Great Britain by TJ International Ltd, Padstow, Cornwall

VARIORUM COLLECTED STUDIES SERIES CS786

CONTENTS

This volume contains xviii + 308 pages

ACKNOWLEDGEMENTS

Grateful acknowledgement is made to the following persons, editors, publishers and institutions for their kind permission to reprint the articles included in this volume: The Oregon Historical Society (I, VII); Real Academia Hispano-Americana, Cadiz (II); Australian Academy of the Humanities, Canberra (III, VI); The Peabody Museum of Salem (IV, XIII); The Royal Geographical Society (V); The University of Alberta Press (VIII); the Scott Polar Research Institute (IX); the University of British Columbia (X); Forest History Society (XI); *Journal of Canadian Studies*, Ontario (XII); The Society for Nautical Research (XIV, XVII); *The Journal of Pacific History* (XV); Duke University Press (XVI); *British Journal of Canadian Studies* (XVIII); Butterworth & Co. Ltd (XIX).

INTRODUCTION

The years between the voyage of Captain James Cook of the Royal Navy to the North Pacific Ocean, specifically to Nootka Sound, Vancouver Island, and to Alaska in 1778, and the commencement of the First World War in 1914 constitute a unique epoch of modern history. This was marked by the lifting of the curtain on a complex world hitherto unknown to Europe and to eastern North America, a revealing process by which aboriginal and native populations and economies were disclosed for the first time. This process of disclosure, or revelation, was to bring dramatic and sometimes fatal results to the indigenous societies, at the same time bringing opportunities frequently embraced by these peoples in the face of modernization and development. This era also was distinguished by international rivalry and competing empires, for all the major powers of the late eighteenth century, the nineteenth century and the early twentieth century came to quest for influence within the Pacific rim: Britain, France, Spain, Russia, the United States and Germany, all had a presence in the North Pacific world. Canada, a legatee of British Empire practices and purposes, came forward in this remarkable epoch, exerting a new position as a North Pacific nation, a disposition dictated by its imperial situation, one mirrored in the actions of Australia and New Zealand in the South Pacific and in the waters of South East Asia.

Historians seeking to understand world history or the global experience can find in the history of the Northwest Coast and the North Pacific world a true example of the interrelatedness of peoples and lands – and their links by sea. But they can also find here the essence of British imperial purposes, which in the late eighteenth century (as in later times) were predicated on commercial influence and political power. It has been one of the old conundrums of history to inquire into whether the flag followed trade or vice versa, and it is left to the reader to establish the truth of the maxim that commerce came first and empire second.

This epoch, in large measure, was characterized by the rise and dominance of British commerce on and over the seas. At the time, Britain was the "workshop of the world," the premier manufacturing and trading nation, the first state in capital formation, insurance and banking, and the leading power in seaborne commerce, merchant trading and, not least, naval power. This influence was never absolute but always was held or displayed against international rivals, individual or in combination. Scientific pursuits and hydrographic inquiries fueled British activities in waters near and far, adding additional incentives and obligations to the fundamental commercial and political requirements of a burgeoning empire and influence, formal and informal. What transpired in the North Pacific littoral particularly reflected a new British preoccupation with diversification in merchant trading by sea and laying to rest any prospect of a western entrance to a navigable Northwest Passage.

Even before the War of the American Revolution, the British were formulating this new empire in eastern seas; and the years after the independence of the United States did not in any way deter British expansion, though in regards to the Canadian provinces it forced accommodation. The British revived their Tudor ambitions beyond the great Capes, always preferring trade to dominion. Vincent Harlow analyzed this achievement in his *The Founding of the Second British Empire, 1763–1793*. The first volume, published 1952, he subtitled *Discovery and Revolution*. The second, published 1964, he called *New Continents and Changing Values*.[1] Harlow's theme was the "swing to the east," which he described as the multiplication or enlargement of British interests beyond the Capes. New branches of trades developed, new alliances of trade and commerce were made, new political purposes were embraced, and new international rivalries occurred. At the time of the Nootka Sound crisis, 1790, the British possessed a spirit of commercial adventure that was unbounded. "We are not contending for a few miles [at Nootka Sound] but a large world."[2] This was the view of Henry Dundas, a principal architect of trade policy.

Of the books that have shaped my views as an historian I believe that Harlow's ranks at the top of the list. He was interested in British statecraft in regard to this widening world of British obligations. In particular, he sought to examine how British politicians and the civil servants who guided or managed political affairs, often at the requirement of Parliament and the press, shaped the nature of imperial purposes in eastern seas. A master of sources, public and private, Harlow revealed the diversification of actions beyond the Capes. He was less concerned with colonies of settlement (and the problems of emerging colonies and dominions) than he was with profit and power. In a very certain way he had the equation right, for the nature of the British imperial purpose was the conjunction of profit and power. As Sir Josiah Child, a scion of the East India Company, put it unerringly, "In all things profit and power ought jointly to be considered."[3] At the very end of the

1. Both published in London by Longmans, Green and Co.
2. Adapted from Ronald Hyam's review of the Harlow pair, in *Historical Journal*, 10, 1 (1967): 113–31; quotation, 118.
3. Sir Josiah Child, *A New Discourse of Trade* (2d ed., London, 1694), 114–15; quoted in C. H. Wilson, *Profit and Power: A Study of England and the Dutch Wars* (Oxford: Clarendon Press, 1957), 1. This became my theme in "The 'Adventurers of England Trading into Hudson's Bay': A Study of the Founding Members of the Hudson's Bay Company, 1665–1670," *Albion*, 2, 1 (1970): 35–47. See also my "Lords of the Northern Forest," *History Today*, 41 (September 1991): 49–56.

period marked by my studies as printed in this collection, we find the Earl of
Selborne saying precisely the same thing. During the period when he was First Lord
of the Admiralty, in 1901, he minuted that on its credit and its strength the existence
of Britain rested, and he noted that these were twin pillars of power.[4]

The profit that drove British enterprise in the North Pacific in the age of James
Cook was the sea otter trade, and Cook even suggested the appropriate
requirements for successful prosecution of such a new branch of business. In fact,
by this blueprint of commercial activity, British maritime fur traders were to find
themselves not only in a largely profitable (though wholly risky) business but to
find themselves in a remarkable rivalry with Spain, Russia, France and the United
States. That fur trade drew the British closer to China, specifically Canton, and to
the Portuguese at Macao. It brought the British in touch with the Russians in Alaska
and Kamchatka and with the ever so reluctant Japanese in their home waters and
islands. In due course, by 1800, British maritime fur traders were supplanted in
their dominance by American traders, and of the several reasons for this we count
the following as premier: first, the preoccupation of the British with waging war
against France and, second, the zeal and ship handling capacities of the Yankee
sailing captains.

It did not take long for the directors of British state policy in regards to
commerce and colonies to take note of these doings in the distant North Pacific;
nothing of value (or threat to same) seems to have escaped their attention, voracious
as they were to enlarge their coffers. But often an abundance of riches faced those
who had to frame policy, and more often than not the British shaped their statecraft
within legal and diplomatic means whenever they could but by force and war if
absolutely necessary. Often in the wars of the eighteenth century they acquired
more than they could conceivably use, and often returned bits and pieces to
previous owners or collaborators, hoping thereby to keep a more steady peace for
the future.[5]

---

4. Quoted in Brian McKercher, ed., *Anglo-American Relations in the 1920s: The Struggle for
Supremacy* (Edmonton: University of Alberta Press, 1990); also, Barry M. Gough, "Profit and Power:
Informal Empire, the Navy and Latin America," in Raymond E. Dumett, ed., *Gentlemanly Capitalism and
British Imperialism: The New Debate on Empire* (London: Addison Wesley Longman, 1999), 68–81.

5. Perhaps I might be allowed a personal note here. My research work at the master's level University
of Montana, 1966, was to unravel the secrets about the respective policies of keeping Canada or keeping
the Sugar Islands in the peace arrangements of 1763. The theme has often charmed students. The central
reality was that Britain wanted Canada in order to protect the northern boundaries of the Thirteen
Colonies from French attack. British motivations were entirely strategic. See Barry M. Gough, *British
Mercantile Interests in the Making of the Peace of Paris, 1763: Trade, War, and Empire* (Lewiston, N.Y:
Edwin Mellen, 1992).

The pursuit of the sea otter pelt and the increasing engagement of the British in imperial rivalries on the Northwest Coast and in the North Pacific brought a new requirement for the premier maritime state: the necessity to chart the waters of the Pacific and its rim and islands. The greatest legacy of the British imperial experience is the charting of the seas for safe navigation and the encouragement of seaborne trade, and to the North Pacific the British sent their explorers and surveyors. The tasks were daunting and difficult but by the end of our period charts and sailing directions had been produced giving a modicum of data suitable for safe navigation, though on shipwreck-dominated shores (such as western Vancouver Island) natural hazards still led navigators to destruction. The British found themselves working cooperatively with the Spanish in the examination and disclosure of the hydrographic details of the Northwest Coast, but unlike the Spanish they were completely willing to share their findings with the public. This was a feature of the evolving free trade world that the British in their wisdom were promoting. Imperial science lay at the root of the quest for geographical details, and science was the handmaid of empire, just as surveying was the harbinger of commerce. The British knew these things implicitly and they invested mightily in scientific pursuits to make seaborne commerce safe and profitable. They also worked strenuously to establish friendly arrangements with indigenous peoples, and at Vancouver Island, Nootka Sound specifically, they took up the task begun by Cook and extended by George Vancouver as partners with indigenous peoples.

Spain and Russia were the two imperial rivals for territorial control in the North Pacific, just as the United States was the rival for commercial dominance. By the Nootka Sound crisis Britain acquired a right of trade and occupation on the Northwest Coast. Spain's exclusive claim to trade and dominion was ended by this event. Russia, already present in the North Pacific as a trading and territorial power, posed less of a difficulty to British traders and statesmen than did the Spanish, for the Russians needed British supplies, principally foodstuffs. Even so, the Russians treated the British as interlopers and acted with guarded suspicion. That rivalry, one that embraced scientific discovery, lasted into the early nineteenth century and cast a long shadow over the search for the Northwest Passage. British traders reached the Northwest Coast from Canton and Macao but they also arrived from Madras and Bombay or directly from London or Bristol. The links of the Northwest Coast with the wider world were extensive, unlimited: even New South Wales was connected to Vancouver Island by a fragile political and commercial connection in the 1790s, though a scheme to introduce convict settlement to Vancouver Island never reached fruition.

The British first came to the Northwest Coast by sea, but by 1793 the spirited fur trader and explorer Alexander Mackenzie of the Northwest Company had crossed overland from the Athabasca country (now northern Alberta) to Pacific tidewater. This conjunction of British enterprises by sea and by land spelled the beginning of British transcontinental dominion, itself presaging the Canadian confederation. The politics of British imperial expansion overland were tied invariably to the struggle between the Canadian traders based on Montreal, of whom Mackenzie was one, and the Gentlemen Adventurers of England Trading into Hudson's Bay, otherwise known as the Hudson's Bay Company, founded 1670, headquartered in London. The corporate wars between these firms is an integral part of the westward expansion of Canada, and long before the United States had extended its reach to the Pacific Coast of North America the Canadian traders had unlocked the secrets of the fur trade and exposed the difficulties of transportation and trade across the Rocky Mountains. Gradually the mouth of the Columbia River came to replace Nootka Sound as the focal point of British statecraft, and the reorganization of coastwise trade brought about the recognition of southern Vancouver Island as the base of steam navigation. The Treaty of Washington, 1846, established a border between the United States and British dominion on the Northwest Coast, and the British set up colonies at Vancouver Island and the mainland of British Columbia in 1849 and 1858 respectively. British naval power was influential on this far shore in a number of ways, and imperial purposes worked themselves out in unique ways, such as the use of forests to enhance sea power. With its abundant forests and superb types of timber Vancouver Island became a source of naval strength in supplies, besides becoming a location from which a new staple trade, in timber exports, developed.

Until the railway age the Northwest Coast constituted one of the world's farthest shores for European states. The finding of a Northwest Passage always had a seductive lure, but as events were to prove it was always a hoax in southern latitudes. Mackenzie disproved its existence, and Captain George Vancouver, RN, did likewise. But distance shaped colonial attitudes and disposition. Until the Panama Canal was completed, just on the eve of the First World War, all seaborne commerce had to go via Cape Horn or the Cape of Good Hope. The distances were remarkable and the times of transit even more so.

From the Tudor era, statesmen and commercial interests watched for the opportunities they knew awaited them in Spain's crumbling New World. Piracy and operations of intrigue aided the British in their unstated goal and helped foment revolution in Latin America. Beginning in the first decade of the nineteenth century, British statesmen depended on commercial activity (including banking and credit arrangements), consular representation, and naval influence to bolster their influence in Central and South America. The passages to the Northwest Coast from say London or Bristol brought British mariners into connection with Latin American ports. In this same epoch the growth of British trade with Latin America was remarkable and significant and the stabilization of republics in a continent noted for upheavals meant that the British paid special attention to Brazil and the many former parts of the Spanish Empire in America. British sea power was signally significant in the winning of Brazil's independence and the keeping of its security. Similarly British sea power remained influential in the commercial activities and financial wealth of the former Spanish colonies. The conveyance of specie, that is bullion, was a task performed by the Royal Navy to the commercial benefit of local merchants and bankers and British capitalists and managers. In this vast informal empire the British through their naval influence provided a remarkable force for stability. The sending of a sloop of war was powerfully effective, representative of abundant British naval power. The influence of the City of London spread directly outwards from the home islands through the agencies of the British merchant marine and the ships of the Royal Navy that provided their protection and assurance. The specie was conveyed in British warships under strict regulation, and the whole forms a unique chapter in world commercial management.

Even before the Canadian Pacific Railway reached Pacific tidewater at Port Moody, east of Vancouver, British Columbia, 1885, a strong colonial economy had developed in Vancouver Island and the mainland. In 1871 the United Colony of British Columbia became a province of the Dominion of Canada, and the federal structure of the Canadian confederation now supplanted the former British imperial edifice. For the next two decades or so Canadian purposes marched side by side with British imperial aspirations and activities. Once the railroad became more than a paper dream Canada found itself with a Pacific portal, ushering in a new era of Canadian aspirations and activities. Until 1914 Canada's Pacific enterprises were locked into Britain's because of political, strategic and commercial reasons. In that era Canada's realities overlapped with those of Britain and vice versa. Yet there was a growing realization, exhibited by Canadians in Halifax, Montreal, Toronto and Winnipeg of a new destiny in the Pacific for the young dominion. British Columbians knew this already, but in this early national period of British Columbia's history the national dream of having a place in the Pacific world became a reality. Because Britain had developed a naval base and arsenal of power at Esquimalt, near Victoria, over many years (Esquimalt was used first by a Royal Navy vessel in 1846 and was Pacific Station headquarters intermittently, first in 1862) Vancouver Island truly became an "anchor of empire" in the Canadian west much as Halifax, founded 1749, was for Canada's eastern seaboard.

British naval power as exercised on the Northwest Coast in the late nineteenth century represented the *Pax Britannica* in all its features. For one thing it encouraged and facilitated seaborne commerce and protected it against piracy; it also promoted lawful trade. By the same token it encouraged alliances with native peoples and implicitly supported Christian missions and education or training of native peoples. It further kept Russian and American rivals or interlopers at a distance. Not least, it introduced systems, political and legal, which were regarded at the time as advantageous, beneficial and productive. Nowadays that would all go under the heading of "imperialistic" or even "colonial" and would be much disparaged in many, though not all, quarters. In due course, the Province of British Columbia, like the Government of Canada of which it is a component and prominent part, would come to wear the mantle of the British Empire on the Northwest Coast. I view the progression as a natural one, far less dramatic in its shifts from the earlier era. As I have come to see Canada as a successor state to the British Empire in North America so too have I come to realize how the first century and a half of British influence in western North America were a natural opening to the longer experience of Canada and the Pacific rim. Even today Canada continues to extend its naval influence from Esquimalt and its commercial and political influence in the Pacific is considerable.

As will be seen from the several essays that form this collection my general argument is that commercial interests, or combinations of such business groupings, were a primary determinant in what the British later undertook as policy. Profit lay at the root of imperial expansion – and was far more important in these lands and seas than colonization and settlement. The latter was a development in British Columbia at a far later era, post-dating the establishment of British colonial administration at Vancouver Island and British Columbia. Practitioners of imperial statecraft responded to commercial pressures. In fact, in formulating their policies British ministers and diplomats had to take into careful consideration all such commercial purposes and influences; but at the same time they were mindful of what rivals were doing – and what threats were possible, even likely, from rival commercial interests and nations. Thus commerce – and its protection – brought state formation of policy. Tied to this was a fear of rival advances and preemption; this, in turn, the British developed their own form, practiced very successfully, of preemptive imperialism. Elsewhere I have written about the British Columbia frontier as a variant of the thesis advanced by R.E. Robinson and J. Gallagher on the "imperialism of free trade."[6] British imperial expansion in British Columbia was more about protecting territorial claims from United States expansion, both real and

---

6. Barry M. Gough, "The Character of the British Columbia Frontier," *BC Studies*, 32 (Winter 1976– 77): 28–40. Barry M. Gough, "'Turbulent Frontiers' and British Expansion: Governor James Douglas, the Royal Navy and the British Columbia Gold Rushes," *Pacific Historical Review*, 41, 1 (February 1972): 14–32. But British policies as worked out on this western margin of empire also were an extension of British practices in turbulent gold fields. See, on this, Barry M. Gough, "Keeping British Columbia British: The Law and Order Question on a Gold Mining Frontier," *Huntington Library Quarterly*, 38, 3 (May 1975): 269–80. Not least British policies focused on the perpetual problem of pacifying the Indians and satisfying their wants. On this, see Barry M. Gough, "Indian Policies of Great Britain and the United States in the Pacific Northwest in the mid-Nineteenth Century," *Canadian Journal of Native Studies*, 2, 2 (1982): 320–37.

imagined, than it was about establishing formal empire in succession to informal empire.

In order to extend such formal empire as was required, the British were obliged to unravel state policy from the corporate empire (and formal licenses and charter) of the Hudson's Bay Company. From the time of Captain Cook's visit to the colonial era of British Columbia commercial interests, individual traders, then the North West Company, and then the Hudson's Bay Company in turn pressed upon the British government the need for protection. The sending of British warships (the first in 1813 to the mouth of the Columbia River) was one form of metropolitan response. Another was British statecraft as projected by British diplomats in relation to their United States counterparts. The whole process was abundantly successful, for it precluded the United States from putting the Stars and Stripes on all lands stretching north from the mouth of the Columbia River to the Gulf of Alaska. Similarly this same process allowed for the British colonies to become, in 1871, the Province of British Columbia of Canada. In short, a combination of commercial impulses, British ministerial (and parliamentary) responses to the same, and British statecraft (through naval posturing and direct diplomacy with the Americans) were the form of British imperialism worked out in regards to this particular imperial frontier. This locale was unique in British imperialism, no doubt, and the same could be said for many other locales – in Africa, India, Australia and New Zealand. These, taken together, defy easy, overarching definitions or descriptions of imperialism.

The essays in this volume are placed under two headings. The first is James Cook and British Enterprise in the North Pacific. The second is *Pax Britannica*: South America, Canada, and the Pacific. The first is marked by those commercial impulses and activities described above. The focus is on British activities and foreign competition right down to and including the Oregon question, ended in 1846. I have portrayed the quest for the sea otter, British commercial activities and Canadian overland developments as part of a larger process along the lines that Harlow described. And I have attempted to show how Canada – and the modern world – came to possess these territories and trades: in short, how they were embraced by imperial purposes and brought into our present-day understanding of the past.

The second cluster of articles takes us to farther lands and seas, into the politics and decolonization of Latin American states (including Alta California) and into the processes whereby Canada as a new-found Pacific nation sought means to extend its own interest into that Pacific world that the British had made so much their own. The Royal Navy was a principal force in this projection, even after British Columbia became a province. That service's influence was world wide, and in that vast desert of waters its influence in various islands, archipelagoes and littorals was mighty. For that reason I have included here the archival guide I prepared many years ago about the records of the Royal Navy's Pacific Station. The theme of this second section is not only the diversification of commerce and nations but the protective and defining role of sea power (and naval force) in the emergence of Canada as a Pacific nation. The maritime foundations of the Canadian state, so abundantly clear in the history of Newfoundland, Nova Scotia and Quebec are similarly revealed in the history of Canada's Pacific province. And so with these concluding chapters we are brought full circle, and the end result, it is hoped, is an appreciation and description of how commerce backed by statecraft and its instrument of naval power forged underpinnings of the Canadian state and gave protection to Canadian commercial endeavors that were based on the empire of the St. Lawrence and on Hudson Bay.

BARRY M. GOUGH

Ontario, 2003

PUBLISHER'S NOTE

The articles in this volume, as in all others in the Variorum Collected Studies Series, have not been given a new, continuous pagination. In order to avoid confusion, and to facilitate their use where these same studies have been referred to elsewhere, the original pagination has been maintained wherever possible.

Each article has been given a Roman numeral in order of appearance, as listed in the Contents. This number is repeated on each page and is quoted in the index entries.

This work is dedicated to
Willard Ireland, Margaret Ormsby and
Vincent Harlow, pathfinders in rigorous documentary
evaluation and all blessed with wide visions.

I

The Northwest Coast In Late 18th Century British Expansion

On July 4, 1776, delegates from the Thirteen Colonies adopted the Declaration of Independence. Two days later, across the North Atlantic, the Lords of the Admiralty signed instructions for Captain James Cook to undertake a voyage to the Northwest Coast of North America. These two momentous events were not unrelated, because by 1776 two great empires were in conflict: one, emanating from growing cities on the eastern seaboard of North America, was penetrating the continent and extending its oceanic commerce; the other, originating from London, was increasing its role in all seas and nearly all continents. Cook's instructions made no explicit reference to the developing troubles with the Thirteen Colonies. This was because the British government feared no American reprisals at sea. As the Secretary at War, Lord Barrington, put it in December, 1774, "A conquest by land is unnecessary when the country can be reduced first to distress, and then to obedience, by our Marine totally interrupting all commerce and fishing and even seizing all the ships in the ports with very little expense and bloodshed."[1] He reasoned that by stifling American seaborne trade the rebel Americans would be reduced to submission. In doing so, he failed to understand that the roots of American colonial strength "lay within the North American Continent beyond the reach of British sea power."[2]

Nonetheless, during the War of the American Revolution and the War of the French Revolution, British interest in trade and territory in distant seas and continents continued. Chief among the areas of concern to the British was the Northwest Coast of North America, a vast quarter of the North American Continent heavily populated by vigorous Indian tribes. This was the ocean's farthest coast for British merchant-

Barry M. Gough, "The Northwest Coast in Late 18th Century British Expansion," in *The Western Shore: Oregon Country Essays Honoring the American Revolution*, edited by Thomas Vaughan (Portland: Oregon Historical Society and American Revolution Bicentennial Commission of Oregon, 1975). © 1975, reprinted with permission.

I

men and sloops of war. However, the British maintained a presence there during the late 18th century in order to develop trade in eastern seas and also to gain an advantage over their European rivals—the Russians, the French and especially the Spanish[3]—all of whom had an interest in this territory. In this relative backwater the British were observing the famous maxim of Sir Josiah Child of the East India Company during the late 17th century, that in all things "Profit and Power ought jointly to be considered." It was for this joint reason that the Northwest Passage was of great potential importance.

I

Ever since the 15th century Florentine geographer Toscanelli had proposed a route to Asia by sailing west through passages separating habitable lands, Europeans were captivated by the idea. As the voyage of Drake in 1579 to the California coast—which he called Nova Albion—had shown, the English were clearly no exception. Tudor geographers thought the legendary Strait of Anian to be the western mouth of the passage. The strait appeared on maps in new places with further discoveries. British geographical theorists, commercial promoters and artful strategists kept the legend alive. On their maps they changed the position of the strait and other bodies of water in the North American Continent as it suited their purposes and as they learned of new discoveries from French, Spanish, American and Russian sources.

By the 1770s the problem of the Northwest Passage remained unsolved. A reward of £20,000, offered by the British parliament after 1745 for finding a route through Hudson Strait to eastern seas, stood unclaimed.[4] As a further inducement, the British government, on pressure from the Royal Society, decided to extend the reward to include ships of the Royal Navy. In 1775 a new Act specified that £20,000 would be paid for discovering a passage north of 52° and £5,000 to the crew of the first ship sailing within one degree of the North Pole, as "such approaches may greatly tend to the discovery of a communication between the Atlantic and Pacific oceans."[5] The Act, it must be pointed out, mentioned that such a discovery would have "many advantages to commerce and science." This announced a shift in motives of geographical exploration away from those of the 1745 Act, which stated the discovery would be "of great benefit and advantage to the trade of this kingdom."[6]

The shift to include science as a motive for discovery reflects the pressures of the Royal Society on government. Already instrumental

48

in sending Captain Cook, R.N., on his first voyage to the Pacific and involved in a variety of endeavors related to exploration, the Society, through its various leaders, was close to the seats of power in Whitehall. Daines Barrington, a member of the Society's council and a jurist, naturalist, antiquarian and geographer, had knowledge through his Swiss scientific correspondent Samuel Engel that the north polar sea was ice free, an idea existing as early as Tudor times. In 1775 and 1776 Barrington wrote a series of pamphlets elaborating the idea, while at the same time he pressed on his friend the Earl of Sandwich, First Lord of the Admiralty, the necessity of sending a naval expedition to find a passage to the East Indies via the North Pole. These pressures were effective, for in 1773 the Admiralty dispatched two vessels, *Racehorse* and *Carcass,* under command of Captain Constantine Phipps, F.R.S., for the purpose. Phipps, assisted by ice pilots from the Greenland whaling fleet, found the ice barrier north of Spitzbergen to be impassable, and he returned to London full of pessimism. Barrington, ever full of optimism, thought Phipps had been sent in a "bad year" and continued to lobby Sandwich on the subject of polar exploration and now revived the idea of a naval expedition to find an approach to the Northwest Passage from the Pacific.

Barrington's new plan, which we may say gave birth to Cook's third voyage, was adopted by the council of the Royal Society in February 1774.[7] Subsequently, on February 17, the secretary of the Society wrote to the Admiralty as follows:

The Council of the Royal Society having last year submitted a proposal to your Lordship, for making discoveries towards the North Pole (which was honored with your approbation), are now emboldened to lay another plan before the Board of Admiralty, for the protection of Science in general, and more particularly that of Geography.

They conceive that a Ship, or Ships, fitted out either in Europe or the East Indies, may be victualled at the Port of Canton in China; from whence the run to the Northern parts of New Albion will not be, probably, longer than from England to Jamaica: such vessels therefore (even if no refreshment could be procured on the Coast of North America) might proceed up the Northwestern side of that continent, so as to discover whether there is a passage into the European Seas.[8]

Although the Admiralty was unable for financial reasons to undertake this very expensive project, the Royal Society at least had the Admiralty's assurance that an expedition would be fitted out when Cook returned from the Pacific, probably in 1775.[9] This decision reflects the conjoint interests of the Royal Society and Admiralty in the pursuit of science and national honor, and is also a testament to

I

Captain James Cook. Portrait at National Maritime Museum, Greenwich.

the determination of Barrington and the sagacity of Sandwich. And Cook's third voyage, like its predecessors, was to represent in a balanced fashion these inseparable goals of science and national advancement.

The 1775 Act had specified that the search was to be concentrated north of the 52nd latitude. This can be explained on the basis of Russian geographical exploration, on new but not necessarily accurate cartography, and on the findings of Samuel Hearne in the employ of the Hudson's Bay Company. In 1774, a new book, entitled *An Account of the New Northern Archipelago, Lately Discovered by the Russians in the Seas of Kamchatka and Anadir,* was written by Jacob von Stahlin, the Secretary of the Russian Academy of Sciences.[10] Originally published in German, it was translated into English in the same year. Stahlin's map of Russian discoveries, published in the volume, was a startling reworking of the geographical theories of Gerhard Friedrich Muller, who had been with Bering and Chirikov in their great discoveries of Bering Strait and Alaska. Muller's map of 1761, regarded in England as the best authority, showed New Albion and Kamchatka to be firmly delineated and the Northwest Coast of North America and Alaska in their presently-known form to be vaguely defined. Stahlin's chart, by contrast, erroneously showed "Alaschka" to be a large island, part of the Northern or Aleutian Archipelago, and separate from the North American Continent. The authority for this map rested in the supposedly accurate surveys of Lieutenant Synd of the Russian Admiralty Office in 1764-1766.

The British reaction to Stahlin's map was generally condemnatory. However, this did not remove the suspicion that a passage might reach north and east from Alaska to the Polar Sea, as Stahlin had proposed. Might not such a waterway join with the partly frozen Arctic Sea discovered by Samuel Hearne, the fur trader-explorer who in 1771 had made his way to the mouth of the Coppermine River? Moreover, would not the findings of Hearne's expedition from Fort Churchill to 71° 55' N without crossing a large body of water confirm that there was no hope of a Northwest Passage in low latitudes? On the evidence, we can say that the influence Hearne's discoveries had on Cook's instructions was great indeed: Admiralty, Hudson's Bay Company and Royal Society were in close cooperation on this subject, and all were anxious to put an end to a riddle of sizable dimensions.

Cook's objective, according to his instructions of July 6, 1776, was to find a Northwest Passage from the Pacific. He was to enter the Pacific by way of the Cape of Good Hope, touch at islands in 48° S

I

in the Indian Ocean near Mauritius, possibly New Zealand, and then Otaheite or the Society Islands. After refreshing his crews and taking on wood and water, Cook was to leave those islands in or before February, 1777, and "proceed in as direct a course as you can to the coast of New Albion, endeavouring to fall in with it in the latitude of 45° 00' north; and taking care in your way thither not to lose any time in search of new lands, or to stop at any time in search of new lands, or to stop at any you may fall in with unless you find it necessary to recruit your wood and water."[11] Cook was not to land on any portion of Spanish lands on the western portions of the Americas unless if by accident or if absolutely necessary; and if he did meet any inhabitants or Spanish subjects, or of any other European nation, he was not to disturb or give offense to them.

In reference to actual discovery of the passage, Cook's instructions specified that upon his arrival on the coast of New Albion he was to put into the first convenient harbor for wood, water and refreshments and

then to proceed northward along the coast as far as the latitude of 65°, or farther, if you are not obstructed by lands or ice, taking care not to lose any time in exploring rivers and inlets, or upon any other account, until you get into the before-mentioned latitude of 65°, where we could wish you to arrive in the month of June next. When you get that length you are very carefully to search for and to explore such rivers or inlets as may appear to be of a considerable extent and pointing towards Hudson's Bay or Baffin's Bay.

If, from his observations or on the basis of information received from native inhabitants, Cook learned of the certainty, or even probability, of a passage, he was to proceed in his ships or boats as he thought necessary, and attempt to discover it. But if certain that no passage existed, he was to repair to Petropavlovsk or Kamchatka for the winter. In the spring of the following year Cook, at his discretion, could make a further search for a passage, either to the northeast or northwest, and proceed, as earlier directed, to England "by such route as you may think best for the improvement of geography and navigation, repairing to Spithead with both sloops, where they are to remain till further orders."

Cook had orders not to interfere with Spanish claims to the Northwest Coast. Nonetheless, with the consent of the inhabitants, he was to take possession in the name of George III of "convenient situations in such countries as you may discover, that have not already been discovered or visited by any other European power, and to distribute among the inhabitants such things as will remain as traces and testi-

52

monies of your having been there. But if you find the countries so discovered are uninhabited you are to take possession of them for His Majesty by setting up proper marks and inscriptions as first discoverers and possessors." This implied that Cook was to extend British claims whenever and wherever possible, but not at the risk of conflicting with those of other European nations or of native tribes not agreeable to such an act of possession.

While Cook was to explore the Pacific Coast for a sea lane to the Arctic, a complementary attempt was to be made from Baffin Bay. In 1776, Lieutenant Richard Pickersgill was sent in the armed brig *Lion* to protect British whalers in Davis Strait from American privateers, capture any vessels belonging to the rebellious American colonies, and explore the coasts of Baffin Bay preparatory to sending guides to help Cook find his way eastwards.[12] By the time he reached the whaling grounds, the British whalers had already left for home. Pickersgill, however, faced difficult conditions. He became ill, was prone to heavy drinking, and the *Lion* returned to England. Early in the following year, she was recommissioned under command of Lieutenant Walter Young, who was given detailed instructions that indicate that his voyage was to be in conjunction with Cook's. Young was to find if Hearne's Polar Sea could be reached from Baffin Bay and also if the natives of that bay used copper.[13]

Young's voyage was as disappointing as that of Pickersgill, and for no known reason he ignored his instructions and abandoned the project. Neither man was the quality of Cook; neither had the strength or determination to discover and chart the eastern access to the passage at the time when Cook himself was in the Pacific completing an even more difficult part of the project.

Cook, in the meantime, had left from Plymouth on July 12, 1776, in H.M.S. *Resolution* accompanied by H.M.S. *Discovery*. The details of their voyage through the South Atlantic and into the Indian and Pacific oceans by way of the Cape of Good Hope are too lengthy to recount here. But enroute to the Northwest Coast Cook called at the Cape, New Zealand, the Friendly Islands, Tahiti, the Sandwich (later Hawaiian) Islands, and made a landfall on "the long looked for Coast of new Albion" at daybreak, March 7, 1778.[14] Cook had come close to the Admiralty's suggested landfall of 45° N latitude; indeed, Cook's newly-named Cape Foul Weather, descriptive of the very bad weather soon met with, was in 44° 50' N. On the following day, light airs permitted Cook to range along the coast, but occasional squally weather forced a change of plans, and a steady examination of the

I

Resolution and *Discovery* off Oregon's coast, 1778. Hewitt Jackson painting (private collection, used by permission).

coast could not be undertaken. On March 11, Cook was in latitude 43° 44', near where the Spaniard Martin de Aguilar was supposed to have found Cape Blanco in 1603. "It is worth observing," Cook recorded in his journal, "that in the very latitude we were in, Geographers have placed a large entrance, or Strait, the discovery of which they ascribe to the same Captain, whereas nothing more is mentioned in the Voyage than seeing a large River,[15] which he would have entered but was prevented by the currents."[16]

Heavy winds and weather from the west and northwest forced Cook away from the shore. In any case, he had made his examination of the coast in and around 45° N latitude, as the Admiralty had suggested, and could now move north in search of a place of refreshment and refit. On the 22nd he was off Cape Flattery, the southern entrance point of access to the Strait of Juan de Fuca, which Cook, for unspecified reasons, did not see. "It is in the very latitude we were now in," he wrote in his journal in words that have been often quoted, "where geographers have placed the pretended *Strait of Juan de Fuca,* but we saw nothing like it, nor is there the least probability that iver any such thing exhisted."[17]

Perhaps the growing darkness of night prevented Cook from sailing into the strait. Had he done so, he might, in his search for a harbor as specified in his instructions, have revealed the insularity of Vancouver Island, in which case he would probably have spent much time in the inland waters, especially Puget Sound, Georgia Strait and the waterways to the northward. As it was, and in the gales, Cook kept off from the land; and on March 29, he reached Point Estevan in latitude 49° 23', which had been visited four years earlier by the Spanish explorer Juan Perez in the corvette *Santiago.*

Cook could see several indentations on the coastline, and would have preferred to have entered what is now known as Kyuquot Sound. But he could not "fetch it" in the winds and entered Nootka Sound instead. The *Resolution* was then in great need of water and Cook decided to anchor and did so at the entrance to Zuciarte Channel.

The Spaniards or other Europeans had already been to Nootka, Cook knew, because of the presence of iron and other metals. This accounts for his not having made a formal declaration of possession. But he remained there long enough—almost a month, from March 29 to April 26—to get a substantial impression of the place and its inhabitants. His journals, available to us in printed form, tell in splendid detail of the geographical features of Nootka Sound, its fine woods well suited for use as ships' spars and decking, its villages, animals,

I

inhabitants, produce, manufactures, foods, artistry, equipment, religion, government and language. Cook found the site quite different from places of his earlier discovery. As Professor Beaglehole has written: "A windy and a rainy place this was, none the less interesting; part of a continental coast so very different from that of Cook's other continent, Australia; a harbour so very different from the warm Polynesian bays; with a vegetation so different from the familiar breadfruit and hibiscus and plantain; a people so almost totally different from the brown and flower-decked islanders."[18]

His voyage north to the Alaskan coast was not easy: heavy weather meant that Cook was driven westwards of the Queen Charlotte Islands, Prince of Wales Island and even the Alexander Archipelago. Finally, in latitude 57° 3' N, near Cape Edgecumbe and the present day Sitka, he began to seek out the coastline. This was adjacent to the pretended strait of Admiral Bartholomew de Fonte or river Los Reyes, supposedly discovered by de Fonte for Spain in 1640 in order to forestall Boston navigators trying to attempt a passage from Hudson Bay to the Strait of Anian. Cook wanted nothing to do with de Fonte's fabrications. "For my own part," he recorded, "I give no credet to such vague and improbably stories, that carry their own confutation along with them nevertheless I was very desirous of keeping the Coast aboard in order to clear up this point beyond dispute; but it would have been highly imprudent for me to have ingaged with the land in such exceeding tempestious weather, or to have lost the advantage of a fair wind by waiting for better weather."[19]

His subsequent explorations on the coast of Alaska, especially in Cook's Inlet, proved similarly unrewarding for finding a Northwest Passage. For Stahlin's map he had nothing but disgust, and he must have felt duped.[20] Alaska, Cook had shown, was no island, but rather a large promontory extending west and north and then northeast from Bering Strait. By July 18, Cook had penetrated into the Bering Sea as far as Icy Cape, Alaska. By the 29th, he had crossed over to the Siberian shore and then made his way to the Hawaiian Islands, which he thought, quite correctly, would be the best place to winter, Petropavlovsk on the Kamchatka Peninsula being unsuitable.[21] In an unfortunate train of events in which Cook seems to have lost his temper, he was killed on February 14, 1779, by the Hawaiians.

Cook's last voyage might be interpreted as one of defeat: defeat in finding a Northwest Passage, defeat in penetrating the Bering Sea, and defeat in Cook's death. But to interpret it as such would surely be wrong. Cook's voyage was a splendid achievement: the rough outline of the Northwest Coast had been defined, several myths had been disproven, and new scientific data had been compiled. Perhaps the most important result was the discovery that the beautiful pelts of the sea otter could be purchased for paltry amounts at Nootka and elsewhere on the coast and then sold for fantastic prices in Asian markets. The subsequent rise of the great maritime fur trade was to change forever the remoteness of the Northwest Coast as traders from various nations sought easy profits. Thus, Cook's third voyage, which had been tied up with finding a means for British commercial aggrandizement in the Pacific, to say nothing of political, strategic and scientific considerations, brought on, in spite of the non-discovery of a Strait of Anian, a new commercial development very beneficial to British trading and therefore national interests.

II

The growth of British interests in eastern seas in the late 18th century, "the Swing to the East," as Professor Vincent T. Harlow called it, reflected two main motives for British interest in the Southern oceans.[22] One was the great voyages of discovery, especially those of Cook. These showed the need for gateways into the Pacific free from Spanish interference. They also revealed that bases suitable for refit, refreshment and repair would be required. For these reasons, the Cape of Good Hope, the Falkland Islands, St. Helena and other places took on a new strategic significance in British policy. The second reason for British interest in eastern seas was commercial. As Harlow said, the Second British Empire was founded on "a conscious revival of an ambition [dating from Tudor times] to open up new fields of commerce in the Pacific and the South China Seas."[23]

The evidence is overwhelming that in the late 18th century discovery was the handmaiden of commerce; and no more clearly can this be seen than in the case of Cook's third voyage and the subsequent development of the international maritime fur trade. As early as 1740 the Russian navigator Vitus Bering had crossed the Pacific from the Kamchatka shore to Alaska and had begun the Russian maritime fur trade. He and his followers erected advance posts for trade on the Okhotsk seaboard, the Kamchatka Peninsula and the Aleutian Islands. Bering's second Kamchatka expedition, in 1741-1742, yielded 1,500 to 1,800 sea otter pelts. These were worth 80 to 100 rubles each at Kyakhta, and defrayed a small portion of the cost of the expedition.[24] Bering's men were perhaps the first Europeans to profit by this trade, and subsequently a large number of Russian promyshlenniks or fur

Nootka Sound native habitations, as seen by Cook. (Cook's *Voyages*.)

hunters were drawn to the Commander, Kurile and Aleutian Islands. Bering's importance in inaugurating this branch of commerce must not be forgotten. As Cook, who met some of these Russian traders on the Alaska coast in 1778 noted,

. . . never was there greater respect paid to the memory of any distinguished person, than by these men to that of Bering. The trade in which they are engaged is very beneficial; and its being undertaken and extended to the Eastward of Kamtschatka, was the immediate consequence of the second voyage of that able navigator, whose misfortunes proved to be the source of much private advantage to individuals, and of public utility to the Russian nation. And yet, if his distresses had not carried him to die in the island which bears his name, and from whence the miserable remnant of his ships' crew brought back sufficient speciments of its valuable furs, probably the Russians never would have undertaken any future voyages, which could lead them to make discoveries in this sea, towards the coast of America.[25]

So extensive was Russian interest in the trade that between 1743 and 1800 some 101 ventures were undertaken by a total of 42 companies, and nearly 187,000 pelts taken (about ten per day) worth in all about ten million rubles.[26] Not surprisingly, therefore, this was then the most popular of Russian merchant trades. What is surprising is that it took the English so long to discover it.

Cook's third voyage, as we have seen, had the primary object of finding the supposed western or Pacific entrance to the Northwest Passage. At the "first convenient port" on the coast of New Albion, Cook was to recruit wood and water and procure refreshments and then proceed northward along the coast to about 65° N latitude, where he was to undertake an extensive exploration of the coastline. These instructions are singularly devoid of any reference to the extension of British commercial interests. Perhaps these were intrinsic motives, but this seems uncertain and we can conclude that any discovery of such a valuable field of commerce as the maritime fur trade must have come as a pleasant surprise to the British.

The first convenient port Cook came across was Nootka Sound where, on March 30, 1778, the English began to trade with the local tribes. "A great many Canoes filled with the Natives were about the Ship all day," he recorded in his journal, "and a trade commenced betwixt us and them, which was carried on with Strict honisty on boath sides."[27] The Indians offered various skins—bear, wolf, fox, deer, raccoon, pole cat, martin and especially the "Sea Beaver" (the Russian name was *bobri morski*) or, more accurately, sea otter, the same kind, Cook knew, that was to be found on the Kamchatka shore.

I

This animal, known properly as *Enhydra lutris,* resembles the *Lutra canadensis* or land otter in size. Four to five feet in length and weighing up to 80 pounds, the sea otter was found, except for small gaps of distribution, along a 6,000-mile crescent from lower California to the Alaska peninsula and across the Aleutians to Kamchatka and Japan. Its beautiful, thick fur consists of hairs an inch to an inch and a half long. In the colder northern waters, the skins are especially attractive, being dark brown to jet black in color. The female produces only one pup at a time and does not do so every year. Accordingly, the slow rate of reproduction did little to offset the steady extermination of the sea otter by human depredations. By the 1830s the animal was virtually extinct. Among kelp beds and along rocky, protected shores, where he thrived on shellfish, sea urchins, clams and crabs, the playful sea otter was found in abundance. And there, in his inquisitive and unsuspecting fashion, he was easy game for a hunter armed only with a club.

The Nootka Indians also traded in clothing, made either from furs or cedar bark or hemp, bows and arrows, carved work, human skulls and hands, animal oil in bladders, and small items. They even offered a child of five or six years. They took, in exchange, knives, chisels, pieces of tin and iron, nails, buttons and any kind of metal. They were not fond of beads, unlike tribes farther up the coast, and would not accept clothing. In their trade patterns, the local Nootka tribes held an apparent monopoly. When, on April 18, six or eight canoes from strange tribes approached the English ships, they retreated at the order of local Indians. "We also found," Cook wrote, "that many of the principals of those about us carried on a trade with their neighbors with the articles they got from us; as they would frequintly be gone from us four or five days at a time and then return with a fresh cargo curiosities and such was the passion for these things among our people that they always came to a good Market whether they were of any value or no."[28]

As mentioned, they held beads in little esteem. As a society thrust suddenly from the stone to the iron age, they had a passion for metals, especially brass, tin and shiny pewter. "Nothing would go down with them but metal, and brass was now become their favourate, So that before we left this place, hardly a bit of brass was lieft in the Ship, except what was in the necessary instruments. Whole Suits of cloaths were striped of every button."[29] Hardware from furniture, copper kettles, tin canisters and candlesticks "all went to wreck." The result was that they got more from the expedition than any other peoples visited by Cook's ships.

60

On the ships' departure from Nootka Sound, Cook had the voluntary promise from a local chief that a stock of furs would be available if the English ships returned. On May 13, 1778, they were at Port Etches, Hitchinbrook Island, Alaska, in about 60° N latitude, where Cook's crew next traded with the Indians for furs. At this place beads were a prized commodity, especially those of sky blue color about the size of large peas and probably of Russian origin. For five or six beads, one might acquire a beaver skin worth 90 or 100 dollars. Later, in September, Cook was at Unalaska in the Aleutians where he learned from Russian furriers what sort of prices might be obtained from the furs; as much as 80 rubles was the price paid for a sea otter pelt at Kamchatka. Cook learned also that these skins were valuable in Japan but not, so he was told mistakenly, in Canton.[30]

Cook, because of his death in the Hawaiian Islands later during this voyage, never lived to see the maritime fur trade thrive in English hands. Thus it is interesting to note that he thought it would be of little promise because of the remoteness of the Northwest Coast from the British Isles. "There is no doubt," he wrote, "but a very beneficial fur trade might be carried on with the Inhabitants of this vast coast, but unless a northern passage is found it seems rather too remote for Great Britain to receive any emolument from it."[31] Cook was right in a way: the Americans and Russians profited from the trade most. But distance was not the sole determinant, for the voyage from Boston to the North Pacific was as long as that from London. What therefore accounts for the British being outtraded? The English private traders, facing monopoly restrictions allowing the East India Company under terms of its charter to control the licensing of all ships trading to China, were unable to exploit the trade to the same degree as did their rivals. And wars with the Americans and then the French, lasting from 1776 to 1783 and 1789 to 1793, kept many English merchantmen from commercial pursuits.

The emolument to Cook's crew was great indeed. At Kamchatka, two-thirds of the skins were sold since they considered them of little value. But at Macao, in January 1780, higher prices were realized, totalling £2,000. Midshipman Trevenen, as has been mentioned, sold one pelt for $300. Captain James King, in charge of the expedition following the deaths of Cook and Captain James Clerke, wrote in his journal that at Macao, sea otter furs brought good prices, better than at Kamchatka, "the Chinese being very Eager to purchase them and gave us from 50 to 70 dollars a skin; that is from 11 £ 5s to 15 £ 15s for what we bought with only a hatchet or a Saw."[32] So great was the excitement over the prospects of making an easy fortune that two men, John Cove, the quartermaster, and Michael Spencer, a seaman, stole the *Resolution's* great cutter with the object of going back to Cook's River in the Bight of Alaska for more furs. They were never heard of again. King, who sold 20 skins for 800 Spanish dollars and who himself worked out a plan for a combined surveying and trading voyage undertaken with the agreement of the East India Company, almost had mutiny on his hands in Macao. And it is not surprising that various officers and men from the *Resolution* and *Discovery* such as John Ledyard, Nathaniel Portlock and George Dixon later became involved either directly or indirectly in the maritime fur trade. As for King, he did not face a mutiny and the ships returned to England in 1780 by way of the Cape of Good Hope.

As soon as the details of Cook's voyage and discoveries on the Northwest Coast were known, especially that a profitable trade in sea otter and perhaps other skins could be obtained, British, French and American subjects entered the trade. Of these the British seem to have been the most energetic in the early stages. The Spanish, incidentally, knew of the trade but did not take advantage of it. Later, they merely, through the acts of possession of Don Esteban Jose Martinez in 1789, sought to reassert Spain's rights to ownership in the face of rival trading activity.[33]

The first Englishman to enter into the fur trade of the Northwest Coast was James Hanna, who in August 1785 reached Nootka Sound in a 60-ton brigantine called, appropriately, the *Sea Otter*. She had sailed from Canton, where she had been equipped by English merchants, probably under East India Company auspices or perhaps, as has been suggested, under Portuguese direction. At Nootka Sound, the *Sea Otter* and her crew of under 30 appeared small by comparison to Cook's ships and crews, and the Indians attacked the ship, but unsuccessfully. This seems to have been the first white-native conflict of the maritime fur trade, and was to be frequently repeated. Once hostilities were at an end, a brisk trade began and Hanna took many furs to Canton, which brought him $26,000. In the following year, he returned to Nootka in a larger vessel also known as the *Sea Otter*. But as rival ships had already arrived, his trade was not so profitable.

In the same year that Hanna made his first voyage, 1785, a syndicate had been formed in London under the name of the King George's Sound Company, although in various licences it is referred to as Richard Cadman Etches and Company. The eight members of this group were mainly merchants and the principal subscriber and prime mover was Richard Cadman Etches, a London merchant. Two other members of the company were Nathaniel Portlock and George Dixon, already mentioned as officers in Cook's ships and now to be masters, respectively, of the group's first two trading vessels, the *King George* and the *Queen Charlotte.*

This syndicate, through some delicate arrangements apparently approved of by the British government, obtained a trading licence from the South Sea Company, which had in theory and by law a monopoly of trade in the Pacific, and similarly got special permission from the East India Company to bring back to London teas in return for Northwest Coast furs traded in Canton.

The instructions to Portlock and Dixon, exactly identical, specified that factories were to be built on the Northwest Coast for safety of settlers and traders of the company. Nootka Sound or King George's Sound as Cook had named it after his sovereign, was specified as the central place of establishment, although the captains were given discretionary powers in this regard. There can be little doubt of the projected permanence of British settlement. A William Wilby was to establish the trading post in a secure site on land purchased on liberal terms from the natives. "You are then to appoint as many men as you shall deem necessary," the orders ran,

and you shall turn out as volunteers, to be companions to Mr. Wilby; you are to give them every possible assistance to erect a log-house, or such other building as shall appear to be necessary for their residence, and for the carrying on traffic with the natives, etc. You are to give them every assistance to make such place tenable against the natives, and provide them with such arms, ammunition, etc. as you shall deem necessary for their defence and protection. You are to leave them such quantities of provisions and other articles for convenience, and the purpose of trade.[34]

The voyage proved to be less successful than anticipated, although the two ships collected 3,552 sea otter skins. These were sold in Canton for $50,000, "well knowing," Dixon wrote, "that the money would be more acceptable to our owners than an account that we had left the furs on commission."[35] But the price was about $20 per skin, well below the usual market price of $80 or $90 each.[36] In London, Etches blamed Portlock and Dixon for letting the furs go at such low prices; but the real culprit seems to have been the East India Company which supervised the sale. Judge Howay, who studied these and other transactions between maritime fur traders and the Company, concluded: "The real root of the loss of the maritime fur trade by the British was not the Napoleonic wars, nor the keen Yankee opposition but the octopus hold and suction of the East India Company."[37] As for the South Sea Company's monopoly, in Portlock's words, it stood "in the mercantile way of more adventurous merchants."[38]

Another development that angered Portlock and Dixon was that when they anchored in Nootka Sound they discovered that another project for opening the maritime fur trade was under way and that they had been anticipated by two English enterprises, from Bombay and Calcutta. Cook's *Voyages,* published in London in 1784, inspired an East India Company servant of the Madras establishment called James Charles Stewart Strange, later the son-in-law of Henry Dundas, First Lord Melville, the prominent statesman. Strange took his proposal to David Scott, an independent merchant of Bombay, who with help from his two partners, Tate and Anderson, got the approval of the President and Council of Bombay for the plan. Two ships, the *Captain Cook* of 300 tons and the *Experiment* of 100 tons, were well-manned and equipped for the expedition, and Strange was placed in sole control of the expedition.

The outline plan, very ambitious in scope, was nothing less than a complete blueprint for the expansion of British trade and dominion in eastern seas. New discoveries for the improvement of navigation, new trade with the Northwest Coast from India and China, and surveys of the coast, Bering Strait and the Asian Coast—all these were laid down in Strange's instructions.[39]

Yet during the voyage, as might be expected, trade took precedence over discovery. Leaving Bombay in December, 1785, Strange was at Nootka on June 27, 1786, and "got possession of every rag of Furr within the Sound."[40] He then proceeded northward, to Cape Scott, Queen Charlotte Sound, Goletas Channel and Prince William Sound, where he met a rival trader from Bengal, Captain William Tipping, in the *Sea Otter.* By late 1786 the two ships had reached Macao where the expedition, grand in design but small in profit, came to an end.

Tipping's *Sea Otter,* a 100-ton vessel sailing from Calcutta, had arrived on the coast in 1786. She was accompanied by the *Nootka,* a 230-ton vessel commanded by John Meares, an unemployed lieutenant in the Royal Navy and the promoter of the expedition. Meares, later notorious as a fur trader "wronged" by the Spanish at Nootka, ranged along the coast from Nootka to Cook's Inlet and determined to winter and build a trading post at Prince William Sound. They experienced a difficult winter, and in the spring, Portlock and Dixon arrived from London. The two expeditions were jealous of each other; Portlock and

64

Dixon dealt harshly and ungenerously with Meares' requests for anti-scorbutics and other supplies. Later, when all three were back in London, this developed into an acrimonious controversy between Dixon and Meares. And the real issue was the fact that Meares, sailing under Portuguese colors, was an interloper, while the King George's Sound Company had government support and was licensed by the East India and South Sea companies.

Meares was not deterred, and on his arrival in Macao he ended his arrangements with the Calcutta group and entered into an arrangement with two "Merchant Proprietors" named John Henry Cox and Daniel Beale and Co. Two large ships, the *Felice* and *Iphigenia,* were fitted out and placed under Portuguese colors; and Meares was given instructions on December 24, 1787. These directed Meares to focus his attention on the trade of Nootka Sound. But they went farther than this. They suggested that rival vessels, "Russian, English or Spanish" might be met with, and if so they were to be treated with civility. If, on the other hand, they interfered with his ship, Meares could, if he had the superiority, take possession of the attackers and take them to China "that they may be condemned as legal prizes, and their crews punished as pirates."[41] The indication is clear that the interlopers intended to vie with the London ships for control of the trade.

Fortunately, the two companies entered into a formal agreement, dated January 23, 1789. This required that all ships were to be on a joint account and the profits to be shared. It was, essentially, a marriage of convenience for it gave both partners government protection and legality under the chartered companies and served to meet the competition of American ships now appearing at Nootka such as the *Eleanora* of New York and the *Columbia* and *Washington* of Boston. This development also allowed the London group to implement their policy of establishing a permanent factory at Nootka and several subsidiary posts along the coast. For this purpose, the *Argonaut,* Captain James Colnett, was dispatched with 29 Chinese artificers to build the factory, which was to be a permanent and solid establishment, not one "to be abandon'd at pleasure."[42]

By 1789, therefore, British activity in the maritime fur trade was far advanced from its earlier uncertain developments of the late 1770s and early 1780s. Cook's voyage had revealed the trade to the English commercial community. Several independent expeditions had been undertaken by the British—from London, Bombay, Calcutta, Canton and Macao. In total, according to Meares' estimates of May 1790 (which are probably on the high side), since 1785 five British ships

I

Launching John Meares' coastal trading vessel *North West America,* built at Nootka Sound, 1788. Europeans, Indians, Chinese carpenters and Sandwich Islanders attended the ceremony. (Meares, *Voyages* . . ., op. p. 220.)

had entered the trade from Europe and nine others from eastern seas.[43] Their sales in furs were worth 288,000 Spanish dollars, while French, Spanish and American rivals had engaged in trade worth only 142,000 Spanish dollars, about half that of the British. But still, Meares' statistics showed that foreign competition was closing in on the British. These figures indicated to the British ministry that the maritime fur trade was worthy of government attention, and that permanent steps should be taken to put the trade on a firm footing. More important, as we shall see below, the British now had a grand project in motion for the extension of British settlement and trade in eastern seas. Furs, settlers, convicts, naval stores, factories and depots were interrelated subjects in this master plan. But largely unknown to the British, the Spanish were taking steps to check the British incursion into their hemispheric preserve, and the Nootka Sound controversy which was to follow was born of rival national ambitions for control and thus trade of the Northwest Coast.

III

The merchant ships engaged in the maritime fur trade of the North Pacific in the four-year period 1785-1789 were mainly English, and it is thus not surprising that when this profitable trade became threatened by Spain in what the English regarded as a high-handed fashion the British government exercised its naval preponderance as a means of forcing the Spanish to acquiesce to their demands for commercial expansion in the Pacific. In the Nootka Sound crisis of 1790 the British played a masterful game of diplomatic chess, and with their sizable fleet they were able to bargain from strength. No matter how accurate the claims of the intemperate trader John Meares, the cabinet of William Pitt the Younger was keen that British merchants be able to trade in what Spain regarded as her sphere of influence in eastern seas; and these statemen intended to have it their way—by peace if possible, by war if necessary.

In 1789, Nootka Sound was well-known in places of profit and power in England. It had the reputation as a place where Cook had been hospitably received by local Indians. It had given birth, after Cook's discoveries, to a new and profitable field of commerce, the maritime fur trade, and this further confirmed the possibilities that awaited British entrepreneurs in the Southern Ocean. Nootka Sound thus symbolized prosperity to the British mercantile interests. This was a fact that the government, ever alive to the wishes of traders, could ill afford to ignore.[44]

Thus in July, 1789, when Captain George Dixon of the *Queen Charlotte,* a fur trading vessel owned by Richard Cadman Etches and the King George's Sound Company, urged the government to send an expedition from England to the Northwest Coast by way of Cape Horn for purposes of trade and settlement, the government was bound to listen. Dixon believed that sending an expedition by way of Quebec or Hudson's Bay would be "only losing time." He argued that foreign competition in the form of Russian activity at Cook's "River" (Inlet) and Prince William Sound, their possible expansion of settlement southward, and the increased activities of Portuguese, American, Swedish and Spanish vessels in the trade all augured badly for British commercial interests. Unless the British government took active measures, he maintained, "this valuable Branch of Commerce will be lost to this Country" and also to Canadian and Hudson's Bay Company fur interests.[45] This information seems to have been accepted by David Scott, previously mentioned as a Bengal merchant in the maritime fur trade, who had returned to London with hopes of getting the East India

Company involved in the trade. Scott had a natural ally in the Hon. Henry Dundas, the Home Secretary, who was organizing an embassy to China to open markets there. And at the Board of Trade also, Lord Hawkesbury was listening to the urgent pleas of Samuel Enderby and others interested in the Southern Whale Fishery who wanted a place of refreshment and repair at some place in the South Pacific and urged that the government send a naval expedition for the purpose.[46] The whale fishery was then more important than the maritime fur trade but it was displaced by the latter in the frantic train of events following the Spanish seizure of British ships at Nootka.

On the subject of the fur trade the Ministry was being influenced from yet another quarter. Alexander Dalrymple, then "Examiner of Sea Journals" for the East India Company, an associate of Duncan's, and a promoter of discovery and trade, was keenly aware of the necessity of finding a Northwest Passage and promoting the maritime fur trade. On February 2, 1790, in a memorandum to the government on the route for discoveries, he compared the access by Hudson Bay with that by Cape Horn. His preference for the former can be imagined for he thought the passage to exist. Thus, he argued, a ship should go from England to Hudson Bay and, if unsuccessful, return to replenish its stores and supplies and make its way by the Horn to the Northwest Coast. Better still, the government could send two ships.[47] Shortly thereafter, on February 11, he was again writing to the government, advising them that his friend Samuel Wegg, the chairman of the Hudson's Bay Company and his weekly dining companion at the Royal Society Club, was agreeable to sending a 90-ton sloop at Company expense "to examine if any outlet can be found from Hudson's Bay to facilitate the communication with the West Coast." Such an expedition, Dalrymple believed, would allow for further exploration of the interior of the Canadian Northwest west to Cook's discoveries; and accordingly Captain J. F. de B. Holland of Quebec submitted plans and estimates for expenses and instruments for a party of 16 men.[48]

Meanwhile, Dalrymple had another project in mind, this one to expand the maritime fur trade on the Northwest Coast. Arguing that British vessels would be forced out of the trade by Spanish, Russian and American rivals, he proposed that a government-supported merger of the Hudson's Bay and East India companies would allow the British traders to dominate the North Pacific and its commerce in furs: an East India Company ship could meet Hudson's Bay Company traders on the Northwest Coast with supplies and receive their furs from the coast itself and the interior of Canada and convey them to China

I

markets.⁴⁹ But while this project was falling on deaf ears, Dixon was
engaged in a Hudson's Bay Company expedition led by Charles Duncan to find possible water communication to the Pacific. But this
proved unrewarding and Duncan, in despair and still believing that
Admiral de Fonte's claims that an inland sea existed had foundation,
attempted to commit suicide on his return to England.⁵⁰

Yet another influence was being brought to bear on the British government which had to do with the expansion of national interests on
the Northwest Coast. After the American Revolution, the British no
longer could send criminals, about a thousand per year, to the Thirteen
Colonies, mainly Virginia and Georgia. In 1788, the government began
its project at Port Jackson, New South Wales. In the same year Richard Cadman Etches wrote Sir Joseph Banks, the President of the Royal
Society on this subject. Banks had supported the voyages of Etches'
vessels, the *King George* and *Queen Charlotte,* in 1788. The government having adopted the colonizing of convicts in New South Wales
as policy for relieving distress at home and reducing the incidence of
crime, Etches urged the application of the idea to the Northwest Coast.

If [the government] wou'd adopt the same idea, and make the attempt
with a certain Number (perhaps 100) under the same regulations,
with a few Soldiers, paying their Freight out, in fact *adopting* every
regulation laid down for the Colonizing New Holland [Australia], and
giving us power *over the Commercial part,* for a *limited time* as *they*
shou'd approve, a plan form'd on such an Idea, I am persuaded wou'd
not only secure the complete discovery of that extensive and unex-
plor'd part of the World, but wou'd open, and secure a source of
commerce of the most extensive magnitude to this Country.⁵¹

Trade and convict settlement Etches saw as going hand in hand;
both would be conducive to the national benefit. His plan suggested
that a small armed government vessel, commanded by a lieutenant,
should be sent to form the establishment, survey the coast from Nootka
Sound to Cook Inlet, develop the timber and spar trade of the coast,
build coasting vessels for trafficking with coast tribes, and promote the
trans-Pacific trade in furs with Asia, especially Japan.

This project had the support of several persons in Britain, including
Patrick Wilson, a professor of astronomy at Glasgow University, and
a medical doctor named Henry Robertson, also of Glasgow. Their
proposals indicate the widely held views of the advantages of this type
of settlement. As Robertson put it, convict settlement would be the
means whereby "the several Members of our Empire might link and
connect together and form a solid and compact whole, comprehending
everything from St. James; and even to Botany Bay." "In such a

I

Station," he wrote, "we shall be possessed of a fixed Point, a *Fulcrum,* on which we may be able to poize and weigh up a World. By beginning in the South-Pacific we are on the wrong Side and must labour unsuccessfully, because working against Nature. Our Province is the North. It is the native and proper Seat of our Strength, whence it may spread far and wide, and be everywhere effectual."[52]

The idea of establishing a convict colony at Nootka Sound or elsewhere on the Northwest Coast does not seem to have been widely considered by the British government. The reason for this is clear: the availability of land in New South Wales for convict settlement meant that the government would not have to look elsewhere in the Empire for new establishments. This did not preclude the possibility that the Northwest Coast might become a convict settlement at some future date. Still, the links between Nootka Sound and Botany Bay were tangible in these days of British expansion in the Pacific, and it is not surprising that the government, ever optimistic and energetic, developed a project to extend the colony of New South Wales to include the area now known as British Columbia.

In 1789, the government decided to implement the various suggestions, as given above, and send the sloop *Discovery* to the South Seas and the Northwest Coast. Captain Henry Roberts was selected as commander and his second officer was Lieutenant George Vancouver. Both had been with Cook on his second and third voyages and were intimately acquainted with the difficulties of white-native contact. Both were well-seasoned navigators.

The objects of the expedition were as follows. Surveys complementary to those of Cook were to be undertaken at Australia, New Zealand and the Northwest Coast, and places suitable for bases were to be reported on. But when the first news of the Spanish seizure of British vessels at Nootka Sound reached London, the ministry decided that an armed escort should be available for the *Discovery,* this to consist of H.M.S. *Gorgon* from England and a frigate from the East Indies station. At Port Jackson, the *Discovery* and *Gorgon* were to be supplied with provisions and reinforced with as many men and provisions as available from H.M.S. *Sirius.* The two ships would then sail for Hawaii and there meet the frigate from India, whose captain would then assume command. The Secretary of State, the Hon. W. W. Grenville, drafted instructions in March 1790. These reveal the intent of the government and are worth quoting at some length.

One of the objects of this expedition being to form a settlement on the nor-west coast of America, it is his Majesty's pleasure that you should select from among the people with you a proper number of persons to compose it, and that you should embark them either on board the *Discovery* or *Gorgon*.

The Extent of this establishment, it is imagined, need not at first exceed thirty persons, a moiety of whom at least should consist of drafts from the new corps, under the command of a discreet subaltern officer, who is to be entrusted with the temporary superintendence of the new settlement. The remainder should consist of two or three of the most intelligent of the overseers, who have lately been sent out, a storekeeper, and any other persons who may be desirous of accompanying them, together with a few of the most deserving of the convicts, to whom you may offer a remission of a part of their service (sentence) as an inducement to go.

And you will be careful to embark on board these ships such articles of stores, provisions, medicines and utensils for building, etc. as you may judge sufficient for their use, in order to enable them to fulfil the object of forming such a settlement as may be able to resist any attacks from the natives, and lay the foundation of an establishment for the assistance of his Majesty's subjects, in the prosecution of the fur trade from the N.W. coast of America.[53]

These instructions reveal that the government had adopted as policy the design to establish a colony proper on the Northwest Coast. The British were acting quickly with a strong expedition. Apparently they were prepared for the consequences should Spain decide on war. Backing the project of the Southern whalers, they were also prepared to overcome any obstruction which might arise from the East India and South Sea companies.

On April 30, when the *Discovery* was about to sail to sea, John Meares arrived in London full of reports of the seizure of British vessels. The expedition was immediately cancelled, and Britain, in George Vancouver's words, "was thrown into a state of intense war fever by the prospect of a renewal of hostilities with Spain."[54] Meares, leading a private venture operating out of Calcutta, had built a trading depot and factory at Nootka. On May 6, 1789, Don Estevan Jose Martinez, in command of the corvette *Princessa,* mounting 26 guns, had anchored in the sound and was joined a week later by the *San Carlos,* a brig of 16 guns. The Spanish did not interfere with the Boston trading vessels *Columbia* and *Washington,* perhaps because of the amicable relations then developing between Spain and the United States. The Spanish, however, did not leave unmolested the British ships *Argonaut* and *Princess Royal,* Captains James Colnett and Duncan respectively, and the coastal trading vessel the *North West America.* They seized these ships and sent them under guard to the Spanish naval base at San Blas, Mexico. At Nootka the Spanish ensign re-

71

I

British, Spanish and American vessels in Friendly Cove, Nootka Sound (Vancouver Island), September, 1792, during Vancouver-Quadra negotiations. (Hewitt Jackson painting at OHS, S. S. Johnson Collection.)

placed the British flag and Martinez proclaimed the coast from Cape Horn to 60° North latitude as belonging to the Spanish crown. Thus he was reasserting Spanish claims on the west side of the Americas as far north as the Russian settlements on Kodiak Island. Although he had been sent, as the English thought, "for the purpose of reconnoitering the new establishments of the Russians in the North of this Continent," the real intent seems to have been "to give notice to all comers," including the Russians, that the Northwest Coast from Monterey, the administrative capital of California, to 60° North latitude was closed to foreigners.[55] Martinez, therefore, was merely acting on the instructions of the Viceroy of Mexico, who, in an era when the dispute over the Falkland Islands in 1766 was an ever-constant reminder of Britain's successful challenge to overcome Spain's claims in the Pacific and the Western Hemisphere, wanted to check the British menace on the Northwest Coast.

The Spanish government in Madrid assumed the offensive in diplomacy, and, in strong language which the English considered highhanded, informed the British government of Spanish claims up to line 60° North and the extremity of Russian interest. "Imagination refuses to picture nearly half the water surface of the world long barred to the shipping of all nations except the most reactionary Powers of the Old World," wrote Professor J. Holland Rose, "Yet that was what was at stake."[56]

The British ministry listened to Meares' complaints at a meeting of inquiry. Pitt, the Prime Minister, Grenville, the Secretary of State, and the Duke of Leeds, the Foreign Secretary, wanted satisfaction for what they considered to be a wrong against their commercial interests. In addition, they wanted Spanish recognition for British commercial expansion in the Pacific. An apology, a compensation, and a subsequent negotiation on territorial claims were the British demands. These were initially rejected by Madrid. Spain, the British Consul-General in Madrid reported, was seeking an alliance with four other states against Britain and was mobilizing a fleet.[57]

Yet the British government was in no position to back down in their demands. Professor Harlow analyzed this situation as follows:

In the circumstances no British Administration dare refrain from resolute action, even if they were privately disposed to temporise, which they were not. Sixty years earlier Sir Robert Walpole had ignored the excited resentment of merchants against the "insolence" of Spanish *guarda costas* and had refused to take official action when Capt. Jenkins had inflamed public opinion with his accounts of ill-usage and his exhibition of a severed ear; and in consequence Walpole

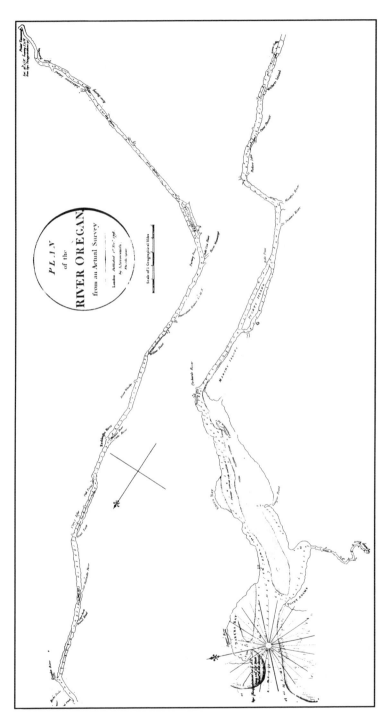

Arrowsmith's published map of the Columbia River, 1798, made from Lt. William Broughton's 1792 exploration during the Vancouver expedition.

had been driven into a war which had terminated his long and useful career. On the present occasion Meares had even more formidable propaganda material at hand than his predecessor: he represented more extensive claims; and the crisis came when the British were penetrating the Pacific from all sides.[58]

The British government had no option but to demand "immediate and adequate satisfaction for outrages" committed by Martinez, and on April 30 the Cabinet adopted this as policy and ordered a squadron of ships to be outfitted "in order to support that demand and be prepared for such events as may arise."[59] On May 5, the King's Message to Parliament explained the Ministry's position and seems to have been well received except by Charles Fox, who wondered why references to British territorial claims to Nootka were not mentioned. And why had Parliament not been informed what the British ships were doing there, "whether they were about to make an establishment, or whether Spain knew that we were about to make an establishment?"[60] This opposition forced the sagacious Pitt to modify policy slightly but still keep a firm stance towards Spain.

Pitt's strength was the British fleet, which he had not neglected in the years of his ministry. He had 93 capital ships available for service, and a fleet of 40 sail were placed in commission and sent to sea shortly after Meares burst into London with his news. On the Spanish side, 34 ships of the line were ready in the summer of 1790, and, if the French government could be persuaded to assist the Court of Madrid and equip the projected 45 sail, then the war at sea would have been hotly contested. But the French, bankrupt, distraught with revolution and their fleet in mutiny, proved unwilling. Spain, in her isolated position and facing British preponderance at sea and possible enemies in Prussia and Holland, backed down and a peaceful settlement followed on October 28.

This mobilization of the British fleet, "the Spanish armament," as it is widely known, was decisive in strengthening British interests on the Northwest Coast. As a later Controller of the Navy wrote, the armament was "a proof of great exertions, and speaks volumes as to the opinions of Mr. Pitt with respect to the necessity of having the navy in great strength and ready for immediate action."[61] The exercise of "fleet diplomacy," which was to be repeated in the Oregon crisis of 1846, had been highly successful, and the wisdom of having a strong navy, useful alliances, strong finances, materiel and manpower, to say nothing of adroit statesmanship, had again been revealed.

In the Nootka Sound crisis Britain had won a diplomatic victory

I

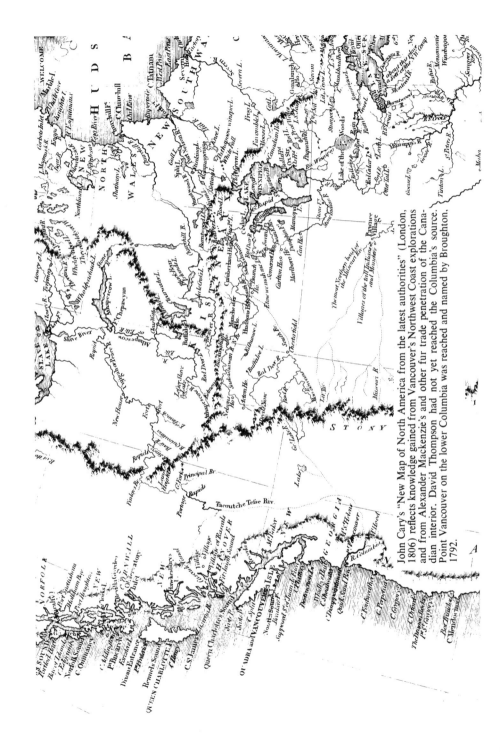

John Cary's "New Map of North America from the latest authorities" (London, 1806) reflects knowledge gained from Vancouver's Northwest Coast explorations and from Alexander Mackenzie's and other fur trade penetration of the Canadian interior. David Thompson had not yet reached the Columbia's source. Point Vancouver on the lower Columbia was reached and named by Broughton, 1792.

important for both her Pacific trade and the extension of her North American dominions, although the full impact of the latter may not have been realized at the time. Only men such as Alexander Dalrymple, Hydrographer of the Admiralty, Sir Joseph Banks, botanist and President of the Royal Society, and Alexander Mackenzie, the fur trader, were thinking in terms of transcontinental British North American dominion. Yet the origins of a Canada from sea to sea were born as a result of the Nootka Convention of 1790. What made this possible? British desires for commerce, a wish to remove Spanish pretensions and, lastly, the exercise, albeit peaceful, of British superiority at sea. The ancient Spanish obstacle had been removed for all time, and it remained for the voyage of Captain George Vancouver in 1791-1794 to explore the coast from Lower California in about 30° N latitude to Cook's Inlet near 60° N. His discoveries ended forever the myth of the Northwest Passage in a southerly latitude but above all gave the British a clear indication of the outline of the coast that they had firm claim to as a result of the Nootka Sound crisis.

By the end of the 18th century, then, British ambitions to expand into the Pacific had been partially realized. The Nootka Sound Convention had eliminated Spain as sole claimant on the Northwest Coast. Thus British merchant adventurers were able to enter into the maritime fur trade and to develop other undertakings in the Pacific without fear of molestation from the Spanish. A wedge had been made into the Spanish hemispheric reserve: British settlement at Nootka could now go ahead unrestricted if British interests warranted it. Canadian fur traders could now move overland from the Athabaska country without fear of trespassing on foreign soil. And English interests in the maritime fur trade and Southern Whale Fishery could operate in the Pacific without worry of molestation. But in the main, the Northwest Coast of North America had now been brought within the perimeter of international rivalry, and by the late 18th century, the British had added further fields of trade and dominion to their imperial interests in eastern seas.

I

FOOTNOTES

1. Quoted in Gerald S. Graham, *Empire of the North Atlantic: The Maritime Struggle for North America* (rev. ed., Toronto, 1958), 194.

2. *Ibid.*

3. Spanish interest in the Northwest Coast of North America has been the subject of numerous recent works. See especially, Warren L. Cook, *Flood Tide of Empire: Spain and the Pacific Northwest, 1543-1819* (New Haven and London, 1973); Christon I. Archer, "The Transient Presence: A Re-Appraisal of Spanish Attitudes towards the Northwest Coast in the Eighteenth Century," *B.C. Studies,* No. 18 (Summer, 1973), 3-32; and Michael E. Thurman, *The Naval Department of San Blas: New Spain's Bastion for Alta California and Nootka, 1767 to 1798* (Glendale, California, 1967).

4. Great Britain, *Statutes at Large,* 18 Geo. II, c. 17.

5. *Ibid.,* 16 Geo. III, c. 6.

6. Quoted in Glyndwr Williams, *The British Search for the Northwest Passage in the Eighteenth Century* (London, 1962), 167.

7. Council Minutes, Feb. 10 and 17, 1774, Archives of the Royal Society, London (hereafter ARS), VI, 214, 216.

8. Dr. Maty (Sec., Royal Society) to Admiralty, Feb. 17, 1774, *ibid.,* 216; see also Williams, *British Search,* 166.

9. Reported in D. Barrington to Royal Society, Mar. 30, 1774, ARS, VI, 227.

10. For a more complete account of Stahlin's theory, see John C. Beaglehole, ed., *The Journals of Captain James Cook on his Voyages of Discovery: Vol. III, The Voyage of the Resolution and Discovery, 1776-1780* (Hakluyt Society, Extra Series No. XXXVI, Cambridge, 1967), lxi-lxiv.

11. Secret Instructions to Capt. James Cook, July 6, 1776, Admiralty Papers, Public Record Office, London (hereafter Adm.), 2/1332, 284-96. Printed in Vincent Harlow and Frederick Madden, *British Colonial Developments, 1774-1834: Select Documents* (Oxford, 1953), 1-4.

12. Instructions to Lieut. R. Pickersgill, May 14, 1776, Adm. 2/101, 89-90.

13. Instructions to Lieut. W. Young, March 13, 1777, Adm. 2/1332, 322.

14. Beaglehole, *Cook's Journals,* III: 289.

15. Perhaps this was the Umpqua River (lat. 43° 40′).

16. Beaglehole, *Cook's Journals,* III: 292.

17. *Ibid.,* pp. 293-94.

18. Beaglehole, *Cook's Journals,* III: cxxi.

19. *Ibid.,* 335.

20. *Ibid.,* cxxxviii.

21. *Ibid.,* 470.

22. Vincent T. Harlow, *The Founding of the Second British Empire, 1763-1793. Vol. I. Discovery and Revolution; Vol. II. New Continents and Changing*

Values (Longman Group, Ltd., London, 1952, 1964). See also David Mackay, "British Interests in the Southern Oceans, 1782-1794," *The New Zealand Journal of History*, III (October, 1969), 124-42.

23. *Second British Empire*, Vol. I: 3.

24. James R. Gibson, *Feeding the Russian Fur Trade: Provisionment of the Okhotsk Peninsula, 1639-1856* (Madison, 1969), 16-17.

25. Captain James Cook and Captain James King, *A Voyage to the Pacific Ocean* (3 vols., London, 1784), III: 497.

26. Gibson, *Feeding the Russian Fur Trade*, 17.

27. Beaglehole, *Cook's Journals*, III: 296.

28. *Ibid.*, 302.

29. *Ibid.*

30. *Ibid.*

31. *Ibid.*, 371.

32. *Ibid.*, 714.

33. Jose Mariano Mozino, *Noticias de Nutka: An Account of Nootka Sound in 1792*, trans. and ed. by Iris Higbie Wilson (Toronto, 1970), xxx-xxxi, 95-97.

34. Printed in F. W. Howay, ed., *The Dixon-Meares Controversy* (Toronto, 1929), 61, and Harlow and Madden, *British Colonial Developments*, 29-30.

35. Howay, *Dixon-Meares Controversy*, 134.

36. Nathaniel Portlock, *A Voyage Round the World; but more Particularly to the North-west Coast of America: Performed in 1785, 1786, 1787, and 1788, in the King George and Queen Charlotte, Captains Portlock and Dixon* (London, 1789), 382.

37. F. W. Howay, "Four Letters from Richard Cadman Etches to Sir Joseph Banks, 1788-92," *British Columbia Historical Quarterly* (hereafter BCHQ), VI (April, 1942), 127.

38. Portlock, *Voyage Round the World*, 4.

39. Instructions to James Strange, Dec. 7, 1785, East India Company Records, Home Miscellaneous Series, India Office Records, London (hereafter H.M.S.), 494 (5), 422-27.

40. Quoted in F. W. Howay, "The Voyage of the 'Captain Cook' and the *Experiment*, 1785-86," *BCHQ*, V (October, 1941), 286. Strange's journal (H.M.S. 800) was published by the Madras Record Office in 1928; see A.V.V. Ayyar, "An Adventurous Madras Civilian: James Strange, 1753-1840," *Proceedings, Indian Historical Records Commission*, XI (1928).

41. Harlow and Madden, *British Colonial Documents*, 30-32.

42. Sailing orders for the *Argonaut*, Macao, April 3, 1789; in F. W. Howay, ed., *The Journal of Capt. James Colnett aboard the Argonaut from April 26, 1789, to November 3, 1791* (Champlain Society, Toronto, 1940), 19-23.

43. John Meares, "Statement of the Value of Furs exported from the North Western Coast of America by British and Foreign Ships Previous to the Year 1790," May 20, 1790, Home Office Papers, Public Record Office, London (hereafter H.O.), 42/16 (24).

44. This section owes much to Harlow's *Second British Empire, 1763-1793*, Vol. II, ch. VII, entitled "The China Trade and the Canadian Pacific Coast." Professor Harlow has little data on activities on the coast but has provided the most comprehensive account, to date, of the official British view during the crisis. See also, John M. Norris, "The Policy of the British Cabinet in the Nootka Crisis," *English Historical Review*, LXX (October, 1955), 562-80, and Lennox

I

Mills, "The Real Significance of the Nootka Sound Incident," *Canadian Historical Review*, VI (June, 1925), 110-22. Of lesser value and now quite outdated is William R. Manning, "The Nootka Sound Controversy," *Annual Report of the American Historical Association, 1904* (Washington, 1905), 279-478.

45. Capt. George Dixon to Evan Nepean (Home Office), July 14, 1789, Q series, vol. 49, p. 354, Public Archives of Canada, Ottawa (hereafter P.A.C.), printed in *Report on Canadian Archives, 1887* (Ottawa, 1890), 29.

46. See Mackay, "British Interest in the Southern Oceans," 131-36, esp. 132.

47. Memorandum by Alexander Dalrymple on the route for Discoveries, Feb. 2, 1790, Q series, vol. 49, p. 368, P.A.C.; printed in *Report on the Canadian Archives, 1889* (Ottawa, 1890), 32-35.

48. "Captain Holland's Plan to Explore from Quebec" [1790], with lists of expenses and instruments, in *ibid.*, 36-37. Howard T. Fry, *Alexander Dalrymple (1737-1808) and the Expansion of British Trade* (London, 1970), 202ff.

49. Alexander Dalrymple, *Plan for Promoting the Fur Trade, and Securing it to this Country, by uniting the Operations of the East-India and Hudson's Bay Companys (sic)* (London, 1789), 31. See also, his "Trade to the N. W. Coast of America" [1791], H.M.S. 494 (5).

50. Williams, *British Search for the Northwest Passage*, 246-48.

51. R. Cadman Etches to Sir Joseph Banks, July 17, 1788, Sutro Branch, California State Library: in Howay, ed., "Four Letters from Richard Cadman Etches to Sir Joseph Banks, 1788-92," *BCHQ*, VI: 132.

52. See Richard H. Dillon, ed., "Convict Colonies for the Pacific Northwest," *BCHQ*, XIX (January-April, 1955), 93-102.

53. Grenville to Governor Arthur Phillip, New South Wales, March 1790, printed in George Godwin, *Vancouver: A Life, 1757-1798* (New York, 1931), 189-90.

54. Quoted in *ibid.*, 25.

55. Harlow, *Second British Empire*, II: 443-44.

56. J. Holland Rose, "Sea Power and the Winning of British Columbia," *Mariner's Mirror*, VII (March, 1921), 78.

57. Anthony Merry to the Duke of Leeds, April 5, 1790, Foreign Office Papers, Public Record Office, London (F.O.), 72/16.

58. Harlow, *Second British Empire* (Longman Group, Ltd., London, 1952, 1964), II: 448.

59. Cabinet Minute of April 30, 1790, copy in Harlow and Madden, *British Colonial Developments*, 33.

60. *Parliament History*, XXVII: 76 ff.

61. *Letters of Sir T. Byam Martin*, III: 382, quoted in Admiral Sir Herbert Richmond, *Statesmen and Sea Power* (Oxford, 1946), 165.

II

NEW EMPIRES OF TRADE AND TERRITORY
IN THE TIME OF MALASPINA

In Malaspina's time Spain had three rivals for the Northwest Coast – Russia, the United States, and Britain. Yet only Britain provided armed opposition to Spanish designs. For its part, Russia was then only a trading power, interested only in commercial pursuits on the shores and islands of the Pacific Ocean. As for the remaining or fourth claimant to sovereignty, the United States, its activities, too, were based in activities of an energetic, growing merchant marine and thoughts of carving out a sphere of influence and a territorial empire on Pacific tidewater crossed only the minds of the most fervent imperialist. A fifth power, France, exhibited only scientific interest in this distant zone. For the time being, accordingly, Nootka Sound and the Northwest Coast was a cockpit of empire in which the main contestants were Spain and Britain with Russia and the United States (in that order) playing minor roles.

Spain's attempt to check British aggrandizement at Nootka Sound was only one of a series of such episodes between the two countries after the Seven Years' War ended in 1763. The Falkland Islands, Tahiti, and Nootka Sound are separated from each other by thousands of kilometres. Nevertheless, they formed focal points of Anglo-Spanish rivalry and integral parts of the contest for trade and dominion in the Pacific.

Spain claimed these and other realms within the Pacific as part of her imperial preserve. However, she was already overextended in Louisiana, Mexico, Central and South America, the Philippines, and West Africa. Given the resources at her disposal, Spain could not maintain her empire everywhere. The Northwest Coast lay on the fringe of her American dominions. She could not hope to check her rivals' ambitions here unless she had adequate naval and financial strength to meet any emergency that might threaten her interests in distant seas or, failing that, unless she had support from her ancient ally, France.

Spain's claims for the Pacific were unchallenged as long as Britain's interest in the southern ocean remained largely sporadic, as indeed it was before 1763. The long succession of English incursions into Spain's claimed oceanic preserve, including the voyages of Drake, Cavendish, Anson, and Byron, were fragile penetrations by armed enemy ships. Bold as they were, they hardly represented a grand design for English commercial and colonial hegemony in the southern ocean. In fact, they were little threat to Spanish claims.

After the Seven Years' War, the greatest chance for imperial aggrandizement lay with the paramount nation at sea. For the British, whose preponderant imperial and maritime authority was now established, the way lay open to renew ancient, largely unsatisfied Tudor ambitions. The nation now possessed an expanding industrial base that needed new markets for manufacturers. Britain wanted to consolidate overseas trade and build trade alliances with native peoples. Not least, she fostered the scientific objective of delineating the most distant of oceans, the one least known to the European world.

In this great swing of British interests that laid the foundations of a new empire in eastern seas, the importance of bases, especially in time of war, seemed obvious to all imperial nations with overseas territories. In respect to both Nootka Sound on the Northwest Coast and Botany Bay in New South Wales, statesmen engaged in the same thinking as they did concerning the Cape of Good Hope and the Falkland Islands. These two imperial beachheads on opposite sides of the Pacific were important to the United Kingdom not simply because they might increase Britain's wealth but also because they would make foreign rivals – Spain or Russia in the case of the Northwest Coast and France or Holland in the case of New South Wales – more dependent on their existing holdings by excluding them from the advantages of trade that actual possession might provide. In other words, British strategists looked at these distant territories from two points of view: firstly, how they would suit national interests, and secondly, as a naval officer wrote, how they would "annoy us in other hands."[1] The British knew that the Cape of Good Hope, for instance, gave the Dutch a place of refreshment and repair for their shipping in the Indian Ocean and eastern seas as well as a place from which to extend their trade in South America. This "tavern of two oceans," as the Dutch affectionately called it, was coveted not only by Britain, but also by France, then smarting under the past humiliation of the loss of Canada. Britain could not afford to let France conquer and keep the Cape, for it was the key to India and eastern trade. During the wars of the late eighteenth century France captured the Cape once and Britain seized it twice, the second time in 1806, and kept it in order to forestall the French.

At the same time the British jealously watched rival ambitions with regard to the Falkland Islands. The importance of the Falklands to Britain had been

---

[1] As Commodore J. Blankett, R.N., had advised London to take the Cape of Good Hope in 1795 (Vincent Harlow and Frederick Madden, eds., *British Colonial Developments, 1774–1834: Select Documents* [Oxford: Clarendon Press, 1953], pp. 19–21).

pointed out by Lord Anson in the 1740's. In time of peace, he said, the islands could be of great consequence to the nation while in time of war they could make the British masters of the southern oceans.[2] Such a base would provide British whalers and other merchant ships with a convenient resting place en route to eastern seas. Subsequently, strategists believed a halfway house to the Pacific corresponding to the Cape should be established to stimulate trade in the Pacific and South America and to advance exploration of the Pacific. This base would counter Spain's head start in Chile, Peru, Mexico, and Manila. Perhaps also, they reasoned, it would check annexation of the Falklands by France or by Spain or, for that matter, by any other rival such as Holland.

In that mercantilist age the underlying national objective was to increase national security and military preparedness through trade. Thus, the Pacific assumed importance as a potential El Dorado, a hitherto unknown world that might have riches that in some rival's hands would damage the nation's trade advantage or upset the delicate balance of power in Europe. Not only did the British want to go to the Pacific; they believed they were obliged to go there.

The rivalry for the Falkland Islands, these "few spots of earth, which in the deserts of the ocean had almost escaped human notice," as the satirist Samuel Johnson called them, were a prelude to the dispute over Nootka.[3] In 1764, after the loss of Canada, France had sent Bougainville to settle Fort Louis in the Falklands with Acadian refugees. Almost concurrently, the British Admiralty had sent Commodore John Byron to survey the islands and to establish a base there at Port Egmont. He found that the French had already established their rival base. The French withdrew, not because of Byron's demands, but because Spain claimed these lands on the basis of the moribund Treaty of Tordesillas. For the time being the British stubbornly maintained their fragile hold.

Meanwhile Spanish authorities in Madrid and Valparaiso watched this growth of British expansion with alarm and suspicion. Perhaps, they argued, Drake's anti-Catholic ambitions were being pursued once more. Perhaps the Falklands in British hands would give their ancient enemies a base from which to attack Peru's wealth or to settle Patagonia. Perhaps the annexation of Terra Australis Incognita, which had haunted French and British imaginations, would occur. Perhaps Tahiti, Hawaii, or even California would

---

[2] Quoted in M. B. R. Cawkwell, D. N. Maling, and E. M. Cawkwell, *The Falkland Islands* (London: Macmillan, 1960), p. 14.

[3] Quoted in Nicholas Tracy, "The Falkland Islands Crisis of 1770: Use of English Naval Force," *Historical Journal* 90 (1975): 40.

be seized. Thus, in 1767, the Viceroy of Peru sent ships to reconnoitre the Patagonian coast in search of British settlers. The Spanish also attempted to garrison the rocky and windswept barrens of Tierra del Fuego. Finally in 1770, a superior Spanish force captured the tiny and beleaguered British garrison at Port Egmont. War was avoided only by negotiations which restored the settlement to the British without prejudicing Spanish claims to prior right of discovery. The British, however, voluntarily abandoned the fort in 1774 and did so for financial reasons, leaving behind only a plaque and a British flag as a feeble register of British title.[4]

The Falkland Islands crisis showed that Britain could challenge Spain's imperial pretentions successfully. The Spanish had suffered, Dr. Johnson boasted, "a breach to be made in the outworks of their empire, and notwithstanding the reserve of prior right have suffered a dangerous exception to the prescriptious tenure of their American territories."[5] The "key to the Pacific," as the First Lord of the Admiralty glowingly described the Falklands in 1765, now became a more frequent port of call.[6] Cape Horn grew as an entry to the Pacific. A varied collection of seafarers now doubled the Horn, including whalers, trepang hunters, pearl fishers, guano traders, and tallow and hide seekers. Missionaries from Spain, France, and the United States bound for Polynesia also passed the Horn. By the 1780's, the Falklands had become a frequent stopping place for some of these ships and for North Pacific whalers and maritime fur traders.

As in the Falklands, the Spanish attempted to check the rise of British activities in the South Pacific islands. Cook's voyages stimulated Spanish fears, for, as Professor Harlow has written, "Generations of painful experience of English *corsarios* and smugglers did not make it easy for Spanish administration to accept the English in the unexpected garb of scientists."[7] The Spanish mistakenly regarded Cook's first Pacific voyage – to observe the Transit of Venus – as a mere pretext for further English raids and conquests. During his third voyage, Cook had possessed strict instructions to avoid

---

4 In 1780 the Spanish destroyed the British buildings. For 50 years thereafter British authority was not maintained which caused Charles Darwin to lament: "Here, we, in dog in the manger fashion seize an island and leave to protect it a Union Jack" (Cawkwell *et al., Falkland Islands*, p. 44). The fluctuations of British policy for the Falklands may be traced in Barry M. Gough, *The Falklands/Malvinas: The Contest for Empire in the South Atlantic* (London: Athlone, 1982).

5 Quoted in Tracy, "Falkland Islands Crisis," p. 72.

6 The usage here is by the First Lord of the Admiralty: Memorandum by Earl of Egmont, 20 July 1765, S.P. 94/253, f. 228, Public Record Office, Kew, England.

7 Vincent T. Harlow, *The Founding of the Second British Empire, 1763–1793* (2 vols.; London: Longmans, 1952–64), 1: 52.

Spanish-occupied dominions on the west side of the Americas and not to give offence to any Spanish subjects. The Spanish, however, aware of how much was at stake, made a feeble and unsuccessful attempt to secure their longstanding interest in Tahiti by sending two Franciscan priests there in 1775 to establish a protectorate and keep out the English.[8] As indicated by the potential costs of war with Britain and the insecurity provided by her unoccupied Pacific possessions' tenuous alliance with France, Spain could not hold these possessions. In these circumstances, British consolidation of claims to trade and dominion – at the Falklands in 1771, New South Wales in 1787, and Nootka Sound in 1789 – could advance steadily, always with the real threat of war but with the margin of safety largely on the side of the British.

Spain's first concern for the fate of her claims to the far Northwest Coast began to mount in the early 1770's.[9] The Spanish ambassador at the Russian court at St. Petersburg warned Madrid that the Russians were advancing eastward across the top of the Pacific horseshoe. He reported that the explorer Alexei Chirikov had made investigations in 1769–71 and found that navigation along the Alaskan shore was less difficult than imagined. Alarmed, he reported that Tsarina Catherine II planned to send a fleet from the Baltic to Kamchatka via the Cape of Good Hope.

Such news brought an immediate response from Madrid. At the same time Spain learned that the British were mounting expeditions to find the Northwest Passage from Hudson Bay. Instructions were immediately issued to the Viceroy of Mexico, the closest authority, to learn if explorations were being pursued. Foreign incursions were to be halted by scouting the coasts for rivals and by developing appropriate plans for Spanish occupation. As the Viceroy put it, "any establishment by Russia, or any other foreign power, on the continent ought to be prevented, not because the king needs to enlarge his realms, as he has within his known dominions more than it will be possible to populate in

---

[8] See B. G. Corey, ed. and trans., *The Quest and Occupation of Tahiti by Emissaries of Spain during the Years 1772–1776* (3 vols.; London: Hakluyt Society, 1913–19), 1: 108.

[9] I owe much of the following account of Spanish motives and activities to Warren L. Cook, *Floodtide of Empire: Spain and the Pacific Northwest, 1543–1819* (New Haven: Yale University Press, 1973), pp. 54–69, 88–134; Michael E. Thurman, *The Naval Department of San Blas: New Spain's Bastion for Alta California and Nootka, 1767 to 1798* (Glendale, Calif.: Arthur H. Clark, 1967), pp. 257–76; and Christon I. Archer, "The Spanish Reaction to Cook's Third Voyage," in Robin Fisher and Hugh Johnston, *Captain James Cook and His Times* (Vancouver: Douglas & McIntyre, 1978), pp. 99–119. A view, giving hitherto neglected economic perspectives is Virginia Gonzálves Claverán, "Malaspina, New Spain and the Northwestern Otter" (paper given to The Vancouver Conference on Exploration and Discovery, 1992).

II

centuries, but in order to avoid consequences brought by having any other neighbours [there] than the Indians".[10]

Vizcaino's 1603 discoveries on the California coast had left the whole northern shore above Cape Mendocino unexplored to Europeans, and it was not until 1774 that Spain's next expedition sought to determine the details of the coastline stretching north and west as far as the 60th parallel for evidence of newly reported Russian settlements and trading activity. To check any such foreign encroachment, in 1774 the Viceroy sent Juan José Pérez Hernandez, then the most able and experienced pilot at San Blas, north on a secret voyage. Pérez was a seasoned navigator and empire builder, for he had crossed the Pacific and had played a key role in the establishment of presidios and Franciscan missions in San Diego and Monterey in 1770. His advice on northern objectives was earnestly solicited by his political superior, the Viceroy, and Pérez initially responded that he was in favour of undertaking a voyage to latitude 45° or 50° North. However, as is often the case in human affairs, the state of international relations impinged on national plans, in this case those of Spain. In the end Pérez was instructed to go as high as the 60th parallel. Possibly this was beyond his personal desires or the capabilities of his ships and supplies, and we will never know this for want of evidence. In the circumstances, however, he made an extensive voyage along the coast in a remarkably short time. He sailed from Monterey in the frigate *Santiago* of 225 tons. He returned to port with little to show in the way of concrete discoveries and with no claim to his credit of having planted the flag of Spain or of having made any claim to the territory he discovered. He made a landfall near the present Alaska-Canada boundary, where he met the Haidas of the most northern of the Queen Charlotte Islands and saw the southernmost point of the Alaska Panhandle, Dall Island. Pérez failed to push north, for the time that he could have used profitably in exploration had been foolishly wasted at San Diego and Monterey. On 20 to 28 July the *Santiago* was off the Queen Charlotte Islands and 7 to 8 August off the Hesquiat Peninsula near Nootka Sound. Pérez did report an encounter with the Haida but rather typical of the man he reported the details with incredible sparseness. All he learned of the Northwest Coast in that latitude was that it consisted of several offshore islands inhabited by vigorous natives. Timorous of proceeding north into heavy weather or of visiting shore to take on water and make a formal act of possession as instructed, Pérez sailed south to Nootka Sound, where he anchored in what he named "Roadstead of San Lorenzo." Pérez and the crew of his ship, the *Santiago*, became the first known whites to visit Nootka

---

10 Bucareli to Julián de Arriaga, 27 July 1773; in Cook, *Floodtide of Empire*, p. 55.

Sound. They traded with the Indians of Yuquot, who came to the ship in their canoes. Several warriors boarded the Spanish vessel, and one light-fingered Indian managed to steal several silver spoons. Four years later, James Cook bought these same spoons, recognized their provenance, and noted in his account that this was proof that the Spanish had been at or near Nootka Sound before him.

Pérez was much impressed with the strategic value of Nootka Sound, but did not send a party ashore to take formal possession. "This fateful omission," Warren Cook has written, "would have profound diplomatic consequences and be much lamented by Spanish officialdom."[11] Sailing south, Pérez missed the Strait of Juan de Fuca and reached his home port of San Blas with only a few charts and some rough notes of his voyage. Francisco Antonio Mourelle, who subsequently commanded a Spanish expedition over much the same track, complained of Pérez's voyage that despite considerable expense to the crown, "we are left almost in the same ignorance."[12] The Viceroy, obviously disappointed, told Madrid that Pérez's meagre accomplishments nonetheless would facilitate a follow-up voyage then in preparation. The following year, 1775, two explorers, Bruno de Hezeta and Juan Francisco de la Bodega y Quadra, were sent to reach 65°N latitude and then, on a southerly course, to take possession of convenient places on shore. They were also to trade with the Indians and demonstrate Spanish friendliness to the natives.

About this time the zealous Minister of the Indies, José de Galvez, learned that Britain was sending James Cook to search for the western opening of the Northwest Passage. Now Galvez recited a whole litany of fears: that the English by discovering the passage would outflank the Spanish on the north; that British traders would conduct illicit trade in these lands; that British settlers would settle the coast; that British agents would foment a revolution among Indians and colonial subjects in Spanish America. Might not "el famoso Capitan Kook" establish British claims to unoccupied territory and rights to trade and navigation and shatter dreams of a Spanish Pacific northwest?

On 20 May 1776, Galvez directed the Viceroy of New Spain, Antonio Maria Bucareli, to take decisive measures to stop Cook's expedition: he was to withhold supplies and all aid to the Englishman. If Cook's ships were encountered, they were to be apprehended and their papers seized so that a diplomatic presentation could be made to London protesting the encroachment. Two months later, after news reached Galvez that Bodega had successfully

---

11 Cook, *Floodtide of Empire*, p. 67.
12 Ibid., p. 69.

explored the Alaska Coast and that Hezeta had discovered a great river on the Northwest Coast, later called the Columbia, he immediately ordered a third exploring expedition to be sent to the coast. This development of Spanish policy by sea was related to a similar growth by land. At the same time, Galvez reorganized the General Command for the Interior Provinces, a new jurisdiction in the American southwest separate from New Spain, one which would allow for the better administration of Texas, California and, in time, the Northwest Coast. Spain's power at Nootka depended on her power in the North American southwest. Eventually Indian raids in northwestern Mexico restricted the strength that Galvez could draw on to extend his dreamed Pacific coastal dominion north and west and even to the Arctic.

For his part, Bucareli in Mexico City was anxious to oblige his superior and follow his instructions, but only if he had the necessary martial support to counter Captain Cook. The Spanish navy, he confessed to Galvez, was too weak to oppose Cook by force, but he agreed to withhold supplies and aid from the British navigator.[13] Bucareli was plagued by a critical shortage of ships. He had few well-trained naval officers and men. His first concern was that Alta California be supplied regularly by sea. With some ships in dock, others in need of repair, and still others bound for the Alta California capital of Monterey with supplies, his slender marine resources were taxed to the limit. He believed that two frigates should be built at the naval yard at Guayaquil and sent north to further explore the Northwest Coast. Eventually the frigates *Princesa* and *Favorita* were readied. However, not until February 1779 did they head north from San Blas under command of Ignacio de Arteaga and Bodega to conduct an expedition ordered two years previously. This prolonged lapse augured poorly for Spanish interests.

In March 1779, one month after the *Princesa* and *Favorita* quit San Blas, Cook's ships left the Hawaiian Islands for the Arctic with no hint that two Spanish armed ships were in pursuit. In fact Arteaga was to be disappointed in his search: he never determined that Cook had visited the Northwest Coast though he explored north from Bucareli Sound (where the Spanish contemplated building a naval base) to Port Etches at Hinchinbrook Island, in Prince William Sound, the northernmost Spanish claim in America at 61°N.

Arteaga's investigations at Afognak Island near Kodiak revealed that the Russians, despite their energetic activities, were apparently confining themselves to the Aleutian Islands. These findings gave Spanish authorities a false sense of security. They allowed Carlos III and his ministerial advisers

---

13 Ibid., pp. 90–91, which reviews Bucareli's dilemma.

"to assume that Madrid could rest on its laurels and still retain dominion over that coastline, by virtue of previous discovery and symbolic acts of possession. No one foresaw that the decade to follow would bring traders of half a dozen nationalities swarming into the very area visited by Arteaga and Bodega."[14] As late as 1779 Madrid saw no reason to occupy the Northwest Coast with a garrison or settlement or even to claim Nootka. Indeed for nine years no Spanish navy ships ventured north from San Blas.

In 1788, however, Estéban José Martínez was given command of an expedition to Alaska. He had instructions to sail from San Blas in the frigate *Princesa* accompanied by the packet *San Carlos*, Gonzalo Lopez de Haro commanding. He was to investigate vague reports that Russian ships were trading for sea otter skins on the Northwest Coast south of Mt. St. Elias in about 60°N. He was to determine if the Russians, as rumour stated, had erected establishments at various ports along the Alaska Coast.

Martínez, a central and controversial figure in the Nootka story, was a Sevillano, born in 1742. At the age of thirteen he began his naval career; and in 1773, at thirty-one, he was serving as second pilot at the Naval Department of San Blas. He had sailed north with Pérez to Nootka in 1774 and would have gone with Hezeta in the following year had not Pérez, no model himself, found him wanting in navigation and seamanship. For twelve years he patiently sailed supply ships between San Blas and Monterey, Alta California, a prosaic existence for such an ambitious man apparently destined to obscurity in the distant Pacific. Eventually his dedication brought him the approval of Viceroy Bucareli as a competent and an able officer. Such an opinion ran counter to Pérez's assessment, and in view of Martínez's subsequent conduct during his Alaska voyage (which provoked the wrath of his fellow officers) and his high-handed actions at Nootka (which the British argued, precipitated the crisis) Pérez's report of incompetence seems the more reliable.

At bottom, Martínez was a patriot. In September 1786, he was in Monterey in command of two regular supply vessels from San Blas, the *Favorita* and *Princesa*, when the French explorer La Pérouse put into port for supplies.[15]

---

14 Ibid., pp. 97–98.

15 France had sent La Pérouse to complete Cook's work. With respect to the Northwest Coast he was to inquire into the prospects of the maritime fur trade north of Spanish possessions, claim a bay suitable for a depot for French traders, and find the western entrance to the Northwest Passage. La Pérouse claimed Lituya Bay, near Yakutat or Bering Bay, known locally as Frenchmen's Bay until the early twentieth century. Port des Français, as La Pérouse called it, remained the only French claim on the Northwest Coast until 1790, when Captain Etienne Marchand left Marseilles in the *Solide* on a private project to visit the Northwest Coast for furs. See John Dunmore, *French Explorers in the Pacific* (Oxford: Clarendon Press, 1965), 1: 262–63, 266–68, and 342–53.

La Pérouse had just called at Yakutat Bay, Alaska, and he gave Martínez first-hand information not only about the Russians' fort locations, but about their military strength and their future plans. Martínez, impatient for an important assignment, made the best of his information and warned both the Viceroy, Flores, and his superior, the Minister of the Indies, Galvez.[16] Meanwhile, several British ships had come after Cook to exploit the sea otter trade. Martínez knew nothing of the details of Hanna's voyages, of Strange's two vessels, or of the Etches project. But from La Pérouse he learned the startling fact that the English were now conducting a highly profitable trade between Nootka and Canton. La Pérouse's news was sufficient to stir the Spanish from complacency. In the summer of 1787 preparations began at San Blas to assemble supplies and outfit ships for a northern voyage to regions hitherto unvisited by Spanish vessels.

At this time the Spanish had good reason to be frightened of Russian southward penetration from the Gulf of Alaska. As early as 1741 the Russian expedition of Bering and Chirikov had crossed the Pacific from the Kamchatka shore to Alaska – known to the Aleuts as the "great mainland" – where among the countless kelp beds they found immense quantities of two of the world's richest furs, Alaska seal and sea otter. The Russians soon erected advance posts for trade on the Okhotsk seaboard, the Kamchatka Peninsula, and the Aleutian Islands. Bering's second expedition, in 1741–42, yielded fifteen to eighteen hundred sea otter pelts. These were worth 80 to 100 rubles each at Kiatka, and defrayed a portion of the cost of the expedition.[17] Subsequently a large number of Russian fur traders were drawn to the Commander, Kurile, and Aleutian Islands. They pushed eastward to the American coast and in 1784 had a fur station at Three Saints Bay on Kodiak Island. The closest European settlement was the Spanish presidio at San Francisco, founded fifteen years earlier.

By land and by sea the Russians pressed forward to establish their own distant dominion on the most northwesterly reaches of America. So extensive was Russian interest in the fur trade that between 1743 and 1800 some 101 ventures were undertaken by a total of forty-two companies, and nearly 187,000 pelts were taken (about ten per day) – worth in all about ten million rubles.[18] This was the most popular of all Russian merchant trades. What is

---

16 Thurman, *Naval Department*, p. 259.

17 James R. Gibson, *Feeding the Russian Fur Trade: Provisionment of the Okhotsk Peninsula, 1639–1856* (Madison: University of Wisconsin Press, 1976), pp. 3–5.

18 Ibid., p. 17. See also, James R. Gibson, *Imperial Russia in Frontier America: The Changing Geography of Supply of Russian America, 1784–1867* (New York: Oxford University Press, 1976), pp. 3–5.

surprising is that it took the Spanish and the English so long to discover that the Russians had established a prodigious new trade in Alaska.

In 1788 Martínez found that not only were the Russian traders building new settlements, as La Pérouse had reported, and sending ships from Kamchatka, but that Tsarina Catherine had outfitted an armed expedition commanded by an Englishman, Joseph Billings, a veteran of Cook's third voyage, to report on North Pacific prospects. Billings had elaborate instructions dated 1785 to explore the extreme northeastern parts of Asia, to visit the Aleutians, to make discoveries on the seas lying between Siberia and America, to report on the Alaskan fur trade, and to claim territory for Russia not previously discovered by any European power.[19]

Martínez's voyage to the Gulf of Alaska confirmed the worst fears of the Spanish court and the Mexican viceroy. From May to August 1788 he made a reconnaissance of the main islands and inlets of that remote coast. He found Russian traders solidly entrenched on many of the continent's island doorsteps east of the Aleutians. Martínez reported six Russian settlements in all, including those on Kodiak and Trinidad (Trinity) Islands. Father east, on the shores of Prince William Sound, he discovered a remnant of a European fort, an indication that Russians or perhaps Englishmen had been there already. The Russians had six small galleons, or "galliots," measuring fifty-three to fifty-eight feet, all armed – useful vessels for the then considerable trade with the natives. The Martínez expedition estimated the number of Russian occupants in the six posts at between 462 and 500, a considerable total in view of the obstacles of distance and environment.[20]

In itself, this information might have been sufficient warning to the Spanish that Russian occupation on the northeastern shores of the North Pacific was not only permanent but sizeable and increasing. As it was, Russian informants now told Martínez that the English were trading vigorously between Nootka Sound and Canton. And they warned him that the Russian sovereign had a

[19] Descriptions of Billings' voyage can be found in H. H. Bancroft, *Alaska, 1730–1885* (San Francisco, 1886), ch. 13, and Raisa V. Makarova, *Russians on the Pacific, 1743–1799*, trans. and ed. by Richard A. Pierce and Alton S. Donnelly (Kingston: Limestone Press, 1975). In 1790 Billings met the Spaniard, Salvidor Fidalgo, near Kodiak, but this encounter of rival imperial interests had no immediate political consequences owing to the then present state of the Nootka crisis. An Anglo-Russian alliance against Spain in the North Pacific, California, and Spanish America with a view to conquests was considered but never came to anything. R. A. Humphreys, "Richard Oswald's Plan for an English and Russian Attack on Spanish America, 1781–82," *Hispanic American Historical Review* 18 (1930): 95–101.

[20] William R. Manning, *The Nootka Sound Controversy* (Washington, D.C.: American Historical Association, 1905), pp. 300–301. López de Haro's estimate of 462 Russians is more accurate; see Thurman, *Naval Department*, pp. 272–73.

better right to the Northwest Coast than any other nation because of the priorities of discovery. A further blow was that the Russian trader Potap Kaikov (or Cumsmich as Spanish accounts call him) candidly told Martínez that two Russian frigates and a schooner from Kamchatka soon would buttress Russian interests on the Northwest Coast by settling at the very focal point of what had now become every interested nation's concern, Nootka Sound. Specifically, the Russians aimed to block English commerce. According to Kaikov, his government intended to act in this way because a British maritime fur trader had boasted in Canton that Cook's priority of discovery gave the British the right to trade at Nootka and to possess land on the Northwest Coast.[21]

Martínez quickly decided to report these developments to his superiors. He recommended that his government forestall the Russians. The Spanish, he advised Flores, should send an expedition with as many forces as the Viceroy could spare for the object of occupying Nootka by May 1789. From his visit there with Pérez in 1774 and from Cook's account, he knew Friendly Cove would satisfy most requirements for a small naval base. By establishing such a garrison the Spanish would gain control of the whole coast from San Francisco to Nootka Sound and authority over all the native tribes.[22] The race to Nootka was on. Not only had Meares established his first, if only temporary, base there, he was also planning a substantial settlement. Yankee merchantmen were visiting the port and, more seriously, the Russians and Spanish intended to occupy the same place.

Spain also had a growing, though only recent, fear that the young United States might support their energetic Yankee fur traders by sending an expedition to cross the continent and establish a colony on the Pacific shore. "Obviously, this is a feat that would take many years," the Viceroy of Mexico warned Madrid, "but I truly believe that as of now we are threatened by the probes of Russia, and those that can be made by the English from Botany Bay, which they are populating."[23]

In fact by 1789, Spanish claims to the Northwest Coast had little chance of being upheld if Britain pressed her interests and if France did not support her Catholic ally.[24] Spain had no substantial interest in the fur trade between the Northwest Coast and Canton, although some pelts were arriving at Canton

---

21 Ibid. Martínez to Flores, 5 December 1788 (Manning, *Nootka Sound*, pp. 300–301).
22 Ibid.
23 Flores to Valdés, 23 December 1788 (Cook, *Floodtide of Empire*, p. 130).
24 Christon I. Archer, "The Transient Presence: A Re-Appraisal of Spanish Attitudes towards the Northwest Coast in the Eighteenth Century," *BC Studies* 18 (Summer 1973): 20.

through Spanish hands.[25] However, in general, Spanish merchants had failed to prosecute a traffic that was giving American, Russian, and British rivals a bona fide claim to diplomatic support from their respective governments.

By contrast, Spain expected to maintain her claims by mere occupation of Nootka Sound and by rights of sovereignty under the Treaty of Tordesillas. She seems to have been outflanked on the coast between Alaska and Mexico by more aggressive commercial rivals, especially Britain, which was dominant in armed ships at sea. The cross and sword of Spain might be sufficient controls in Spanish America, but they would not answer on a maritime frontier. There the economic wealth and the facts of oceanic geography dictated that a mere fort on the edge of the vast Pacific rim could not be held against all rivals, especially a great maritime power such as Britain, unless sufficient Spanish merchantmen and frigates could hold it through trade or by force. Thus all too late the Spanish came to realize, as Martínez had warned, that the Northwest Coast had a potential of its own and that true sovereignty over it could only be acquired by more than a small military garrison.

---

[25] Meares complained of "a prodigious number of otter skins" brought to Manila by the galleon and thence to China. He thought they had not been obtained on the Northwest Coast north of 46°N, for nowhere during his voyages had he met with Spanish trade items (Meares to Douglas, 20 September 1788, in John Meares, *Voyages made in the Years 1788 and 1789 from China to the North West Coast of America* [London, 1790], app. 5). For further explanation and development of this imperial rivalry, see Barry M. Gough, *The Northwest Coast: British Navigation, Trade, and Discoveries to 1812* (Vancouver: University of British Columbia Press, 1992).

PACIFIC EXPLORATION IN THE 1780S AND 1790S

To the historian, the task of commenting on the exploration of the Pacific in the 1790s is one riddled with complexities. The following *reconnaissance* does not attempt to exhaust the subject for the indefinite dimensions of the task do not permit that. Rather, three sub-themes suggest themselves: one, George Vancouver as symbolic of his age; two, other nationals, French, Spanish, Russian and American, who were making incursions into the Pacific world; and three, what I have chosen to call "cultural relativism", viz. the perception held by some Europeans of the peoples of the wider world. These three subjects might be likened to three intercircling rings. In this configuration we see European man facing competition in pushing his nation's and continent's interests into new geographical areas, and evaluating his perception of who he is vis à vis new native worlds.

This is not a new theme. J. C. Beaglehole in his *Exploration of the Pacific* (first edition 1936, and subsequent editions) attempted a composite portrayal of the subject, long before he began to view the world through James Cook's eyes. J. M. Ward, too, explained the growing authority of national and international law in the South Pacific. Other scholars – Vincent Harlow, K. Dallas and Michael Roe – pioneered the study of economic motivations for the expansion of the second British Empire in the Pacific, and they also drew Australian studies into the larger world network, that characterized by this age of discovery. More recently, David Mackay, Alan Frost, Margaret Steven and others have looked at this subject and this era with greater scrutiny, and have added to our understanding of their complexities, more especially of the multiplicity of British purposes and the polyglot nature of the Pacific, not only of its peoples but of its places. Small wonder that my mentor, the late G. S. Graham, cautioned me against studying Pacific history and, in a fit of despair, even handed over to me his bulging file of notes on the subject – and intimated that the Pacific was too large a body of water, too large a littoral of varied lands for the historian to come to grips with. The whole, he warned, defied historical narrative and analysis. Maybe he was

III

100

right: perhaps the whole is too large to encompass, for there are worlds
within worlds in the Pacific.   Some intrepid scholars, however, Emeritus
Professor Oskar Spate among them, have not shied away from such a
forbidding challenge – and all the more power to him and his Herculean
endeavours.   Would that others would approach the history of the Pacific
with the appreciative humility of Professor Spate, who wrote: "Of course,
on the scale of treatment dictated by so large a design as a history of the
Pacific, the specialist will find superficialities and perhaps downright
error in his or her own particular field;   certainly errors of detail.   This
is the hazard of the generalist game;   but *it is a game which may bring
great rewards in unsuspected linkages, new insights into the
altogetherness of things.*   I have tried to summarize fairly various
interpretations some valid and some not, and give the reader some hints as
to which, in my opinion, is which" (italics added).[1]   My purpose here,
which is to look at the 1790s, is much more constrained.

I

George Vancouver was a child of his times.   He was schooled in that
classic age of English seamanship of which the legendary James Cook was
but one example.   This was also the age of Anson, of Palliser and of
Vernon.   This was the era of a navy that was in time of war and peace the
determinant of the nation's objectives (which were necessarily maritime
and overseas – both   in trade and dominion).   The Lords of the Admiralty
who directed these affairs were reliant on Parliamentary votes for ships,
supplies and men and, more, on Cabinet's direction as to national
priorities.   In all things, profit and power had jointly to be considered, as
an early East India Company director, Sir Josiah Child, remarked: and
this was as true in the time of Vancouver as in those of Palmerston,
Salisbury or Thatcher.   Thus, for Vancouver's age, whaling for oil – a
strategically necessary commodity – held a high position in national
priorities;   so, too, did Oriental trading in teas, silks, porcelain and
opium, which promoted the coastwise or country trade between Indian and
Canton;   so, moreover, did doing business in commodities American and
Pacific such as the sea-otter pelt, the ermine of Asia and a luxury for the
Mandarins, and bêche-de-mer, the edible sea-slug, and sandalwood.   All
these trades and navigations added to the profit and power of the British
nation-state.

However, making more complex these needs for profit and power were
the domestic requirements of the United Kingdom.   Dean Jonathan Swift's
proposal for dealing with the surplus of Irish babies was out of the
question.   In consequence, precursors of Thomas Malthus were already
pondering schemes of assisted emigration, of "shovelling out paupers" as
one critic put it so bluntly.   Bernard Bailyn has reminded us that the
peopling of British North America was not only promoted by the
availability of new American lands but by urgent needs that had to be met
at home.   In this regard, indentured servitude grew as a common mode of
"transportation" to America.   Then, too, there is the convict question.
This was one cause for Australia's founding under British auspices.   It
represented an imperial impulse that likewise and later affected the
history of the Falklands and of Bermuda, and had an unfulfilled prospect
in the history of British Columbia.[2]   Such perplexing and complicated
domestic needs necessitated overseas settlements, and these needs became

abundantly apparent to policy makers in the last decades of the
eighteenth century.

Vancouver was schooled by Cook. But so too were Bligh, Broughton,
Colnett, Meares, Portlock and Dixon. All of them were seasoned Pacific
voyagers before they themselves were entrusted with government projects
or corporate schemes. We can wonder at their contributions to enlarging
the European understanding of the wider world. William Bligh of
breadfruit fame practised the arts of seamanship during Cook's third
voyage and was Master of the *Resolution*, and he left for posterity many
legacies, not least the first English chart of Nootka Sound. William Robert
Broughton, Vancouver's second in command (in the *Chatham*), sounded the
Columbia River's channel and left for posterity the first English plan of
the great western American river (the Spaniard Hezeta had preceded him
by a few years). Broughton also surveyed the San Juan Islands lying
between Vancouver Island and the mainland, the source of so much Anglo-
American tension in 1859. Perhaps most important, under broad
discretionary powers delegated to him, he undertook a general survey of
Japanese seas in the mid 1790s, the last such serious survey before
Captain Matthew Flinders and F. W. Beechey were to resume exploration of
the Pacific. James Colnett we best remember for his intemperate nature,
and his incarceration by Spain's Nootkan Commandant Martínez in 1789.
Yet he was an explorer too. He investigated the Galapagos and looked in at
Juan Fernandez and other islands seeking a haven for British whalers
ranging the Southern Ocean. John Meares sailed from Bombay to Alaska
and Nootka Sound, and then, based on Macao and Canton, unlocked the
secrets of the maritime fur trade as advertised by James Cook and James
King eleven years previously. Nathaniel Portlock and George Dixon
followed from London and left notable narratives of their sea ventures.
And think, too, of the contemporaries of these persons who knew of or
were influenced by Cook: John Ledyard, who shaped United States
thinking about the Northwest Coast and the North Pacific; Joseph Billings
who sailed for the Russians; James Trevenen who also went into Russian
service; and Wilhelm Bolts who got up a scheme from Ostend and Trieste
to challenge British pre-eminence in the eastern Indian Ocean and trade
to distant Alaska and Nootka Sound.

This school left important legacies, and clearly that of Vancouver was
significant. Vancouver was solidly middle-class, the son of a customs
officer. Illness (and impatience) marred his command, and he flogged his
social superior, a young man of the quarterdeck, Lord Camelford, whose
family stood in high places. This was an act that guaranteed that
Vancouver would never be entrusted with command of a similar expedition
again. Indeed, Greg Dening has demonstrated that Vancouver flogged more
frequently than Bligh or Cook.[3] As a diplomat in dealing with the Dons at
Nootka Sound, Vancouver was inconclusive, though admittedly he carried
vague orders. His contributions to surveying are several, and in this
category I would count especially his charting of south-western
Australia, his circumnavigation of Vancouver Island, and his surveying of
the Hawaiian Islands.

More generally we can say that Vancouver and his contemporaries
were the successors of Cook: they were the second wave, so to speak, of
this Georgian, or Hanoverian, age. What we can admire best about them is

their scientific scepticism.   For example, let me quote James Cook on the prospect of a Strait of Anian in March 1778.   "It is in this very latitude we were now in [48°15'N] where geographers have placed the pretended *Strait of Juan de Fuca*, but we saw nothing like it, nor is there the least probability that ever such thing existed."[4]   Truly, these explorers derided the "closet philosophers".[5]   The ideas of these persons, Vancouver complained, "have been adopted for the sole purpose of giving unlimited credit to the traditionary exploits of ancient foreigners and to undervalue the laborious and entertaining exertions of our own countrymen in the noble science of discovery."[6]   These navigators had been trained as empiricists.   To question, to evaluate, to record, to conclude: these were their tasks.   They were sceptics and rationalists, sons of the age of reason.   And this, above all other reasons, is why we regard their journals and voyages as historical evidence of unquestionable meritorious value, a fact long ago appreciated by antiquarian booksellers.

II

The late eighteenth century was a time of acute international rivalry. Lapérouse sailed for France in 1785 on a number of interrelated assignments: to make claims to sovereignty, to promote the maritime fur trade, to "show the flag", and to advance the many causes of science. Gray and Kendrick sailed from Boston on more pecuniary pursuits: to develop a round-the-world trade in luxury items, and they succeeded mightily. Spain's Bodega y Quadra, Vancouver's more diplomatic and more astute counterpart, extended the survey of the Northwest   Coast – a work also undertaken by his fellow countrymen Martínez, Quimper, Eliza and Narvez (among others).   Like America's, Russia's interests were fundamentally business-like, and in 1799 the Russian-American Company received St. Petersburg's royal charter and a free hand to develop the trade and dominion of Alaska.[7]

If the 1790s saw a four-power struggle to open the Pacific it is also important to note that this state of affairs was dramatically dependent on a state of peace in European and North Atlantic waters.   Once France and Britain went to war, as they did in 1792, this bore on the relationships of these powers with the native peoples of the distant Pacific.   The Americans gained an ascendancy in the maritime fur trade as British merchantmen and sailors were drawn off for other national obligations. Abandoned by revolutionary France during the Nootka Sound crisis, Spain could not sustain the same degree of imperial authority, especially in the Pacific and in western North America.   Preoccupied in the Baltic, Russia did not renew her Pacific interests until after 1815 and then did so in remarkably energetic ways – in the waters of the Antipodes as in the little known, icy reaches of the Bering Sea and Alaskan littoral. War, therefore, closed the era of exploration in the Age of Vancouver.   Hostilities cut short what would have been a gradual extension of European knowledge about the wider world.

But war and revolution had another effect, a deleterious one on the advances of distant exploration.   The French revolution and its warlike aftermath – that shook the continent of Europe and challenged every political order (including that of Great Britain) – ushered in a new era where private societies, scientific institutions and publication societies became more broadly interested in exploration. Vancouver's voyage, undertaken during the French Revolution, can be regarded as the last expedition of the Age of Reason. However, for almost fifteen years scientific enquiry overseas was practically halted and only then resumed under the arguments of pressing hydrographic work to make uncharted seas safer for navigation and, to a lesser degree, of providing naval employment. The deep-seated motivation for these voyages was economic and strategic advantage, and these voyages bore a more wide-ranging nationalistic purpose than those of their predecessors. The reason for this is that oceanic exploration was becoming less the work of fixers such as Sir Joseph Banks, Bart, and Captain Hugh Palliser, R.N. It was becoming more the endeavour of the Hydrographic Office, first under Thomas Hurd then under Francis Beaufort and Admirals Washington and Richards, and the Admiralty Office under Sir John Barrow. This change came about partly from pressure from the Royal Geographical Society, the Colonial Office, and even corporations such as the Hudson's Bay Society and East India Company. Funding for such scientific research, in comparison to that of the Age of Reason, was more widely borne by the private sector and even government expenditures on such worthwhile endeavours came under closer parliamentary control than ever before.

In closing this discussion on international influences on discoveries at the end of the eighteenth century I should like to return to the relative state of activities between Britain and the principal European power in the Pacific, Russia. We who have studied the British imperial ethos throughout time are at once aware of the uniqueness of the British experience. We are also – but here I think we always need be reminded – cognizant of the fact that foreign rivalry shaped the character of British responses. Think of English-Dutch-Portuguese rivalry in the Indian Ocean in the sixteenth century, or English-Spanish-French rivalry in the Caribbean in the seventeenth and eighteenth, or of English-French-German-Russian rivalry in the Pacific in the nineteenth. If we take the date 1791 – when Vancouver's new instructions had been finalized (and not those of 1789-1790 which had a different purpose)[8] – we may be aware of French interests in the Pacific through Lapérouse's expedition and of Dutch and Spanish activities earlier in that century. So often British policy was shaped by the psychological realities of the pre-emptive impulse.

We should remember, too, that this was an age that sought order; not that it *had* order, mind you, but that it *pursued* it. This we hear in the "classical" music of Bach, Mozart and Salieri; and this we see in the formal gardens of Capability Brown, and in the Georgian houses built along Greek and Roman lines. Edward Gibbon the historian, a contemporary of Vancouver's, was similarly concerned with order, and one of his constant themes was fear of savage people battering at the gates of European civilization.[9] The Swedish botanist Carolus Linnaeus was seeking to order the natural world; taxonomy, now derided in certain circles, was then of premier importance to the ordering of the natural world. To these could be added the search for accuracy in cartographic technique and in time-keeping. All, indeed, were part of this search for precision. Another contemporary, James Hutton, a precursor of Darwin's, announced a theory of the earth (published in the *Transactions of the Royal Society of Edinburgh* in 1788), in which he argued that the earth's surface was moving towards a static order. "Uniformitarianism" was triumphant in the thinking of that age.[10] The enlightened thinkers of that age, the creative human forces as it were, sought and lauded order, perhaps out of the social chaos of war and revolution that they witnessed all around them.

III

Because the European world – by which again is meant its educated and learned leadership – sought to develop order and regulation and to define European standards of taste and perception, it tended to judge other civilizations in relative terms, as is done today. The men of Vancouver's age judged other civilizations in comparative terms and did so almost invariably. From their own particular points of reference Cook and Vancouver, the latter more so than the former, evaluated the societies they were meeting. But they suffered human frailties. They were too often just *voyeurs*, ethnographers *en passant*, making casual reconnaissances, and recording in their journals their perceptions. But how weightily we hang on their every word two centuries later while the likes of the more cautious Howe, Dening and Fisher desperately try to see the other side of the frontier, from the other side of the beach, to use Dening's mighty metaphor.[11]

Let us here consider two examples of Vancouver's perceptions. His account of his landfall in south-western Australia is one eye-opener on this score.[12] He first discovers an Aboriginal dwelling, and from a few scraps of evidence about this dwelling and signs of life puts the locals in the "wretched" category. He even goes so far as to make reference patronizingly to how sorry he feels for their wretched, savage condition. The Aborigines are nowhere to be found, being away on a seasonal migration or perhaps having decided that if they stayed to welcome the newcomers the guests might, unhappily, decide to stay. Vancouver coasts eastwards and in so doing leaves a whole new cluster of place names, superimposing European terminology for bays, bights and barriers for native terms. Happening upon the remains of a temporary native settlement Vancouver again returns to the world-of-the-wretched scenario. He also is mystified by why these people are not fishermen or oyster gatherers. Puzzled, he continues his course, changes his mind about calling at Botany Bay (thus disappointing his shipmates who sought time ashore and a chance to see what the infant convict colony was doing), and shapes a course for Dusky Bay, New Zealand, having concluded that a Bass Strait must have existed, even if *he* could not navigate the passage. How Eurocentric, how *Vancouver*-centric!

A less harsh view of the environment and inhabitants of south-west New Holland and King George's Sound is provided by botanist Archibald Menzies.[13] A man of wider, more inclusive vision, Menzies had been employed in the Edinburgh Botanic Garden, had been trained as a surgeon in Edinburgh University, and had entered the navy as a young man. He was appointed naturalist with Vancouver's expedition through the interest of Sir Joseph Banks, scientist and patron. Menzies' journal of his perceptions of King George's Sound, 27 September to 13 October 1791, portrays a rich land, initially approached by rocky bluffs. On 29 September a brief excursion ashore brought Menzies, who accompanied

Pacific Exploration in the 1780s and 1790s 105

Vancouver, to a land that was not infertile as has been expected. Rather, Menzies recorded, "we were soon impressed with a very rich idea of its fertility from the richness and abundance of its vegetable productions".[14] Menzies mentions the hut but does not pass comment, and goes on to describe the beauty of hills and valleys beyond – "a rich picturesque prospect boldly drawn by nature's manly pencil".[15] They found, too, the gum tree and other species, and Menzies notes for the first time that "the place had been burnt down here and there, particularly about the stems of the gum plant which bore its marks more than any other".[16] He admires the oyster beds and the watering places, and the verdant woods as far as the eye could see promised "luxuriency [sic] of vegetation in many places", and the land capable of "sustaining thousands of inhabitants with the necessaries as well as the comforts of life, though at this time it appeared destitute of any".[17]

On 7 October Menzies found a thick wood of *Eucalyptus* with naked stems, or trunks. These too were burned – culturally modified trees, or "C.M.T.'s" to the archaeologist. "...we conceive it probable", Menzies wrote with willing understanding,

> that the natives are at this trouble for the purpose of collecting a kind of redish gum which this tree produces, is it not probable that this substance may in its milder state form a part of their food, as it seemed to be so much in general request, that we seldom met with these trees or the other gum plants anywhere about the Sound without observing their stems burnt or scorched with fire, on purpose no doubt of causing a quicker excretion of these concentrations by means of heat.[18]

A second village was entered, this one having been more recently occupied, and here too stood those strangely scorched trees – "many of the larger trees had been scorched by it and deep cuts made in their bark as has been already mentioned in other places – but no residue of the food of the natives could be seen any where".[19]

His further reconnaissance over the next few days revealed to Menzies an excellent range and good feeding area for domestic animals "of every denomination".[20] Deeper coloured, richer soil also promised cultivation with moderate labour. "In short", he concluded,

> the island colony of this part or New Holland has a very delightful and promising appearance and we therefore conceive it an object well worth the attention of government in a more particular investigation of it, as it offers fair to afford an eligible situation for a settlement which, on account of its nearness and easy access to our settlements in India, possesses peculiar advantages not to be derived from the opposite shore.[21]

Concerning the Aborigines, Menzies was not prepared to state categorically, but he was prepared for hypothetical reasoning of a careful nature. They were probably not numerous, he surmised, for otherwise the British would have seen more signs of their encampments. That they were migratory he thought likely, and dependent on "roots of the fields, the fruits of the forest or the productions of the different lakes". This, he reasoned, would explain the temporary nature of their huts.[22] The British remained perplexed. Menzies again was left guessing:

> In the few places of their encampment we met with our not being able to find out any traces of their food was a matter of no little astonishment to enquiry, for we examined with the greatest care round their huts and fire places and could find no vestiges of the bones of birds, animals or fish, no shells or any remnant whatsoever that might enable us to form a criterion of their means of subsistence. This leads me to suppose that they live in a great measure on the vegetable kingdom and perhaps at particular seasons not a little on the different gums in their plant state with which the country every where abounds....[23]

And he clinched his conclusion by remarking that otherwise he would not have found so many trees singed by fire.[24] Menzies was of the opinion, not held by Vancouver, that the Aborigines had capabilities of crossing rivers and bays by some sort of marine transport, that they exploited the oyster beds, and that they drew considerable sustenance from the sea.[25] Thus was a new world being disclosed to Europe by scientists such as Menzies. Truly Australia afforded, as Menzies had promised Banks, "a fine field for Botanizing!"[26]

A second example of Vancouver's thinking in relative terms occurs when he makes his reconnaissance of Puget Sound on the Northwest Coast of North America – again stamping the names of Lords of the Admiralty and political friends, acquaintances, patrons, and other worthies on every mountain and bay he could see. About the time when he proclaims British sovereignty for His Majesty King George III in the Strait of Georgia – heretofore Salish Indian country – he gives away yet another European concept: that the wilderness of trees and mountains are undeveloped, and only await European enterprise to bring the land into productivity.[27] Little did he realize or choose to realize, as the archaeological findings at nearby Ozette, Washington State, or the tree-use surveys on Meares Island, British Columbia, have shown recently, that the Indians were using the forests, and that culturally modified trees allowed for tree use without tree cutting – something the great foresting timber giants have yet to discover. All that is needed, Vancouver remarks, is a population (by which he means a European one) to open the land to productive use. Even the solemn, grey-green-blue forested landscape bothers his eye. The misty shoreline, the primeval beach, the untouched forested hills, rolling away into the distance – the stuff the Sierra Club reminds us is too quickly disappearing – this offered a savage, unwelcoming, untutored coast to Vancouver. No parkland this, and probably even Brown was incapable of bringing it to order. We are left with an unsatisfactory perception in Vancouver (not found in Cook) that he is short on sympathy and empathy, that he is inwardly angry and judgmental, that he lacks Cook's simple, uncomplicating urbanity, that his vision is narrower and less generous.

Even so, his contribution to his age was significant. In the year 1792, George Vancouver completed most of his Northwest Coast survey. Precisely three centuries had passed since Columbus's discovery of America. Those three hundred years had brought a conclusion to the end of the search for a northwest passage in certain latitudes. Nonetheless, the polar shore and passage had yet to be plotted and traversed. That the Inuit and Indians knew these physical dimensions of America all along is obvious but not trite to recount. For some 25,000 years – about half the time the Aborigines had lived in Australia – Northwest Coast Indians had developed one of the most remarkable cultures of the Americas. This was a non-industrial, heavily ordered, finely balanced system of human existence that Europeans with their brief and facile commentary were prepared to describe and dismiss as savage. Christian missionaries had not yet followed the explorers, though this was soon to happen. Yet the period had brought guns, disease and new expectations. Moreover, it foreshadowed an age of commercial development, imperial rivalry and national growth that would lead to the largest naval battles in history within its littoral and the dropping of the only atomic weapons against civilian populations. "It was indeed sincerely to be wished", scientist George Forster, a veteran of Cook's second voyage, wrote with telling solemnity, "that the intercourse which has lately subsisted between Europeans and the natives of the South Sea islands may be broken off in time, before the corruption of manners which unhappily characterizes civilized regions, may reach that innocent race of men, who live here fortunate in their ignorance and simplicity." To this he added his own plea for a halt to Time's advance: "If the knowledge of a few individuals can only be acquired at such price as the happiness of nations, it were better for the discoverers, and the discovered, that the South Sea had remained unknown to Europe and its restless inhabitants."[28] But Time could not stand still; and the 1790s perhaps saw the last moments of native innocence in the Pacific.

NOTES

Abbreviations

ARA	Algemeen Rijksarchief, The Hague
BL	British Library, London
BM (NH)	British Museum (Natural History), London
BN	Bibliothèque Nationale, Paris
Dixson	Dixson Library, State Library of New South Wales, Sydney
GC	*The Great Circle* (Perth, 1979-)
Guildhall	Guildhall Library, London
Historical Studies	*Australian Historical Studies* (Melbourne, 1940-)
HRA	*Historical Records of Australia*, series 1 (Sydney, 1914-25)
HRNSW	*Historical Records of New South Wales* (Sydney, 1892-1901)
Huntington	Henry E. Huntington Library, San Marino
IOR	India Office Records, London
JAS	*Journal of Australian Studies* (Melbourne, 1978-)
JRAHS	*Journal of the Royal Australian Historical Society*
Mitchell	Mitchell Library, State Library of New South Wales, Sydney
NLA	National Library of Australia, Canberra
NMM	National Maritime Museum, Greenwich
PMC	*Portugaliae Monumenta Cartographica*, ed. Armando Cortesão and Avelino Teixeira da Mota (Lisbon, 1960)
PRO	Public Record Office, London
La Trobe	La Trobe Library, State Library of Victoria, Melbourne
Sutro	Sutro Library, California State Library, San Francisco
VOC	Dutch East India Company

III

Notes

1. O. H. K. Spate, "The History of a History: Reflections on the Ending of a Pacific Voyage", *The Journal of Pacific History*, 23(April 1988), 12.
2. B. M. Gough, *Distant Dominion: Britain and the Northwest Coast of North America, 1579-1809* (Vancouver, 1980).
3. Greg Dening, *The Bounty: An Ethnographic History* (Parkville, 1988).
4. Cook, *Journals*, III, 293-94. Spelling corrected from original.
5. Quoted in Gough, *Distant Dominion*, p. 125.
6. Quoted in Howard T. Fry, *Alexander Dalrymple (1737-1808) and the Expansion of British Trade* (London, 1970), p. 221.
7. James R. Gibson, "Russian Expansion in Siberia and America", *The Geographical Review*, 70(1980), 127-36.
8. Gough, *Distant Dominion*, ch. 7.
9. Gibbon's *Decline and Fall of the Roman Empire*, published 1787, announced: "The savage nations of the globe are the common enemies of civilized society; and we may inquire with anxious curiosity whether Europe is still threatened with a repetition of those calamities which formerly oppressed the arms and institutions of Rome. Perhaps the same reflections will illustrate the fall of that mighty empire and explain the probable causes of our actual security." And again, "... the experience of four thousand years should enlarge our hopes, and diminish our apprehensions" – quoted in H. G. Wells, *The Outline of History*, rev. ed. (New York, 1961), II, 677-81.
10. James Hutton, "Theory of the Earth; Or An Investigation of the Laws Observable in the Composition, Dissolution and Restoration of Land Upon the Globe", *Transactions of the Royal Society of Edinburgh*, I(1788), 209-304. Loren Eiseley, *Darwin's Century: Evolution and the Men who Discovered It* (Garden City, N.Y., 1958), pp. 69-75.
11. K. R. Howe, *Where the Waves Fall: A New South Sea Islands History from First Settlement to Colonial Rule* (Sydney, 1984). Greg Dening, *Islands and Beaches: Discourse on a Silent Land: Marquesas, 1774-1880* (Honolulu, 1980), "Possessing Tahiti", *Archaeology Oceania*, 21(1986), 103-118, and *The Bounty*. Robin A. Fisher, *Contact and Conflict: Indian-European Relations in British Columbia, 1774-1890* (Vancouver, 1977).
12. George Vancouver, *A Voyage of Discovery to the North Pacific Ocean and Round the World, 1791-1795*, ed. W. Kaye Lamb (London, 1984), 1, 325-57.
13. *Dictionary of National Biography*, XXXVII, 258.
14. BL Add. MS 32641, ff. 41-73; typescript in Mitchell, B1135; (microfilm of journal FM4/17, quotation at f. 43).
15. *Ibid.*
16. *Ibid.*, f. 44.
17. *Ibid.*
18. *Ibid.*, f. 54.
19. *Ibid.*, f. 57.
20. *Ibid.*, f. 59.
21. *Ibid.*, ff. 59-60.
22. *Ibid.*, f. 61.
23. *Ibid.*, f. 62. In evaluating Aboriginal native uses of trees, Menzies mentions these publications: Phillip, *Voyage to Botany Bay* (London, 1789) and Hawkesworth (1773).
24. *Ibid.*, ff. 62-63.
25. F. 63.
26. Menzies to Banks, 10 August 1791, Mitchell MS A79/2.
27. Douglas Cole and Maria Tippett, "Pleasing Diversity and Sublime Desolation: The 18th-Century British Perception of the Northwest Coast", *Pacific Northwest Quarterly*, 65(1974), 1-7.
28. George Forster, *A Voyage Round the World, in His Britannic Majesty's Sloop "Resolution"* ... *1772-75* (London, 1777), pp. I, 303, 368.

IV

James Cook and the Origins of the Maritime Fur Trade

A MONG his many feats Captain James Cook of the Royal Navy is best remembered for his three great world-circling voyages between 1768 and 1779. His exploratory expeditions for the British government opened to European enterprises certain lands in the Pacific suitable for settlement, particularly New South Wales and New Zealand. They also opened new branches of commerce within the Pacific rim.

Cook's third voyage revealed for the first time a general delineation of the Northwest Coast of North America from Oregon to Bering Sea but also inaugurated a great sea link between present Canadian territory on the west coast and the markets of China, one which grew in time with Asiatic desires for Canadian staples, particularly beaver pelts, wheat and minerals and Northwest Coast Indian demands for trade items. This trade grew from small beginnings, and it began not through any great design of merchants in the City of London or even by some preliminary trade mission authorized by the government. It began in fact by accident, and its repercussions were greater than Cook's men could have foreseen.

When Cook's ships, H.M.S. *Resolution* and H.M.S. *Discovery* reached Nootka Sound on Vancouver Island's west coast in March 1778, natives approached the ships in their canoes, crying '*Macook*'—will you trade? Cook's crews had not come to trade in any organized way. Yet this is not to say that they were unprepared to trade, for out of custom, officers and seamen bound for the Pacific brought nails, knives, and trinkets with them for the purpose of buying favor with native women or acquiring articles of food and clothing. Among sailors there were always a few curio hunters wishing to purchase items scarce in their homeland, souvenirs of their personal penetration into new and far-off lands. At Nootka, Cook's officers and men traded their nails and knives, then their buckles and buttons, and even may have taken to robbing their ship's metal

IV

JAMES COOK

fastenings to satisfy the insatiable demand of the Indians (in a land largely untouched by the industrial revolution) for brass, iron, tin, copper, pewter, and shiny precious metals.

The British seamen had come to Nootka prepared to trade in an incidental way in beads. But the Nootka held spherical glass in little esteem. 'Nothing would go down with them but metal,' Cook wrote in his journal, 'and brass was now become their favourate, So that before we left this place, hardly a bit of brass was left in the ship, except what was in the necessary instruments. Whole suits of cloaths were stripped of every button....' Hardware from furniture, copper kettles, tin canisters, and candlesticks—all these, he mused, 'went to wreck.'[1] The result was that the Nootka got more from the expedition than any other Pacific peoples visited by Cook's ships. There are stories, too, which tell of the natives' passionate desire for metal. Midshipman James Trevenen, by chance holding a broken buckle in his hand, was approached by a Nootka man who wanted to trade a sea-otter skin for the object, which he tied on his wrist and bought as a bracelet. The same otter pelt sold for as much as three hundred dollars in China, sufficient for Trevenen to buy his own necessities at Macao, as well as silk gowns, teas, and other oriental objects and items which he took home for family and friends. In this case Trevenen had quite accidentally established his own round-the-world trade of metals from Europe, furs from the Northwest Coast, and teas from the Orient—paying cargoes on each leg of the voyage and commodities sufficiently in demand at each destination to make profitable a new global commerce. As for the Indian in question, he believed he had made an advantageous bargain.

The Nootka had in their midst a great economic resource, the pelts of the sea otter. They also had (and offered) others, including bear, wolf, fox, deer, raccoon, cougar and martin. But none was so precious and none so attractive as the sea-otter pelt, beautiful, delicate and thick, soft to touch, almost luminous in appearance. The hairs of the fur are an inch to an inch and a half in length, and in colder northern waters are especially attractive in color being dark brown to jet black, surely a gorgeous material to enrich milady's or a gentleman's wardrobe. The British sometimes called them the 'sea beaver,' taking the term from the Russian *bobri morski*. In actuality they were sea otter (*Enhydra lutris*) which resembles the land otter (*Lutra canadensis*) in appearance. The sea otter attains a mature size of from four to five feet in length and eighty pounds in weight.

1 J. C. Beaglehole, ed., *The Journals of Captain James Cook on His Voyages of Discovery: The Voyage of the* Resolution *and* Discovery, *1776-1780* (2 parts; Cambridge, England: The Hakluyt Society, 1967), pt. 1, p. 302.

At the time of Cook's visit, sea otters inhabited, except for small gaps of distribution, the whole 6,000-mile crescent littoral of the North Pacific from Baja California to Japan. The animal prefers waters of the open coast and bays of the outer seacoasts, never occupying inland waters far from the ocean such as Puget Sound or the inside passage of Alaska. The sea otter favors rocky coasts where points of land, large bays, underwater reefs, and large rocks or islets provide feeding and resting places. In these locations abundant invertebrate bottom fauna—clams, abalones, sea urchins—are taken usually a half mile from shore; in some areas fish and king crabs are their diet. But always their activities are gregarious. They congregate in large groups known as 'rafts,' floating happily on their backs eating and playing. In the late eighteenth century when they were still plentiful in number they afforded an attractive and easy target for a sea hunter carrying a spear. The maternal care and solicitude for the young meant that the adult female sea otter would seldom leave her pups during an encounter with a hunter, a fact which hastened the despoliation of the breed. Moreover, because the female produces only one pup at a time and does not do so every year, the slow rate of reproduction could not offset the steady extermination of the sea otter by human depredations. In Cook's time these points counted little, but by the close of Chief Maquinna's era in the early 1800's they bulked large in the declining wealth of the Nootka and the sea-otter trade generally.

In 1778, however, the Indians took sea-otter pelts with ease and little concern. They traded, according to the estimate of the Royal Marine John Ledyard, 1,500 sea-otter skins, an average of 7.5 skins per sailor. The whites took only the best, Ledyard said, 'having no thoughts at that time of using them to any other advantage than coverting them to the purposes of cloathing.' They bought other skins—weasel, mink, and wolverine—but only a small part of what they might have done had they known of the possibility of marketing them at 'such an astonishing profit.'[2] By the end of their visit to Nootka Sound the British knew that the Indians hoped they would return once more to trade; indeed as an encouragement they promised to lay in a good stock of skins. Cook had no doubts but that they would.

Farther north, on the Alaska coast, the British again traded for sea-otter skins. Cook's search for the western entrance to the Northwest Passage took him to Cape Hitchinbrook near the northernmost reaches of the Gulf of Alaska. Here there was a mingling of aboriginal people—the

2 James Kenneth Munford, ed., *John Ledyard's Journal of Captain Cook's Last Voyage* (Corvallis: Oregon State University Press, 1963), p. 70.

IV

Eskimo and the Tlingit—and Cook's men saw from time to time people very different in dress and manner from those of Nootka Sound. But, like the Nootka, they came to trade in the sea otter which here was a lustrous black and bred in plenty. Cook thought these natives had not traded with the Russians from Kamchatka. He reasoned that the Russians had never been among them or traded with them, for, if they had, the natives would not be wearing such valuable skins as the sea otter; 'the Russians,' he wrote acidly, 'would find some means or other to get them all from them.'[3] Here, unlike at Nootka, colored beads, especially sky blue beads, were a prized commodity. Ironically, however, the British had come armed with only the clear crystal kind. The blue beads, about the size of large peas, were apparently of Russian manufacture and handed down in trade from other natives to the west. For five or six blue beads one might acquire a sea-otter skin worth ninety or one hundred dollars.

Farther west, the English traded with natives at Unalaska in the Aleutian Islands, the principal commercial center of Alaska where Russian influence had long been strong. Here Cook met the Russian G. Ismaylov, who in addition to telling him what he knew about Alaska and the American continent, informed him that his countrymen had made several unsuccessful attempts to get a foothold on the continent but had always been repulsed by natives regarded as treacherous. Ismaylov had once voyaged to the Kurile Islands, Japan and China; and Cook suspected that the Russians had tried to open up a seaborne trade with Canton but had been unsuccessful. He also learned from Ismaylov that the sea otter was valuable at Japan but not at Canton. Cook was suspicious of this, and he hints in his journal that his opposite was trying to induce him to trade at Kamchatka by offering him the present of a sea-otter pelt worth eighty rubles at the Russian port. Cook declined this offer, wishing not to remain in his debt on that point. They parted as friends, however, Cook bearing a letter of introduction from Ismaylov to the Russian governor at Petropavlovsk and the useful warning that when Cook's ships approached the Kamchatka port they were not to go by ship unannounced, for they would surely be shot at, but rather to announce their arrival by sending in a boat with Ismaylov's letter.

But now Cook knew the Russians were entrenched on the doorstep of the American continent, operating an emporium of trade with the help of a schooner sailing out of Petropavlovsk, 1,500 miles distant. At Unalaska about thirty Russians and seventy Kamchatka natives were pursu-

[3] Beaglehole, ed., *Cook's Journals*, pt. 1, p. 371.

ing a branch of commerce developed by Vitus Bering and his Russian successors.

Cook's explorations on the Northwest Coast and Alaska did not disclose, as was hoped, a northwest passage which would allow the British to undertake a world revolution in trade by a new and shorter route to Asia. They did reveal, however, the absolute requisite to carrying on any British trade in this region—profitability. Cook did not yet know of the possibilities of the China market when he wrote in his journal on 5 June 1778, 'There is no doubt but a very beneficial fur trade might be carried on with the Inhabitants of this vast coast, but unless the northern passage is found it seems rather too remote for Great Britain to receive any emolument for it.'[4] He knew that the sea otter was the prized pelt of the North Pacific and available in quantity. Moreover, he knew that the Indians would hunt them in order to trade for foreign luxuries. If a high enough price could overcome the costs accrued by long-distance trading perhaps the trade could indeed become profitable. After all, were not the Russians already trading here?

Cook, because of his death in the Hawaiian Islands later during this voyage, never lived to see the maritime fur trade thrive in English hands as it did during the years 1785 through 1789. But at Kamchatka and again at Macao Cook's men came to realize, all too late, that they had been on the very doorstep of wealth without knowing it. At Petropavlovsk in Kamchatka they disposed of two-thirds of their skins but not knowing their value had naïvely traded away freely with an exceedingly eager Russian merchant named Fedositch. It was a surprisingly brisk traffic, carried on between decks, and eventually the price rose and good skins yielded thirty-five rubles or £7. The most made by any of the officers or men was £60, a pleasant and unexpected return. Eventually they learned to their surprise and disappointment that the Russians got more than double the price for their skins in China, and that Fedositch was specializing in Russian trade with northern China. Perhaps the British would have been wise to await their arrival in Macao. On the other hand, there was no certainty if or when Macao would be reached, and indeed not until November 1779 did *Resolution* and *Discovery* sail into the Typa of the Macao Roads, and then only for a brief call for supplies.

The Typa lay near the entrance to the Chu or Canton River, leading upriver some twenty-four leagues distant to the great imperial city. Here trading connections were difficult. For one thing, the Portuguese had a

4 Ibid.

virtual monopoly on commerce with the Chinese, making the situation
of the English merchants, the East India Company, one of little influence. For another, protocol had to be observed, a protocol based on an
ancient fear of the West. Here, frustrated East India agents complained
to Captain John Gore, now in command, that 'delay and form take place
of activity and effectual service.'⁵ Yet a third reason making trade difficult was that international relations were now at flash point: the War of
American Revolution had not ended and hostilities had spread to eastern
seas. Britain and France were in an undeclared state of war in the Indian
Ocean. In these circumstances the Chinese objected to the presence of
two British warships that had not come to trade but were now armed and
prepared to defend themselves against the French or their probable
allies, the Spanish.

Nonetheless, the British were able to dispose of their valuable cargo.
A box of sea-otter skins was given to the East India Company for its use
as a favor to the mandarins. Gore sent Captain James King to Canton to
expedite the tricky arrangements for supplies, and as this seemed likely
to be the best place to sell furs, King took some twenty pelts with him,
chiefly the property of the late Captains Cook and Clerke. This commission gave King, he wrote sarcastically of the expedition, opportunity of
becoming acquainted with 'the genius of the Chinese for trade.'⁶

King was required to meet with a representative of the Hong, a society
of Canton merchants, who boldly told him that he could depend on his
integrity. Then, when King produced his wares, the Chinese agent
studied the peltry, examining them with care over and over again, and
eventually, after some delay, telling King that he could offer but 300
Spanish dollars for the lot. King now knew he had to drive a hard bargain,
for knowing the prices got at Petropavlovsk the Chinese had not offered
nearly half of their valued worth. He demanded a thousand in return.
His opposite advanced to 500 dollars, then offered a private present of
tea and porcelain worth 100, then 100 more in cash, then advanced to
700 dollars. King reduced his demand to 900. The Chinese trader then
produced a list of India goods King should take in exchange, but this
King refused because he did not wish to deal in this mode. Now the Chinese gave the surprising demand, his ultimatum, that they would divide
the difference, and King now quite wearied by business settled for 800
dollars.

There is more to this transaction than meets the eye. The Chinese

⁵ English Factory, Canton, to John Gore, 3 December 1779, ibid., pt. 2, p. 1549.
⁶ James Cook and James King, *Voyage to the Pacific Ocean* (3 vols.; London, 1784), III, 437-40.

specie supply was closely guarded by imperial regulation and for years the Chinese had demanded that if westerners were to trade with them they would have to receive commodities in return such as silks, teas and porcelain. All too frequently, as in King's case, the Europeans were looking for cash settlements. Nonetheless, the Hong merchant had bought the sea-otter skins for cash, for they were prized items of clothing and ornamentation in China among persons of wealth and influence, being made into splendid robes or cut and sewed on as borders for greatcoats. Sea otter were the ermine of Asia and highly in demand at the Chinese court.

King was not alone in completing a transaction, for other sailors sold what they had brought to Macao. One seaman sold his stock for 800 dollars. Some prime skins, clean and well preserved, yielded 120 dollars each. Trevenen's pelt, acquired for the broken brass buckle, brought the splendid sum of 300 dollars, perhaps the highest price of the lot. Another index of capital gain is William Bligh's purchase of thirty large green Spanish beads from Tahitians for a shilling hatchet; at Prince William Sound he bought six sea-otter skins with twelve of the beads, skins which sold in China for fifteen pounds each. This constituted a quick return of £90 for a one-shilling investment. In all, King estimated, the value of furs in both ships in specie and goods counted not less than £2,000, and this acquires additional significance when we understand that many of the poorer quality had been given away or traded at Kamchatka. 'When in addition to these facts,' King wrote in summary, 'it is remembered, that the furs were, at first collected without our having any idea of their real value; that the greatest part had been worn by the Indians, from whom we purchased them; that they were afterward preserved with little care, and frequently used for bed-clothes, and other purposes, during our cruize to the North; and that, probably we had never got the full value of them in China; the advantages that might be derived from a voyage to that part of the American Coast, undertaken with commercial views, appear to me of a degree of importance sufficient to call for the attention of the Public.'[7]

The new opportunities presented by the maritime fur trade were immediately known to the men of *Resolution* and *Discovery,* and among those who would soon lead major trade ventures were Nathaniel Portlock and George Dixon, both veterans of this voyage, who in 1787 became partners in the King George's Sound Company and commanders of *King George* and *Queen Charlotte* respectively. Others did not wait so long.

7 Ibid.

IV

One sea-otter pelt was worth the equivalent of an ordinary seaman's wages for two years. Thus, just before *Resolution* and *Discovery* left the Typa, two men—John Cave, a quartermaster, and Michael Spencer, a seaman—stole *Resolution*'s great cutter under cover of a dark morning and made their way unopposed to sea, bound for the Northwest Coast. They were neither heard of nor seen again, the first casualties of the new trade. Now the officers and watch were on their guard against desertions of this sort, and, although a few did occur, the ships were soon at sea. But the crews had been 'not far short of mutiny,'[8] he said. He described in the authorized published version of the *Voyage* a scheme for a surveying and fur-trading expedition to the Northwest Coast how he was well aware that the men knew they could make their fortune by going to Cook's River, obtaining another cargo of the black, lustrous sea-otter pelts, and returning to Macao or Canton.

Here was the design of future voyages, some of them originating in Macao, others in Bengal and Calcutta, still others in Europe and the United States, but all of them certain to concentrate on Nootka Sound and on Cook's River. Who knew what peltry lay uncaught in the coastal waters between 50° and 60° North not investigated by Cook? If the peltry of Cook's River and Nootka were an indication what regal fortunes might be acquired given strong ships, proven and healthy crews, adequate supplies, and, not least, the nails, buttons, and beads held in such high esteem by the Northwest Coast Indians? In short, Cook's last voyage had demonstrated the basis of a new trade. It had given promise of wealth for those who could overcome obstacles of distance and who could serve the needs and answer the peculiarities of consumers on both sides of the Pacific.

8 Ibid.

V

INDIA-BASED EXPEDITIONS OF TRADE AND DISCOVERY IN THE NORTH PACIFIC IN THE LATE EIGHTEENTH CENTURY

In the late eighteenth century two great oceans, the Indian and the North Pacific, were joined by voyages of trade and discovery. The merchant seaborne endeavours of Bombay and Bengal were linked with Canton and Macao on the western rim of the Pacific and, more, with Nootka Sound, Vancouver Island, and Cook Inlet and Prince William Sound on the far distant, eastern shores of the Pacific. To a much lesser extent, these voyages encompassed Unalaska, Kamchatka and Japan, reference to which in the documentation is unfortunately marginal and therefore receives little attention here.

Such voyages – conducted in 200- to 400-ton ships, otherwise known as snows – consumed nearly half a year outward bound from Bombay harbour or the Hughli River to Nootka Sound. A return passage from the Northwest Coast of North America to Canton or Macao – 13 500 kilometres distant – could count half that time, say three months. Consequently, distance stamped its own tyranny on profitable commerce, and in the process reduced scientific discovery to a minimum. Certainly Captain James Cook's reconnaissance of the North Pacific in 1778 had given the wider world but an inkling of the intricacies of navigation and of the multitude of cartographic problems and geographic riddles of the North Pacific. During subsequent years Lapérouse, Vancouver, Broughton and others came to define more completely the ocean's characteristics (Dunmore, 1965–9; Ritchie, 1967; Ruggles, 1967). Still, in large measure, these India-based voyages were to little-known or unrecorded waters.

Historians of late eighteenth-century European expansion have stressed the 'swing to the east' theory of Professor Vincent Harlow, and modified or corrected it in regard to certain areas of Asian and Pacific seas. One branch of this literature exists on the motivation and characteristics of British settlement of New South Wales beginning in 1788 (Frost, 1975, 1980; Steven, 1983; Mackay, 1974). Another branch, older in provenance, is on the nature of British East India Company operations on the subcontinent, in the Indian Ocean and towards China (Furber, 1951). From the other side of the Pacific, and especially from the pens of Canadian and American scholars, flows the work of the maritime fur trade historians and those interested in Anglo-Chinese relations (Howay, 1973; Gough, 1980; Morison, 1921; Pritchard, 1936; Wilbur, 1945). This present contribution to the literature rests mainly on unpublished East India Company records, on British ministerial papers,

V

and on voyage accounts by the principal participants. It does not strain for any explanation of a grand design. Rather, it modestly argues that India-based voyages of trade and discovery to the North Pacific in the years 1785–1800 were significant in the progress of that branch of commerce and were part of a larger British, American and indeed international interest in the North Pacific. This paper also demonstrates the eastward shift of Company interest to Canton and Macao, and seeks to explain why these ports grew in commercial ascendancy during the late eighteenth century (Fairbank, 1978).

Two coasts, two continents

Three presidencies constituted British India at that time: Bengal, Madras and Bombay. Of these Bengal was the most important, the seat of the Governor-General, and the base of the Honourable Company's prestige and power. Madras and Bombay made important contributions to the marine prowess of the Company, but in the 1780s Bengal was assuming an increased ascendancy, not only on mainland Asia, the first large area of the subcontinent subjugated by a European power, as Professor P. J. Marshall has explained, but as a base for further expansion by sea to the east (Marshall, 1976, 1988). The business of Bengal was trade, and the key families were predominantly highly educated and enterprising Scots. The Company's regulations permitted a well ordered Europe-to-Asia trade and allowed a 'country trade' within Asia, one in which servants enjoyed by permission considerable latitude in individual trading. In the year 1785 Bengal ships, lying idle, were available for distant trading, and local merchant traders were taking shares on ships as well as cargoes. Among these traders were a number of free merchants who were sufficiently powerful to resist being displaced by Company servants. These investor-sailors were searching out new trades, but, more, were seeking means of profitable outward-bound cargoes from India or elsewhere, perhaps even Nootka Sound or Alaska, that would satisfy China market requirements and allow the vessels to purchase and carry tea for London. The Chinese preferred cash, but did acquire Indian opium, cotton, tin and pepper. Beginning in 1785 they began to trade with the 'foreign devils' for additional items – sandalwood, ginseng, and sea otter pelts.

In the late eighteenth century the pelt of the sea otter, or *Enhydra lutris*, was the ermine of Asia (Kenyon, 1969; Rickard, 1947). On occasion but not always, Chinese mandarins paid a king's ransom for a fur that embellished hat, cape or gown. Russians also held this pelt in high esteem. Truly it was a beautiful and lustrous fur. One sagacious American mariner in the business remarked that it would 'give him more pleasure to look at a splendid sea-otter skin, than to examine half the pictures that are struck up for exhibition, puffed up by connoisseurs'. He regarded these pelts as among 'the most attractive natural objects' that could be placed before him, 'excepting a beautiful woman and a lovely infant' (Sturgis, 1846). Delicate, thick, soft to touch, and mysteriously luminous in appearance, the sea otter also spawned an international rivalry of trade and eventually for dominion. Captain James Cook's third voyage to the Pacific introduced the possibilities of such a trade – though Cook himself was uncertain of the profitability of it, given the immense distances involved, that is, unless a navigable Northwest Passage be found (Gough, 1978). The Russians, trading overland from Kamchatka and Siberia to the Chinese empire via Kiatka, enlarged their trade eastwards from the Sea of Okhotsk and Kamchatka and built the basis of an American empire in Alaska. The Spanish voyaged north from Mexico to Nootka Sound, Vancouver Island, expecting to find and oust the Russians. Instead, they discovered British traders, one of them John Meares who features in this present account. The Spanish seized ships, shore establishment and property, and in so doing commenced the celebrated Nootka Sound crisis. The Americans, chiefly Bostonians, initiated a celebrated golden round in which Yankee hardware, wheat and rum, North American ginseng, and sea otter pelts, Pacific island sandalwood, Chinese porcelain, teas and silks became paying propositions on the various legs of a voyage of circumnavigation. By 1790 the profits of the sea otter had placed Nootka Sound and the Gulf of Alaska securely on the maps of the world and enlarged Western understanding of the North Pacific Ocean and littoral.

A new branch of seaborne commerce

James Cook's finding of sea otters on the Northwest Coast was 'as if a new gold coast had been discovered', wrote the American man of letters, Washington Irving in 1836. HMS *Resolution* and HMS *Discovery* visited Nootka Sound, where sea otter were abundant in March and April 1778. Subsequent transactions with the natives of Alaska confirmed the prevalence of the sea otter which seemed to be, like Falstaff said of reasons, 'as plenty as blackberries'. However, the Russians at Unalaska endeavoured to deflect Cook from thinking that the trade could be profitable (Gough, 1980; Svet, 1973; Liever, 1934). This, however, did not deter individual mariners such as Quartermaster John Cave and Able Seaman Michael Spencer from stealing the *Resolution's* cutter under cover of a dark morning in the Typa, in Macao's estuary, and sailing away to sea. Cave and Spencer were never heard of again, and can be classified as the first human casualties of the new trade.

V

News of the prospects of a rich trade spread quickly to the key ports of the world. In the formative years of the trade, several expeditions, such as that of the *Resolution's* cutter, disappeared from the face of the globe, and of history. The snow *Lark*, for instance, owned by the East India Company, with a crew of 70, sailed from her home port Bengal in March 1786 via Canton and Petropavlovsk. She was wrecked on Copper or Bering Island with a loss of all but two hands (Meares, 1790; Sauer, 1802). Other vessels were mystery ships: one such was the Bengal barque *Phoenix*, master Hugh Moore, whose voyages in 1792 and 1794 to the Northwest Coast are seen fleetingly in the records of other mariners; another was the Bengal brig *Arthur*, captain Henry Barber, which arrived on the coast by way of Port Jackson, New South Wales, and was met by Captain George Vancouver at Cross Sound, Alaska, in 1794 (Howay, 1973). She was wrecked on Oahu, 1796. Then there is the brig *Halcyon*, probably of Calcutta and commanded by Charles W. Barkley, which in 1792 carried to Alaskan waters the diarist Mrs Francis Hornby Trevor Barkley and their small son (*Halcyon*, ms., Barkley, 1978). Lastly, mention might be made of the fast-sailing snow *Fairy* of Calcutta, captain William Rogers, which traded on the coast in 1791. She sailed from Calcutta to Canton and then was chartered as 'a foreign bottom' by the Americans Ingraham, Rogers and Coolidge, renamed *Sea Otter*, and shipped tea for Boston. She sailed again in 1792 for Canton, perhaps via the Northwest Coast (Howay, 1973). In later years most vessels came from Boston, Providence or New York.

By count there seem to have been at least nine India-based vessels in the trade *Lark, Phoenix, Arthur, Halcyon, Fairy, Captain Cook, Experiment, Nootka* and *Sea Otter.* The *Argonaut* was Calcutta-built, but sailed from Macao/Canton. In the early years, many British vessels were London-based, though others came from Bristol, or were Canton-based; the *Ruby* and *Jenny* are the Bristol vessels; the pioneer Canton vessel was James Hanna's *Harmon*, or *Sea Otter* (1785). From time to time French, Swedish and Austrian vessels joined the trade, giving credence to the argument that this was an international commerce.

None the less, the variety of ports of origin masks the fact that this was initially a British trade and eventually an American one. During the earliest phase the octopus-like regulations of the East India Company – which possessed the full and free privilege of British commerce between the Cape of Good Hope and the Straits of Magellan – and to a lesser degree the control of the nearly moribund South Sea Company – which possessed the monopoly of licensing all British shipping on the west coast of the Americas and from the mainland to 300 leagues at sea – meant that these companies, more particularly the former, dominated the affairs of these voyages. The British trader could acquire sea otter only within the limits of one company and sell it only within the monopoly of the other. The Company preferred to have private traders outfit and man the vessels and not to enter into the trade directly. This can best be explained by tracing the voyages and fortunes of one James Charles Stuart Strange. In addition, the dominance of the Company obliged others to attempt to circumvent the monopoly regulations by sailing under foreign colours. This can best be explained by tracing the first voyages of Captain John Meares and William Tipping.

James Strange's misfortunes

Strange's expedition was based on Bombay; Meares's, on Calcutta. For a variety of reasons, Indian ports proved to be disadvantageous as places from whence to mount exploring and trading expeditions to the Northwest Coast. Labour and ships were cheap, and supplies and provisions bountiful. By contrast, profitable cargoes outward-bound from India to Canton and Macao were hard to manage, opium not yet being a large trade. There were also the seasonal difficulties of monsoons and of ill-charted islands and reefs. There were, too, the dangers of pirates and of hostile Dutch and French ships. Accordingly, the Asian base of operations, as in the case of Meares's expedition, tended to shift from India to Canton and Macao, a further 'swing to the east', if you like, and to be based under the Portuguese flag. The Company residents in Canton tended to supplant those in Bombay and Bengal as prime movers in the trade, and several India-built vessels came to trade out of Macao and Canton.

The first major India-based maritime fur trading voyage was headed by James Strange (Ayar, 1978). Son of the distinguished engraver Sir Robert Strange and brother of Sir Thomas Andrew Lumisden Strange, Chief Justice of the Supreme Court of Madras, Strange eventually rose high in the Indian Civil Service and was at one time a British Member of Parliament. His papers and allied correspondence, as of yet unavailable in definitive edition, recount that he ranks among the first to perceive the possible financial rewards and imperial benefits of a Northwest Coast voyage. He had read James Cook and James King's *Voyage to the Pacific Ocean* (3 vols.; London, 1784) wherein a design for a trading and exploring expedition, consisting of two vessels, was put forth by James King. Strange's imagination must have been caught by King's statements that a rich commerce might ensue. Strange prepared a memorandum on such a voyage, and presented it to his friend and patron David Scott. Scott was a rising Bombay merchant, an influential publicist of projects of this sort, and on his way to becoming Chairman of the Court of

V

Directors of the East India Company. Scott became convinced of the scheme's viability and successfully solicited aid from his partners, Tate and Adamson ('Bombay Expedition', 1785). More, he advanced the scheme before the President and Council of the East India Company in Bombay. The East India Company's officials considered the project, gave consent, and granted Strange a leave of absence from Madras (Minutes of Consultation). One reason the expedition was authorized is because other merchants and shipping interests were pressing for permission from the Company for the liberalization of trade. These interests included the London merchants headed by Richard Cadman Etches who formed the King George's Sound Company and John Meares and James Colnett, British naval officers on half pay, who also planned an expedition from India. Another reason the Company acquiesced was the fear of foreign rivals in the trade – Dutch, Austrian, Russian, French and American. A third reason is that the British Government was exerting considerable pressure through Henry Dundas, President of the Board of Trade, to open up the East India Company's operations to private and coastal traders with a view to advancing the interests of British and Indian trade in China and the Pacific seas.

Though the Company gave permission, the financial costs were born by Strange and his backers. Scott advanced Strange a loan of £10 000 for the project. They purchased two Bombay-built vessels. These were the *Betsey*, renamed the *Captain Cook*, 350 tons, sheathed with plank and then with copper, commanded by Henry Laurie, formerly in the Royal Navy, and the newly-constructed *Experiment* of 100 or 120 tons, commanded by Henry or John Guise, another former British naval officer. The Madras Establishment provided all-European crews, stores for several years and provisions for 15 months, besides guns, ammunition, instruments and charts. The Bombay Government provided 15 men of the Bombay Regiment who were to serve less as mariners than as artificers and to build a shore establishment and depot on the Northwest Coast, should trade and circumstances prove promising. In charge of the soldiers, and presumably to be first governor of this British factory, was Alexander Walker, an ensign in the Bombay Army, whose account richly supplements Strange's own narrative, particularly in regard to Nootkan ethnography (Walker, 'Account' and 'Log').

Strange's instructions of 7 December 1785, based on James King's plan, called for the vessels to proceed from Bombay to Goa on the Malabar Coast. There the resident Portuguese Captain-General would provide passes and letters to ensure the ships' safe reception at Macao during the season when intercourse with English ships was not allowed at Canton. On the Malabar Coast, too, Strange was to purchase sandalwood and tinware for the China market. Leaving the river at Canton he was to proceed to the Northwest Coast, conduct trade at Nootka Sound and Alaska, make discoveries, and shape a course via Bering Strait, the Arctic Ocean as far as the North Pole, then Kamchatka, and finally Canton. There it was to be left to his discretion as to whether or not a second Northwest Coast voyage be made and if not to return to Bombay ('Instructions').

It need hardly be said that this was an ambitious project. Strange's instructions specified that discovery constituted the principal object. In fact, the investors understandably came to look on the commercial advantages as the main goal. To serve in due proportion the interests of discovery and trade was an unrealistic assumption given the distances involved, and in the end Strange served neither with distinction. The voyage from Bombay via the Malabar Coast, Batavia, Borneo, the Celebes and thence to Nootka Sound was marred by both vessels grounding on a reef in the Straits of Macassar. Some advances in discoveries were made, for some charting of the north-western coast of Vancouver Island, Prince William Sound and Alaska, was undertaken, and recorded in the manuscript charts of Samuel Wedgborough, some of which were later engraved. The expedition also made ethnographic contributions, and Strange and Walker compiled additions to, or enlargements of, Captain Cook's vocabulary of the Nootkan language ('Journal and Narrative'). Strange thought a North-West Passage might exist near the northern extremity of Vancouver Island, and he called the passage separating the island from the mainland, Queen Charlotte Sound (now Strait). On nearby Nigei Island he nailed a copper plate to a tree to announce his having taken possession of the place on behalf of the British Crown. It may be of interest to note that this plate was found in 1956, 150 years later, by Bruce McKelvie, and is in the Provincial Archives of British Columbia.

In terms of profits, the expedition accorded no success. Strange needed a paying cargo in each leg of the voyage, and the outward bound trade to Malabar and thence China was unsuccessful. Moreover, the expedition garnered only 604 skins, an insufficient quantity to offset the costs of the voyage. Strange faced personal financial ruin, and endeavoured, unsuccessfully, to get compensation from the Company. His subsequent application for a second venture, this one with Company backing, for further trade on the Northwest Coast and for forming a settlement there, failed to gain the approval of Sir Archibald Campbell, the Governor of Madras and the Council (Strange to Council, Strange to Campbell; also Madras Public Proceedings).

The Strange expedition, we can conclude, is important in several ways. First it serves as an example of attempts by the likes of David Scott to enlarge and liberalize the Company's trade to include private investors or promoters. In that sense, the Strange voyage demonstrates Professor Holden Furber's dictum that at this time the East India Company had become a mere device for the achievement of private ambitions (Furber, 1951). Secondly, the Strange expedition affords an explanation of how the Company developed its interests in China and the Pacific in response, to the nascent maritime fur trade. In that regard, it was prepared for a conjoint commercial venture and was obliged to get into the business, for it would have been severely chastized by British political leaders for failing to take advantage of a new and profitable branch of commerce. That the Directors rejected Scott and Strange's 1787 follow-up scheme for direct investment in distant Pacific voyaging throws light on the Company's unwillingness to liberalize trade or to curtail the private profits of individual merchant partners (Minutes, Court Book; Philips, 1951). Thirdly, the Strange expedition demonstrates some of the ways in which pioneering expeditions can be less than successful owing to poor planning, lack of knowledge, and unfortunate circumstances. Certainly Strange was no mariner, and his superiors knew little if anything about long distance voyaging and had little or no intelligence of what Northwest Coast Indians had to trade and at what prices. Fourthly, and last, the Strange expedition exhibits that which certain historians delight in, a further extension of British and European interest in distant and eastern seas in the late eighteenth century. In that sense the Strange voyage was a noteworthy case in point.

John Meares's hazardous undertakings

The last India-based voyages that came under our scrutiny are those of the snow *Nootka* of 200 tons, of Bengal, owned by the Bengal Fur Company, John Meares, formerly of the Royal Navy, master, and the snow *Sea Otter*, also of Bengal and owned by the Bengal Fur Society, William Tipping master. They were almost simultaneous rivals to the Strange project. Little hitherto has been known of these voyages, and the extant documentation remains scanty. Meares in his *Voyages* makes but brief reference to his pioneering voyage. However, in his *Memorial*, presented to the House of Commons on 13 May 1790 during the Nootka Sound crisis, he stated:

> That early in the year 1786, certain merchants residing in the East Indies, and under the immediate protection of the Company, desirous of opening a trade with the North West Coast of America, for supplying the Chinese market with furs and ginseng, communicated such design to Sir John Macpherson, the Governor-General of India, who not only approved of the plan, but joined in the subscription for its execution, and two vessels were accordingly purchased, and placed under the orders and command of your memorialist (Meares, Appendix 1).

Meares also stated that in March 1786 he dispatched one of the vessels, which he named the *Sea Otter*, under Tipping, and followed in the *Nootka*, which he also named.

Meares's sworn testimony before the Privy Council in 1791 represents previously neglected data on this voyage. Meares testified that the Governor General of Bombay permitted two gentlemen of the Bengal Establishment to accompany him to render assistance in surveying the country. The destination was the Gulf of Alaska, for Meares rightly knew that better pelts were to be procured there, in more northern waters. He did not anticipate Russian resistance, however, and was woefully ignorant of the Alaskan climate.

Tipping's *Sea Otter* traded successfully on the Alaskan shore, and Meares's *Nootka* arrived shortly thereafter but never encountered the companion vessel. Meares first entered Cook Inlet, or River as it was then called, but found 40 or 50 Russians entrenched in an ill-fortified redoubt against local native attack, the site of modern Anchorage. The Russians dominated the trade, and accordingly Meares shifted his attention to Prince William Sound where he decided to hazard a winter frozen up in what became known as Sutherlands or Snug Corner Cove. This was a fatal mistake which cost dearly the lives of 23 men from scurvy and other diseases and, moreover, reduced his trading time. In May 1787, when Captain George Dixon of the *Queen Charlotte* chanced upon Meares, his mate Ross, and eight surviving crew, humanitarian necessities tipped the scales against trading priorities and what Dixon and his companion captain Nathaniel Portlock of the *King George* regarded as their exclusive trading domain. To them Meares was an interloper. Here in the Gulf of Alaska London traders had arrived to compete with Calcutta interests, and merger or association became the necessary consequence (Privy Council Evidence, 1791; Beresford, 1789; Harlow, 1952–64).

None the less, the Calcutta syndicate's ships completed their initial trading round. Tipping reached Macao in February 1787, and sold his sea otter furs for 8000 Spanish dollars. Meares also made his way to Macao, a few months later, and sold his 350 pelts for $14 000, double the price Portlock and Dixon gained for theirs a few months later (Gough, 1980).

It may be mentioned here that in January of the following year, 1788, Meares sold the *Nootka* and in conjunction with investors in India, purchased and outfitted two vessels, the *Felice Adventurer* and *Iphigenia Nubiana* under Portuguese colours and registered under the name of Juan Cawalho of Macao (Howay, 1973). They sailed for Nootka Sound and Cook Inlet, Alaska, respectively, arriving in May and June. During that trading season, Meares enhanced his relations with Maquinna at Nootka Sound and extended his relationships to the southwards, especially with the powerful Wikinanish of

Clayoquot Sound. He also made several claims to discovery, some fictitious, others borrowed, from which ensued a paper war (Howay, 1929). He was back in China by December to undertake a further reorganization of his concern, under the title of the Associated Merchants trading to the North West Coast of America in conjunction with the Messrs Etches concern and others 'making a joint stock of all the vessels and property employed in that trade'. The Associated Merchants were Meares, John Henry Cox, Richard Cadman Etches, John Etches, William Fitzhugh, Henry Lane, and Daniel Beale. They purchased a ship built in Calcutta, the *Argonaut*, and sent her and the sloop *Princess Royal* to Nootka Sound under the direction of James Colnett, to form a base of operations. This was Meares's design to establish a beach-head of the British empire on the Northwest Coast, the very same scheme that invited the intervention of the Spanish commandant Esteban Martínez who had sailed north from San Blas to intercept Russians rumoured to have designs on Nootka Sound. Martínez captured Meares's ships and shore establishment, but he did not molest recently arrived American ships. Details of the dramatic Nootka Sound crisis belong elsewhere. Suffice it to say that the bold schemes of Meares and the highly successful enterprises of his several vessels got him into trouble with the Spanish. As for Tipping's command, the *Sea Otter*, she made another voyage in the trade but was lost on the Kamchatka coast.

Profit and power

As the above evidence shows, India-based expeditions of trade and discovery to the North Pacific were fraught with difficulties and did not always yield sufficient profit that would allow subsequent voyages. Distance alone mitigated against ready success; another was navigational hazards. Paying cargoes on each leg was the prized goal of the merchant mariner. However, India-based sea otter seekers trading half a world away from home port discovered to their costly ruin the secret that soon became so well understood by American rivals. Strange and Meares were literally 'in the dark' as regards the geography of the Northwest Coast, except where James Cook had previously been and charted. They also knew little of the needs of North American native consumers, from whom they would acquire furs. To some degree their voyages were trial and error: however, although Strange's plan for a second voyage came to naught, Meares's scheme grew to substantial, profitable proportions in the intervening years before Spanish seizures at Nootka Sound halted the British trade. What dramatically differentiates the two expeditions is the fact that whereas Meares came to base his operations on Canton and Macao, Strange's Bombay design had no sequel.

Comparisons between Indian-based voyages and Canton/Macao expeditions should not be made in a vacuum, for London-based expeditions, especially those of the Etches concern, namely Portlock and Dixon, were making dramatic inroads into the trade, as were the American expeditions from Boston. Even then, with the Meares syndicate reorganization as described, Macao/Canton became the base of organizing and outfitting such expeditions. Rough estimates of furs exported from the Northwest Coast and sold in China indicate that India-based ships held a strong minority position in British trade in the years 1785–1788 but by the latter date had begun to lose even that as the trade became more heavily based on Macao/Canton and London and Boston (Meares, 'Rough Estimate').

Next, we come to judge the East India Company itself. It did not stand in the way of this new branch of trade. Octopus-like as it was in its control it did not restrict the initiatives of the James Stranges and John Meares of that world. The maritime fur trade offered the Company opportunity: it gave vent to new enthusiasms, provided avenues for shipping interests, both in vessels built and in vessel building. It was also good business for outfitters, and for those merchants endeavouring to improve the coastwise Asian trade eastwards from Bombay and Calcutta.

What marred the Company and led to its subsidiary position in the maritime fur trade is that it was slow and cumbersome. Not initiatory in new trades, it tended to be reactive and sometimes reactionary. Small wonder then that David Scott, Strange's patron, was seen to be in league with Henry Dundas and the British ministry when it came to reform – with a view, it should be stressed, of enhancing trade with China and of opening up new branches of commerce in eastern seas (Philips, 1961).

From the point of view of discovery, India-based voyages added some new accurate findings but contributed some confusions. Strange placed northern Vancouver Island securely on the chart, and Alexander Dalrymple soon added the plans of master Samuel Wedgborough to his growing folio of Northwest Coast material. However, Strange continued to believe in the possible existence of a North West Passage, perhaps through Queen Charlotte Strait. When opportunities to advance geographical knowledge presented themselves, Strange remained timid or otherwise preoccupied with questions of profit. To repeat: the design of Strange's expedition was faulty, for making a profit by trade was the only means for Strange to continue a sea-trader's career. Meares, too, was a poor discoverer. Indeed, he seems to have misappropriated place names, claimed priority of discoveries at the expense of others, and perpetuated the myth of the North West Passage in the latitudes of Vancouver Island.

V

Lastly, these voyages contributed to the general reduction of the East India Company's corporate and regulatory power. The British Government reduced East India Company licensing powers in American waters by statue in 1802 and in 1793 and 1833 modified the Company's charter so that a British vessel could sail from Canton to the Columbia River without the necessity of a license (Gough, 1980). In the meantime, foreign competition in the maritime fur trade, principally American, grew in ascendancy. The North Pacific world, opened to the wider world by British scientific discovery in the age of Cook, was fast becoming an area for the rivalry of trade and dominion for the Russians, the Spanish and especially the Americans. In the process the India-based voyages had made their own contribution.

Acknowledgements

An earlier version of this paper was presented to the Joint Meeting of The Society for the History of Discoveries and The Hakluyt Society, at the Royal Geographical Society, London, England, 4 September 1987. In locating certain archives held at the sources on which this work is based, I acknowledge, with thanks, the assistance of Andrew S. Cook, India Office Library and Records, British Library, London, and of Brian Young, Provincial Archives of British Columbia, Victoria.

References

Manuscript sources
British Columbia, Provincial Archives, Victoria
    Halcyon ms. AA 20.5 L92W.
British Library, India Office Library and Records, London
India Office Records:
    'A Bombay Expedition to North West America', Scott, Tate and Adamson [for James Strange] to Hon. Sir and Gentlemen, 17 September 1785, *Bombay Secret and Political Consultations* 1785, vol. 72.
    China: *Factory Records* II, vol. 1, XVI, notes, 4 April 1787.
    Court Book Minutes 21 and 27 June 1787, No. 96.
    Home Miscellaneous Series 'Instructions to James Strange, Esq., Director of the Exploring Expedition to the N. West Coast of America and Towards the North Pole'. Bombay, 7 December 1785, *H.M.S.* 494, (5). 'Outlines for an Exploring Expedition', 1 September 1785, *H.M.S.* 494 (3).
    Strange, J. 'Journal and Narrative', 1 January–15 November 1786, copy, *H.M.S.* 800, pp. 1–145 (vocabulary at pp. 147–61).
    Madras Public Consultations Strange to Council, 15 January 1788, vol. 147; Strange to Sir Archibald Campbell, 22 February 1788, vol. 148; Campbell to Court of Directors, E/4/317, paras. 23, 24, 25.
    Madras Public Proceedings range 241, vol. 5, pp. 603–19.

V

Minutes of Consultations 30 September and 18 November 1785; President etc. to Scott and
Co., 30 September 1785; Scott and Co. to President, 15 and 18 November 1785, pp.
271–334.
National Library of Scotland, Department of Manuscripts, Edinburgh
Walker, Alexander Mss. 13778, 'Account', and 13779, 'Log' with additional comments,
circa 1817.
Public Record Office, London
Meares, J. Rough Estimate of Value of Furs Exported from the NW Coast (to 1789) and
statement of the Value of Furs exported from the North-western Coast of America by British
and Foreign Ships previous to the Year 1790, 20 May 1790, *H.O.* 42/16 (24).
Meares, J. Evidence before Privy Council, 8 February 1791, *P.C.* 1/63/(B22).

Printed sources
Ayar, A. V. Venkatarama 1928 An Adventurous Madras Civilian: James Strange (1753–1840).
Proc. Indian Hist. Rec. Commn 11: 22–9.
Barkley, F., 1978 *The Remarkable World of Frances Barkley, 1764–1845.* Sydney, B.C.: Grays
Publishing.
Beresford, W. 1789 *Voyage Round the World . . . by George Dixon.* London.
Dunmore, H. 1965–69 *French Explorers in the Pacific,* 2 vols.; Oxford: Clarendon Press.
Fairbank, J. K. 1978 T*he Cambridge History of China, vol. 10: Late Ch'ing, 1800–1911, Part 1.*
Cambridge: CUP.
Frost, A. 1975 The East India Company and the Choice of Botany Bay, *Hist. Stud.* 16, 65: 606–11.
—, 1980 *Convicts and Empire: A Naval Question, 1776–1811.* Melbourne: OUP.
Furber, H. 1951 *John Company at Work.* Cambridge: Harvard Univ. Press.
Gough, B. 1978 James Cook and the Origins of the Maritime Fur Trade, *American Neptune,* 38,
3: 217–24.
—, 1980 *Distant Dominion: Britain and the Northwest Coast of North America 1579–1809.*
Vancouver: Univ. British Columbia Press.
Harlow, V. T. 1952–64 *The Founding of the Second British Empire, 1763–1793,* 2 vols. London:
Longmans Green.
Howay, F. W. 1929 *The Dixon–Meares Controversy.* Toronto: Ryerson Press.
Howay, F. S. 1973 *A List of Trading Vessels in the Maritime Fur Trade,* Richard A. Pierce (ed.).
Kingston, Ontario: Limestone Press.
Irving, W. 1836 *Astoria,* 2 vols. Philadelphia.
Kenyon, W. 1969 *The Sea Otter in the Eastern Pacific Ocean.* Washington: Govt Print. Off.
Leiver, E. (ed.) 1934 The English in Kamchatka, 1779. *Geogrl J.* 84: 417–19.
Mackay, D. 1974 Direction and Purpose in British Imperial Policy, 1783–1801. *Hist. J.* 17:
487–501.
Marshall, P. J. 1976 *East India Fortunes: The British in Bengal in the Eighteenth Century.*
Oxford: Clarendon Press.
—, 1988 *Bengal, The Bridgehead: Eastern India 1740–1822.*
Meares, J. 1790 *Memorial* app. XII.
Morison, S. E. 1921 *The Maritime History of Massachusetts, 1783–1860.* Boston: Houghton-
Mifflin.
Philips, C. H. (ed.) 1951 Correspondence of David Scott, Director and Chairman of the East
India Company . . . 1787–1807. *Camden Society Third Series, vol. XXV,* London: Roy. Hist.
Soc.
—, 1961 *The East India Company, 1784–1834.* Manchester: Manchester Univ. Press.
Pritchard, E. H. 1936 The Critical Years of Early Anglo-Chinese Relations, 1750–1800. *Research
Studies,* Washington State University. Pullman, Washington.

Rickard, T. A., 1947 The Sea Otter in History. *British Columbia Hist. Q.* 11: 15–31.

Ritchie, G. S. 1967 *The Admiralty Chart: British Naval Hydrography in the Nineteenth Century.* London: Hollis and Carter.

Ruggles, R. I. 1967 Geographical Exploration by the British. In Herman R. Friis, (ed.) *The Pacific Basin: A History of its Geographical Exploration.* New York: American Geogrl Soc.

Sauer, M. 1802 *Expedition to Northern Russia.*

Steven, M. 1983 *Trade, Tactics and Territory: Britain in the Pacific 1783–1823.* Carleton, Vic: Melbourne Univ. Press.

Sturgis, W. 1846 The Northwest Fur Trade. *Hunt's Merchants' Magazine*, 16.

Svet, Y. M. 1973 *Cook and the Russians.* London: Hakluyt Soc.

Walker, A. 1982 *An Account of a Voyage to the North West Coast of America in 1785 & 1786 by Alexander Walker*, Robin Fisher and J. M. Bumstead (eds). Vancouver: Douglas and McIntyre.

Walker, Alexander 1899 *Dictionary of National Biography*, vol. 59.

Wilbur. M. E. 1945 *The East India Company and the British Empire in the Far East.* Palo Alto, Ca.: Stanford Univ. Press.

WILLIAM BOLTS AND THE AUSTRIAN ATTEMPT TO ESTABLISH AN EASTERN EMPIRE

In the 1770s, 1780s and 1790s European powers continued that vigorous commercial expansion beyond the Cape of Good Hope that had characterised English, Portuguese, Dutch and French activities in the Indian Ocean for the previous century and a half. All the same, this enterprise took on new characteristics. The Peace of Paris (1763) had consolidated Britain's hold on certain areas of the Indian subcontinent, where indigenous rulers permitted the maintenance and enhancement of East India Company trade. British trade in the Indian Ocean, meanwhile, shifted eastwards, and the Arabian Sea yielded to the Bay of Bengal as the place of energized interest by East India traders. A general swing to the east was occurring in British commercial and imperial activities. This was not confined to the absolute growth of metropolitan influences on the distant oceans but was also exemplified in the shift of inter-coastal trade in the annexes of the Indian Ocean, along the coast of the subcontinent and south-east Asia, among the lesser known islands of the Bay of Bengal, including the Nicobar Islands, and through the more commonly used sea-lanes leading to Batavia, Macau and Canton, and even the distant shores of Australia and the north-west coast of North America [Fig.17].

The process of commercial and imperial growth was not the result of British activities only; French activities intensified after 1763, not only in entrepreneurial endeavours but in scientific ones too. The Dutch also continued their trade and empire-building. Running parallel to these national activities were those of the private or semi-private persons, those who worked between the cracks of chartered company or state regulation. These were the *entrepreneurs extraordinaires*, the businessmen whose allegiance to king and country was but a matter of convenience, ashore or afloat. They used the system when it suited them; they sought to raise

For supplying certain sources and references for this work, the author acknowledges with thanks the assistance of Alan Frost, P.J. Marshall and Margaret L. Waddington.

capital and obtain insurance for their ventures from international sources; they stood outside of the national state corporation, British, French or other, and were sorely disliked by regulators at various national boards of trade.

One such entrepreneur was William (or Wilhelm) Bolts. This "fixer" or promoter seldom escapes the pages of histories of late eighteenth-century British overseas expansion in the Indian and Pacific Oceans. Yet his strange and uncertain passage through time and space resembles that of a firefly on a hot and dark summer's night: we see him here, and then there, as he makes his progress. His light shows when he gets into trouble, or when he causes others alarm. He is the interloper, the strangely moving force that poses problems for strongly structured rivals. He is the problematic threat to British designs on the eastern Indian Ocean and even the sea-otter trade of the north-west coast of North America. But his curious career tells much about money-making and imperial rivalry in eastern seas, and illuminates the multifaceted characteristics of how and why Australia became a focus of British activity.

William Bolts, according to Holden Furber who corrects his biographer Hallward,[1] was a German whose father was from Heidelberg.[2] He himself wrote that he was a subject of the Elector Palatine, though in 1768 he claimed himself as "freeman and loyal subject of Great Britain". He seems to have been born in 1740, and in 1759, according to his deposition, "went out to Bengal in the station of a factor, in the service of the Honourable the East India Company".[3] He learned to speak Bengali, was employed in Calcutta and introduced double-entry bookkeeping. Later he was appointed to Banaras Factory, where he opened a woollens mart, developed saltpetre manufacturing, established opium works, imported cotton, and promoted the advantages of Banaras diamonds.[4]

A man of many talents, some of them exhibiting deviousness, Bolts fell foul of the East India Company. He was sent back to England on the first boat after Company officials found him bankrupt in 1770, "to the irretrievable loss of his Fortune", he later claimed.[5] He never seems to have been able to redeem himself in the eyes of the Company, and in London and perhaps elsewhere fought a rearguard action against his many opponents within it.[6]

Nonetheless, Hallward praised him as "among the most remarkable civilian adventurers of the eighteenth century in the territories of the East India Company".[7] Holden Furber termed him "a German 'Nabob'," "a European adventurer *par excellence* of the mid-eighteenth century in Bihar and Bengal".⁸ Bolts never tired of describing his own skills to would-be backers or employers, and classified himself as "regularly bred to business, almost from his childhood, in a merchant's accompting-house".⁹ Against the exemplary stood the views of critics, official and otherwise. An anonymous contemporary pamphleteer labelled him "a full-grown mercantile monster".¹⁰ Recently Catherine Gaziello described Bolts's role in this way:

> Though he was scarcely scrupulous, Bolts was a valuable person where commercial and colonial questions were concerned, for the interesting information he was able to offer.¹¹

Throughout the mid and late-1770s Bolts pursued a number of projects, none of them particularly lucrative, but all of them having the goal of reasserting his own personal presence in eastern seas. In 1775 he accepted an offer made by the Empress of Hungary, Maria Theresa, and sailed out to India in command of an Imperial ship, the *Joseph and Theresa*. This was one of ten intended ships. Bolts took with him a ten-year charter authorizing him to trade under Imperial colours in the Adriatic and to Persia, India, China and Africa, and to trade in slaves from Africa and Madagascar to America. This grand design required substantial capital, for which Bolts brought in Charles Proli and Company, merchants of Antwerp. Leghorn and Trieste, London and Lisbon were other places where Bolts outfitted ships or otherwise raised capital. In the next few years he established three factories: one on the Malabar coast, one on the African coast at Delagoa, and another at the Nicobar Islands.¹² During his voyages he obtained cochineal on the Brazilian coast and transported it to the east coast of Africa, thereby predating the introduction to Bengal of this insect for the making of scarlet dyes and carmine.

In the course of voyages in the Indian Ocean, Bolts arrived at the Nicobar Islands or Nicobars, in June 1778. Lying between Sumatra and the Andaman Islands, these islets in the Bay of Bengal were at various times the subject of Danish, French, Austrian and British attention, and all these powers had more or less shadowy rights to them, the Danish being the most persistent until 1869, when they relinquished their claims in favour of the British who put down local piracy and established a penal settlement. With a keen eye to profitable possibilities, Bolts discovered a hitherto overlooked species of the breadfruit, known locally as *mellori*. In addition, his several branches of commercial enterprise seem to have promised further expansion; and in 1781, in Antwerp, partners in the reconstituted Imperial Company of Trieste for the Commerce of Asia agreed to send six ships to China and India, two to East Africa, and three for the southern whale fishery. Proli and Company continued as the key backers, and they opened the company to public subscription.[13]

Characteristically Bolts found himself in trouble with rival interests. The Grand Duke of Tuscany also gave him a charter, dated 29 May 1781, for exclusive trade between Tuscany and all countries beyond the Cape Verde Islands. Serving two masters Bolts found himself subverted by his naturally suspicious Antwerp backers. This led to a second bankruptcy, and to his additional debt to Messrs Proli.[14] These circumstances reduced him to little more than a supercargo on board the remaining ships.

Bolts's eastern activities had not gone unwatched by British government and Company officials, who feared Danish, Austrian but especially French aggrandisement in the Indian Ocean. "We are now mortified in knowing that Mr Bolts has made a settlement for the Austrians on one of the Nicobar Islands", wrote a nervous Laurence Sulivan, sometime Chairman of the East India Company, to Lord Macartney, Governor of Madras, on 5 February 1781, "and it's my anxious wish to secure the others."[15] The Company's Court of Directors aimed at expanding trade eastwards towards the river port of Achin, or Acheen, the key to the Malacca Strait. This place was the occasional resort of ships of the Royal Navy. It lay on Sumatra's northern extremity where the Sultan's favour was being courted by a number of nations for access to the place as an entrepôt and for its commercial prospects in rice, cattle and pepper, among other products. "The importance of an Establishment at Acheen", the Court of Directors asserted,

> would be greatly increased by small settlements upon the Nicobar and Andaman Islands; where Ship Timber, of which Acheen is deficient, is procurable in great abundance. The Harbours of the Nicobars are also safe, and capable of receiving Ships of any magnitude; and from Acheen, Ships will have the advantage of being able to proceed to any part of India at all seasons.[16]

The British considered the relative merits of the Nicobars and Achin. In 1784 Pitt possessed information from Admiral Howe and from the East India Company that Bolts had made an establishment at the Nicobars, which constituted the most eligible station for ships of war though somewhat less commercially advantageous.[17] Bolts's presence deflected British interests away from the Nicobar Islands and eastward to Achin. The Court of Directors had proposed raising English colours there, but not if rivals threatened, for the Court wanted a secure, self-sufficient entrepôt that would provide a base for merchant-marine operations in Further Asia, near the crossroads of east Asian trade.[18] But the Company could not get dominion at Achin, and had to content itself with consular presence, for Warren Hastings reminded the Company heads that palace revolutions tended to be shortlived, and that ousting the Sultan in favour of a pretender might backfire. As regards the Nicobars, in 1785 British ministers recommended a full examination of the islands, more especially the harbour of Nancowery, with a view to annexing the place against Danish or Austrian designs. The Governor-General and Council of Bengal replied that only in time of war would the Nicobars, which were hilly, rainy and unhealthy and inaccessible in monsoon seasons, be of material advantage to British fortunes in those seas.[19]

The British gained paramouncy neither in Achin nor in the Nicobars. The French came to dominate affairs at the former, and Bolts and the Austrians possibly at the latter. The British knew of French desires: Admiral Suffren "had been heard to give it as his opinion that the possession of Trincomali and Acheen would be regarded by his royal master as testament to receiving the keys of Hindustan".[20] But such rivalry and failure of British intentions at Achin meant that the British could then concentrate on trying to obtain Rhio, where the Dutch foothold was insecure, and to acquire Penang off Malaya's north-west coast, thought to be a means of relieving the Dutch commercial stranglehold on the Malacca Straits.[21] Eventually Penang gave way to Singapore, and even after Trafalgar Dutch power remained sufficiently strong in those seas for the British to adopt in 1824 a scheme to assert formal influence over Bathurst Island, Melville Island, and the Coburg Peninsula on Australia's north coast.[22] Such was the natural extension of imperial rivalries long after Britain had made its decision to found a convict settlement at Botany Bay.

Bolts's activities in the Nicobars thus caused British expansionists considerable trouble. The Nicobars were not his only concern, and as mentioned his several ships were seeking new avenues of trade in a variety of places. For instance Bolts, with two Imperial ships, reconnoitered Tristan da Cunha in the South Atlantic, and this deflected some British opinion towards establishing the necessary convict settlement at Madagascar.[23] In addition, Bolts actively pursued a project for the maritime fur trade of the north-west coast of North America. In 1780 James Cook's ships were returning to England after the celebrated third expedition. Bolts, at Mauritius, learned of the possibilities of a lucrative commerce in sea-otter pelts and seems to have been among the first to develop a scheme for entering the trade.[24] Bolts's project – embracing as it did a scheme of French support by Fleurieu, and leading as it also did to Lapérouse's voyage – has been well treated by Catherine Gaziello and by Admiral Brossard who saw that Bolts's purely commercial scheme of merchant ships grew to an official expedition of two naval ships, and studying the possibilities of the fur market became only one part of a scheme of discovery and commerce embracing the whole Pacific.[25] Bolts's contribution to this enlarged French design was not inconsiderable.

Meanwhile we have a few fleeting glimpses of Bolts's three other ventures in the sea-otter trade. In 1781 he outfitted the large ship *Count Cobenzell* and was to have sailed her from Trieste with four officers bred under Cook, but corporate intrigues wrecked the scheme and caused enormous loss. It was, Nathaniel Portlock said, a "feeble effort of an imprudent man".[26] Bolts attempted to refinance this scheme.[27] In 1784 his ship *Imperial Eagle* was seized by creditors at Cadiz. His scheme, however, survived, for in November 1786 another ship named the *Imperial Eagle* (otherwise the former East Indiaman *Loudoun*), under Captain Charles William Barkley, sailed from Ostend for the north-west coast of North America. She was owned by supercargoes in China in the East India Company's service and by several Company directors in London. She was outfitted by the Austrian East India Company, carried Austrian colours out of Ostend, and bore the appropriate name. This was really a poaching expedition, financed by East India Company servants intending to trade in ports and waters controlled by the East India and South Sea companies. The scheme ended in disaster mainly because Barkley sold his furs on an over-stocked Canton market.[28]

In certain respects, Bolts never found himself far away from the power of the East India Company. Even by working along the margins or seams of the Company's endeavours he was obliged to take cognisance of their policies. His Austrian scheme, and the eventual withdrawal of Proli money and the bankruptcy of the Imperial East India Company of Trieste in 1784-5, led him first to seek France's support, and then to open another chapter in European affairs in the Indian Ocean: the also little-known Swedish East India Company's scheme for an eastern entrepôt and a trading factory on the coast of Sind. But Bolts's factory – Boltsholm, with Bolts as governor – and the Swedish scheme, like its earlier French variant, never came to pass. "In taking leave of him", concluded Furber in his assessment of the Swedish chapter of Bolts's life, "let us hope that he was never deprived of his library and could have most of it beside him, looking out at the Seine while letting his mind range over his past,

VI

William Bolts and the Austrian Attempt 79

mingling the real with the unreal – Rhineland, Banaras, Patra, Calcutta, London, Antwerp, Stockholm, Isle de France, Botany Bay, Nootka, Canton, Sind, and Boltsholm."[29] To this list should be added the Nicobars and Tristan da Cunha; indeed, whether or not Bolts acquired the Nicobars has never been determined. The Austrian scheme for eastern empire remained very much one of trade, as witnessed by the sending of an agent to Nanking in 1842.

It is said that Bolts died in Paris in 1808 in great poverty. Doubtless in his later years he was, as his biographer suggests, "probably engaged in fresh intrigues against the East India Company".[30] More likely he was endeavouring to work along the margins of corporate policy, to bring in backers and interested private individuals. It was a costly and high-risk business frequently inviting bankruptcy and involving fleeting pledges of loyalty to kings and countries. Like John Meares, James Colnett, John Ledyard, and Peter Pond – all of whom had designs for north Pacific trade and in some cases dominion – men like Bolts were pressing the larger corporation and the nations into action. The challenges of individual merchants such as Bolts deserve wider attention in the story of imperial expansion, for it was their goadings and their initiatives that in many cases supplied the *raison d'être* for claims to sovereignty by European states in eastern seas.

NOTES

1. N.L. Hallward, *William Bolts* (Cambridge, 1920).
2. Holden Furber, "In the Footsteps of a German 'Nabob': William Bolts in the Swedish Archives", *The Indian Archives*, 12 (1958), 7-18.
3. William Bolts, "A Short Chronological Narrative of Events [1801]", Cleveland Public Library, John G. White Zamboni ms Wq 091.92, B 639s, p. 1.
4. See ibid.; and P.J. Marshall, *East India Fortunes* (Oxford, 1976), p. 221.
5. Bolts, Narrative, p. 4.
6. Bolts, *Consideration on India Affairs* (London, 1772-5), I, passim; Harry Verelst, *A View of the Rise, Progress and Present State of the English Government in Bengal* (London, 1772), passim; L.S. Sutherland, *The East India Company in Eighteenth-Century*

Politics (Oxford, 1952), pp. 219-22, 255-8.
7. Hallward, op. cit., p. 3.
8. Furber, op. cit., p. 7.
9. Quoted in Hallward, op. cit., p. 5.
10. Ibid.
11. Catherine Gaziello, *L'expédition de Lapérouse, 1785-1788* (Paris,1984), p. 49 (my translation).
12. Quoted in Hallward, op. cit., p. 193.
13. Ibid., pp. 192-4.
14. Ibid., p. 193.
15. BL Add ms 29147, f. 310.
16. Chairman of the EIC to Hillsborough, 16 November 1781, IOR H155, pp. 364-5.
17. Pitt to Howe, 24 December 1784, Howe to Pitt, 25 December 1784, Suffolk RO, Howe Papers, Bundle T 108/33.
18. Court of Directors, Draft of Proposed Instructions to the Indian Presidencies, 28 November 1781, IOR H155, pp. 423-4.
19. Secret Court of Directors to the Bengal Council, 9 April 1785, PRO FO 41/1; India Board, Secret Minutes, 9 April 1785, IOR L/P &S/2/1, p. 3; Bengal Government to Secret Court, 27 October 1785, IOR H555, pp. 283-9.
20 Harlow, II, 348.
21. Gerald S. Graham, *Great Britain in the Indian Ocean* (Oxford, 1967), pp. 332-3.
22. See ibid., pp. 408-9.
23. Blankett to Howe, 6 August 1786, NMM HOW 3.
24. Gaziello, op. cit., pp. 49-50.
25. Ibid., and M. de Brossard, "Lapérouse following the path of Cook on the north-west coast of North America", paper given at the conference Captain James Cook and his Times, Simon Fraser University, April 1978.
26. N. Portlock, *A Voyage Round the World* (London, 1789), p. 2.
27. See his letters of 31 July and 31 August 1782 in the Provincial Archives of British Columbia, ms 223.
28. See, variously, Mackay, p. 61; B.M. Gough, "Charles William Barkley", *Dictionary of Canadian Biography*, VI, 36-7; and Holden Furber, *John Company at Work* (Cambridge, Mass., 1948), p. 137.
29. Furber, "In the Footsteps of a German 'Nabob'", op. cit., p. 18.
30. Hallward, op. cit., p. 202.

VI

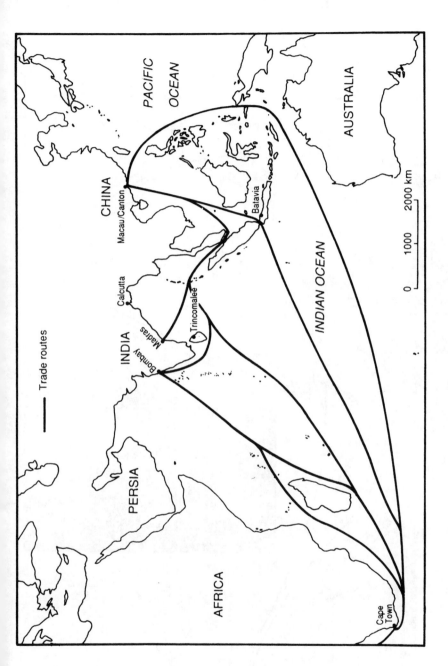

Figure 17   Sailing Routes to and from China

VII

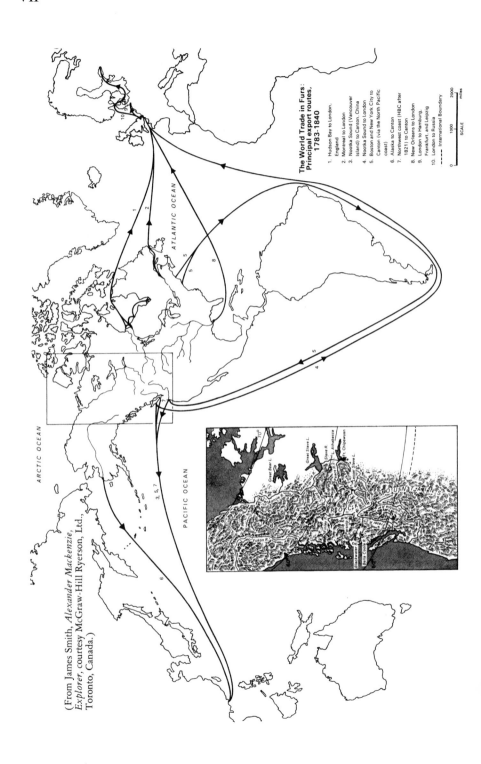

The World Trade in Furs: Principal export routes, 1783-1840

1. Hudson Bay to London, England
2. Montreal to London
3. Nootka Sound (Vancouver Island) to Canton, China
4. Nootka Sound to London
5. Boston and New York City to Canton (via the North Pacific coast)
6. Alaska to Canton
7. Northwest coast (HBC after 1821) to Canton
8. New Orleans to London
9. London to Hamburg, Frankfurt, and Leipzig
10. London to Russia
- - - International Boundary

(From James Smith, *Alexander Mackenzie, Explorer*, courtesy McGraw-Hill Ryerson, Ltd., Toronto, Canada.)

The North West Company's "Adventure to China"*

THE EUROPEAN INVASION of the Pacific Ocean and its littoral, beginning with Magellan's voyage and extending down to our times, is among the most significant events of human history.[1] This invasion may be looked upon as a moving frontier comprising peoples, animals, plants, diseases and institutions. As this frontier reached out from lands adjoining the Atlantic Ocean into and across the Pacific, new areas for European settlement were found, such as Australia, New Zealand and British Columbia; and new depots for trade were established, as in the case of Hong Kong. All of this caused international rivalry for trade and dominion. From the mid-18th century on, most major wars of the western world, including the Seven Years' War, the War of 1812, and the Crimean War, had the Pacific as a place of conflict—even though this was a sidelight to battles in Europe and eastern America. As the 18th century advanced, the importance of the Pacific became more fixed in the minds of European and American statesmen and men of commerce. By 1846, the modern destinies of such areas as Oregon, California, Hong Kong, Macao, Tahiti, New Zealand and Australia had been largely determined by the course of events associated with the western European invasion of the Pacific Ocean and its continents.

The growth of Canadian interests in the Pacific Ocean and its littoral in the late 18th and early 19th centuries represents but a small chapter in that large story. Yet now we are beginning to

*I acknowledge, with thanks, the assistance of Mrs. J. Craig and Mrs. S. A. Smith of the Hudson's Bay Company Archives, London. Quotations from the Company Archives are by kind permission of the Hudson's Bay Company. I also acknowledge the assistance of R. Comeau and A. B. McCullough of the Public Archives of Canada, Ottawa, and of Miss Joan C. Lancaster of the India Office Records, London. (Ed. note: this article was a lecture given at the Oregon Historical Society Center, November, 1974.)

1. A. Grenfell Price, *The Western Invasions of the Pacific and Its Continents: A Study of Moving Frontiers and Changing Landscapes* (Oxford, 1963), 1-5.

Barry M. Gough, "The North West Company's 'Adventure to China'," *Oregon Historical Quarterly* 76:4 (December 1975): 308–31. © 1976 Oregon Historical Society. Reprinted with permission.

appreciate the importance that East Asia has played and continues to play in the evolution of modern western societies. It is a chapter of history which shows that from the beginning of European development in Canada the economic promise of the Pacific and the China market drew explorers west in search of the "Western Sea" and the "Southern Ocean." Their migrations were prompted by thoughts of profit rather than of adventure. Their efforts in extending trade routes stimulated scientific surveying and mapmaking. Skilled cartographers such as David Thompson worked tirelessly to lay down the principal topographical features of northwestern North America, and one of their objects was to find some sort of northwest passage—a navigable waterway that would facilitate trade with the Orient, whose fabled riches described by Marco Polo never ceased to lure these men.

In Canadian history, the China market, mythical or not, plays not an insignificant role, because it drew Canadian business interests across a vast land mass stretching westward some 3,000 miles from Montreal to Pacific tidewater. This movement had its origins in the period 1784 to 1821 when the North West Company, a group of Canadian traders operating principally out of Montreal but with trading contacts in New York, Philadelphia, Boston and London, extended their interests to the Pacific and to Canton. These traders, actually the first "Canadians" in the Pacific, came by land and by sea. Their exploits, which developed partly in response to the competitive activities of their American rivals headed by John Jacob Astor of New York and of their British rivals in the employ of the Hudson's Bay Company, deserve to be better known in the larger story. Though their activities on the North American continent have already been well described elsewhere,[2] it is not generally understood how the Nor'westers were lured across the Pacific to China, how they

2. The best works on the history of the North West Company are: L. R. Masson, ed., *Les Bourgeois de la Compagnie du Nord-Ouest: récits de Voyages, lettres et rapports inédits relatifs au nord-ouest canadien* (2 vols., Quebec, 1889 and 1890; reprint New York, 1960) ; Gordon C. Davidson, *The North West Company* (Berkeley, 1918; reprint, New York, 1967) ; W. S. Wallace, ed., *Documents Relating to the North West Company* (Champlain Society, No. XXII, Toronto, 1934) ; W. S. Wallace, *The Pedlars from Quebec* (Toronto, 1954) ; Marjorie Wilkins Campbell, *The North West Company* (New York, 1957) ; E. E. Rich, *Montreal and the Fur Trade* (Montreal, 1966; E. E. Rich, *The Fur*

attempted to shape the direction of Canadian and British trade across the Pacific, and what difficulties they encountered during that development which they called their "Adventure to China."

In its search for profits in the China market, the North West Company, derived from a group of Montreal traders operating together under a series of agreements going back to 1776,[3] was obliged to observe mercantilist regulations emanating from London. They did not enjoy the privileges of trade that their great rivals, the Gentlemen Adventurers of England Trading into Hudson's Bay, had possessed by charter since 1670. And, as will be seen, the Nor'westers had to resort to subterfuge in order to circumvent the powers of the British East India Company, another chartered firm whose monopoly also dated from the 17th century. At one time or another, these two giant chartered companies and, to a lesser degree, the South Sea Company (which had some rights of licensing ships sailing in the Pacific between Cape Horn and the Cape of Good Hope), sought to keep rival British traders out of their domains. Even though, as was the case with the East India Company, they allowed the North West Company to trade in China, stringent regulations were imposed. No doubt the monopolistic nature of British colonial and commercial policy was detrimental to the growth of the Canadian fur trade to China. On the other hand, competition with the Hudson's Bay Company on its northern flank and with the Astorians on its southern flank (both in the Old Northwest and on the Pacific slope) pushed the Nor'westers westward. Essentially, the Nor'westers had to choose between expansion or elimination: but the latter was out of the question to the Nor'westers, whose motto was "Perseverance."

The "Adventure to China" seems to have originated in the 1760s, shortly after Canada came under British control in the Treaty of Paris, 1763. In 1768, Sir Guy Carleton, the Governor

Trade and the Northwest to 1857 (Toronto, 1967); and E. E. Rich, *The History of the Hudson's Bay Company, 1670-1870*, Vol. II (Hudson's Bay Record Society [hereafter HBRS], London, 1959), chs. 5-16 *passim;* and Harold A. Innis, *The Fur Trade in Canada: An Introduction to Canadian Economic History* (rev. ed., New Haven, Conn., 1962), sec. III.

3. The first reference to their corporate name seems to be 1776. Wallace, *Documents Relating to the North West Company,* 5. The syndicate may well have been formed before that time, however.

of Quebec, advised Lord Shelburne, the President of the Board of Trade, that British traders should proceed across the continent to the Pacific Coast. There, Carleton wrote, they would select "a good port, take its latitude, longitude, and describe it so accurately as to enable our ships from the East Indies to find it out with ease, and then return the year following."[4] Here was a concrete proposal, perhaps the first, for trans-Pacific trade emanating from the St. Lawrence. Similar schemes involving a search for a northwest passage by sea and land, as well as the founding of a post near the mouth of the Strait or Straits of Anian, were proposed by Major Robert Rogers, Jonathan Carver and others. Carver, for instance, believed that a British settlement on the Northwest Coast of North America would aid trade, discovery and communication with China and English settlements in the East Indies.[5] Although the various partners and traders in the North West Company eventually undertook expansion toward the Pacific at their own cost, they never tired of sending memoranda to the home government for British support for their enterprises: this was especially true of Peter Pond who realized that Athabaska (north central Alberta and Saskatchewan) could be a base for a new trade to the Pacific Coast and the far east.[6] Pond's vision inspired Alexander Mackenzie to set out on voyages that would bring him in 1793 to the Pacific Coast.

Simultaneous with this transcontinental growth of empire, a new approach to the Pacific was being made by Captain James Cook in His Majesty's ships *Resolution* and *Discovery*. Sailing from Plymouth on July 12, 1776, Cook had instructions to find the western entrance to the northwest passage. Neither he nor his fellow officers and crew expected that they would open a new branch of commerce for the British—the North Pacific maritime fur trade. The Russians, beginning with Bering, had already dis-

---

4. Sir Guy Carleton to Lord Shelburne, Quebec, March 2, 1768; quoted in Lawrence J. Burpee, *The Search for the Western Sea* (2 vols., Toronto, 1935), I: 303.

5. *Ibid.*, I: 289-90. Also, Major Rogers' Instructions to Captain Tate . . . for the Discovery of the North West Passage, Sept. 12, 1766, Public Archives of Canada, Ottawa [hereafter P.A.C.], Baby Collection, M.G. 24, L3, vol. 40.

6. Memorial by Peter Pond, April 18, 1785, P.A.C., Q/24-2, p. 418; also in *Report on Canadian Archives, 1890* (Ottawa, 1891), 52-54. At this time, the North West Company was seeking a 10-year monopoly in the Northwest. *Ibid.,* 403, 405.

covered the Pacific's vast wealth in fur seal and otter. However, Cook's crew were the first British subjects to profit from the sea otter pelts, which they sold at Kamchatka and Canton. As for Cook himself, who did not reach these trading ports owing to his death in Hawaii, he believed that although a fur trade could be carried on with the Indians of the North Pacific Coast, that locale was too remote from Britain for *lucrative* trade—unless of course a northwest passage could be found, and Cook did not believe one existed.[7] Cook, in his brilliance, had put his finger on the problem, so to speak: he recognized the difficulties of distance and the effect it would have for successful enterprise in this trade. Nevertheless, the trade in marine peltry did expand with profit for Americans, Canadians and British alike, though in various phases;[8] and this resulted from prices that these furs could command in China.

As soon as the details of Cook's voyage and discoveries on the Northwest Coast became known in various mercantile circles, traders from various nations sent ships to the coast. Although the East India Company showed no interest in the trade, it gave grudging assent to certain British entrepreneurs trading under the name of the King George's Sound Company. The East India Company disliked and feared this intrusion; to them it seemed to foreshadow the advent of free trade.[9] Thus the Court of Directors framed regulations to protect their interests.[10] This resembled what the British expansionist Alexander Dalrymple called "that left-handed policy all too visible." He would have preferred a union of the East India Company and the Hudson's Bay Company for the prosecution of the trans-Pacific fur trade.[11]

---

7. J. C. Beaglehole, ed., *The Journals of Captain Cook: III, The Voyage of the Resolution and Discovery, 1776-1780* (2 pts., The Hakluyt Society, Cambridge, 1967), 371. On the extent of Russian trade, see James R. Gibson, *Feeding the Russian Fur Trade: Provisionment of the Okhotsk Peninsula, 1639-1856* (Madison, 1969), 16-17.

8. *Ibid.*, 372n.

9. Vincent T. Harlow, *The Founding of the Second British Empire* (2 vols., London, 1952, 1964), II: 423.

10. "A Report on . . . Regulations . . . concerning the Trade of Private Adventurers . . . ," India Office Records, London [hereafter I.O.R.] Home Misc. Series 494(5), pp. 385-417. Also, Harlow, *Founding of the Second British Empire*, II: 423-25.

11. "Trade to the N.W. Coast of America," I.O.R., Home Misc. Ser., 494(5), 429.

VII

Though there was at least one attempt, in 1793, for East India Company cooperation with the Hudson's Bay Company,[12] the East India Company's regulations remained in force until they were relaxed later in that year by government demand.[13] Nonetheless, the maritime fur trade fell increasingly from British into American hands.[14] While it is easy to blame this development on British mercantilist regulations, it is also true that in 1793 Britain was at war with France and in 1812 was again at war, this time with the United States, and both conflicts were detrimental to commerce in the North Pacific.

Meanwhile, the North West Company had commenced its China trade. They did so through Moscow, Irkutsk and thence to Peking. Indeed, a quarter of all furs that came on to the English market were destined for Russia, and from there the largest portion went on to China. Not only did the Nor'westers seek to expand this trade, but they wanted to trade directly with Canton. Thus in 1792 they lobbied the government to request that Lord Macartney, the British emissary to Peking, would negotiate with the Manchu emperor Ch'ien-lung for admission of furs to China.

Also, A. Dalrymple, *Plan for Promoting the Fur-Trade, and Securing it to this Country, by Uniting the Operations of the East-India and Hudson's Bay Companys* (London, 1789). He did not support the North West Company; see *ibid..*, 31-32. There is an obvious link between Dalrymple's plan and that of the geographer Alexander Maconochie. See the latter's memo of 29 January 1817 to the East India Company, printed in *The Journal of Pacific History*, I (1966), 195-98; also his *Summary view of the Statistics and Existing Commerce of the Principal Shores of the Pacific Ocean* (London and Edinburgh, 1818).

12. Hudson's Bay Company Archives, London [hereafter H.B.C.A.], A. 1/47, fol. 8, Minutes of a meeting of the Governor and Committee, 6 February 1793, and A. 5/3, fols. 96, 97 d. See also Rich, *History of the Hudson's Bay Company*, II: 161-62, and A. S. Morton, *A History of the Canadian West to 1870-71* (2nd ed., Toronto, 1973), 401, 402, 410. I am obliged to Mrs. Shirlee A. Smith, the Archivist of the Hudson's Bay Company, for these references.

13. By the Statute 33 *Geo*. III, c. 52, independent traders could ship furs from the Northwest Coast of North America to China in vessels which the East India Company licensed. The company was obliged to grant such a license unless the cause of rejection was confirmed by the Board of Control. David Macpherson, *Annals of Commerce* (4 vols., London, 1805), IV: 273-74.

14. Judge Howay tabulated this change as follows:

	BRITISH VESSELS	AMERICAN VESSELS
1785-1794	25	15
1795-1804	9	50
1805-1814	3	40

F. W. Howay, "An Outline Sketch of the Maritime Fur Trade," *Canadian Historical Association Annual Report, 1932* (Ottawa, 1932), 7.

Macartney's mission was unsuccessful: he refused to *kowtow*. Consequently, the Nor'westers had to continue conducting their trade via Russia, and during the period 1792-1795 they sent furs to the annual value of £40,000.

This method of trading with China seems to have terminated in 1797, by which time the company had found a less indirect, more lucrative way of doing business. This involved smuggling furs from Montreal into the United States from whence John Jacob Astor of New York forwarded the cargo to Canton. At Canton, agents effected sales wherever they could and arranged return cargoes. Gradually, the "Adventure to China" ran into trouble: by 1794 McTavish, Frobisher and Company, leading partners in the North West Company, had run up a deficit of £23,000 on their China account. As for the China trade via Russia, this was similarly disappointing.[15]

While these difficulties were being encountered, the Canadian traders pushed westward to the Pacific, among these being Peter Pond, already mentioned. Pond sold his interest in the North West Company in 1787, returned to Connecticut where he discussed at Yale University his project for a fur empire of the West and a trans-Pacific commerce, and sought, unsuccessfully, the support of Congress. Meanwhile, the company deliberately took up his plan and, as one historian put it, "engrossed it for the rest of its career."[16] In particular, it was Alexander Mackenzie of Gregory, McLeod and Company, partners in the North West Company, who prosecuted Pond's plan. In two great explorations—the first in 1789, the second in 1793—Mackenzie uncovered the principal geographical secrets of the Canadian Far West. These were firstly that a great river, the Mackenzie, flowed northward to the Arctic Ocean, and secondly that the Pacific could be reached by crossing the Rocky Mountains—through the Peace River—Fraser River and West Road (Blackwater) River —Bella Coola River watersheds to tidewater at North Bentinck Arm.[17]

Mackenzie, with a great deal of energy, now pressed on gov-

15. Gordon, *North West Company*, 195-97. Rich, *History of the Hudson's Bay Company*, II: 206-207.
16. Rich, *Montreal and the Fur Trade*, 86.
17. See W. Kaye Lamb, ed., *The Journals and Letters of Sir Alexander Mackenzie* (The Hakluyt Society, extra ser. no. 41, Cambridge, 1970), 373.

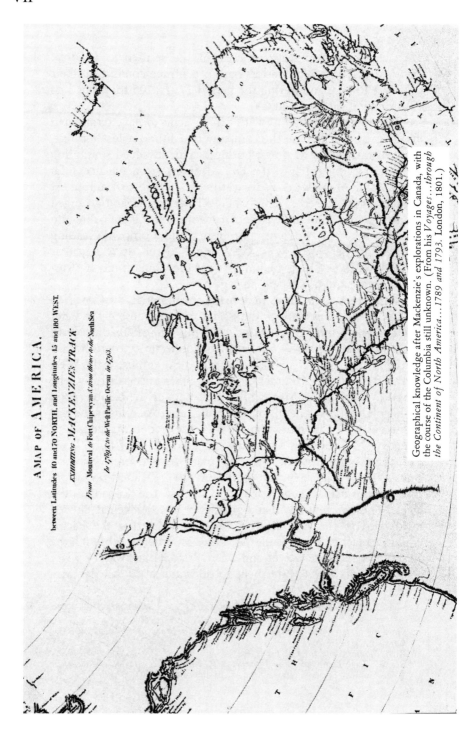

Geographical knowledge after Mackenzie's explorations in Canada, with the course of the Columbia still unknown. (From his *Voyages...through the Continent of North America...1789 and 1793.* London, 1801.)

VII

ernment and public the necessity of developing the trans-Canada trade route. In his now famous book, *Voyages from Montreal*,[18] first published in 1801 and for which he was knighted, Mackenzie put forward his suggestions, which deserve to be quoted here at some length:

The discovery of a passage by sea, North-East or North-West from the Atlantic to the Pacific Ocean, has for many years excited the attention of governments, and encouraged the enterprising spirit of individuals. The non-existence, however, of any such practical passage being at length determined, the practicability of a passage through the continents of Asia and America becomes an object of consideration. The Russians, who first discovered that, along the coasts of Asia no useful or regular navigation existed, opened an interior communication by rivers, & through that long and wide-extended continent, to the strait that separates Asia from America, over which they passed to the adjacent islands and continent of the latter. Our situation, at length, is in some degree similar to theirs; the non-existence of a practicable passage by sea, and the existence of one through the continent, are clearly proved; and it requires only the countenance and support of the British Government, to increase in a very ample proportion this national advantage, and secure the trade of that country to its subjects.

... the Columbia is the line of communication from the Pacific Ocean, pointed out by nature, as it is the only navigable river in the whole extent of Vancouver's minute survey of that coast:[19] its banks also form the first level country in all the Southern extent of continental coast from Cook's entry, and, consequently, the most Northern situation fit for colonization, and suitable to the residence of a civilized people. By opening this intercourse between the Atlantic and Pacific Oceans, and forming regular establishments through the interior, and at both extremes, as well as along the coasts and islands, the entire command of the fur trade of North America might be obtained, from latitude 48 North to the pole, except that portion of it which the Russians have in the Pacific. To this may be added the fishing in both seas, and the markets of the four quarters of the globe. Such would be the field for commercial enterprise, and incalculable would be the produce of it, when supported by the operations of that credit and capital which Great Britain so pre-eminently possesses. Then would this country begin to be remunerated for the expenses it has sustained in discovering and surveying the coast of the

18. *Voyages from Montreal, on the river St. Laurence, through the continent of North America, to the Frozen and Pacific oceans; in the years 1789 and 1793. With a preliminary account of the rise, progress and present state of the fur trade of that country* (London and Edinburgh, 1801).
19. Here the reference is to the voyage of exploration of Capt. George Vancouver, R.N., 1791-1795. Mackenzie is confusing the Columbia with the Fraser: at that time the course of these two rivers had not been delineated.

317

VII

Pacific Ocean, which is at present left to American adventurers, who without regularity or capital, or the desire of conciliating future confidence, look altogether to the interest of the moment. They, therefore, collect all the skins they can procure, and in any manner that suits them, and having exchanged them at Canton for the produce of China, return to their own country. Such adventurers, and many of them, as I have been informed, have been very successful, would instantly disappear from before a well-regulated trade.

It would be very unbecoming in me to suppose for a moment, that the East India Company would hesitate to allow those privileges to their fellow-subjects which are permitted to foreigners, in a trade that is so much out of the line of their own commerce, and therefore cannot be injurious to it.

Many political reasons, which it is not necessary here to enumerate, must present themselves to the mind of every man acquainted with the enlarged system and capacities of British commerce, in support of the measure which I have very briefly suggested, as promising the most important advantages to the trade of the united kingdoms.[20]

In Mackenzie's scheme of things, trade via the Pacific would be less expensive and less difficult than through the St. Lawrence. A post at Cook Inlet and another at the southern limits of British trade would secure the Pacific coastal trade by a conciliatory Indian policy. The China trade would increase, a matter of importance to the East India Company, because the importation of furs would lessen the need for the importation to China of silver from India or England. British martime interests would also advance with the development of trade via Hudson Bay, and in time of emergency Upper Canada might be made more secure.

He pressed this plan on the government in Upper Canada, where he was a sometime member of the legislative assembly. He solicited the support of Col. John Graves Simcoe, the lieutenant governor of Upper Canada, who in turn submitted the project to the Privy Council for Trade and Foreign Plantations.[21] Mackenzie also brought his project before Sir Guy Carleton, already mentioned but now named Lord Dorchester. Dorchester in his

20. Lamb, ed., *Journals and Letters of Sir Alexander Mackenzie,* 415, 417-18.
21. Simcoe's report to the Lords of the Committee of the Privy Council, for Trade & Foreign Plantations, 1 Sept. 1794, encl. in Simcoe to the Hon. Henry Dundas, 11 Sept. 1794, Public Record Office, Colonial Office papers [hereafter P.R.O., C.O.], 42/318, pp. 227, 266-69 (P.A.C. microfilm reel B-281) ; printed in Brig. Gen. E. A. Cruikshank, ed., *Correspondence of Lieut. Governor John Graves Simcoe, 1789-1796* (5 vols., Ontario Historical Society, Toronto, 1923-1931), III: 68-69.

capacity as Governor in Chief of British North America passed the information on to the British minister responsible for colonial affairs, the Duke of Portland.[22] From these documents it is clear that the advancement of trade and dominion was an idea to which Governors Simcoe and Dorchester, but especially Simcoe, gave their support. However, Mackenzie's plan seems to have gathered dust in London.

While Mackenzie was advancing his plan the North West Company was proceeding to effect the grand design. In 1792, two years before Mackenzie met with Simcoe and a year before Mackenzie reached the Pacific Coast, the partnership of McTavish, Frobisher and Alexander Henry, and possibly Astor, chartered the ships *Washington* and *America* to convey pelts to China via Cape Horn. The return cargo of yard goods, tea and semi-porcelain purchased in Canton was sold to Astor.[23] This direct and profitable Canadian venture to China was followed by a second and more ambitious undertaking. The outlay for this was estimated at £279,894. The trade, involving the conveyance of 4,000 beaver pelts, was undertaken by an 800-ton vessel chartered in New York.[24]

One can readily appreciate the difficulties associated with carrying on commerce across the North American Continent and the vast Pacific Ocean: these included a large capital outlay for a long period, the risks of war and storms (beaver pelts could and did get wet and spoiled), the need to develop roads and canals in Canada to encourage the export of the staple, and the reliance on American ships and illegal means of commerce to circumvent the stringent British commercial regulations. However, despite these obstacles this trade continued.

The trade was, in fact, given added impetus when Mackenzie, now a principal partner in McTavish, Frobisher, began to implement his plan. As E. E. Rich has suggested and W. Kaye Lamb has supported, Mackenzie was "confirmed in his view that the salvation of the fur trade lay in the north-west, in access to the Pacific and in the absorption of the Hudson's Bay Company's

---

22. Mackenzie to Lord Dorchester, 17 Nov. 1794, P.R.O., C.O. 42/101; printed in Lamb, ed., *Journals and Letters of Sir Alexander Mackenzie*, 456-58.
23. Campbell, *North West Company*, 89-90.
24. *Ibid.*, 90.

Alexander Mackenzie. (*Voyages*, London, 1801.)

rights; not in collaboration with the Americans."[25] Having convinced his partners to extend their capital outlay, Mackenzie went to New York in 1798 where he purchased in the name of William Seton and William Magee Seton, citizens of the United States and residents of New York, the 340-ton ship *Northern Liberties.* He had her coppered and fitted out, and also convinced Messrs. Seton, Maitland & Co. of New York to invest $25,000 in the project.[26] Mackenzie's breakdown of the costs was as follows:

The Ship value at . .	25,000			
Outfit, Guns, Provisions		Dollars in		
and 2 months Advance		specie	40,000	
to the men	10,000	Furs .	40,000	80,000
	35,000			115,000 dollars[27]

25. Rich, *History of the Hudson's Bay Company,* II: 210-11; Lamb, ed., *Journals and Letters of Sir Alexander Mackenzie,* 28.
26. Simon McGillivray later wrote that the North West Company had an arrangement with Messrs. Nicklin and Griffiths of Philadelphia and later Messrs. Seton, Maitland & Company of New York to ship at least $100,000 annually to China. By the new agreement (1804), no shipments were sent. H.B.C.A., A. 7/1, fols. 38 d.-39, Memo. of Simon McGillivray, 1 Sept. 1823.
27. Mackenzie to McTavish, Fraser & Co., London, March 10, 1798, in Lamb, ed., *Journals and Letters of Sir Alexander Mackenzie,* 470.

He had the venture insured for the total cost and for a voyage from New York to Canton and thence to any European port with leave to call at Falmouth, England, for "orders warranted American property."[28] Thus was the subterfuge of using foreign cargo ships complete.

The success of this voyage encouraged the Nor'westers to consign furs of the first quality to China. Regretably, however, the company had insufficient first quality pelts for both London and Canton markets: in consequence, the former began to suffer, much to the regret of the London partners. Thus the Montreal interests soon were at odds with their London counterparts—the "Canadians" (McTavish, Frobisher) wanted to extend the new field of commerce, while the "British" (McTavish, Fraser) warned that the enterprise would weaken their position on the London market *vis à vis* the Hudson's Bay Company, to say nothing of running afoul of East India Company regulations and French warships at large on the high seas. As Marjorie Wilkins Campbell put it: McTavish, Frobisher would be obliged to "juggle the demands of the Far East with those of Europe and somehow to retain both."[29]

This actual extension of markets tied in naturally with Mackenzie's strategy of extending, with deliberate speed, company trade across the continent. Athabaska was the farthest west that furs could, with profit, be sent east to Montreal and then to markets. Why not send the Athabaska returns westward to the Pacific? Here was the origin of what later became known as the "Columbian enterprise." At this germinal stage, Mackenzie was pressing for a division of company exports: on the one hand, pelts could be sent via Hudson Bay (thus avoiding the expensive Montreal route); on the other, western furs would be taken to the Pacific, where company ships would transport them to China ports.

Mackenzie was also thinking in global terms of how he could outflank the East India, South Sea and Hudson's Bay companies. He reasoned, and rightly, that the fishery of the North Pacific Coast offered a field of commerce of immense possibilities. He planned to set up a new company, "The Fishery and Fur

---

28. *Ibid.*
29. Campbell, *North West Company*, 115-16.

Company." Whale ships would take trade items to the Northwest Coast. An entrepot of trade and an organizational center would be built at Nootka Sound, with smaller posts on the Columbia River in the south and at Sea Otter Harbor in the north in latitude 55 degrees. Mackenzie laid his plan before the Secretary of State for War and the Colonies, Lord Hobart, in January 1802, under the title, "Preliminaries to the Establishment of a permanent Fishery & Trade in Furs &c. in the interior and on the West Coast of North America."[30] Eight months later, on October 25, 1802, Mackenzie again appealed to the Colonial Office for support—this time military—for the building of an establishment on the Northwest Coast and for forestalling foreign rivals.[31]

At this stage, Mackenzie met the greatest opposition not from the government nor perhaps from the chartered companies but from certain Montreal traders. Mackenzie had told Lord Hobart that a coalition between the North West Company and its Montreal rival, the XY Company, would be necessary to achieve the desired end. As he anticipated, his scheme for company union met resistance, especially from Simon McTavish, who did not want his own role and that of Montreal reduced.[32] With McTavish's death in 1804 and the rise of his nephew William McGillivray to a position of authority in the reorganized firm of McTavish, McGillivray and Company, conditions became more propitious for implementing Mackenzie's scheme. In 1806, Mackenzie and his associates formed the Michilimackinac Fur Company to forestall the expansion of John Jacob Astor and the Pacific Fur Company in the Old Northwest.

The rise of Astor's larger intentions of trade to the Pacific alarmed the Nor'westers because they did not wish to see their

---

30. Encl. in Mackenzie to Hobart, Jan. 7, 1802, P.R.O., C.O. 42/120. This project, Mackenzie knew, had two legal obstacles: (1) getting rights of fishing and navigation from the East India Company and South Sea Company (which commerce neither company had exercised) ; (2) obtaining a license of transit for trade goods through Hudson Bay and Rupert's Land. *Ibid.*

31. Sir Alexander Mackenzie to John Sullivan (for Lord Hobart), 25 Oct. 1802, P.A.C., Q/293, p. 225; printed in *Report on Canadian Archives, 1892* (Ottawa, 1893), 150-51.

32. W. Kaye Lamb, ed., *Journal of a Voyage to the North West Coast of North America during the Years 1811, 1812, 1813 and 1814*, by Gabriel Franchère (The Champlain Society, vol. XLV, Toronto, 1969), 3.

Columbia enterprise preempted. They refused to agree to Astor's 1809 proposal that the Canadians buy one-third of the stock in his Pacific plan. In common parlance, they preferred to go it alone. However, five disgruntled Nor'westers, dissatisfied with the company reorganization in 1804,[33] fell in with Astor[34] and were included in the Pacific Fur Company trade agreement of June 23, 1810. Thus was born the great American company which sent the *Tonquin* to the Northwest Coast (she arrived at the mouth of the Columbia March 22, 1811), built Astoria, and forestalled the Nor'westers at the very mouth of the Columbia River.

Until 1813 and the British purchase and occupation of Astoria (Fort George), the Astorians proved that the "golden round"—from Europe, eastern North America, the Northwest Coast and Canton—was highly profitable.[35] What Mackenzie had warned of, and in fact proposed for British commerce as late as 1809,[36] had been achieved. No doubt some Nor'westers must have been greatly concerned at first that the British government failed to heed the appeal of their London agent, Simon McGillivray, dated November 10, 1810, to send a British warship and to build a military fort or settlement at the mouth of the Columbia, thereby securing to Great Britain rights of possession.[37] That, however, was a development the government, in conjunction with the company, would pursue in 1813 during wartime, and pursue with success.[38]

In the meantime, beginning in about 1800, the Nor'westers had been extending their operations to the Pacific slope.[39] Mac-

---

33. Masson, ed., *Bourgeois de la Compagnie du Nord-Ouest*, II: 482-99; Wallace, ed., *Documents Relating to the North West Company*, 143-57.

34. Alexander McKee, Donald McKenzie, Duncan McDougall, David Stuart, Robert Stuart.

35. See Lamb, ed., *Franchère's Journal*, intro. Also, Peter Corney, *Early Voyages in the North Pacific, 1813-1818* (Fairfield, Wash., 1965), 93-98.

36. Mackenzie's last appeal to the Board of Trade, probably in 1809, is considered in Campbell, *North West Company*, 176-77. On this occasion, Mackenzie proposed to pay a reasonable rent for the East India Company's exclusive right of trade to the Orient.

37. P.A.C., Q/113, pp. 221-23, S. McGillivray to Lord Liverpool, 10 Nov. 1810.

38. Barry M. Gough, *The Royal Navy and the Northwest Coast of North America, 1810-1914: A Study of British Maritime Ascendancy* (Vancouver, 1971), 12-28.

39. In that year, 1800, Simon McTavish and Duncan McGillivray on an abortive expedition to open trade west of the Rockies. Wallace, ed., *Documents Relat-*

kenzie's route to North Bentinck Arm was unsuitable, and the
Nor'westers continued to search for a navigable river to the
Pacific. By the winter of 1807-1808, William McGillivray could
write that the company had "commenced a project for extending
their researches and trade as far as the South Sea" and that the
company intended to "form an establishment for the trade of
that country on the Columbia river, which . . . receives and con-
ducts to the Ocean all the waters that rise West of the Mountains."[40] In keeping with these objectives, David Thompson,
geographer *extraordinaire,* crossed the Rockies in 1807 to set up
the Columbia trade. During the next year, Simon Fraser, under
instructions to determine the course and character of the Columbia, delineated the river bearing his name. Subsequently, the
company built a number of posts west of the Rockies, including
Fort St. James in 1806, Kootenai House in 1807, Kullyspell
House in 1809, Spokane House in 1810 or 1811, and Fort
Thompson in 1812. And the company was there because it had
to be: as Mackenzie noted in 1812, the Pacific cordillera was
"our only remaining Beaver country." The scarcity of beaver, he
commented, "has been so much felt for the last two years that
the country in its present state cannot support our establishment
of partners, clerks and canoemen, so that there is a necessity for
extending the field, were there no intruders in the country to
menace us."[41]

Because of the nature of the Pacific Coast drainage basin
with its short, swift rivers, the company had to develop a practicable link between the interior, which Fraser called New Caledonia, and the sea. Over a decade, they developed the Okanagan
Trail, which went from Alexandra on the Fraser to Kamloops
and through the Okanagan Valley to the Okanagan River, a
tributary of the Columbia. In 1813, traders left Fort St. James on
Stuart Lake in search of a trail to Kamloops. As one Nor'wester

ing to the North West Company, 19. Perseverance "paid off." For a description of the establishment of posts west of the Continental Divide, see Innis,
Fur Trade, 203-204.
40. William M'Gillivray [?], "Some Account of the Trade Carried on by the
North-West Company," fol. 20, Library, Royal Commonwealth Society,
London.
41. Quoted in Roy Daniells, *Alexander Mackenzie and the Northwest* (London,
1969), 189-90.

wrote, "we shall, for the future, obtain our yearly supply of goods by that route, and send our returns out that way, to be shipped directly for China."[42]

The destination of these land traders was the mouth of the Columbia River, where Astor's company had built Astoria in 1811 and the Nor'westers had supplanted them in 1813. This was the focal point of the "Adventure to China." Not only was it a place where furs were collected for export but it served as the entrepot where supplies and trade items for the vast interior were received. In short, it was the linch-pin of the trans-continental–trans-Pacific fur trade. Rivalry with the Astorians, the military assistance of Britain during wartime, the continual westward expansion of the Canadian fur trade—all had brought the Nor'westers to the Pacific in 1813. There they were some 3,000 miles from Montreal overland. And they were some 18,000 miles from London via long, tenuous sea lanes. Across the Pacific, some 8,000 miles directly, lay the lucrative China market.

Though the North West Company's fortunes continued to expand in the first decade of the 19th century, the lack of a charter remained detrimental to any great advance in company trade. Although this is a larger subject than can be considered adequately here, it must be stated that the company repeatedly pressed on the government the advisability of issuing such a charter.[43] At one time, in 1812, the Board of Trade came very close to granting a charter to the company for the rights of trade to the Mackenzie River watershed and the Pacific slope.[44] Evidently such a charter was not granted because the full extent of American interests and claims on the Northwest Coast was not known. Certainly the British ministry knew of Lewis and Clark's penetration to the Pacific and of the role of the United States government in that expansion. And they were ready to grant such a charter provided it did not interfere with United States terri-

---

42. Quoted in Donald W. Meinig, *The Great Columbia Plain: A Historical Geography, 1805-1910* (Seattle and London, 1968), 53-54.
43. One such appeal originated in Montreal. See P.A.C., M.G. 11, Q/113, pp. 228-30, McTavish, McGillivrays & Co., John Ogilvy, Thomas Thain to McTavish, Fraser & Co., Inglis, Ellice & Co. and Sir Alexander Mackenzie, 23 January 1810. For subsequent appeals, see Davidson, *Northwest Company*, 124-32.
44. P.R.O., Board of Trade 5/22, pp. 17-19, Report to Privy Council, 16 Nov. 1812.

tories in the Pacific Northwest, the limits of which were not precisely defined.[45]

The plight of the Nor'westers was somewhat relieved when they entered into an arrangement with the East India Company. How this came about seems to be as follows. On July 13, 1811, when the Nor'westers were at their Fort William rendezvous on Lake Superior, discussion centered around correspondence with the British ministry and the East India Company "relative to a licence solicited from the latter on the part of the North West Company—to enable them to dispose of such Furs & Skins in China as they might collect in course of their intended trade on the North West Coast of America."[46] Three days later they resolved to enter "into adventure and a Trade from England, and China to the North West Coast of America," if a suitable license could be acquired from the East India Company.[47] This application was successful, much to the satisfaction of the North West Company. "We are happy to hear," wrote the North West partners to William McGillivray, "that part of the difficulties that existed between us and the East Indian [sic] Company are done away."[48] But it must be noted that not all difficulties were done away with.

How did this change come about and what benefit accrued to the Nor'westers? It may be suggested that because the government could not grant a charter to the Nor'westers they may have prevailed upon the East India Company to ease its restrictions.[49]

---

45. The United States was similarly aware of the relation of the Pacific Northwest to commercial potential of the Orient. See R. W. Van Alstyne, *The Rising American Empire* (Oxford, 1960), 93-96, 124-46. There can be no doubt that the push toward Oregon and California in the 1840s was tied to a lure for China markets. See Charles Vevier, "American Continentalism: An Idea of Expansion, 1845-1910," *American Historical Review,* LXV (January, 1960), 323-25, and Norman A. Graebner, *Empire on the Pacific: A Study in American Continental Expansion* (New York, 1955), *passim.*
46. Wallace, ed., *Documents Relating to the North West Company,* 266.
47. *Ibid.,* 267-68.
48. P.A.C., Selkirk Papers, M.G. 19, E1, vol. 28, p. 8627, North West Company partners to William McGillivray, 18 July 1812. The date of permission is uncertain but it was probably in 1811. See Davidson, *North West Company,* 130n37.
49. For evidence of opposition to the East India Company in the Cabinet, see Viscount Melville to Earl Bathurst, 6 April 1812, encl. G[eorge] Rose to [Viscount Melville], 3 April 1812, in Historical Manuscripts Commission, *Report on the Manuscripts of Earl Bathurst, Preserved at Cirencester Park* (London, 1923), 170-72.

The principal, perhaps sole, concession seems to have been that the Nor'westers could be certain of getting dollars rather than Oriental products in exchange for their beaver skins.[50] This they greatly preferred because dollars gave them an immediate freedom from competition with the East India Company.

Immediately the Montreal agents learned the good news, they instructed their London associates that a ship, the *Isaac Todd,* would be sent from Montreal to London and then to the Columbia and Canton. They sought and acquired naval support, with the result that H.M.S. *Racoon* reached Fort George on November 30, 1813, and the *Isaac Todd* on April 23, 1814.[51] The *Isaac Todd* subsequently took *all* the Columbia furs from Fort George to Canton[52] and returned to England with tea on account for the East India Company. Evidently, the success of the venture did not exactly meet expectations for in reference to the trader Angus Bethune, who had gone with the *Isaac Todd* to Canton, one Nor'wester wrote another: "Bethune is returned from China where he sold his furs, but not at a flattering price."[53] The total value of furs sold on this occasion amounted to $101,155.40.[54]

This first legitimate trans-Pacific British trade from the Columbia to Canton was followed by a venture in 1814 by a schooner aptly named the *Columbia,* which twice conveyed Northwest Coast furs to Canton.[55] Certainly, information from "the Gentlemen of the Columbia" indicated that the state and resources of the Columbia region were highly satisfactory.[56] Not only did the *Columbia* trade with China, she initiated the Canadian company's trade with the Spanish in Alta California, the Russians at Bodega Bay, the Hawaiians at Kailua, and with the

50. P.A.C., M.G. 19, E1, 1(30), p. 9123, Wm. McGillivray to Wintering Partners, 9 April 1812. This was a removal of a barrier which McGillivray previously considered "insurmountable."

51. Gough, *Royal Navy and the Northwest Coast,* 20-24.

52. P.A.C., Selkirk Papers, M.G. 19, E1, vol. 30, p. 9022, A. Macdonnel to J. Severeght, 6 March 1815.

53. *Ibid.,* vol. 29, p. 8843, J. Haldane to J. Leith, 21 Feb. 1816.

54. *Ibid.,* vol. 31, pp. 9209-10, "Canton Sales, 1815."

55. Marion O'Neil, "The Maritime Activities of the North West Company, 1813 to 1821," *Washington Historical Quarterly,* XXI (October, 1930), 254-63. This vessel under consignment to the company, was owned by her captain, Robson.

56. Wallace, ed., *Documents Relating to the North West Company,* 283.

VII

Painting of Canton, China, with foreign factories or "hongs" indicated by flags. British second from right. From Chinese lacquered tray made for American market, ca. 1825. Metropolitan Museum of Art, Rogers Fund, 1946.

Russians again at Sitka.[57] The "golden round" was not now dependent only on British manufacturers, Northwest Coast furs, and Chinese tea. Such items as sandalwood, rum, livestock, tallow, provisions, naval stores, and tobacco were conveyed by the *Columbia* within the broad confines of the Pacific rim. A third company ship, the *Colonel Allan*, visited Fort George and took furs and specie to Canton in 1816.

Nonetheless, after these three vessels were sent, the company, for reasons of cost, reverted to the system of having an American house facilitate their business in China.[58] Such an arrangement, which lasted through 1821, involved a partnership with the firms of Perkins & Co. of Boston and J. & J. N. Perkins of Canton.[59] Five or six ships sailed under this arrangement in 1815-1821.[60] To make more legal this trade, the company in 1817 considered the territory as belonging to the United States in order to circumvent the East India Company monopoly.[61] American independence favored the company's achievement.

But whether the trade was legal or not, it was still expensive. Simon McGillivray, writing in 1823, put it this way:

... the restrictions imposed on the private trade by the E. I. Co. and the disadvantageous manner of remittance caused expences which the trade could not bear & subsequently in 1813 & 1814 the case was the same, when the NW Co sent the skins to Canton in British ships and subject to the regulations of the E. I. Co. In both cases the result was the same, the trade was thrown into the hands of the Americans & after paying their heavy charges & large commissions, it was still more profitable to the Proprietors than to continue it on their own acct.[62]

Thereafter, with the merger of the North West Company with the Hudson's Bay Company in 1821, Company ships continued

---

57. The *Columbia's* voyage is recounted in Corney, *Early Voyages in the North Pacific*, 93-188.

58. Wallace, ed., *Documents Relating to the North West Company*, 283.

59. "Diary of Nicholas Garry ... 1821," *Proceedings and Transactions of the Royal Society of Canada*, ser. 2, vol. VI (1900), sec. 2, p. 81.

60. For an excellent account of these "Boston Ships," see O'Neil, "Maritime Activities of the North West Company," 265-67.

61. P.A.C., Baby Collection, M.G. 24, L3, vol. 16, Inglis, Ellice & Co. to Messrs. Sir Alexander Mackenzie and Co., 5 Nov. 1817.

62. H.B.C.A., A. 7/1, fol. 39, "Memo of Simon McGillivray, 1 September 1823."

Two sides of North West Company trade token. (OHS Collections.)

to send supplies from London to Fort George on the North Pacific Coast, supplanted in 1825 by Fort Vancouver, and to new entrepots developing such as the first Port Simpson (1831) and later Fort Victoria (1843). Furs from the Columbia Department were invariably sent to the London auctions by return ship. Until 1828 at least, the Company continued to sell high quality furs to Canton, though with some difficulty, especially because of the East India Company's tenacious position regarding their rights in the China trade.[63] Nonetheless, the Company continued to trade throughout the Pacific rim—at such diverse places as San Francisco Bay, Bodega Bay, Sitka, and Honolulu.

On reflection, the North West Company's "Adventure to China" proved to be a success, if a qualified success. The Nor'-westers overcame almost insurmountable obstacles of topography and distance to market Columbia furs in Canton by the thousands, for instance, 98,240 pelts in 1817[64] and 21,826 in 1820.[65]

---

63. See H. A. Innis's introduction in R. Harvey Fleming, ed., *Minutes of Council Northern Department of Rupert Land, 1821-31* (HBRS, vol. III, London, 1940), xxx-xxxi, lxx.

64. H.B.C.A., A. 7/1, fol. 27, "Importation into Canton in 1817."

65. Compiled from P.R.O., C.O. 40/367, J. G. McTavish to Agents and Proprietors of the North West Company, 22 April 1821; printed in Davidson, *North West Company,* 304.

Their achievement reflected the strategy they employed in carrying on trade through American corporate auspices in order to avoid British, mainly East India Company, restrictions.[66] Further, it demonstrated the ability of the North West Company to determine market needs, to obtain capital, and by no means the least, to ensure cheap bulk transportation across 3,000 miles of land and 8,000 miles of water. True, the company faced high capital expenditures, costly insurance, and long-term financial outlay. But these were offset by the good prices received for furs. When the North West Company finally closed its ledgers on the "Adventure to China" upon its merger with the Hudson's Bay Company in 1821, it left a legacy of trans-Pacific trade that now amounts to billions of dollars a year and is based mainly on another staple, wheat, rather than on furs as was the case in the days of the Nor'westers.

---

66. The East India Company privileges were suspended by an Act of Parliament in 1833. But from 1821 to 1833 the restrictions plagued the expansion of commerce from the Canadian Pacific Coast to China. This and related matters are considered in Frederick Merk, ed., *Fur Trade and Empire* (rev. ed., Cambridge, Mass., 1968), 71, 78-86, 120; John S. Galbraith, *The Hudson's Bay Company as an Imperial Factor, 1821-1869* (Berkeley and Los Angeles, 1957), 123-24 and 447n36; Frederick Merk, *The Oregon Question: Essays in Anglo-American Diplomacy and Politics* (Cambridge, Mass., 1967), x, 142-46, 157-59; and Edward J. Stapleton, ed., *Some Official Correspondence of George Canning* (2 vols., London, 1887), II: 71-116.

VIII

Peter Pond and Athabasca

Fur Trade, Discovery, and Empire

Much has been written by historians of discovery concerning official voyages by sea and land and their consequences to the evolution of trade, to the enlargement of geographical knowledge, and to the progress of national ambitions and imperial rivalries. Less is known about the contribution to these fields of human endeavour by individual persons unsupported by government, by learned societies, or by corporations. Marginally literate and largely unskilled in the scientific principles of cartography, persons such as Peter Pond left behind to historical researchers little documentation. In consequence, their lives can only be tracked, so to speak, like the intermittent flashes of a firefly at night. Here and there we see rare illuminations, but in between them lie large black spaces.

Nonetheless, as a class of individuals, merchant traders merit attention as discoverers and mapmakers. They were pathfinders in the sense that they were expanding the sphere of business capitalism and searching out new areas of commerce. In certain cases, largely unappreciated, they were pioneers of empire. As the distinguished historian of the Hudson's Bay Company's role as an imperial agent, John S. Galbraith, put it, the energies of the mercantile class were largely responsible for British imperial expansion. "Far more important to the shaping of British Imperial policy than the secretaries and undersecretaries of state often credited with its formation," wrote Professor

Galbraith in 1957, "were hundreds of men in the commercial community, most of them unknown to history, who created the conditions
upon which that policy was based."[1]

The fur traders of North America contributed markedly to the exploration of the continent. By experience they gathered a geographical
knowledge of the continent, especially its river basins, mountain passes, and native peoples. Moreover, they existed largely on suffrance of
the native people, and their profits as well as their survival depended
on the Indians among whom they travelled and traded. They learned
of the land's resources and how to survive in the wilderness. They
built trading posts and established networks of communications. Easy
as it would be to dismiss these fur traders as "unscientific," they led
lives on the frontier that required a pragmatic disposition. As the
celebrated American scholar of frontier exploration, William H. Goetzmann, has recently stated of fur traders as explorers, "they were
seriously engaged in the process of empirical information gathering,
and their very lives depended upon the testing of geographical hy-
potheses formed for very practical reasons."[2] Throughout North
America's river valleys and mountain passes fur traders enlarged the
world's knowledge about hitherto inaccessible or little known peoples
and places.

Peter Pond is among the names of the fur trade explorers of the
North American northwest that deserve to be better known. He frequently stands in the shade of Sir Alexander Mackenzie, David
Thompson, and Simon Fraser. Yet this resilient, violent, and ambitious man made a significant contribution to opening the trade of
Athabasca to the nascent North West Company based in Montreal. He
added to the trading domain of that concern which under Mackenzie
extended its interests throughout the Mackenzie River valley and later
to the Pacific Coast of what later became Canadian territory. His
actions also compelled trading rivals to enter into a partnership, a
revised North West Company, which by 1790 constituted the most
aggressive trading concern in North America west and south of the
Hudson's Bay Company's Rupert's Land. Pond's accomplishments
rested on his discovery and use of the Methye or La Loche Portage,
linking two of the continent's main river systems, the Churchill and
the Mackenzie. His skills as a mapmaker were largely unscientific; however, his maps of the northwestern regions of North America remain
among the principal visual references for our knowledge of the river
systems and trading posts for the last quarter of the eighteenth century.

Pond's life was a paradoxical one, and so too were the times in which he lived. His wilderness career spanned those years that witnessed a phenomenal turnaround in North American history and is commensurate with much of the second half of the eighteenth century for we are introduced to Pond fighting as a British colonial soldier against the French in Canada. Then we watch his progress as a merchant trader, mapmaker, and political geographer in what would become the Canadian northwest under the security of the British Empire. Finally, we view him in retreat from that same empire, partly consumed by the difficulties he brought upon himself, partly engulfed by the rivalry, jealousy, and suspicion of others, and ultimately dismissed by government authorities as a native-born American of dubious loyalty. In large measure, Pond was a victim of the dissolution of the old British Empire in America. Like the Royal Marine John Ledyard, who was at Nootka Sound with Captain James Cook in 1778, or like Benedict Arnold, who sought advancement in what he considered would be a better professional service, Peter Pond was an opportunist. We cannot admit the fact that his being a New Englander or Yankee necessarily stood in his way, for otherwise we should have to exclude the likes of Peter Pangman, both Alexander Henrys, Simon Fraser, and Daniel Harmon—all born in British American colonies and all, in time, prominent in the fur trade. Though particulars on Pond's later years are sparse we can nonetheless demonstrate, first, that Pond made a specific contribution to the annals of discovery through his trading activities; second, that his maps were significant if somewhat inaccurate representations, though contradictory from edition to edition, of the main waterways of the Canadian northwest; and third, that his contribution to the scientific delineation of the main features of the North American continent is as enigmatic as the man himself.

On 18 January 1740 Pond was born under the British flag at Milford, Connecticut, where his father was a shoemaker, and the descendant of a family which traced its ancestry in the New World to the 1630s. Little is known about Pond's childhood, except that he too became a shoemaker, a trade presumably learned from his father. To paraphrase Pond's own curious prose, he took pride in the fact that he was born to a family whose menfolk had for five generations acquired a reputation for being warriors either by land or by sea.[3] When the Seven Years' War commenced, Peter, age sixteen, ignored the protestations of his parents, left a growing number of brothers and sisters, and enlisted in the British Colonial Army. In 1758 he fought against

The Narrative

[*I was born in*] Milford in the countey of New Haven in Conn [*the 18 day*] of Jany 1740 and Lived thare under the Goverment and [*protec*]ton of my Pairans til the year 56 a Part of the British troops which Ascaped at Bradixis [Braddock's] Defeat on ye Bank of the Monagahaley in Rea the french fortafycation which is now Cald fort Pitmen Cam to at Milford to ward Spring Goverment Bagan to Rase troops for the Insewing Campain aGanst Crounpoint under the Command of [*G*]enarel Winsloe [1] Beaing then Sixteen years of age I Gave my Parans to understand that I had a Strong Desire to be a Solge that I was Detarmend to Inlist under the Ofisers that was Going from Milford & joine the armey But thay for bid me and no wonder as my father had a Larg & young famerley I Just Began to be of Sum youse to him in his afairs Still the sam Inklanation & Sperit that my Ansesters Profest Run threw my Vanes it is well Knone that from fifth Gineration downward we ware all waryers [warriors] Ither by Sea or Land and In Dead Both So strong was the Popensatey for the arme that I [*c*]ould not with Stand its Temtatons One Eaveing in April [*the*] Drams an Instruments of Musick, ware all Imploid [*to th*]at Degrea that thay Charmd me I Repaird to a Publick [*hou*]se whare Marth & Gollatrey was Highley Going on I found [*ma*]ney Lads of my Aquantans which Seamd Determined [*to*] Go in to the Sarvis I talkt with Capt Baldwin & ask him [*we*]ather he

[1] General Edward Braddock was defeated by the French when he attacked Fort Duquesne in 1755 at the beginning of the French and Indian War. When the fort was recaptured by the British three years later, it was named Fort Pitt. General John Winslow, a native of Massachusetts, was commander of the provincial troops in the unsuccessful campaign of 1756 against Ticonderoga and Crown Point which Pond describes.

Pond's narrative suggests the flavour of the speech of the Yankee at the time of the American Revolution. (From Charles M. Gates, ed., *Five Fur Traders of the Northwest*, 2nd ed. (St. Paul: Minnesota Historical Society, 1965), p. 18.)

the French at Ticonderoga; in 1759 he was with British troops that took Fort Niagara; and in 1760 he was in Montreal when the city surrendered to General Jeffrey Amherst.[4] Pond was much taken by Canada and its prospects. But, as he wrote in his narrative, in consequence of the conquest of Quebec, there was evidently "no business left for me in Canada." He went on a trading voyage to the West Indies, and considered making seafaring a profession, a natural occupation for one born in a New England seaport. This plan was stopped short, for on his return from this voyage he found not only that his father had left Milford to begin life as a fur trader at Detroit, but also that his mother had died. The Pond family was parentless, and it fell to Peter to assume the duties of head of the household, a task he performed until 1765 when presumably his siblings were able to fend for themselves.[5]

In that year, Pond began his career in the interior of North America. For some years he traded privately or in partnership with others who made Albany, New York, their base.[6] Detroit was one advance interior headquarters for this trade. Others were Grand Portage and Michilimackinac on Lake Superior, and Prairie du Chien at the junction of the Wisconsin and Mississippi rivers. Between 1765 and August 1775 Pond roamed this vast wilderness, known as the Old Northwest, invariably bringing in large cargoes of trade goods to the Indians.[7] In addition, he became a capable wilderness survivor, enduring difficult environmental circumstances. He was skilled in his relations with native peoples, and on one occasion was employed by other traders as a diplomat to bring peace among warring Dakota (Sioux) and Chippewa.[8] In some cases, such as with the Yankton Dakota, he claimed to be the first white to have visited them in the Upper Mississippi River watershed, and his brief account of these peoples is still regarded by ethnologists and anthropologists as an invaluable record.[9]

In 1775 Pond decided to extend his successful trade north and west. His route lay inland of the "lakehead," as it then was, at Grand Portage, Lake Superior. In 1775 many traders were using Grand Portage as their forward base of operations, from whence they were moving across the upper Mississippi watershed and into the Missouri country. Others were skirting the southern margins of the Canadian shield. Pond had decided that he was bound for the northwest beyond Lake Winnipeg and west of Hudson's Bay Company trading operations. English traders from Montreal such as James Finlay in 1767 and Thomas Curry in 1771 had already been pathfinders on the Saskatchewan River. But the Hudson's Bay Company largely confined its operations to the shores of Hudson Bay. The presence of "pedlars" from Quebec and Grand Portage in the interior led the Hudson's Bay Company to send certain traders, including Matthew Cocking in 1772 and Samuel Hearne in 1774, to reconnoitre. The latter went to the Pas in 1774 and subsequently established Cumberland House, the first Hudson's Bay Company initiative in the building of inland posts in the northwest.

That late summer and autumn of 1775 Pond went into the interior accompanied by other "Canadians" bent on peddling their wares in untrapped areas. One such person, though on a separate trading venture, was Alexander Henry the Elder, who recorded that at that time Pond was already known as a trader of some "celebrity" in the northwest.[10] Pond's aggressive trading practices had earned him a bona fide reputation as a man not to be antagonized, as he had a tendency to take the law into his own hands. Some years before, he had killed a man in the wilderness of the Old Northwest, and had told authorities in Detroit of the crime. For reasons unknown, the case had gone unprosecuted. It was precisely this violent streak in the man which was to be his undoing. Twice in the next few years he was involved, though not at first hand, in the murder of rival traders. This was to have consequences for him as a trader at a time when the North West Company partners were endeavouring to establish monopoly and order.

Pond spent that first winter in the northwest at Lake Dauphin. Here he intercepted Indians bound for Cumberland House to trade with the Hudson's Bay Company. Here also he found plenty of buffalo meat, which he prepared for his portable pemmican supplies for the next summer's voyage into distant parts. Pond now used Grand Portage rather than Michilimackinac as his supply base, and in conjunction with a number of other traders, he began to advance his scheme to exploit Athabasca. In the spring of 1778, according to Alexander Mackenzie, who had evidence of this from Pond, several traders who had goods to spare put them into common stock. The trading interests in this new partnership gave the management of the enterprise to Pond. They instructed Pond to enter the Churchill River and to make his way into the heart of the Athabasca country, then little known to the "pedlars" except by reports that had reached them from Indians.[11] This new arrangement was probably the direct forerunner of the North West Company. By the association of capital, the minimizing of competition, and the pursuit of a common commercial objective, a monopoly was established and a profit could be achieved. Otherwise, endless feuds would ensue, and profit was not likely.

In late 1778 Pond crossed into the Athabasca watershed from the lakes and rivers of the Saskatchewan and Churchill systems. Perhaps Indians told him the way, or he may have followed a well-worn native trail. In any event, his was the first crossing of the La Loche or Methye Portage by a white trader. Pond set up his winter post known as Pond's House on Athabasca River, at a site about sixty kilometres south of Athabasca Lake. This establishment, Alexander Mackenzie wrote, "was the only one in this part of the world till the year 1785." That winter, 1778-79, Pond did not come out to warmer climes nor did he enjoy the company of fellow traders at the Grand Portage rendezvous. Rather, at his house on Athabasca River, he saw, in Mackenzie's words, "a vast concourse" of Cree and Chipewyan tribes bound on their annual excursion to Fort Churchill on Hudson Bay by way of the long and difficult route to salt water. These tribes were very pleased to see Pond, for his presence meant that this would save them from making the long, troublesome journey.[12] They were prepared, also, to adjust their prices accordingly. They would accept less from Pond than they would otherwise have got at Fort Churchill. Herein lay the trading secret of the Athabasca Country. By his commercial enterprise Pond had unlocked the door to the little known distant trade of the Athabasca and Peace river deltas and the lands to the west and north. Not least, he had stopped the Hudson's Bay Company trading lifeline near its source.

The trading rewards of discovery now came to Pond. Like Radisson and Groseillers north of Lake Superior in the 1650s who were "Caesars in the wilderness," there was no one to compete with him or challenge his trade. He traded freely and on beneficial terms. In the spring of 1779, at the completion of a voyage that had taken two summers, Pond came out of Athabasca heavily laden. On 2 July he arrived at the Hudson's Bay Company's Cumberland House, "with three Canoes from the Northward very much distressed for want of food having had success on his Journey down his Canoes being broke upon the falls." From the HBC factor William Walker, who treated him civilly in exchange for previous kindnesses, Pond acquired tobacco, powder, and meat. He told Walker that he had gone far enough north to trade with Matonabee and the Northward Indians among whom Samuel Hearne had been. During trading he had made 140 packs of 90 pounds each

VIII

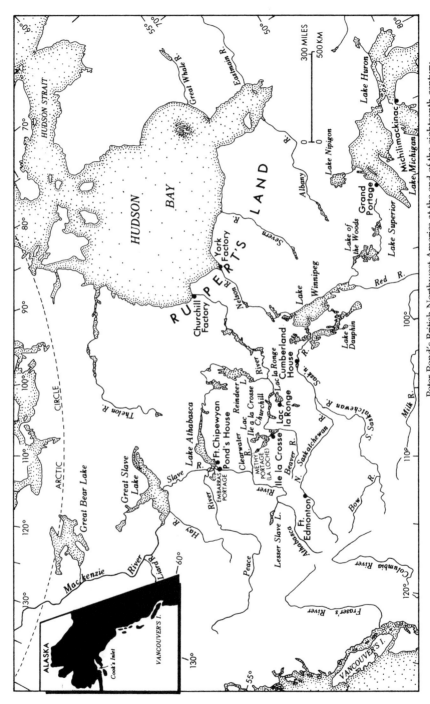

Peter Pond's British Northwest America at the end of the eighteenth century.
(Map courtesy of G.A. Lester, Cartographic Section, Geography, University of Alberta.)

VIII

but was obliged to leave most of them, mainly parchment and coat beaver, behind.[13] The Indians with whom Pond traded had been so distressed and eager to trade that Pond had traded even the clothes off his back. Pond, evidently unconcerned about secrecy, told Walker freely of his discoveries, and informed him of his famous find, Portage La Loche or Methye Portage, which he described as about twelve miles in length and so steep—it rises twelve hundred feet—that it had taken his party eight days to complete the passage. Pond came out of Athabasca to Grand Portage, and returned there directly to bring out the furs which he had left in Athabasca. He spent the winter of 1780-81 at Michilimackinac.[14] He then returned toward Athabasca to winter with Jean Etienne Waden at Lac la Ronge.

Pond's expedition to Athabasca brought new information for securing the northern trade. Other traders grasped the significance of Pond's findings. For instance, Alexander Henry the Elder, who used Pond's discoveries for his own benefit and without acknowledgement, envisioned a new transcontinental route of commercial importance, indeed one of national and imperial significance. Henry asked the influential president of the Royal Society in London, Sir Joseph Banks, to whom in a memorandum dated 18 October 1781, he had proposed the exploratory expedition, that he be entrusted with the leadership of the expedition, if the king, George III, approved of the project.[15] However, the scheme did not go forward immediately in this form.

Pond's newly expanded trade to Athabasca also invited competition from other pedlars. Accordingly, to keep out or at least control rivals, Pond sought both partnerships and a general monopoly that would eliminate ruinous competition for a business with extended lines of communication, costly transportation, and numerous risks. First, after leaving his old Detroit-based association with Felix Graham in 1775, he developed one with George McBeath, a former Albany trader whose Montreal connections were being exercised through the energizing auspices of Simon McTavish. In 1781 he was selected by larger interests as their representative to trade in joint-stock with Jean Etienne Waden, already mentioned. This partnership grew, in 1783, into the larger association, the first declared North West Company. In 1783 Pond had one share of sixteen held by northwest traders who "joined their stock together and made one common interest."[16]

In March 1782, Pond and Waden were encamped at Lac la Ronge, trading with the natives. They represented different yet interrelated commercial interests: Pond's was the larger, and built around the

10

bigger houses of Montreal, that is, the Frobishers, McGills, Ellices, and McTavish along with McBeath and Company, and Phyn and Ellice. By contrast Waden's was the smaller and represented Waden and St. Germain, Oakes and Company, Ross and Company, and perhaps Holmes and Grant. The two groups were nonetheless affiliated, and in 1779 Waden had been chosen to replace Pond in trading with the Athabasca Indians. However, rivalry between the two groups lay unresolved, and in an intended compromise the two agreed to trade side by side at Lac la Ronge. This was easier said than done. According to Mackenzie's narrative, Pond and Waden were of distinctly different character. Ill-will developed between them, doubtless because of commercial rivalry. In February 1782 the two of them fought, but the details are not known. At the beginning of March, Waden was shot and mortally wounded, perhaps by Pond or by his clerk, Toussaint Lesieur. Waden's widow pressed charges against Pond and Lesieur but at the trial both were acquitted, partly on evidence supplied by a deposition made 19 May 1783 by Joseph Faignant, Waden's clerk.[17]

Pond, his map shows, wintered on Ile a la Crosse Lake in 1783. Probably in the spring he proceeded to Athabasca, wintered, and in 1784 went to Grand Portage and to Montreal. During this his third winter in Athabasca, Pond probably learned from Indians about the approximate location of Great Slave and Great Bear lakes and perhaps the courses of the Peace and Mackenzie rivers. During his Athabasca winters, especially 1783-84, he came into contact with many Indians of the Mackenzie district, and secured for the Nor'Westers a trade which ended Hudson's Bay Company attempts to control Athabasca. After 1782 fur shipments from the area flowed not to Fort Churchill but to Grand Portage. In 1784 Pond came out of the *pays de la mer d l'ouest* to Grand Portage. Disaffected at not being given appropriate shares in the reorganized North West Company, he considered joining former rivals John Ross and Peter Pangman, for whose earlier defeat he had been so largely responsible. In 1784-85 Pond was at Montreal, possibly, if Mackenzie is to be believed, for the trial of the murder of Waden. On 18 April 1785 a memorial, probably written by the Frobishers and signed by Pond, was presented at Quebec. This memorial urged the Governor of Canada, Frederick Haldimand, to support a scheme for discoveries of the northwestern reaches of North America under Pond's leadership.[18]

In 1785 Pond returned to Athabasca via Grand Portage. Another trader, John Ross, also went there, to compete with Pond. In the

VIII

Peter Pond and Athabasca 11

subsequent summers of 1786 and 1787 Pond made excursions from his post, extending trade up the Peace River and organizing his base of provisions. In the winter 1786-87 competition became more severe. Sometime during this winter Ross was "shot in a scuffle with Mr. Pond's men."[19] The effect of this news was a decision made by leaders of rival interests to join forces. Two of Pond's men were arrested, and brought to Quebec for trial, but were acquitted. Peter Fidler had no doubts about this and stated categorically in his journal of 1791: "Mr. Ross was shot by one Peshe, a Canadian, by order of Pond."[20] Henceforth, Pond was a marked man, largely regarded by fellow traders as untrustworthy and dangerous.

Meanwhile, during the winter of 1784-85, Pond had prepared his celebrated map. In Montreal he had come in contact with narratives of Cook's voyage to the North Pacific, possibly W. Ellis, *An Authentic Narrative of a Voyage performed by Captain Cook and Captain Clarke* published in London in 1782. Doubtless these accounts inspired Pond with visions of Cook's Inlet, of Prince William Sound, and King George's Sound. And the maps in such accounts described the location of Bering Strait and the Arctic Ocean. There exist four versions (in various states) of Pond's map. Of the first version he is said to have submitted a copy (what we might call the first state) to the United States Congress on 1 March 1785. [21] This showed the rivers and lakes from the Great Lakes and Hudson Bay westward to the Rocky Mountains and northward to the Arctic, called by Pond the Mer du Nord West." This map also shows a large river flowing from Lake Athabasca to Slave Lake and thence to the Arctic. A note on a surviving copy of this map states that "from his own discoveries as well as from the reports of Indians," Pond "assures himself of having at least discovered a Passage to the N[ord] O[uest] Sea."[22]

In April 1785 Pond submitted a revised version of his map to the Lieutenant Governor of Quebec, the Honourable Henry Hamilton. This map shows that in the interval he had become aware of the discoveries of Captain James Cook, R.N., who mistakenly identified Cook Inlet as a river draining from Athabasca. Governor Hamilton, anxious to support Pond and prevent him from aiding the United States or another country, more probably Russia, urged the British government to support Pond and the Nor'Westers. In due course the British organized an expedition under Captain John Frederick Holland to cross the continent in 1790. However, this was cancelled when news reached Quebec and London that Mackenzie had explored the

12

Mackenzie River and found its course very different from that suggested by Pond.[23]

Pond's first map correctly suggested the course of the Mackenzie River; however, accounts of Captain James Cook's unsubstantiated discovery of Cook's "River" evidently deflected Pond from his earlier belief, and on his map he sketched in a course of the Mackenzie River as draining to the Pacific.[24] This change severely hurt his credibility as a mapmaker.

Pond continued, however, to produce or allow others to produce copies of his map. One such copy,[25] dated 6 December 1787, he presented to Lord Dorchester, Hamilton's successor as governor at Quebec. This version shows a gigantic Great Slave Lake, perhaps leading to the Pacific. Dorchester sent this to London in November 1790.

A simplified copy of this map was published in London in *The Gentleman's Magazine* of March 1790.[26] This map has no known draftsman, and exhibits no tell-tale signs, though it is necessarily engraved for the purpose of reproduction. It is based on a drawing doubtless prepared on the basis of evidence contained in a letter, dated 7 November 1789, and written by the well-informed Mr. Justice Isaac Ogden of Quebec to his father David Ogden of London, who in turn conveyed a lengthy extract of it to Mr. Evan Nepean, principal secretary to the Honourable W.W. Grenville, member of the British cabinet responsible for trade and colonial matters. As was customary, when such reports contained enticing data, the letter was passed on to a responsible periodical, in this case *The Gentleman's Magazine*.

Another copy of Pond's original map was made by J. Hector St. John de Crevecoeur for the Duc de la Rochefoucauld-Liancourt, who published it, in 1799, in an account of his recent travels in eastern North America.[27] Yet another copy, prepared by Pond in July 1787, was intended for the Empress of Russia, Catherine II, and may have been carried by Alexander Mackenzie on his voyage down the Mackenzie River.[28]

By 1789 knowledge of Pond had reached interested quarters. In that year Pond extended his connections in Quebec, and came into the company of several people, not the least of whom was Dr. John Mervin Nooth, a correspondent of the previously-mentioned Sir Joseph Banks, who was a botanist, president of the Royal Society, and "fixer" of various colonial enterprises. On 4 November 1789 Nooth wrote Banks explaining how James Cook's discoveries and the dreams of finding a sea passage to the Pacific had consumed Pond, as it had so many:

VIII

a very singular person of the Name of Pond is arriv'd in Quebec. This man has been some years in the western parts of America on a trading Expedition with the Indians, and positively asserts that he has discover'd an immense Lake nearly equal to Great Britain that communicates in all probability with Cooks River on Sandwich Sound. In the River which was form'd by the Water that was discharg'd from this Lake he met with Indians that had undoubtedly seen Cooks Ships and who had with them a variety of European Articles evidently of English manufacture. The country which Pond pass'd thro' after leaving the neighbourhood of Montreal was altogether level no mountains or even Hills any where appearing till he came near the Lake above mention'd and to which the Traders have given the Name of the Great Slave Lake....[29]

Nooth added that a map of Pond's journey had been presented to the governor, Lord Dorchester. The latitudes of this map were well laid down, Nooth assured Banks, "as Pond himself was very capable of ascertaining that circumstance."[30] As to longitudes, he regarded Pond's observations as "guesswork" and hence unreliable. We know Banks' response to this intelligence. To Nooth's letter he added: "A Mr. Pond set out from Quebeck in the Spring 1785 Alone with intention of Crossing America Westward and returning by Siberia, he had before traveld [sic] till he met the Tide in a river which ran to the west and supposes he then was within three days Journey of the Sea in the Neighbourhood of Jesuits harbour."[31] This data, Banks noted, he had obtained from his informant Captain Bentinck when he visited Banks' house, Revesby, in 1788.

Meanwhile, Pond had left Athabasca in the spring of 1788 never to return. The murder of Waden and the death of Ross led to Pond's withdrawal or forced retirement from the fur trade. Roderick McKenzie, at Fort Chipewyan on Lake Athabasca in 1788, wrote that at that time Pond "being accused, at different times, of having been instrumental towards the death of two gentlemen who were in opposition to his interest,...was now on his way out of the country on his defence."[32] Whether or not he retired of his own volition is not known; however, Pond was not included in the 1790 reorganization, having sold his share in that year to William McGillivray for 800 pounds.[33] Lord Dorchester had knowledge that Pond quit the Province of Quebec owing to his dissatisfaction with the North West Company. Pond's intention, Governor Dorchester said, was to seek employment in his

VIII

native United States.[34] Little is known about Pond in retirement. We do know that in 1790 he visited President Ezra Stiles of Yale College, and Stiles made a copy of Pond's map.[35] Pond spent later days reading the western travels of such persons as Baron Lahontan and Jonathan Carver.[36] He may have been aware of Mackenzie's famous *Voyages from Montreal on the River St. Lawrence, through the Frozen and Pacific Oceans*, published in 1801. This book brought its author a knighthood and gave depreciated value to Pond's preliminary findings, rather tending to detract from his significant contributions.

Nonetheless Pond had attained a position of eminence in regard to his knowledge of the Canadian northwest. In consequence he was in demand by certain trading and government interests. On November 1791, for instance, Pond was offered a share in a projected "Company for the N.W." in opposition to the North West Company.[37] Pond's response to this proposal does not survive, and we do not know if he went to the interior. On 9 January 1792, to cite another example, Captain Peter Pond and William Steedman were instructed by Henry Knox, the United States secretary of war, to go to Niagara and Detroit to seek from warring Indians a request for peace.[38] Again we do not know whether or not Pond went there or into any other interior portions of the continent. Pond spent the latter years of his life in the United States, most probably at Milford, where he died in 1807.

Pond was the first white man to cross La Loche or Methye Portage and to discover the Athabasca River and Lake Athabasca. These discoveries linked the Mackenzie watershed to waters flowing to the Churchill and Saskatchewan rivers. The first white to trade in Athabasca, he opened what Mackenzie and others called the "new eldorado" of the North West Company. Around this great find their future prospects revolved. Pond's use of supplies, including pemmican, and his good organization were keys to his success. Indeed, they enabled him to travel farther and to trade better than his predecessors. His energizing enterprises in opening Athabasca were of fundamental importance to the North West Company.

Pond was also the first to outline the general features of the Mackenzie River system. This had important consequences for Alexander Mackenzie, who profited from Pond's pioneering enterprises and geographical suggestions, and went on to build a career and reputation on business activities and commercial expansion suggested by Pond's postulations and proceedings. Pond's findings fired Mackenzie with the possibilities of discovery in the Mackenzie water-

VIII

shed and led to Mackenzie following the course of the great river to
its mouth in 1789. Pond's maps belong to the pre-survey type and are
largely unreliable as to specifically accurate longitudes; yet they remain as valuable contributions to the process of delineation of the
features of northern North America at a particularly interesting time.
Their findings, for instance, were used by Alexander Dalrymple, and
by London engravers.

Pond's contemporaries rather consistently regarded him with a
curious mixture of admiration and suspicion: admiration for his energetic activities; suspicion for his association with murders and foreigners. After the War of the American Revolution his loyalty to
Britain was suspect. Alexander Dalrymple, for instance, doubted his
loyalty to the Crown.[39] The Nor'Wester Alexander Henry the Elder
thought him a "trader of celebrity."[40] Dr. John Mervin Nooth, who met
him in Quebec in 1789, classified him as "a very singular person."[41]
Judge Isaac Ogden of Quebec favoured him as "a Gentleman of Obser-
vation and Science."[42] Trader Roderick McKenzie said Pond "thought
himself a philosopher, and was odd in his manners."[43] Surveyor-
trader David Thompson wrote of Pond: "He was a person of industri-
ous habits, a good common education, but of a violent temper and
unprincipled character."[44] This vilification formed a common thread
for later historians and writers, including Patrick Small, Charles Lind-
sey, J.N. Wallace and E.E. Rich. Even his biographer, Harold Adams
Innis, classified him as "one of the sons of Martha," a common toiler.[45]

Doubtless Pond was an unusual man. Lured by profits of rich
northern furs, he advanced farther north and west than any other
trader in the 1770s and 1780s. Overcoming competition from rivals and
problems of supply over lengthy distances, he and his men pushed
their wares into little-known river valleys and lakes of the northwest.
They made them tributary to the commerce of Montreal. In so doing
he induced rivals into his lucrative trade. Others benefited from his
geographical findings. Pond pursued a career in the northern forest in
common with that of other celebrated names such as Samuel Hearne,
Alexander Mackenzie, and David Thompson. He ranks among the
leaders in opening branches of fur commerce and in uncovering
secrets of the fur bearing regions of the northwest. Certainly none was
earlier in laying the groundwork for the successful operations of that
first great transcontinental business, the North West Company. His
violent conduct invited the suspicion of other traders both inside and
outside of the concern, and eventually forced his withdrawal from the

VIII

16

Company. Yet his maps and his suggested course of the waters of Athabasca remain as testaments to this pioneer in what was then the last great fur-bearing area of North America.

Notes

1. John S. Galbraith, *The Hudson's Bay Company as an Imperial Factor, 1821-1869* (Berkeley and Los Angeles: University of California Press, 1957), p. 3.
2. William H. Goetzmann, *New Lands, New Men: America and the Second Great Age of Discovery* (New York: Viking Penguin Inc., 1986), p. 128.
3. Pond's manuscript narrative is in the Beineke Rare Book Manuscript Library, Yale University, New Haven, Connecticut, and I have used copies that are in the University of Toronto Library. A remnant of this narrative was published in *The Connecticut Magazine* 10, No. 2 (1906), pp. 239-59, and reprinted, with annotations by Reuben G. Thwaites, in the *Wisconsin Historical Collections* 18 (1908), pp. 314-54. To date the best edition is Charles M. Gates, ed., *Five Fur Traders of the Northwest*, 2nd ed. (St. Paul: Minnesota Historical Society, 1965), pp. 18-59.
4. Ibid., pp. 21-26, and *Wisconsin Historical Collections* 18, 320n. On this campaign, see also Harold Adams Innis, *Peter Pond: Fur Trader and Adventurer* (Toronto: Irwin and Gordon, 1930), pp. 2, 6-13, and John Knox, *Historical Journal* (Toronto: The Champlain Society, 1916), p. 189. Further particulars of his military career are given in my biography of Pond in *The Dictionary of Canadian Biography* V (Toronto: University of Toronto Press, 1983), p. 681.
5. Gates, p. 26.
6. Ibid., p. 29; also Innis, *Pond*, pp. 20, 67, 150.
7. Gates, p. 30.
8. Trader Joseph-Louis Ainsse was sent as an emissary when fighting resumed in 1785.
9. Gates, pp. 27-28.
10. Alexander Henry the Elder, *Travels and Adventures in Canada, 1760-1776*, J. Bain, ed. (Boston, 1901; reprint, New York: Burt Franklin, 1969), pp. 251 and 263n.
11. On this, see Arthur S. Morton, *A History of the Canadian West to 1870-1*, 2nd ed. (Toronto: University of Toronto Press, 1973), p. 311, Henry R. Wagner, *Peter Pond: Fur Trader and Explorer*, Western Historical Series, No. 2 (New Haven, Conn.: Yale University Library, 1955), p. 7; Gregg A. Young, "The Organization of the Transfer of Furs at Fort William: A Study in Historical Geography," Thunder Bay Historical Museum Society, *Papers and Records* 2 (1974), p. 30; and Harold Innis, "The North West Company," *Canadian Historical Review* 8, No. 4, (December 1927), p. 312.
12. W.K. Lamb, ed., *The Journals and Letters of Sir Alexander Mackenzie* 41, (Cambridge: The Hakluyt Society, 1970), p. 73. Also, Alexander Mackenzie, *Voyages from Montreal* (London, 1801), pp. xii-xiii.
13. E.E. Rich, ed., *Cumberland House Journals* 15, 2nd Ser. (London: Hudson's Bay Record Society, 1953), pp. 5-6.
14. Harold Innis, "Peter Pond in 1780," *Canadian Historical Review* 9, No. 4 (December 1928), p. 333.
15. "Memorandum by Alexander Henry on an Overland Route to the Pacific," 8 Oct. 1781, in L.J. Burpee, comp., *The Search for the Western Sea* 2 (Toronto: Macmillan of Canada, 1935), pp. 587-96.
16. Quoted in Innis, "The North West Company," p. 312.

17. Innis, *Pond*, pp. 92-93, 97; Lamb, *Journal and Letters of Sir Alexander Mackenzie*, p. 75; E.E. Rich, *Montreal and the Fur Trade* (Montreal: McGill University Press, 1966), pp. 172-73; see also W.S. Wallace, "Was Peter Pond a Murderer?" in *The Pedlars from Quebec and Other on the Nor'westers* (Toronto: Ryerson Press, 1954), pp. 19-24.

18. Innis, *Pond*, pp. 99-100, 104, 106, and 109; Wagner, *Peter Pond* p. 14. Also, Wallace, "Was Peter Pond a Murderer?" p. 24.

19. "Reminiscences of Roderick McKenzie," In L.F.R. Masson, comp., *Les Bourgeois de la Compagnie du Nord-Ouest: Recits de Voyage* 2, premiere ser. (Quebec: 1889-90,) p. 18.

20. Wallace, "Was Peter Pond a Murderer?" p. 25; J.B. Tyrrell, ed., *Journals of Samuel Hearne and Philip Turnour* 21, (Toronto: The Champlain Society, 1934), p. 394n.

21. Lamb, *Journals and Letters of Sir Alexander Mackenzie*, p. 9; Innis held similar opinions. However, Malcolm Lewis has cautioned me (letter of 15 March 1982) that the problem of the Congress version is unsolved. Perhaps Crevecoeur somehow intercepted it (for the British Library's version [Add. Ms. no. 15, 332-C] "is in one of Crevecoeur's two quite different hands.")

22. W. Kaye Lamb, late Dominion Archivist of Canada, states that this note is a contemporary one. Lamb, *Journals and Letters of Sir Alexander Mackenzie*, p. 9.

23. Holland's report, 10 November 1790, C.O. 42/77, f. 274-5v. Public Record Office, Kew, England.

24. Harold A. Innis, "Peter Pond and the Influence of Captain James Cook on Exploration in the Interior of North America," *Transactions of the Royal Society of Canada*, Sec. 2 (1928), pp. 131-41, esp 139-41.

25. C.O. 700 [America] 49 (dated "Araubaska," 6 December 1787), P.R.O. See Williams, *British Search*, p. 232.

26. *The Gentleman's Magazine*, Vol. 60, p. 197.

27. Burpee, *Western Sea* 2, p. 343.

28. Glynn Barratt, "Alexander Mackenzie and the Empress," *The Beaver* 315, No. 1 (Summer 1984), pp. 42-46.

29. The Banks correspondence is printed in Richard H. Dillon, ed., "Peter Pond and the Overland Route to Cook's Inlet," *Pacific Northwest Quarterly* 42 (October 1951), pp. 324-29.

30. Ibid.

31. Ibid.

32. "Reminiscences of Roderick McKenzie," in Masson, *Bourgeois* 1, p. 3.

33. Ibid., p. 38.

34. Lord Dorchester to the Hon. W.W. Grenville, 23 November 1790, M.G. 11, ser. Q Vol. 50-51, Public Archives of Canada (P.A.C.), pp. 1-2; also in Wagner, *Peter Pond*, pp. 34-38.

35. Franklin Bowditch Dexter, ed., *Literary Diary of Ezra Stiles* 3 (New York: Scribner's, 1901), pp. 383, 385. Wagner, *Peter Pond*, pp. 19-22.

36. Innis, *Pond*, p. 141. Lahontan (1666-1715), soldier and author, in 1688-89 voyaged down the Wisconsin and Mississippi into unexplored territory. His *Voyages* were published in 1703. Carver (1710-80), Connecticut-born traveller, in 1766-68 was among the first Europeans to travel in and publish an account about the region now known as Wisconsin when it was under the British regime. His *Travels*, published in 1778, attracted much attention, alluding as they did (quite incorrectly) as *a great river* flowing westwards into the Pacific from the central part of the continent. In 1774, it may be noted, Carver was one of several persons, including Richard Whitworth, who planned to cross the American continent with a large party, to examine the Pacific Coast northwards to the Arctic, and to search for a northwest

passage. The American Revolution caused the scheme to be abandoned, though Cook's departure from Plymouth, England, in 1776 represents the government's desire to determine if such a passage existed in about latitude 60 N.

37. Samuel Birnie Letter Book, 7 January 1792, P.A.C.; also Wagner, *Peter Pond*, p. 103.
38. *American State Papers* 1, Class 11, Indian Affairs, p. 227, in Wagner, *Peter Pond* 98-102.
39. See Howard T. Fry, *Alexander Dalrymple (1737-1807) and the Expansion of British Trade* (Toronto: University of Toronto Press, 1970), pp. 199-200, 200n, 202, 212, and 219.
40. Henry, *Travels*, p. 251.
41. Quoted in Williams, *British Search*, p. 232.
42. Ibid., p. 234.
43. Quoted in Burpee, *Western Sea* 2, p. 340.
44. Quoted in Innis, *Pond*, p. 113.
45. Innis, *Pond*, p. 113.

IX

BRITISH-RUSSIAN RIVALRY AND THE SEARCH FOR THE NORTHWEST PASSAGE IN THE EARLY 19th CENTURY

Received May 1985

ABSTRACT. British-Russian rivalry along the North Pacific littoral after 1815 was at once an extension of 18th century ambitions, commercial and geopolitical, and an enlargement of the interests of both nations in the existence of a Northwest Passage. John Barrow in Britain and Adam John von Krusenstern in Russia exhibited the opposing yet complementary interests of the two powers. British Admiralty activities resulted partly from a fear of Russian pre-emption, partly from ambitions for territorial and commercial aggrandizement. The Russian government supported the Russian American Company, and consolidated its overseas empire in Alaska. This paper describes the maritime activities and plans of both nations concerning the North Pacific and Northwest Passage, explaining political and territorial ambitions of the two powers that underlay the exploration, and their expansion of territorial empire and commerce in this area.

Contents

Introduction

During the 1820s two major maritime powers, Great Britain and Russia, were involved in the search for the Northwest Passage, the ice-bound seaway through northwestern North America. Russian navigators had already searched the northern Pacific Ocean, Bering Strait and Bering Sea for over a century and a half; Russia knew considerably more of these coasts than any other nation (Figure 1). Britain's search in northern Pacific waters had extended over little more than a generation, though her involvement on the Atlantic Ocean side dated from Tudor times. After 1815, and particularly during the 1820s, rivalry developed between the two powers for northwestern North America (Gough 1971, 1973). Britain especially renewed its ancient dream, in the past pursued by Cabot, Chancellor and Willoughby, William and Stephen Borough, Frobisher, Davis, Pet and Jackman and many others, for a northwest or northeast passage to Cathay, though the search in the early 19th century was confined between Cook's Icy Cape (Alaska) and Baffin Island. Meanwhile, Russia was developing a high degree of competence in Pacific and South Seas exploration under Captain, later Admiral, Adam John von Krusenstern, an Estonian-born officer of the Russian navy who had trained as a cadet in the Royal Navy (Figure 2).

This article first appeared in Polar Record 23 (144): 301–317 (September 1986). It is reprinted with permission of the Scott Polar Research Institute.

302   BRITISH-RUSSIAN RIVALRY AND THE NORTHWEST PASSAGE

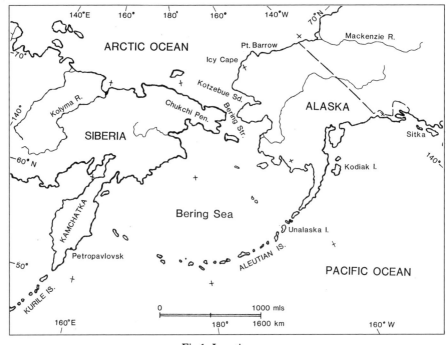

Fig 1. Location map.

Krusenstern's 1803 expedition with Yuriy Lisyanskiy through the southern oceans to
Japan, Yesso, Sakhalin and the northern Kuril Islands won him pre-eminence as the
leading Russian hydrographer and maritime surveyor of his age. Under his direction in
1807 Golovin was ordered to Kamchatka, Russian America and the Kuril Islands (where
he was incarcerated by the Japanese until 1813) and in 1817–19 circumnavigated the world
by way of Kamchatka. Lieutenant Otto von Kotzebue (Figure 3) was sent on expeditions
in 1815–18 and 1823–26 to the South Sea and Bering Strait, and Bellingshausen explored
the South Pacific and Southern Ocean in 1819–20. In short, Russia was extremely active
in exploration at this time, and much credit must be given to Krusenstern; of him was
written:

> ...he saw the welfare of Russia and Britain were not inconsistent or antagonistic, but in fact
> identical. He had too lofty an order of intellect to partake in those small prejudices of race or
> political illusions, which, at the commencement of his career, were professed by many of his
> contemporaries. (Dawson 1885).

The findings of the Russian navigators and scientists were made readily available to
the European public in English, German and French. At the British Admiralty these
reports gave rise to an uneasy awareness that a rival was making discoveries in the
northern Pacific. Though still one of the least known quarters of the world, this brought
them uncomfortably close to British possessions and British spheres of influence, an
unsatisfactory business that had to be stopped.

Fig 3. Otto von Kotzebue. From Kotsebu (1948), by courtesy of Alaska and Polar Regions Dept., University of Alaska, Fairbanks.

Fig 2. Admiral Ivan Krusenstern (1770–1846). From an engraving in the Scott Polar Research Institute, Cambridge.

Science and empire

In the years of Pax Britannica following Waterloo, the Royal Navy had resumed the exploration, hydrography and scientific survey that had been its strength since the days of James Cook and George Vancouver. There was popular enthusiasm in Britain for scientific knowledge, especially among the broadening middle classes, and scientific societies were flourishing; as Kirwan (1959) wrote:

> In so far as the new societies were concerned with the promotion of travel and exploration and with the accumulation of knowledge about foreign and unknown lands, they provided a most welcome avenue of actual or vicarious escape after thirty years of national isolation.

The early 19th century needed more exact and specialized expeditions than the broad studies of the late 18th century, and the Royal Navy was not backward in promoting them. That the aims of science and empire were identical was recognized by Sir John Barrow (Figure 4), Secretary to the Admiralty for most of the period 1804–45, who in 1830 was one of the founders of the Royal Geographical Society. Often regarded as the father of Arctic exploration, Barrow had a general interest in exploration. Motivated by the Tudor adage 'Knowledge is power', he considered science a means of acquiring power (Barrow 1846; Lloyd 1970), and subservient to naval and commercial interests.

One who shared these interests was Captain Thomas Hurd, RN, who as Hydrographer to the Navy had the duty of preparing accurate charts for British and world shipping. In a memorandum of 1814 Hurd spelled out some of the current problems of his office:

> The return of Peace to this country makes me consider it as an official duty to represent to the Lords Commissioners of the Admiralty the great deficiency of our nautical knowledge in almost every part of the World, but more particularly on the coastline of our own Dominions and also with the hopes that the present favourable moment for remedying these evils will be made use of, by calling into employment those of our Naval Officers, whose scientific merits point them out as qualified for undertakings of this nature–of which description of Officers there are I am happy to say many who stand eminently conspicuous (Day 1967).
> Hurd saw the need for surveys of the China and eastern Seas, Kamchatka, Tasmania, East Africa, the Mediterranean and Great Britain. His memorandum made no particular reference to the Arctic, though he noted that surveyors had been sent out to the 'Newfoundland and American Stations'. He concluded:
> In acquiring the nautical knowledge here recommended, much good might also result therefrom in other points of view as an excellent opportunity would thereby be afforded for the exertions of abilities both scientific and commercial... such an undertaking would keep alive the active services of many meritorious officers whose abilities would not be permitted to lie dormant [and] also be the means of acquiring a mass of valuable information that could not fail of being highly advantageous to us in any future War...
> (ibid 1967).

The views expressed by Barrow and Hurd were by no means ignored, for the Royal Navy's role in hydrographic surveying was generally accepted as important to Britain. Accurate charts facilitated trade overseas and economic expansion at home, and helped to maintain British pre-eminence. During the first sixty years of the 19th century no fewer than 190 Admiralty ships were employed on missions of discovery. In the 1820s alone, 26 ships sailed on exploration missions (Admiralty List: 5–19), at a time when economies ensured that warships sailed only to maintain or promote national security and prosperity. Even the Arctic was included; before Sir John Franklin's third visit in 1845, the Admiralty had been responsible for ten expeditions to find a northwest passage or a seaway to the North Pole (Table 1). Britain's interests were worldwide, and the northern Pacific Ocean was one of many areas that could legitimately be explored and surveyed by the Royal Navy.

Russian incursions into the northern Pacific Ocean brought them close to the borders

Table 1. British naval expeditions to the Canadian Arctic, 1815–48, excluding privately financed, whaling and non-Admiralty overland expeditions. Pages cited are from Cooke and Holland (1978).

1818 (NWP)	John Ross, HMS *Isabella*
	William Edward Parry, HMS *Alexander* (p 139)
1819–20 (NWP)	William Edward Parry, HMS *Hecla* (p 142–43)
	Matthew Liddom, HMS *Griper*
1819–22 (land)	John Franklin
	John Richardson (p 143–44)
	George Back
	Robert Hood
1820 (Labrador)	Hercules Robinson, HMS *Favorite* (p 144–45)
1821–23 (NWP)	William Edward Parry, HMS *Fury* (p 149)
	George Francis Lyon, HMS *Hecla*
1824 (Arctic coast)	George Francis Lyon, HMS *Griper* (p 149)
1824–25 (NWP)	William Edward Parry, HMS *Hecla* (p 151)
	Henry Parkyns Hoppner, HMS *Fury*
1825–28 (land)	John Franklin
	John Richardson
	George Back (p 151–52)
	Edward Nicholas Kendall
	Thomas Drummond
1825–28 (Bering Strait)	Frederick William Beechey, HMS *Blossom* (p 152–53)
1836–37	George Back, HMS *Terror* (p 163)
1845–48	Sir George Franklin, HMS *Erebus* (p 174–75)
	Francis Rawdon Moira Crozier, HMS *Terror*

of British North America, causing anxiety in Britain's Colonial and Foreign Offices. To the south of Upper and Lower Canada, the United States had fought a frustrating war with Britain; US expansion into Canada had been checked and in 1818 the continent had been divided along the 49th parallel from the Lake of the Woods to the Rocky Mountains. Only the Pacific slope remained open to both nations, leaving the Oregon question unsettled. By the Monroe Doctrine of 1823, the US was prepared to challenge any future European attempts at colonization in North America. Anglo-American rivalry over fur trading in the area had been intense during the war of 1812, and British interests clearly needed support.

Russia and the North Pacific

Well north and west of the 49th parallel, Russians were solidly entrenched on the Alaskan shore. At the close of the Napoleonic wars they had plans for colonizing western North America from San Francisco Bay northward (Barratt 1981). Their aspirations were based on the discoveries of Vitus Bering, a Dane in the employ of the Imperial Russian Navy, who in 1728 sailed from Kamchatka to ascertain, on behalf of Tsar Peter, 'the separation, contiguity, or connection of Asia and America'. Sailing through Bering Strait to a latitude of 67° 24′ N, Bering concluded that the continents were separate. On a later expedition in summer 1741 Bering and Chirikov discovered the northwest coast of North America.

Bering's voyages were not the first Russian expeditions in the North Pacific. As Bering himself discovered, in 1648 Semen Dezhnev had sailed from the Kolyma River to a point south of the Anadyr River mouth, rounding the eastern tip of Asia (Fisher 1981); other 'Columbuses of the Arctic' (Romanov 1982) had explored, charted and traded along the north Asian coast from Archangelsk to Bering Sea (Barrow 1818; Coxe 1804; Romanov 1982). As Fisher (1977) has demonstrated, Peter wanted a route to extend commerce to New Spain, to secure his Pacific frontiers, and to expand his settlements toward the

Fig 5. Alexander Baranov, chief manager of the Russian American Company 1799–1818. Photo: Scott Polar Research Institute, Cambridge.

Fig 4. Sir John Barrow Bart., FRS (1764–1848). Portrait from the frontispiece of his *Autobiography* (Barrow 1847).

uncolonized northwest coast of North America. The 1741 expedition of Bering and Chirikov aimed to establish sovereignty on the continent and offshore islands so that furs and other resources could be exploited. Indeed both the Bering voyages were in Fisher's view searches for new economic spheres of exploitation, trade and colonization rather than for geographical discovery. Armstrong (1979) has rightly noted that I. K. Kirilov's 1735 memorandum on the second expedition gives a higher priority to the discovery of a sea link between the Arctic and Pacific oceans than Fisher has admitted, but Russian territorial expansion and economic growth were clearly involved, and indeed acknowledged objectives from the early 18th century onward.

In 1799 the Russian American Company was chartered by imperial ukase to extend the commerce and territory of Russia, regulate the sea-otter trade and prevent its destruction, and spread the Greek Orthodox faith (Okun 1951; Tikhmenev 1978). From company headquarters in New Archangel (Sitka), on Baranov Island, trade was conducted along the northwest coast of North America and with the Hawaiian Islands. There were other posts at Unalaska, Pavlovsk Harbour (Kodiak) and at Yakutat Bay, gateway to the sea-otter trade. The major problem for the Russians, as it had been on the Okhotsk seaboard and Kamchatka, was provisioning the posts. For this reason in 1804 Commander Krusenstern, leading the first Russian expedition to the Hawaiian Islands, was pleased when King Kamehameha of Hawaii promised food shipments to Sitka in exchange for sea-otter skins. Henceforth, under the direction of Aleksander Baranov, chief manager of the Russian American Company (Figure 5), Russian ships were frequently sent to Hawaii for food supplies.

In 1815 a Russian agent on Hawaii, Dr Georg Anton Schäffer, ill-advisedly built a fort and raised the Russian flag, but Hawaiians, Britons and Americans united and caused his precipitate departure to China. Later, Russian sympathizers Peter Dobell and A. Ljungstedt saw the islands as the key to the Pacific and tried unsuccessfully to secure Russian domination. The Russian government was well aware of the resistance that Britain or the United States would have made to Russian annexation (Gibson 1976). However, on the northwest coast of North America, Russian expansion was under way. Baranov intended to advance from Sitka to Nootka Sound as soon as possible, but for economic reasons this came to nothing. In 1806 Baron Rezanov planned to establish a colony at the mouth of the Columbia River and thereby drive out the Boston traders, who at that time dominated the maritime fur trade of the coast; however, native resistance caused the project to be abandoned. But farther south, with the consent of Spain, the Russian American Company in 1812 founded Fort Ross on Bodega Bay in Upper California. From this easternmost post of the Russian Empire agricultural supplies were sent to Sitka, and a seal-hunting expedition went to the Farallone Islands near San Francisco Bay. None the less, the centre of Russian influence in North America remained Alaska, where by 1817 the Russian American Company had 500 trappers and 16 posts (Pierce 1965; Golder 1930; Gibson 1969). This did not preclude, as British and United States governments well knew, the possibility of future Russian settlement farther north in Oregon or Nootka Sound.

In controlling Alaska, Russia dominated the western end of any northwest passage, and the explorations of Kotzebue in 1815–18 showed her intentions of discovering the passage to the Atlantic Ocean. Kotzebue's instructions specified that in 1816 he was to explore the Alaskan coast and find a suitable harbour as a base for the following year, when he would try to penetrate northeastward in small boats. He was then to repair to San Francisco and Honolulu. As it happened, his major find was Kotzebue Sound, which the British were subsequently to use as a base for their coastal surveys. Kotzebue was anxious to find such a refuge in order to penetrate farther to the east, for he knew that

IX

the Hudson's Bay Company was trading far to the west of Hudson Bay; in his view, the Russian government ought to establish settlements on the coast of Bering Strait (Kotzebue 1821 1: 238–39).

British activities

Aware of these plans and movements, Barrow in 1817 gave warning that the Russians were 'strongly impressed with the idea of an open passage around America', and commented that 'It would be somewhat mortifying if a naval power but of yesterday should complete a discovery in the nineteenth century, which was so happily commenced by Englishmen in the sixteenth' (Kirwan 1959). Not surprisingly, Parliament offered a substantial reward in 1818, similar to that of 1775, for finding a Northwest Passage or for attaining the farthest north should a westward route to Bering Strait be impossible.

There were other reasons for the renewal of British Arctic exploration at this particular time. Barrow and Sir Joseph Banks of the Royal Society had heard from a reliable whaling captain, William Scoresby (the second to bear this distinguished name) that in the two years since his previous voyage to Greenland seas the ice there had disappeared. Lest this opportunity be lost, Barrow proposed to Viscount Melville, First Lord of the Admiralty, a two-fold assault on the passage. In consequence, HMS *Dorothea* and HMS *Trent*, commanded respectively by Capt David Buchan and Lieut-Cdr John Franklin, and with Lt F. W. Beechey (Figure 6) in *Trent*, sailed in May 1818 (Beechey 1843). These vessels were to make their way as close to the North Pole as possible and thence to Bering Strait. The expedition was unsuccessful, ending near Spitsbergen, but on return Franklin and Beechey proposed to the Admiralty an expedition to reach a high northern latitude by travelling over the ice from Spitsbergen. The Admiralty rejected this proposal; it was not until 1827 that Sir William Edward Parry sailed on a mission of this kind, reaching 82° 45′ N.

Meanwhile a second expedition, consisting of HMS *Alexander* (Commander John Ross) and *Isabella* (Lt William Edward Parry), entered Lancaster Sound in August 1818 and went no farther to the west than what Ross claimed were the 'Croker Mountains'. Evidently these mountains were a mirage, or so the gossip which reached London following this voyage would tend to indicate, and the Lords of the Admiralty immediately sent Parry, in command of *Hecla* and *Griper*, to investigate. This voyage was quite remarkable. In addition to proving the Croker Mountains to be non-existent, the ships sailed all the way to 'Parry's West' in September 1819. This position was near Cape Hay on Melville Island. They were unable to complete the passage because of massive ice to the west and south, the last barrier, and were forced home. Henceforth, as in Parry's next expedition, in 1821, the search was mainly directed south of Lancaster Sound, where it was hoped a seaway would be discovered along the continental shore.

So important had the Canadian Arctic shoreline now become that Franklin was sent in 1819 to explore by land the shores of the polar sea between the mouth of Coppermine River and the eastern extremity of the continent. He reached home in October 1823, then wrote his famous *Journey to the shores of the polar sea in the years* 1819–22, published in London in 1823, and began planning yet another expedition. By his 1819–22 voyage, Franklin had outlined the general trend of the coastline eastward from the Coppermine, and Parry, now Hydrographer to the Admiralty, had good reason to expect a seaway west from Fury and Hecla Strait (between Melville Peninsula and Baffin Island) to the Coppermine and, hopefully, beyond to Bering Strait and the Pacific (Parry 1826: 18–20; Caswell 1969: 29).

About the time that Parry was making his recommendation to the Admiralty for a sea expedition, John Barrow was putting additional pressure on Lord Melville to approve it. Barrow thought a passage via Fury and Hecla Strait, Prince Regent Inlet, the Polar Sea and then Bering Strait might be possible. Fearing again that Russia would prosecute the discovery if England did not, Barrow warned the First Lord:

> To give up the attempt before this point be tried, would indeed be to have opened the door, at a great expense and labor, for some other nation to reap the honor and glory, and to triumph over us who have for two Centuries and a half endeavoured in vain to accomplish it. (Barrow 1823).

Franklin was alive to these proceedings and as aware of the Russian 'menace' as Barrow. On 26 November 1823 Franklin made a detailed proposal to Barrow. This laid down plans for sending an expedition overland in 1825 to the mouth of the Mackenzie River, far to the west of the Coppermine, and thence along the coast to the northwest extremity of America to get a clearer knowledge of it and prevent the encroachment of Russia. The 'objects to be attained', he advised, 'are important at once to the Naval character and the Commercial interests of Britain'. Franklin proposed to reach Icy Cape, Alaska, in the summer of 1826, 'in the autumn of which a ship might be directed to meet it in Kotzebue's Sound, or any known part of the mainland of America to the Northward of that place to bring the party home or furnish it with supplies for its return by land'.

Franklin was convinced that a land expedition could carry out a better survey of the coasts than could ships, because of the number of islands and the difficulties of distinguishing between straits and inlets. Even if Parry's ships, due to sail in the spring of 1824, were successful in completing the passage, the land party would reach the Arctic Sea first and thereby keep to a minimum the extent of the northern shore open to Russian investigation. Franklin knew that Kotzebue was shortly to undertake a second voyage to re-survey part of his earlier discoveries in Alaska, to double Icy Cape, and possibly to explore eastward. He informed Barrow:

> It is plain from the letters of Admiral Krusenstern addressed to you (which Captain Parry has shewn me) that the exertions of Russia are directed to the increase of her Fur trade and the extensions of her dominions in the northern part of America; but I am gratified to perceive that with great liberality of sentiment he recommends to you, the course I have proposed. (Franklin 1828).

Franklin was fully aware of the need to check Russian power in North America in order that it should not expand into the rich fur-bearing region of the Mackenzie River basin.

Russian activities and British responses

But what of Russian aspirations at this time? Franklin was rightly concerned, for, as we have seen, Kotzebue in 1815–18 had searched for an entrance to the Northwest Passage at the northwestern extremity of the continent. Furthermore, Count Romanzov, Grand Chancellor of the Russian Empire, and Captain Krusenstern, his principal naval adviser, had thought that an examination of the Northwest portion of North America would be advantageous to Russian possessions in that area. Thus in March 1823 Alexander I ordered Kotzebue and the *Predpriatiye [Enterprise]*, a 'frigate' carrying 24 6–pound guns and including the latest astronomical apparatus, to leave Kronstadt for Kamchatka and Sitka on the northwest coast of North America to protect the Russian American Company from smuggling carried on by foreign traders (Kotzebue 1830 1: 1–8). Kotzebue never entered Bering Sea on this voyage; the expedition seems to have become one to protect Russian American Company trade and extend scientific knowledge, rather than to find the Northwest Passage.

It seems possible that British and American reactions to the tsar's ukase of 1821 (for territorial sovereignty along the coast from Bering Strait to 51° N, and for dominion over adjacent seas 115 miles from the shore) were so strong that Russia was unwilling to pursue discoveries for strategic advantage which would be counter to those of the British. We know that the ukase, which if successful would have enlarged and protected Russian American Company privileges dating from 1799, brought protests from the Foreign Office, British whaling interests, officials of the Hudson's Bay Company, and John Barrow. They decried the fact that the Russian act had ended free coastal navigation (Temperley 1925: 104–05; Galbraith 1957: 133).

The Hudson's Bay Company at the same time had its own means of forestalling Russian expansion by land and sea. In 1822, the governor and committee had already determined on pushing company interests as far north and west of the Fraser River as possible, in order 'to keep the Russians at a distance' (Fleming 1940: 303). Subsequently Samuel Black explored the waterways parallel to and west of the Mackenzie River and Rocky Mountains with a view to drawing Indian trade in the Stikine territory away from Russians on the coast. This began for the company a successful and little-known programme to stabilize and push back the northwestern frontier of its operations, a process which began first on land, and after 1826 was extended to water. Incidentally, by 1839 American and Russian competition in the fur trade of both the coast and interior had been removed and the company was without rival on the northwest coast of North America.

The Foreign Office was likewise successful in negotiating with the Russians. By a convention signed on 28 February 1825, Britain and Russia entered into an agreement which established the southern boundary of Russian America at 54° 40′ and its eastern limits along Portland Canal to 56°N latitude, and thence by the height of mountains parallel to but no nearer than ten leagues from the coast to the 141st meridian, on which line it would run to the Arctic Ocean. The Russians acknowledged British navigation rights on the coast and on rivers cutting through the Russian lisière or coastal strip. The British could also trade at Sitka and on the Russian coast south of Mount Saint Elias for a 10–year period. These terms, essentially the same as those of the Russian-American Convention of 17 April 1824, stayed Russian progress eastward and southward while they restored British and American maritime rights. By trade and diplomacy, therefore, the British had entrenched their own position in northwestern North America, including the northwest coast.

But what about the navy? The Admiralty was also well aware of Russian pretensions, and politicians such as Henry Goulburn, Sir George Cockburn, and Lord Bathurst at the Colonial Office, supported the Franklin scheme (Gell ms: 256, 257). So too did the Hudson's Bay Company. J. H. Pelly, a company director, advised Barrow that Franklin's intended voyage 'might be the means of preventing a claim on the part of Russia to that part of the continent of America, to the prejudice of British interests', and offered company support for the project (Hudson's Bay Company Archives A 8/1: 220). This was accepted; and early in 1824 the Admiralty, Colonial Office and the Company cooperated in preparing the shipments of scientific instruments, stores and equipment for the Franklin expedition. By May the plan had been decided on. However, not until 16 February of the following year did Franklin with his colleagues George Back and Dr John Richardson leave Liverpool on a journey that they hoped would take them to New York, Great Bear Lake, the Mackenzie River, and ultimately Kotzebue Sound.

Meanwhile instructions for Captain William Edward Parry had been drafted by the Admiralty. Dated 12 May 1824, they noted the objectives in view: discovery of the Northwest Passage and geographical inquiry into the northern boundaries of the continent. Their Lordships favoured a route via Lancaster Sound, Prince Regent Inlet, the Polar Sea and thence to the Pacific. In the Pacific, Parry was to proceed to Kamchatka, where dispatches and journals were to be sent overland via St Petersburg to London. He was assured that Arctic provisions would be available 'in the most advanced situation' to which they could safely be conveyed. Parry's instructions noted that he would be able to meet a ship with provisions in Bering Strait in August or September of 1827. This ship would go round Cape Prince of Wales to latitude 68° 30′N where Kotzebue had found anchorage in the large sound which bears his name (Admiralty 3/262).

The use of British ships in the Pacific in seeking a passage was not new. On his third voyage of discovery James Cook possessed instructions to attempt a passage from the Pacific to Hudson Bay or Baffin Bay beginning at latitude 65°N or higher, and failing that, to seek a Northeast Passage (Admiralty 2/1332: 284–96). He found nothing in this latitude, made a farthest north of nearly 71° in 1778, but found the ice impregnable to the east near Point Barrow as well as to the west south of Wrangel Island and along the Siberian coast (Williams 1962; Beaglehole 1967). It remained for Capt George Vancouver in 1792 to prove the non-existence of a passage eastward from the Alaskan shore south of Bering Strait. If any passage existed, therefore, it would have to be inside Bering Strait, either east from Kotzebue Sound, or east and southeast of Point Barrow, the northernmost tip of northwest America.

In September 1823, the Admiralty sent instructions to the commander-in-chief, South America station, to dispatch a vessel to Bering Strait. News had not then reached England that Parry's *Fury* and *Hecla* expedition, begun in 1821, had been forced to turn for home. The Admiralty named HMS *Aurora*, a 46–gun frigate, to undertake the task. If she was not available, another frigate of the same class was to be sent. At first sight the choice of a frigate seems unusual, because in most Arctic work small bomb-vessels, whalers, brigs and sloops were used. The only explanation seems to be that the Admiralty may have had in mind a display of power in the region which would make British intentions clear to the Russians both in Alaska and in St Petersburg. In any event her commander, Henry Prescott, was to provision fully on the coast of America. If he heard no news of Parry on the northwest coast or at Hawaii, he was to proceed to Bering Strait and remain there from mid July to mid September 1824. He was to keep towards the Alaskan shore, for according to Kotzebue's experience, a river existed there. Near the entrance of Kotzebue Sound, Prescott was to ask the local 'Indians' if a British ship had appeared, then he was to go as far east as Icy Cape, taking care not to be trapped in the ice. Finally, if time permitted, he was to examine Kotzebue Sound to see if a passage existed through it to the 'Polar Sea' (Admiralty 3/262). *Aurora* was never dispatched to Bering Strait and seems to have sailed no farther north than San Blas on the west coast of Mexico.

Plans to send *Aurora* were premature. Neither Parry nor Franklin could have been at Kotzebue Sound by the summer of 1824. In any case, the Admiralty realized that two years might elapse before either could reach the Pacific. Furthermore, the geographical positions of several islands in the South Pacific, especially the Tuamotu Archipelago, were uncertain. Why not send a vessel 'on particular service' to conduct the surveys but, more important, be in the area of Kotzebue Sound during the summer months of 1826 and, if necessary, 1827?

The grand design for the assault on the Northwest Passage therefore fell into three sections. The first was Parry's attempt to find a seaway via Prince Regent Inlet. The second was Franklin's expedition, which was to descend the Mackenzie River to its mouth where Franklin would move west while his companion Dr John Richardson would proceed east. Ancillary to this, Capt G. F. Lyon in *Griper* was to sail to Repulse Bay in Hudson Bay, proceed overland across Melville Peninsula to the Arctic coast, and follow it westward to Franklin's Point Turnagain. (But on reaching Repulse Bay late in the summer of 1824 in bad weather, her officers, quite dispirited because of near shipwreck on two occasions, agreed to return home without wintering.) The third part of the plan was to be the Pacific approach, and the Admiralty chose Cdr Frederick William Beechey and HMS *Blossom* for this task.

Blossom arrived at Petropavlovsk, at Avacha Bay, Kamchatka Peninsula, on 29 June. The gig was despatched with a message to the Russian governor and to collect any mail from England. She brought back the news that Parry's *Fury* had been abandoned at Somerset Island in August 1825 after heroic attempts to save her. Severe ice conditions had resulted in her destruction, but the crew had returned safely to England in the companion vessel *Hecla*. Franklin was presumed to be still making his way westward along the shores of the polar sea, and the officers and men of *Blossom*, according to Peard, 'confidently trusted to meeting Captain Franklin that season, so that there would be no occasion for a second voyage to Behring's Straits' (Gough 1973: 140).

Blossom had put into Petropavlovsk for the purposes of obtaining an interpreter to accompany the intended party northward from Kotzebue Sound overland, of getting information, and of procuring supplies. At Petropavlovsk the health of the crew improved considerably. It seems fortunate that the Russians at Petropavlovsk proved so hospitable and helpful, and although an interpreter could not be found, provisions were purchased as available. *Blossom* left the harbour for Bering Strait on 4 July, somewhat behind time but still able, if the prevailing southwest winds proved steady, to keep the rendezvous in Kotzebue Sound at the appointed time.

After experiencing poor winds *Blossom* reached Kotzebue Sound on 22 July 1826 and the rendezvous at Chamisso Island on the 25th, only five days behind the time agreed to by Beechey and Franklin eighteen months before. There was no trace of Franklin. Numerous explorations were conducted. The barge was sent to examine Hotham Inlet on the north side of the sound near Cape Krusenstern. Reconnaissance showed the country to be impenetrable, uninhabitable and infested with mosquitoes. Beechey left provisions for Franklin at Chamisso and sailed northward in the hope of meeting Franklin and of delineating the coastline. *Blossom*'s course was within sight of the shore, while the barge skirted along as close as possible, her crew periodically erecting cairns and leaving bottles with messages for Franklin. They were within twenty miles of Icy Cape when heavy weather set in, forcing *Blossom* away from shore and into ice floes. Later she returned to the coast and joined the barge on 17 August. The barge was then sent under command of Thomas Elson, the master's mate, along the coast to find Franklin, now expected daily. *Blossom* returned to Chamisso to wood and water; strong westerly winds had prevented her further use along the northern coast.

Elson's logbook of the difficult voyage of the barge, telling of problems with the natives, of heavy weather and of crushing ice, is one of the most remarkable documents in Arctic exploration (ibid 1973: 159–67). On 23 August the farthest east reached was 156° 21′ 30″ W at Point Barrow, named after the architect of the venture. Elson had added 126 miles of new coastline to the chart. But pack ice, moving sea ice astern, and warlike Inuit forced Elson to turn back. Franklin, meanwhile, had been making his way westward with Back, examining the coast to Beechey Point in 149° 37′W longitude. Franklin decided to go no further than what he called Return Reef. This, his farthest west, was reached on 18 August, five days before Elson made Point Barrow, only 146 miles to the west. It would have been an historic meeting at that end of the earth, but there is no doubt that Elson and Franklin acted wisely in not pressing on in the approaching early winter conditions. Neither knew, of course, of the other's position, and, in any case, had Franklin continued he might not have been able to overtake Elson and the barge (Franklin 1828).

Franklin was now forced to retrace his steps to Fort Franklin on Great Bear Lake. Richardson meanwhile had been to the mouth of the Coppermine River and back to Fort

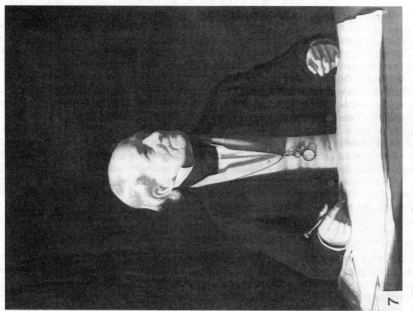

Fig 7. Sir Francis Beaufort KCB, FRS. From a portrait by Stephen Pearce in the National Portrait Gallery, London.

Fig 6. Frederick William Beechey (1796–1856). From a portrait by Stephen Pearce in the National Portrait Gallery, London.

IX

Franklin overland, leaving for Great Slave Lake before Franklin's arrival from the north. In June 1827, they met at Cumberland House, a Hudson's Bay Company post, and returned to England by way of Montreal and New York. Franklin's objective had again eluded him. It remained for two Hudson's Bay Company servants, Peter Warren Dease and Thomas Simpson, to complete the exploration of the western Arctic between Cape Barrow and Return Reef. Dease and Simpson mapped the remaining coastline in 1837, thus completing the outline of the polar sea (Rich 1953: xxiv-xxv).

While Franklin was retracing his steps Elson quitted Point Barrow and made a difficult retreat to the west and south. The barge was reunited with the *Blossom* in Kotzebue Sound on 9 September and, even at that later date, the possibility existed that Franklin might still arrive at the intended rendezvous. Beechey waited a month. *Blossom* left Kotzebue Sound on 14 October. As late as the 16th Beechey was hoping for a change of wind which would allow him to return to Cape Krusenstern 'in order to give Captain Franklin the last chance'. But circumstances would not permit this and reluctantly Beechey abandoned the idea. His immediate requirement was for provisions and he shaped a course for San Francisco Bay. He made a second visit to Kotzebue Sound in 1827, but by this time Franklin was en route home to England.

Results, rivalries and conclusions

Though the two British parties had failed to meet on the north coast of North America, their scientific results were extremely profitable. Undoubtedly the most important for the advancement of navigation and trade were the charts drawn during the voyage and completed under Beechey's direction. Of specific importance in Arctic discovery was the mapping of the coast of Russian America from Point Rodney to Point Barrow and also of Kotzebue Sound and its environs. Elson's expedition to Point Barrow added 126 miles to the chart of the polar sea, and British knowledge of Kotzebue Sound was measurably increased. Beechey's discoveries resulted in the delineation of the north and northwest coasts of Alaska. Despite these contributions, the British survey of the Pacific was far from complete. The requisites of a whaling port in the northeastern Pacific meant that the Hydrographic Department could draw on Beechey's brief surveys of the Bonin Islands.

Yet much remained to be surveyed, and in spite of Anglo-Russian rivalry in the Alaskan Arctic, in 1830 Capt (later Sir) Francis Beaufort (Figure 7), Hydrographer since 1829, exchanged data and charts with his opposite number, Admiral Krusenstern. Pleased to receive Captain Kotzebue's observations on his discoveries made during his circum-navigation of 1823, Beaufort presented Krusenstern with a copy of the *North Polar Chart* with Beechey's additions (Beaufort 1830).

As for Mr Secretary Barrow, the fundamental paradox of his position must not pass unexamined. As noted above, he promoted British discoveries to pre-empt Russian ventures. However, strange though it may seem, it was not contrary to his policies to share all information with his rivals, as Hydrographer Beaufort did with his Russian opposite number Krusenstern. To quote Barrow himself on this, with regard to the 1818 Buchan, Parry and Franklin venture to find a water communication to Bering Strait and the Pacific:

...from the zeal and abilities of the persons employed in the arduous enterprize, everything may be expected to be done within the scope of possibility. Of the enterprize itself it may be truly characterized as one of the most liberal and disinterested that was ever undertaken, and every way worthy of a great, a prosperous, and an enlightened nation; having for its primary object that of the advancement of science, for its own sake, without any selfish or interested views. On this account it has justly excited the attention, and called forth the approbation, of maritime Europe; for it is well known that whatever new discoveries may be made, will be for the general benefit of mankind; and that if a practicable passage should be found to exist from the Northern Atlantic into the Northern Pacific, the maritime nations of Europe will equally partake of the advantages, without having incurred either the expense or the risk of exploring it. (Barrow 1818: 378–79).

Yet this view calls for caution, for the '*oracle* on all matters of inquiry', as one anonymous critic called him, thought it quite false that Barrow should propose a commercial motive, that is, a practicable route for British commerce, when the scientific, especially hydrographical, objectives were sufficient in themselves to justify expeditions to 'any quarter of the Globe requiring survey', including the North Pole (Alman 1826: 44–46).

After his return from the Pacific Beechey persisted with his old idea of attaining a high Arctic latitude. He wanted to match the achievement in the Antarctic of Cdr James Clark Ross, who in 1826 had reached 79° 9′ 30″S in longitude 101° 27′W. But Barrow's main object remained the Northwest Passage, and Beechey's proposition was shelved. In late 1831 Beechey and Franklin were corresponding on further Arctic discovery. Beechey proposed to the Admiralty a relief and search expedition for Sir John Ross (the Ross expedition was finally picked up by *Isabella* of Hull in Lancaster Sound in the summer of 1833 after four winters in the Arctic). The mission would also complete the outline of the American continent. This dual object would be advantageous, Beechey advised Franklin, 'especially as the system of rigid economy pursued, at present, to the detriment of laudable discovery and even to our naval establishment, may hereafter form an insurmountable obstacle to another expedition...' But while Beechey, Franklin and Richardson remained anxious to have employment in the Arctic, for the time being the Admiralty could not approve of the proposal (Lefroy Bequest; Gell ms 301). Eventually Franklin made his third expedition, this time by sea, and with the fatal consequences that are so well known and deserve no repetition here.

As for Beechey, he never returned to the Arctic, but the rest of his life until his death in 1856 was full of naval service and scientific enquiry (Dawson 1885: 114–15). In his last annual address as president of the Royal Geographical Society in 1856, he indirectly summed up the scientific aims of his life and lifetime. He told his audience that after forty years, 'the major problem', the Northwest Passage, had at last been solved 'and Science at least has reaped her harvest' in geography, magnetism, botany, and climatology. Arctic discovery had shown what men can endure with little loss of life, Sir John Franklin and his men notwithstanding. 'They have, in short', he concluded, 'expunged the blot of obscurity which would otherwise have hung over and disfigured the history of this enlightened age' (Beechey 1856: ccviii–ix). Perhaps in saying so he was mindful of Dr John Rae's recent (1852) acerbic critique on Arctic discovery, that the way to get credit was to plan some scheme, '... and after having signally failed, return with a lot of reasons–sufficiently good to gull John Bull–for your failure' (Wallace 1980: 13).

Russian activities in North America and its northwestern coasts continued into the 1860s, decreasing in force with the years. The energizing activities of Shelikhov, Baranov, Rezanov and others led to an extensive Russian American colony and trade. Yet by 1825 the southern limits of that colony were set at 54° 40′N and the Fort Ross food-producing base in California had proved unsuccessful; it was easier to buy food from Yankee ships or the Hudson's Bay Company agricultural subsidiary, the Puget's Sound Agricultural Company. Russian America was never a sizeable colony in terms of numbers–563 males and 64 females in 1833 and a subjugated native population of upwards of 50,000 (Khlebnikov 1973: 1–13). Russian treatment of these natives was brutal and in need of reform, Capt Golovin reported in 1862. Even more so, the colony was becoming too expensive to retain, despite its imperial prestige value (Jensen 1975: 49). In 1866 a decision was made in St Petersburg to sell the colony and cede Russian sovereignty to

IX

the United States. However, the Russian retreat from North America was well advanced before the United States purchased Alaska from Imperial Russia in 1867 for $US7,200,000. Also in that year, it is relevant to note, the federation of British North American colonies was achieved under the name of the Dominion of Canada. This not only consolidated British self-governing colonies in North America but provided for the addition of others, notably British Columbia in 1871.

In retrospect it may be said that the British government, more especially the Lord Commissioners of the Admiralty, sometimes pressured into action by officers such as Franklin and Beechey on half-pay and enforced idleness, sometimes badgered into action by the Hudson's Bay Company, the Colonial Office and the Foreign Office, resumed an interest in the search for the Northwest Passage. That search, dating from Tudor times and interrupted by the Napoleonic wars, had turned into rivalry on the return of peace in 1815. The new rival for science and empire, ambitious and competent, was Russia. The struggle for dominion in far-western North America brought either side a victory—for the Russians temporary dominion in Alaska, and for Britain enhanced knowledge of the main coastal features of northern North America by 1830–all but the fateful passage itself. Such contests involved the national pride of 'being first', the same motive that drove (and still drives) polar investigators to limits of endurance. However, in the end it was the fruits of scientific research that were the most lasting.

Acknowledgements

I thank the following for assistance: David Drewry, Terence Armstrong, Robert Headland and especially Clive Holland, of the Scott Polar Research Institute, Cambridge; Lt Cdr Andrew David, RN, and M. J. Perry, Hydrographic Department, Ministry of Defence (Navy), Taunton, Somerset; the Public Record Office, Kew; the National Library of Scotland, Edinburgh; the Hudson's Bay Company Archives, Winnipeg; and the Royal Geographical Society, London.

References

ADMIRALTY. N.D. List of Admiralty ships employed on missions of discovery etc 1669–1860. R 3/34, Public Record Office, Kew.
ADMIRALTY 3. N.D. Rough and special minutes. Public Record Office, Kew.
[ALMAN]. 1826. *A letter to John Barrow... on the late extraordinary and unexpected hyperborean discoveries.* London, privately printed.
ARMSTRONG, T. E. 1979. Review. *Canadian Journal of History* 14(1): 115– 16.
BARRATT, G. 1981. *Russia in Pacific waters, 1715–1825.* Vancouver, University of British Columbia Press.
BARROW, J. 1818. *A chronological history of voyages into the Arctic regions.* London, John Murray.
BARROW, J. 1823. Memorandum, 14 November. Melville Papers, National Library, Scotland.
BARROW, J. 1846. *Voyages of discovery and research within the Arctic regions, from the year 1818 to the present time.* London, John Murray.
BARROW, J. 1847. *Autobiographical memoir of Sir John Barrow.* London, John Murray.
BEAGLEHOLE, J. C. (editor). 1967. *The journals of Captain James Cook on his voyages of discovery: III, The voyage of the Resolution and Discovery 1776– 1780.* 2 pts., Cambridge, Hakluyt Society, Extra series 36.
BEAUFORT, F. 1830. Letter to Admiral Krusenstern, 25 June 1830. HH2, 619, Hydrographic Department, Ministry of Defence (Navy), Taunton, Somerset.
BEECHEY, F. W. 1831. *Narrative of voyage to the Pacific and Beering's Strait... 1825–28.* New edition, 2 vols. London, Colburn and Bentley.
BEECHEY, F. W. 1856. Presidential address. *Proceedings of the Royal Geographical Society* 26: ccviii-ix.
CASWELL, J. E. 1969. The sponsors of Canadian Arctic exploration, III, 1800– 1839. *The Beaver* 300: 26–33.
COOKE, A. AND HOLLAND, C. 1978. *The exploration of Northern Canada: 500 to 1920; a chronology.* Toronto, Arctic History Press.
COXE, W. 1804. *Account of the Russian discoveries between Asia and America.* 4th ed. London, T. Cadell.
DAWSON, L. S. 1885. *Memoirs of hydrography.* Eastbourne, Henry W. Keay.
DAY, A. 1967. *The Admiralty Hydrographic service, 1795–1919.* London, HMSO.
FISHER, R. H. 1977. *Bering's voyages: whither and why.* Seattle, University of Washington Press.

FISHER, R. H. (editor). 1981. *The voyage of Semen Dezhnev in 1648 : Bering's precursor, with selected documents*. London, Hakluyt Society, Second series 159.
FLEMING, R. H. (editor). 1940. *Minutes of Council of the Northern Department of Rupert Land*, 1821–31. London, Hudson's Bay Record Society 3.
FRANKLIN, J. 1823. Letter to J. Barrow, 26 November 1823. No 1, Letter Book, Vol 1, MS 248/281. Scott Polar Research Institute archives.
FRANKLIN, J. 1828. *Narrative of a second expedition to the shores of the Polar Sea*, 1825–27. London, John Murray.
GALBRAITH, J. S. 1957. *The Hudson's Bay Company as an imperial factor*, 1821–1869. Berkeley and Los Angeles, University of California Press.
GELL. MSS 255, 256, 257, 301 (Bundle C), SPRI Archives.
GIBSON, J. R. 1969. *Feeding the Russian fur trade ; provisionment of the Okhotsk seaboard and the Kamchatka Peninsula*, 1639–1856. Madison, University of Wisconsin Press.
GIBSON, J. R. 1972. Russian America in 1833: the survey of Kiril Khlebnikov. *Pacific Northwest Quarterly* 63(1): 1–13.
GIBSON, J. R. 1976. *Imperial Russia in frontier America*. New York, Oxford University Press.
GOLDER, F. A. 1930. Proposals for Russian occupation of the Hawaiian Islands. *The Hawaiian Islands*. Honolulu, Archives of Hawaii.
GOLOVIN, P. N. 1979. *The end of Russian America : Captain P. N. Golovin's last report*, 1862. Translated by B. Dmytryshyn and E. A. P. Crownhart-Vaughan. Portland, Oregon Historical Society.
GOUGH, B. M. 1971. *The Royal Navy and the northwest coast of North America 1810–1914 : a study of British maritime ascendancy*. Vancouver, University of British Columbia Press.
GOUGH, B. M. (editor). 1973. *To the Pacific and Arctic with Beechey : the journal of Lieutenant George Peard of HMS Blossom 1825–1828*. Cambridge, Hakluyt Society, Second series 143.
HUDSON'S BAY COMPANY ARCHIVES. N.D. Correspondence. Manitoba Archives, Winnipeg.
JENSEN, R. J. 1975. *The Alaska purchase and Russian-American relations*. Seattle and London, University of Washington Press.
KHLEBNIKOV, K. T. 1973. *Baranov, chief manager of the Russian colonies in America*. Translated by Colin Bearne. Kingston, Ont., Limestone Press.
KIRWAN, L. P. 1959. *White road, a survey of polar exploration*. London, Hollis and Carter.
KOTSEBU, O. E. 1948. *Puteshestviya vokrug sveta*. Moscow.
KOTZEBUE, O. VON. 1821. *A voyage of discovery into the South Sea and Beering's Straits for the purpose of exploring a North-East Passage, undertaken in the years 1815–1818*. 3 vols. London, Longman, Hurst, Rees, Orme and Brown.
KOTZEBUE, O. VON. 1830. *A new voyage round the world...* 1823–26. 2 vols. London, Colburn.
LEFROY BEQUEST. N.D. MS 248/347. SPRI Archives.
LLOYD, C. 1970. *Mr Barrow of the Admiralty : a life of Sir John Barrow*, 1764–1848. London, Collins.
OKUN, S. B. 1951. *The Russian-American Company*. Trans. C. Ginsburg. Cambridge, Mass., Harvard University Press.
PARRY, W. E. 1826. *Journal of a third voyage*. London, John Murray.
PIERCE, R. A. 1965. *Russia's Hawaiian adventure*, 1815–18. Berkeley and Los Angeles, University of California Press.
RICH, E. E. (editor). 1953. *John Rae's Arctic correspondence*, 1844–55. London, Hudson's Bay Record Society 16.
ROMANOV, D. M. 1982. *Kolumby Arktiki*. [*Columbuses of the Arctic*.] Tula, Priokskoye Knizhnoye Izdatel'stvo.
STEVENSON, SURGEON LT. RN. 1822. *Voyage to St Petersburg in 1814 with remarks on the Imperial Russian Navy*. London, Sir Richard Phillips.
TEMPERLEY, H. V. 1925. *The foreign policy of Canning*, 1822–1827. London, G. Bell.
TIKHMENEV, P. A. 1978. *A history of the Russian-American Company*. Translated by R. A. Pierce and A. S. Donnelly. Seattle, University of Washington Press.
WALLACE, H. N. 1980. *The Navy, the Company, and Richard King : British exploration in the Canadian Arctic*, 1829–1860. Montreal, McGill-Queen's University Press.
WILLIAMS, G. 1962. *The British search for the Northwest Passage in the eighteenth century*. London, Longmans.

X

The Royal Navy
and the Oregon Crisis, 1844-1846

The division of Oregon as announced in a treaty signed by Great Britain
and the United States of America on July 15, 1846, brought to a conclusion the protracted contest for the sovereignty of the region, a rivalry
in which the Royal Navy played a significant part, especially in the latter
stages. The Anglo-American Convention of 1818, the terms of which
were renewed in 1827, recognized the historic claims of Britain and the
United States to Oregon but did not allow for any means whereby the
matter could be resolved by arbitration. War would be the alternative
should diplomacy fail, and in this regard naval and military preparedness
were important considerations at the height of the crisis from late 1844
to June 1846.

The diplomatic issues involved in the Oregon question are well known,
even if interpretations of the outcome vary.[1] But the Royal Navy's role in
the crisis has been strangely neglected on two counts. The one is that it
has not been explained how British naval power was largely responsible
for achieving an equitable settlement for Britain. The United States
government could ill afford to neglect British primacy at sea and diplomatic developments reflected this. The other is that the activities of
British warships on the Northwest Coast of America — which were so
beneficial in supporting national political and commercial interests at a
time of turbulence on the frontier — have not been examined or narrated
at length. The purpose of this essay is to correct these deficiencies by
demonstrating how British naval primacy influenced the course of Anglo-

---

[1] See especially, Frederick Merk, *The Oregon Question: Essays in Anglo-American
Diplomacy and Politics* (Cambridge, Mass., 1967); H. C. Allen, *Great Britain and
the United States: A History of Anglo-American Relations (1783-1952)* (New
York, 1955), 409-14; and Charles Sellers, *James K. Polk: Continentalist, 1843-
1846* (Princeton, 1966), 235-58 and 357-97.

X

American relations and showing how British warships protected national interests and claims, provided naval intelligence important in formulating Foreign Office policy, and made their influence felt, perhaps out of all proportion to their numbers, on the Northwest Coast and in the Pacific at a time when relations with both the United States and France brought the government almost to the point of war before the Oregon crisis subsided and the area was partitioned by treaty.[2]

The territory in dispute in 1844-1846 lay west of the Continental Divide between the northern boundary of California (42°N) and the southern extremity of Russian America (54°40′N). Britain and the United States each claimed this region by virtue of exploration, discovery and trade.[3] Each nation realized that a solution to the Oregon question probably would be found in an equitable division of the country. Apart from the often exaggerated vote-getting election slogan of the Democratic Party in America — "Fifty-four Forty or Fight" — that swept James K. Polk into the presidency in 1844, each nation eventually saw the advisability of compromise. Essentially, therefore, the issue was how to divide Oregon between the two claimants. In other words, should the boundary extend along the 49th parallel from the ridge of the Rocky Mountains to the sea, as the United States insisted? Or should it follow the Columbia River from where its course intersects the 49th parallel to the Pacific, as Great Britain initially contended?

If war were to be avoided, as each party wished, it was necessary to limit the area in contention to that which extended west and north of the Columbia River to the 49th parallel, including the southern tip of Vancouver Island. Within this territory were three geographical regions of importance to fur trade, settlement and maritime development. The nucleus of British commerce on the Northwest Coast was Fort Vancouver, situated about 100 miles inland near the head of navigation on the Columbia River for ocean going ships. Fort Vancouver was built on the north bank of the river in 1826, as the Foreign Office and the Hudson's Bay Company realized that the Columbia might become the international

---

2 The influence of France on Britain's position in the Oregon crisis cannot be ignored. See George V. Blue, "France and the Oregon Question," *Oregon Historical Quarterly*, XXXIV (1933), 39-59 and 144-63; also, John S. Galbraith, "France as a Factor in the Oregon Negotiations," *Pacific Northwest Quarterly*, XLIV (April 1953), 69-73.

3 The full claims are given in "Correspondence Relative to the Negotiation of the Question of the Disputed Right to the Oregon Territory," *Parliamentary Papers*, 1846, LII (Cmd. 695). On the British case, see Travers Twiss, *The Oregon Question Examined, in Respect to Facts and the Law of Nations* (London, 1846) and Adam Thom, *The Claims to the Oregon Territory Considered* (London, 1844).

boundary. Nearly opposite Fort Vancouver, the Willamette River joined the Columbia after draining the Willamette Valley. The Columbia River basin may have been rich in furs and lands for settlement, but it was not readily accessible to shipping owing to dangerous, shifting shoals at the river's mouth.

The second area of contention was Puget Sound, reaching southward from the Strait of Juan de Fuca. In addition to offering fine anchorages, this body of water offered possibilities of great maritime expansion for the nation that could control its shores. It also furnished, from the north, a more sheltered and safe approach to the Columbia Country than that via the Columbia's estuary. Ships could anchor near Fort Nisqually at the head of the sound and from there travellers and traders could reach Fort Vancouver by going through the Nisqually and Cowlitz river valleys.

The third district of importance, especially to the British, embraced the southern tip of Vancouver Island. This area had several fine harbours readily accessible to ships and arable land nearby. For these reasons, the Hudson's Bay Company, whose maritime operations on the coast and in the Pacific were hindered by the difficult navigation of the Columbia River up to Fort Vancouver, built Fort Victoria in 1843. The Island was also almost certain to be in British territory after an agreement was reached with the Americans.[4] Vancouver Island was therefore the focal point of British concern and the last line of defence against American expansion in Oregon.

Throughout Oregon, the Hudson's Bay Company held a British commercial monopoly. The Company successfully destroyed competition by American and Russian traders on the Northwest Coast in the 1820's and 1830's. However, they were unable to halt the flow of American settlers who came overland by way of the Oregon Trail after 1842; settlement spelled the end of the fur trade in the Columbia River Basin in more ways than the destruction of habitat for fur-bearing animals. Although the implications of the influx of Americans received scant attention in discussions between the British and American governments in reaching a compromise over the Oregon boundary, it must be remembered that Britain could not have controlled an area populated by Americans. In retrospect, the only feasible method of permanent defence that Britain could have employed in this region was British settlement. This view is supported by reports from British naval and military officers, submitted in 1845 and 1846, which described American settlements on the south

---

[4] W. Kaye Lamb, "The Founding of Fort Victoria," *British Columbia Historical Quarterly*, VII (April 1943), 71ff.

X

18

bank of the Columbia River and in the Willamette Valley. The British ministry knew that Company interests, at least south of the Columbia, would have to be sacrificed for the preservation of peaceful Anglo-American relations.

The Company understandably opposed a surrender of the Columbia River Basin and Puget Sound, and warned the Foreign Office accordingly. It felt that the British would lose a valuable field of commerce, and, more important, that the Americans would gain the upper reaches of the region giving them "the command of the North Pacific and in a certain degree that of the China Sea, objects of the greatest commercial & political importance to Gt. Britain."[5] The Company also fully realized that New England commercial and shipping interests sought these ports.[6] It appeared to Dr. John McLoughlin, Director of the Company's Western Department, that the United States Navy also hoped to develop a base on Puget Sound.[7] In view of this, the British government was caught between the appeals of the Hudson's Bay Company for support and the demands of the American government for "All Oregon."

While diplomatic developments ran their course, the Royal Navy protected British interests on the Northwest Coast. The first mention of plans to support the British position in Oregon was contained in instructions to the Commander-in-Chief, Pacific, written in late 1842, which ordered a warship "to the coasts of the Territory of the Columbia River, the Straits of San Juan de Fuca [sic] and Gulf of Georgia."[8] Why no ship carried out this duty remains obscure; most likely, the demands of the station were such that no vessel was available for this service. However, the plans were fulfilled late in 1843, when the Foreign Office advised the Admiralty to instruct the British Admiral in the Pacific to send a warship to the Northwest Coast, to "show the flag" at the main centres of Hudson's Bay Company trade.[9] The task fell to the 18-gun sloop *Modeste*, Commander the Honourable Thomas Baillie.

5 John H. Pelly (Gov., H.B.C.) to Lord Palmerston (F.O.), 26 February 1840, copy, C[olonial]. O[ffice Records, Public Record Office, London]. 6/14.
6 See Norman Graebner, "Maritime Factors in the Oregon Compromise," *Pacific Historical Review*, XX (November 1951), 331-46.
7 J. McLoughlin to Governor, 28 March 1845, B.223/b/33, fos. 170-72, H[udson's]. B[ay]. C[ompany]. A[rchives, London]. The writer acknowledges, with thanks, permission granted by the Governor and Committee of the Company to examine and quote from pertinent documents in the Company Archives.
8 These instructions, noted in IND[ex].4761, Public Record Office, were received by Rear-Admiral Richard Thomas on February 11, 1843.
9 Lord Aberdeen's instructions to the Admiralty, 23 October 1843, are in R. C. Clark, *History of the Willamette Valley, Oregon* (Chicago, 1927), 327-28.

H.M.S. *Modeste* arrived at the mouth of the Columbia River on July 7, 1844; her object was to indicate to the Americans that Britain would not tolerate interference with her trading interests and territorial claims in Oregon. Baillie rightly believed that his mission could best be achieved by taking the *Modeste* upstream to Fort Vancouver. Aided by a Company pilot, he navigated the treacherous waters as far as the post, where he learned that most of the two thousand settlers — of whom only 450 were British — lived south of the Columbia and that only a few lived north of the river. His report strengthened the view of the British government that only the territory south of the river should be relinquished to the United States.[10]

After a three-week stay at Fort Vancouver, Baillie sailed downstream for the river's mouth, where the *Modeste* grounded on the notorious bar and narrowly escaped disaster. After repairs were made at Baker's Bay, he pointed the *Modeste* to the north and Fort Victoria. But the harbours of Vancouver Island's southern tip were as yet uncharted, and Baillie was forced to run in to Captain Vancouver's old anchorage, Port Discovery, across the Strait of Juan de Fuca from Fort Victoria. After receiving provisions from the Company off the entrance to Victoria harbour, the *Modeste* sailed for Port Simpson, the main trading centre on the north coast, near the northern extremity of British claims. There a further examination of her hull revealed more extensive damage than had been disclosed at Baker's Bay, but successful repairs eliminated the possibility that she might have to return to England.[11]

Having completed her mission, the *Modeste* sailed for the Hawaiian Islands. Her visit to the disputed district was significant in that it marked the first of a series of visits by the Royal Navy to show the Americans, and, indeed, the Hudson's Bay Company, that Britain intended to protect her interests in Oregon, notwithstanding Lord Aberdeen's conciliatory foreign policy.

This was the first use of "gunboat diplomacy" in the Oregon crisis and it coincided with the formation of plans in London to reinforce the defences of British North America. In the event of war with the United States, the critical areas of operation would be the Atlantic seaboard, the St. Lawrence River, and Lakes Ontario and Erie. In preparing for hos-

---

10 See "HMS *Modeste* on the Pacific Coast 1843-47: Log and Letters," *Oregon Historical Quarterly*, LXI (December 1960), 408-36, and T. Baillie to Thomas, 4 Aug. 1844, Adm[iralty Records, Public Record Office], 1/5550.

11 F. V. Longstaff and W. Kaye Lamb, "The Royal Navy on the Northwest Coast, 1813-1850, Part I," *British Columbia Historical Quarterly*, IX (January 1945), 19.

tilities, the Admiralty and the War Office were reminded of the experiences of the War of 1812. During that war waterways were essential to communications, and sea power on the Lakes played a decisive role. Consequently, in 1845, the Royal Navy sent Captain F. R. "Bloody" Boxer to examine American military establishments on the Great Lakes. This officer advised the Admiralty that Britain's defence of Canada and the "exposed frontiers of Canada West" depended on maintaining "the command of the navigation of the lakes."[12] He suggested methods, which were largely implemented, of increasing British maritime strength on the Lakes and of conveying troops thereto. His reports and those of other investigators reflected the need for increased military preparations during the gravest foreign crisis to face Britain since the War of 1812.

The problem of sending troops to the remote Northwest Coast would be a major one in the event of military operations there. Soldiers would have to be transported overland from Canada or sent by sea. As a matter of fact, Baron Metcalfe, the Governor-General of Canada, thought that European and native troops from India would assist the British cause.[13] When the United States Congress passed an Oregon bill to incorporate the territory to 54°40′ in the Union, the Prime Minister, Sir Robert Peel, considered sending to Oregon secretly a frigate bearing Royal Marines and a small artillery force.[14] But this remained only an idea as the Foreign Minister, Lord Aberdeen, believed that the strength of the Royal Navy in the Pacific was sufficient to deal with any incident. Simultaneously, Sir George Simpson, the Governor of the Hudson's Bay Company Territories in North America, thought that the British position could be strengthened by stationing four warships (two sail and two steam) in the Columbia with a large body of marines and two thousand Métis and Indians on board.[15] The ambitious proposal of the "Little Emperor," as Simpson was called, did not bear fruit. However, he did convince the Governor

12 This report and those of other officers, naval and military, relating to the defences of British North America at this time, are in Adm. 7/626.

13 Baron Metcalfe to Lord Stanley, 4 July 1846, confidential, W[ar]. O[ffice Records, Public Record Office]. 1/552.

14 Sir Robert Peel to Aberdeen, 23 February 1845, Aberdeen Papers, Add. MSS 43,064, fols. 178-81, B[ritish]. M[useum, London]. Peel referred to this ship as "an additional frigate"; he must have known that the *America* 50 was then bound for Oregon.

15 Sir G. Simpson to Pelly, 29 March 1845, copy, F[oreign]. O[ffice Records, Public Record Office]. 5/440; on this proposal see E. E. Rich, *The History of the Hudson's Bay Company, 1670-1870* (2 vols.; London, 1958-59), II, 724, and C. P. Stacey, "The Hudson's Bay Company and Anglo-American Military Rivalries during the Oregon Dispute," *Canadian Historical Review*, XVIII (September 1937), 285-301.

X

and Committee of the Company, the Governor-General of Canada, the Duke of Wellington and the Foreign Office that the British should have a military post near Fort Garry, Red River, to counteract American influence in the Canadian Northwest.[16] And finally, "in deference to the earnest entreaties of the Company,"[17] the British government sent 346 troops of the 6th Regiment of Foot, the Royal Warwickshires, from Cork to Lower Fort Garry by way of York Factory in Hudson Bay. These soldiers reached their destination September 18, 1846.

As an aid to this expedition, two British officers stationed in Canada were sent to Fort Vancouver "as private travellers." They were to report to London and Montreal on the feasibility of sending troops overland to Oregon in the event of American encroachment on British rights there. They were also instructed to gather information on American settlers, and in cooperation with officers of the Royal Navy, to ascertain the possibilities of defending British interests on the Northwest Coast from an American attack. This hasty investigation was promoted by Simpson, who met with Peel and Aberdeen in London on April 3, 1845, and sailed for Montreal three days later with complete authority from the Ministry to arrange details of the military reconnaissance of Oregon. Lieutenants Henry J. Warre and Mervin Vavasour were chosen for the undertaking, and Simpson accompanied them from Montreal to Fort Garry.[18]

The first stage of the trip presented so many difficulties that these officers immediately advised the Secretary of State for War and the Colonies that a route via York Factory would be much better for any cavalry or artillery which might be dispatched to the Canadian Northwest.[19] Warre and Vavasour then began their journey on horseback across the plains and through the difficult passes of the Rockies, accompanied by their guide, Chief Factor Peter Skene Ogden, and seven Company servants. They hoped to reach the Pacific by mid-August, in advance of Lieutenant John Frémont of the United States Army, who was thought to be on a similar mission for the United States.[20]

[16] See Simpson to Lts. Warre and Vavasour, 30 May 1846, confidential, W.O. 1/552, and Alvin C. Gluek, Jr., *Minnesota and the Manifest Destiny of the Canadian Northwest* (Toronto, 1965), 60-71.

[17] C.O. Memorandum on H.B.Co. Defence, 27 November 1845, C.O. 537/96.

[18] H. U. Addington (F.O.) to J. Stephen (C.O.), 3 April 1845, confidential, W.O. 1/553. The planned meeting with officers of the Royal Navy is mentioned in Henry J. Warre, "Travel and Sport in North America, 1839-1846," typescript, R.G. 24, F71, 52, P[ublic]. A[rchives of]. C[anada, Ottawa]. Simpson to Pelly, 4 May 1845, D. 4/67, fols. 13-15, H.B.C.A.

[19] Warre and Vavasour to Sec. of State for the Colonies, No. 1, 10 June 1845, W.O. 1/552.

[20] Simpson to P.S. Ogden, 30 May 1845, confidential, copy, *ibid.*

X

22

The hazards they faced convinced Warre and Vavasour that Simpson's proposal to send British soldiers overland to Oregon was impracticable to say the least and certainly optimistic. Alternatively, they realized that Oregon could be defended best by establishing control over the strategic waterways of the area, chiefly the Columbia River and Puget Sound, in order to exclude American warships from the region. They assessed Fort Victoria as "ill-adapted either as a place of refuge for shipping or as a position of defence."[21] But not so with Fort Nisqually, which Vavasour described as having fine harbours, accessible at any season to ships of any size and therefore the most suitable place for disembarking British troops.[22]

Warre and Vavasour found Cape Disappointment to be the key position in the defence of that part of Oregon. Perhaps with some exaggeration, Simpson had emphasized that British fortification of this headland on the north bank of the Columbia would be advantageous, for enemy warships entering the river would have to "pass so close under the Cape" that shells from a battery "might be dropped almost with certainty" upon their decks.[23] On the other hand, the merits of Simpson's proposal became evident to Warre and Vavasour when they reached the river entrance. Consequently, they recommended that Chief Factor Ogden buy the land from two American settlers under the pretence that it would be used as a Hudson's Bay Company trading post.

Subsequently, Vavasour submitted plans to his commanding officer in Canada for three batteries of heavy guns at Cape Disappointment, and an additional battery of similar guns at Tongue Point on the south bank of the river.[24] With these fortifications, it was believed the British would be able to control the entrance to the hinterland from the sea. Moreover, as Warre so cogently pointed out, they could control "the whole of the country south of Puget's Sound, there being no other harbour or place of landing between the Columbia River and St. Francisco [sic], where ships of sufficient tonnage to navigate the Pacific could enter or remain at anchor in safety."[25] Nothing came of these plans, for reasons that remain obscure. Probably the British Ministry realized that the military defence

21 Warre and Vavasour to Sec. of State for the Colonies, No. 2, 26 October 1845, ibid. (Received 7 July 1846).
22 Vavasour to Col. N. W. Holloway, R.E. (Officer Commanding, Canada), 1 March 1846, copy, F.O. 5/457.
23 Simpson to Pelly, 29 March 1845, copy, F.O. 5/440. See the sketch of the river entrance in Warre Notebook, R.G. 24, F71, P.A.C.
24 Vavasour to Holloway, 1 March 1846, copy, F.O. 5/457.
25 Warre, "Travel and Sport in North America," 143, P.A.C.

of Oregon was impracticable. In any event, in a war over Oregon, the decisive theatre would not be the Northwest Coast but the Atlantic seaboard and Great Lakes region. In other words, a war over Oregon was unlikely to take place there.

Meanwhile, what Peel had referred to in September 1844, as "a good deal of preliminary bluster on the part of the Americans" continued to grow in intensity.[26] By early March 1845, the Prime Minister, although unable to persuade Aberdeen of the merits of sending a secret force from Britain to the Columbia by sea, did convince him that a British warship should appear on the Northwest Coast from time to time, and that the flagship of the Commander-in-Chief, Pacific, should also call there. Subsequently, the Foreign Office advised the Admiralty that "Rear Admiral Sir George Seymour should himself visit that Coast at an early period in the *Collingwood* with a view to giving a feeling of security to our own Settlers in the Country, and to let the Americans see clearly that H.M.'s Govt. are alive to their proceedings, and prepared, in case of necessity to oppose them."[27] With these words, the British ministry gave its first indication of being ready to use the Royal Navy to oppose the American "bluster."[28] The change of policy prompted Aberdeen to write to the British Minister in Washington: "At all events, whatever may be the course of the American Govt., the time is come when we must endeavour to be prepared for every contingency."[29]

The British ministry could be assured that Rear-Admiral Sir George Seymour, appointed Commander-in-Chief, Pacific, in May 1844, would employ warships to their best effect in support of British policy. Seymour was an outstanding officer whose forcefulness and ability made him the choice of Lord Haddington, the First Lord of the Admiralty, and Sir Robert Peel as Commander-in-Chief, Pacific. He knew a good deal about the Northwest Coast. Before he sailed for the Pacific on September 7, 1844, he had read Vancouver's *Voyages*, Robert Greenhow's *Memoir* . . . *on the N.W. Coast of North America*, and the Secretary of the Navy's report to Congress, November 1843, on American activities in the Pacific.

---

[26] Peel to Aberdeen, 28 September 1844, no. 270, Add. MSS. 44,454, B.M. He suggested that the flagship *Collingwood*, "When she has leisure," might visit the mouth of the Columbia.

[27] Addington to Corry, 5 March 1845, secret, encl. in W.A.B. Hamilton (Adm.) to Seymour, 10 March 1845, confidential, Adm. 172/4.

[28] The hardening of policy was announced in the Commons, April 4, 1845. *Hansard*, Third Series, LXXIX, 199.

[29] Aberdeen to Pakenham, 2 April 1845, private, Aberdeen Papers, Add. MSS 43,123, fol. 2476, B.M.

He had also studied the events leading to joint occupation of Oregon, examined charts of the Columbia, discussed the importance of the region with Sir John Barrow at the Admiralty, and visited Hudson's Bay House in London. He was anxious that the ships under his command should do everything within Foreign Office instructions to keep Oregon and California out of the American hands and as many South Pacific islands as possible from falling under French control.[30]

But the Commander-in-Chief, Pacific, was acting under a handicap which had plagued his predecessors and would plague his successors until the advent of the telegraph and wireless telegraphy. Several months must elapse before a reply to his most urgent message could reach him from the Admiralty. At the time of the Oregon crisis, outwardbound dispatches were conveyed from London to Jamaica and Colon by monthly steam packet, then across the Isthmus of Panama by mule or horse, and on to Callao, which was the port for Lima, and Valparaiso by Pacific Steam Navigation Company ships. This took 55 days, considerably shorter than the 120 days previously required on the route around Cape Horn but still a long time. There was no certainty that a reply would reach the Admiral immediately, however, for he might be absent from port at the time. Furthermore, sending ships from point to point in the vast Eastern Pacific was time-consuming. The passage from Valparaiso to Hawaii was at least 60 days, and from Hawaii to the Northwest Coast a further 21 days under the best conditions. In view of these limitations, the responsibility placed on the flag officer as an interpreter of British diplomacy was great indeed. He had to assess the validity of old intelligence in relation to his latest instructions and make the best possible disposition of his forces under the circumstances. Similarly, captains under his command frequently were required to exercise judgment concerning their actions and movements.

Seymour was at Lima, Peru, on July 6, when he received orders to sail for Oregon. He had to decide whether to sail first for Tahiti, where he hoped to forestall the French who were planning to establish a protectorate, or to sail directly for the North Pacific. He decided to wait at Lima for news of events in London and Washington. On July 14, he read a Liverpool paper reporting that no action on the Oregon issue could occur

---

[30] Seymour, Private Diary, CR 114A/374/21, *passim*, W[arwickshire]. R[ecord]. O[ffice, Warwick]. Statements from the Seymour of Ragley Collection in the W.R.O. are published herein by permission of the Marquess of Hertford. On Seymour's career and the Pritchard Affair at Tahiti, see *Dictionary of National Biography*, LI, 321.

for some time, no matter how arrogant President Polk might be.[31] He therefore decided to sail for Tahiti and then for Honolulu, where he could obtain further intelligence on the state of the Oregon question.

Seymour knew, in setting a course for Tahiti, that the British frigate *America* 50, Captain the Honourable John Gordon, was bound directly from England to the North Pacific because of the Oregon crisis and would soon be in the Strait of Juan de Fuca.[32] Seymour realized that the *America* could not cross the bar of the Columbia, because she drew more than fifteen feet of water. Therefore, she would have to take up her station in the less hazardous, albeit less influential, position at Port Discovery, near the entrance to Puget Sound. From there a party could go by water and land to Fort Vancouver. Seymour believed that this would suffice to show the British in Oregon that their government was "well inclined to afford them protection."[33]

When Chief Factor John McLoughlin at Fort Vancouver received news that the *America* was on her way, he complained to the Governor of the Hudson's Bay Company in London that a frigate would be absolutely no use to the Company in Oregon; instead a smaller vessel was required, which could ascend the river to Fort Vancouver.[34] McLouglin's complaint was legitimate, but he did not know that Seymour intended to send the sloop *Modeste* back to the coast of Oregon and to Fort Vancouver, if necessary, to strengthen the British position.

The *America* did not reach the Strait of Juan de Fuca until August 28, 1845, because of calms and contrary winds. Captain Gordon of the *America* was the brother of the Earl of Aberdeen, the Foreign Secretary, and one of his officers was Lieutenant William Peel, son of the Prime Minister and an able officer in his own right.[35] The presence in the ship of two persons with such prominent connections caused at least one official, Thomas Larkin, the United States Consul in Monterey, Upper

---

[31] Seymour, Private Diary, CR 114A/374/22, 14 July 1845, W.R.O.

[32] For a more detailed account of this mission, see Barry M. Gough, "H.M.S. *America* on the North Pacific Coast," *Oregon Historical Quarterly*, LXX (December 1969), 292-311.

[33] Seymour to Corry, 14 July 1845, Seymour Order Book I, CR 114A/414/1, W.R.O. A copy of Seymour's instructions to Gordon, 13 February 1845, are in *ibid.*

[34] McLoughlin to Governor, 28 March 1845, B. 223/b/33, fols. 170-72, H.B.C.A.

[35] On Peel, see Capt. J. Gordon to Seymour, 22 October 1845, Adm. 1/5564; *Dictionary of National Biography*, XLIV (London, 1895), 224; and Admiral Sir Albert H. Markham, *The Life of Sir Clements R. Markham* (London, 1917), 39-41. Markham thought Peel "the perfect model of what a British naval officer ought to be."

California, to ponder the purpose of the *America*'s visit to the Pacific Northwest.[36]

From the *America*'s anchorage in Port Discovery, Lieutenant Peel went by launch to Fort Victoria. He had two purposes. His first was to deliver a letter given to Gordon in England and addressed to the Officer-in-Charge of the Fort, explaining that the principal object of the *America*'s visit was to assure Company authorities that the British government would oppose American encroachments in the Columbia River basin. The second purpose was to request the use in Puget Sound of the Company steamer *Beaver*.[37] The *Beaver* was away on a trading cruise so the request could not be granted; consequently, Peel and his party were forced to take the frigate's launch to the head of the sound and then travel overland to Fort Vancouver.[38]

Peel had been ordered by Captain Gordon — and may even have been selected by Seymour — to report on the settlements on the banks of the Columbia and Willamette Rivers.[39] His two reports are well known and reveal the judgment that distinguished him as an officer. In the first, addressed to his captain, he gave details on the territory investigated.[40] In the second letter, to Richard Pakenham, the British Minister in Washington conducting talks with the United States government on Oregon, he expressed agreement with Gordon's belief that Vancouver Island must be retained by Britain if the 49th parallel became the demarcation line. Gordon's contention was based on the fact that the northern channel around Vancouver Island was unnavigable for sailing ships, and thus Britain would lack access to the inland passages from the Strait of Juan de Fuca to latitude 51°N.[41] Peel noted that the Island commanded the Strait of Juan de Fuca, possessed a good harbour and had been selected by the Hudson's Bay Company as the eventual hub of trading activities on the Northwest Coast. In his description of growing settlements between

36 T. Larkin to Dr. John Marsh, 19 August 1845, Marsh Collection, California State Library, Sacramento; in John A. Hawgood (ed.), *First and Last Consul* (San Marino, Calif.; Huntington Library, 1962), 33.

37 Gordon to Officer-in-Charge, Fort Victoria, 31 August 1845, Port Discovery, B. 226/b/1, fols. 35-36d, H.B.C.A.

38 Lieut. Thomas Dawes, "Journal of HMS 'America'....," JOD/42, MS 57/055, 85, N[ational]. M[aritime]. M[useum, Greenwich, England].

39 Gordon to Lt. Wm. Peel, 2 September 1845, encl. in Corry to Addington, 13 February 1846, F.O. 5/459.

40 Wm. Peel to Gordon, 27 September 1845, encl. in Hamilton to Addington, 10 February 1846, F.O. 5/459. Inscribed on the back, probably in Aberdeen's hand, is "a very good report."

41 Gordon to Admiralty, 19 October 1845, Adm. 1/5564.

X

the Willamette and Sacramento Valleys, he foretold the inevitable American control of the port of San Francisco which would give the United States a decided maritime superiority in the Pacific.[42] Peel reached the Admiralty with vital dispatches from Gordon and McLoughlin on February 10, 1846. On the same day, copies were sent to the Foreign Office. It is not known if this intelligence had any influence on the British ministry or the discussions then taking place in Washington. Undoubtedly it did add greatly to British information on the Oregon country as a critical stage in negotiations with the United States.

Before the *America* sailed from Fort Victoria for Honolulu on October 1, 1845, Captain Gordon and other officers enjoyed the hospitality of Roderick Finlayson, Officer-in-Charge of Fort Victoria.[43] According to Finlayson's account of Gordon's visit to Fort Victoria, Gordon claimed he would not exchange "one acre of the barren hills of Scotland for all he saw around him."[44] What especially disgusted Gordon was that the salmon were caught by baits or nets, and not by the fly as in his beloved Scotland. "What a country," he is reported to have exclaimed, "where the salmon will not take to the fly."[45] His negative reactions were not shared by all the naval officers on the coast, and Finlayson stated that several who visited Fort Victoria earnestly desired to be sent on a mission of conquest, claiming "that they could take the whole of the Columbia country in 24 hours."[46] Gordon's apathy in regard to British and Company interests in Oregon was also noticed by James Douglas, then Chief Factor at Fort Vancouver, who now had good reason to wonder to what degree the promised naval protection would be made available should circumstances require it.[47] Gordon evidently saw no reason to extend his visit to the Strait of Juan de Fuca or visit Nootka Sound and by October 1 the *America* had cleared Cape Flattery bound for Honolulu and the ports on the west coast of Mexico.

42 Peel to R. Pakenham, 2 January 1846, F.O. 5/459.
43 R. Finlayson to McLoughlin, 24 September 1845, Fort Victoria, B. 226/b/1, fol. 37d, H.B.C.A.
44 [Roderick Finlayson], *Biography of Roderick Finlayson* (Victoria, [1891]), 15; see also, his "History of Vancouver Island and the Northwest Coast," typescript, 34, B[ritish]. C[olumbia]. A[rchives], Victoria].
45 From Finlayson's Journal, B.C.A., quoted in John T. Walbran, *British Columbia Coast Names* (Ottawa, 1909), 210. See also, Leigh Burpee Robinson, *Esquimalt: "Place of Shoaling Waters"* (Victoria, B.C., 1947), 29-30.
46 Finlayson, "History of Vancouver Island," 35.
47 James Douglas to Simpson, 20 March 1846, private, D. 5/16, H.B.C.A.; Douglas was indeed correct in his views on Gordon, for the latter thought Oregon of little importance, especially in contrast to California. See Gordon to Sec. of Adm., 19 October 1845, Adm. 1/5564.

About a week later, the *Modeste*, Commander Baillie, then returned to the Strait of Juan de Fuca to continue protection of the Hudson's Bay Company.[48] The obvious reason for her reappearance lay in the fact that she was more manoeuverable and had a more shallow draft than the *America*. She therefore could enter the Columbia to support the British position, if required. Rear-Admiral Seymour knew that the Hudson's Bay Company would require assistance to maintain law and order, especially in view of the great tide of immigration then flowing into Oregon. He had already informed the Admiralty that he was willing to stop the Americans if circumstances required drastic action, despite his inability to send even small ships such as the *Modeste* into the Columbia without some degree of hazard.[49]

At Fort Nisqually, Commander Baillie found Hudson's Bay Company officials most anxious for him to take his ship into the Columbia. James Douglas, for one, told him of McLoughlin's warning to Gordon that unless the government took "active measures" they would lose Oregon.[50] Under these pressures, Baillie sailed for the river mouth and eventually brought the *Modeste* to anchor off Fort Vancouver on November 30, 1845, the passage having taken almost a month owing to difficult winds and currents in the river.

What were the reactions at Fort Vancouver to the reappearance of the British sloop? Warre and Vavasour considered the arrival of a British warship extremely timely as it encouraged British subjects to support their rights. Moreover, it discouraged Americans from taking the law into their own hands; and it gave protection to Hudson's Bay Company property.[51] In other words, they believed that the presence of the *Modeste* achieved the desired effect: American immigrants who had arrived recently were acting peaceably. A similar view was held by McLoughlin, who wrote that the ship's presence "has both a moral and political effect and shows that our government is ready to protect us."[52] The importance of stationing a British warship at Fort Vancouver is best revealed by the fact that

48 Baillie's instructions from Seymour, 12 August 1845, are in Adm. 1/5561.

49 Seymour to Corry, 14 July 1845, Y 158, Adm. 1/5550.

50 Douglas to Baillie, 8 October 1845, copy, B. 223/b/33, fols. 107-107d, H.B.C.A.

51 Report No. II of Lieuts. Warre and Vavasour to Sec. of State for the Colonies, 8 December 1845, in Joseph Schaefer (ed.), "Documents relative to Warre and Vavasour's Military Reconnoissance [*sic*] in Oregon, 1845-46," *Oregon Historical Quarterly*, X (1909), 64.

52 McLoughlin to Governor, 20 November 1845, in E. E. Rich (ed.), *The Letters of John McLoughlin from Fort Vancouver to the Governor and Committee, Third Series, 1844-46* (London, 1944; Hudson's Bay Record Society, vol. VII), 48.

the *Modeste* remained until May 1847. She was indeed indispensable to British authority in the Lower Columbia.

The Oregon crisis was on Seymour's mind continually while he attended to affairs in Tahiti. On August 19, 1845, he instructed Captain John Duntze of the frigate *Fisgard* 42 to prepare to sail with the steamer *Cormorant* 6 to Puget Sound during the spring of 1846 if the United States and Great Britain did not soon come to an agreement. With this possibility in mind Seymour also considered a plan "to push our Steamers" into the Columbia. There they would be beyond any gun batteries that the Americans might have built on Cape Disappointment.[53] The *Cormorant* and *Salamander*, both paddlewheel sloops, were the only steamers then available to Seymour. There seems to have been not more than two steamers on the station until about 1857 when some screw-frigates and corvettes became available.

His fears were somewhat allayed when the *Collingwood* reached Hawaii in September 1845. He believed that news of the British flagship's presence at Honolulu would eventually reach Oregon and convince Americans there that Britain attached great importance to her interests on the Northwest Coast.[54] At Honolulu, he met his American counterpart, Commodore John F. Sloat. Naturally, each was suspicious of the other, but each also expressed hope that the two nations could reach a peaceful agreement on the definition of the Oregon boundary. Seymour was especially concerned for the fate of Upper California after his conversation with Sloat.[55] At this time, Sloat told him that if the Oregon question were not settled it would be entirely the fault of the American government.[56]

When Seymour returned to Valparaiso on February 15, 1846, he learned that Sloat's squadron was being reinforced from the East Indies station by the ship-of-the-line *Columbus* and the frigate *Constitution*. This information substantiated his fears that the United States Navy was soon to act against either the British in Oregon, or the Mexicans in Upper California — or perhaps both. Therefore, he immediately sailed north to Callao with the brig *Spy* 6 to await news and dispatches from London and New York. There he learned of President Polk's "arrogant declaration" of December 2, 1845 to the United States Congress.[57] Polk had reasserted the Monroe Doctrine, called for an end to the joint occupation

---

[53] Seymour to Gordon, 12 August 1845, private, Tahiti, CR 114A/418/1, W.R.O.
[54] Seymour to Corry, 3 October 1845, Honolulu, Y7, Adm. 1/5561.
[55] *Ibid.*
[56] Seymour, Private Diary, CR 114A/374/22, Appendix, W.R.O.
[57] Seymour, Private Diary, CR 114A/374/23, 26 February 1846, W.R.O.

of Oregon and proposed that Federal jurisdiction be extended to that territory. Such expansionist views hardly could fail to provoke a war, Seymour believed.[58] "To provide for war taking place," he sent the *Cormorant* north, along with a supply of coal in the chartered freight ship *Rosalind*, made arrangements for the provisioning and deployment of the squadron in case of war, and issued instructions for part of the squadron expected at Valparaiso — particularly the frigate *Grampus* 50 on her way from England.[59]

Before the *Collingwood* left Callao for the North Pacific to meet the growing crisis, Seymour penned a lengthy report to the Admiralty informing their Lordships of the situation and appealing for additional naval support. In essence, he expressed concern over the inadequacy of his squadron for guarding British interests in the vast Pacific. At a time when the possibility of war with the United States and France was so great, he had only fifteen ships under his command: one ship-of-the-line, two frigates, ten sloops, one brig and one storeship.[60] The inferiority of the squadron was substantiated in his "Account of Foreign Naval Force at present employed in the Pacific" which accompanied his letter to the Admiralty. This listed the French naval vessels at sixteen (two frigates, nine sloops and five smaller ships) and the American vessels at eleven (one ship-of-the-line, two frigates, five sloops, and two schooners, with an additional frigate, the *Congress*, expected). Clearly, the British would be at a disadvantage in the Pacific if France and the United States joined forces in a war.

To counteract the growth of rival sea power in the Pacific, especially American influence in Oregon, Seymour made a bold appeal to the Admiralty to assign two more ships-of-the-line for duty in Puget Sound. He also requested an arsenal or port for his squadron, as well as a naval-stores depot somewhere between the Northwest Coast and New Zealand. Seymour realized, however, that enlarging his squadron would not overcome the limits of the role that the Royal Navy could play in supporting the British position in the Pacific Northwest. As he admitted to the Admiralty, the rapid increase of American settlers would give them control of the Lower Columbia without the aid of the United States government. Unless a British military force opposed them — and Seymour was reluctant to send naval brigades a great distance from their ships — the

[58] *Ibid.*
[59] *Ibid.*, 7 March 1846.
[60] Seymour to Sec. of Admiralty, 6 March 1846, Adm. 1/5568.

Royal Navy could do very little beyond the areas accessible to ships.[61] This was a fact the Americans knew very well.[62]

Nevertheless, he sought to strengthen his case for an increase in the number of British men-of-war in the Pacific by sending a private letter to his friend, the Earl of Ellenborough, the First Lord of the Admiralty. Seymour could not ignore the deteriorating situation in Oregon, even though some of his acquaintances at the Admiralty considered Polk's address to Congress "mere blustering." It was essential, as he explained to Ellenborough, that "a force commensurate with the superiority of our Navy over that of all other Nations should be sent to these seas. . . . "[63]

These words achieved their desired effect. The Admiralty supported Seymour's urgent demands and informed the Foreign Secretary on June 6, 1846, that it was necessary to increase the Pacific squadron to give it "a decided preponderance" over that of the United States.[64]

The decision was made with some reluctance. Their Lordships feared that strengthening the force in the Pacific would weaken the Royal Navy in home waters, for the French had sixteen or seventeen ships-of-the-line in commission.[65] Fear of French intentions arose two years earlier, in 1844, when the Prince de Joinville published his famous *Note sur l'état des forces navales de la France*, in which he contended that French steam-power could transport thirty thousand French troops across the English Channel at night. This pamphlet touched off a stormy debate in England on national defence, in which alarmists such as Palmerston had warned that steam had "bridged the channel."[66] Thereafter the Admiralty kept a sharp eye on the strength of the French at sea.

These developments prompted the Lords of the Admiralty to explain to the Foreign Office that the Royal Navy was placed in an awkward position by the possibility of a French invasion of England and a war with the United States over Oregon. Henry Corry, the Secretary of the Admiralty, explained the gravity of the situation in these words:

My Lords consider that it would be inconsistent with the character this country has hitherto borne as a Predominant Naval Power, and with that

[61] *Ibid.*
[62] See, for example, Report of William Wilkins (Secretary of War), 30 November 1844, *Senate Documents*, 28th Cong., 2nd Sess., vol. I, 113 ff.
[63] Seymour to Lord Ellenborough, 7 March 1846, Ellenborough Papers, PRO 30/12/4/20, P.R.O.
[64] Corry to Smythe, Under-Secretary of State for Foreign Affairs, 6 June 1846, F.O. 5/461.
[65] *Ibid.*
[66] For a critical evaluation of the crisis, see C. J. Bartlett, *Great Britain and Sea Power, 1815-1853* (Oxford, 1963), 148-74.

X

32

degree of prudent precaution which under the most flattering circumstances of amity with France we ought still to observe, were we to exhibit our Naval Force at home as inferior to that of France, and this too at a period when there are unsettled differences with America, which may unfortunately terminate in war.[67]

But if an increase in force for the Pacific were authorized by the Foreign Office, more ships would have to be commissioned for protection at home, a difficult matter owing to the shortage of seamen.[68]

The reply of the Foreign Secretary, Lord Aberdeen, to the recommendations of the Admiralty indicated that war with the United States seemed then to be unlikely. He disagreed with Seymour's proposal for strengthening the Pacific squadron on the "supposed probability of war with the United States or with France, or with both countries."[69] Although Aberdeen could see the wisdom in a small increase in the forces for the Mexican Coast to protect British merchants and trade — especially as war between the United States and Mexico appeared imminent — in his opinion the Oregon question provided no threat to British interests. In fact, owing to diplomatic developments, Seymour's fears were now believed to be unfounded.[70]

Aberdeen's confident answer regarding the state of Anglo-American relations can be explained by the fact that Britain gained the upper hand in her diplomatic dealings with the United States by June of 1846. In these negotiations she was able to use her supremacy at sea as a threat. The British ministry, like Seymour, was outraged by Polk's statement, mentioned earlier, to the United States Congress on December 2, 1845. Certainly Peel decided that the time had come for action when on January 6, 1846, he informed a friend, "We shall not reciprocate blustering with Polk but shall quietly make an increase in Naval and Military and Ordnance Estimates."[71]

From January to June, Ellenborough at the Admiralty repeatedly urged the Prime Minister to further increase the estimates to prevent the Royal Navy in the Pacific and elsewhere from becoming inferior to the American force.[72] Concessions were made to Ellenborough in this regard

67 Corry to Smythe, 6 June 1846, F.O. 5/461.
68 Ibid.
69 Addington to Corry, 19 June 1846, confidential, Adm. 1/5568.
70 Ibid.
71 Peel to Lord Egerton, 6 January 1846, Peel Papers, B.M.; quoted in Wilbur D. Jones and J. Chal Vinson, "British Preparedness and the Oregon Settlement," Pacific Historical Review, XX (November 1953), 360.
72 Ellenborough to Peel, 5 March 1846, Peel Papers, Add. MSS 40,473, fols. 78-78b, B.M.

but finally Peel was forced to state categorically that he could not sanction further demands on the Treasury in time of peace. He concluded his sharp rejoinder to the First Lord by declaring that Britain was far in advance of her American rival in actual preparedness for war.[73] Peel assured his colleague that the United States knew this, and would see the advantage of signing a treaty ending the dispute over the Oregon boundary. Nevertheless, Ellenborough, the most belligerent member of the cabinet, remained unconvinced. Eventually, in July of 1846, he resigned in objection to the unwillingness of his "timorous colleagues" to be ready for war.[74]

The strength of the Royal Navy may well have been inadequate in Ellenborough's view. It is now clear, however, that Britain's superior strength at sea was the decisive factor in precipitating an agreement between the two powers over Oregon. On January 6, 1846, Louis McLane, the American *chargé d'affaires* in London, met with Aberdeen to discuss the points of dispute. His report of this meeting to officials in Washington warned that the British planned to commission immediately some thirty ships-of-the--line in addition to steamers and other vessels held in reserve.[75] In all likelihood, this alarming news induced the Americans to adopt a less belligerent attitude.[76]

Meanwhile, at the Foreign Office, plans were underway for a carefully calculated diplomatic manoeuvre. The intent was to draw from the American delegate to the negotiations in Washington a proposal that the boundary west of the Rocky Mountains should be the 49th parallel to the middle of the Strait of Georgia, and then the middle of channel leading to the Pacific, thereby leaving Britain in full possession of Vancouver Island. Under the threat of British sea power, the Americans accepted these terms, which formed the basis of the Oregon Treaty signed on June

---

73 Peel to Ellenborough, 17 March 1846, secret, Peel Papers, Add MSS 40,473, fols. 120-23, B.M. The naval estimates of 1846 were 12 per cent higher than those of the previous year because of developments in steam engineering, fear of war with France, and, according to Peel, "relations with the United States." Julius W. Pratt, "James K. Polk and John Bull," *Canadian Historical Review*, XXIV (1943), 346.

74 Ellenborough to Seymour, 28 June 1846, Ellenborough Papers, PRO 30/12/4/20, P.R.O. On Ellenborough at the Admiralty, see Albert H. Imlah, *Lord Ellenborough: A Biography* (Cambridge, Mass., 1939), 236-38, and Bartlett, *Great Britain and Sea Power*, 182.

75 See Hunter Miller (ed.), *Treaties and Other International Acts of America*, V (Washington, 1936), 58, and Merk, *Oregon Question*, 341-42.

76 On this point, see the convincing article by Jones and Chal Vinson, "British Preparedness and the Oregon Settlement," 361-64. Merk (*Oregon Question*, 362-63), in discounting the importance of sea-power in this crisis, makes no reference to the above-mentioned work.

15, 1846. The final partitioning of the continent between Britain and the United States therefore was achieved by an adroit combination of British diplomacy and naval primacy.

Throughout the period when the ministry was reaching an accord with the United States government, Rear-Admiral Seymour possessed sufficient strength on the Northwest Coast to protect British interests in the region. After the *Congress* 54, flagship of Commodore Robert F. Stockton, arrived in the Pacific, Seymour concluded that the Americans were about to take action against the British in Oregon.[77] Consequently, he had carried out his plan, discussed above, of sending the *Fisgard* and the steamer *Cormorant* to join the *Modeste* in those waters. He was confident that they would reach the Strait of Juan de Fuca before the *Congress*, thus forestalling an American occupation of Oregon.[78]

The difficulty of sending ships into the river mouth handicapped the Navy in supporting the Hudson's Bay Company at Fort Vancouver. Ships that drew more than fifteen feet could rarely pass over the bar, and most ships at Seymour's disposal had a draught in excess of this. Because of this, the *Fisgard*, on April 30, 1846, was forced to take up a station at Fort Nisqually at the very head of Puget Sound, after reaching the Strait of Juan de Fuca and receiving supplies at Fort Victoria. Her captain, John Duntze, had instructions that emphasized that he was to send the *Cormorant* and even, if circumstances warranted, the *Fisgard* into the Columbia in order to "afford British subjects due security."[79] However, the matter continued to disturb Seymour, who noted in his diary on July 19 that his sleep would improve if, somehow, he could put the *Fisgard* into the Columbia River without danger.[80]

By this time, other ships had been sent north to check American influence in Oregon and Upper California.[81] The *Grampus* 50 was to join the *Talbot* 26 at Honolulu; the *Collingwood*, *Juno* 26, *Frolic* 16 and *Spy* 6 were in Californian and Mexican waters.

Seymour also expected the *America* to be in the Northeastern Pacific. To his surprise and disgust he learned that she had sailed for England "without orders, with money."[82] In this, Captain Gordon had acceded to

[77] Seymour to Corry, 7 April 1846, San Blas, Y 63, Adm. 1/5561.
[78] *Ibid.*
[79] Seymour to J. Duntze, 14 January 1846, copy, Adm. 1/5561.
[80] Seymour, Private Diary, 19 July 1846, CR 114A/374/22, W.R.O.
[81] On Seymour's policy for California, see Ephraim D. Adams, "English Interest in the Annexation of California," *American Historical Review*, XIV (1909), 756-61. Seymour to Corry, 7 April 1846, San Blas, Adm. 1/5561.
[82] Seymour, Private Diary, 14 August 1846, CR 114A/374/23, W.R.O.

the pressure of British merchants on the Mexican coast. They feared a Mexican-American war and thought their funds would be endangered if sent in H.M.S. *Daphne* 18 to England. Gordon evidently thought this was the best means of protecting British interests. The *America* reached the English port of Spithead on August 19, 1846. According to Seymour, Captain Gordon had made an "ill-judged decision which might have turned the fate of war with the United States against us by taking off the station the only strong ship except the *Collingwood* when he was aware I considered war most probable."[83]

When the *America* reached Portsmouth, a court martial was assembled, "and after due deliberation to the pros and cons," as a junior officer recalled somewhat sarcastically, "our worthy old Chief was doomed to be reprimanded, as indeed if a war with the United States had been brought on, he would have deserved to have been shot. Fortunately for him Polk and Aberdeen made it up somehow."[84] The charge of "leaving his station contrary to orders of his Admiral" was "fully proved" and Gordon was "severely reprimanded."[85] At the court martial, pecuniary gain from the freight monies he received for conveying funds to England was ruled out as a motive. Gordon retained command of the *America* for a brief time and then returned to take advantage of a newly-instituted retirement scheme.

As for Seymour, his anxieties ended on August 23, when he learned that Britain and the United States had resolved the Oregon question. With obvious relief that there would be no further need to send warships over the bar of the Columbia, he wrote to the senior naval officer on the Northwest Coast to inform him of the Treaty. His frustration with the whole crisis was revealed when he added, " . . . the terms are what I understand our Government were ready to give two years ago without all the bluster which has since occurred."[86]

The Treaty effectually signified the end of the Hudson's Bay Company's territorial — but not commercial — domination in Old Oregon. Important provisions in the agreement allowed them to retain full navigation rights south of the 49th parallel and to enjoy access to the harbours

---

[83] *Ibid.*, appendix, 129. Seymour expressed his displeasure on this subject to Capt. H. Byam Martin, C.B., of the *Grampus*, and the latter knew that "with so great a probability of an American war" Gordon would be "called to account." *Grampus* Journal, Byam Martin Papers, Add. MSS 41,472, B.M.

[84] Dawes, "Journal of HMS 'America' . . . ," 107, N.M.M.

[85] Court Martial Books, Adm. 13/103 and 104 for 26 August 1846.

[86] Seymour to Senior Naval Officer of H.M. Ships in Oregon, 3 October 1846, Honolulu, CR 114A/481/2, W.R.O.

X

of Puget Sound.[87] Although it could be argued that the Treaty did not
limit the Company's enterprise, the interests of the Hudson's Bay Company in Oregon declined understandably after 1846.[88] The new depot at
Fort Victoria soon began to flourish as it took the place of Fort Vancouver, which was outliving its usefulness as the hub of Company trade on
the Pacific. Indeed, Fort Victoria constituted a more suitable port than
Fort Vancouver for an organization whose interests west of the Rockies
were becoming increasingly involved in coastal shipping, trade with the
Hawaiian Islands and commerce with London by way of the sea lane
round Cape Horn.

The Royal Navy continued to safeguard the property rights of the
Company in Oregon for three years after the signing of the Treaty.
Because the terms were variously interpreted in Oregon, the *Modeste*
remained at Fort Vancouver until May 3, 1847; she left only after Captain Baillie received information that cleared up all confusion.[89]

Thereafter, Seymour pursued a policy based on the conviction that the
security of Company interests in what had become American territory
could not depend on the continued presence of a ship of the Royal Navy
in the Columbia River. He recommended to his successor that a ship
should "show the flag" in Puget Sound in the summer of 1848 as an
alternative to a Hudson's Bay Company request for a small force to
replace the *Modeste*.[90] In recognition of the continuing presence of the
British at Fort Vancouver, Seymour also advised that the Royal Navy
make occasional visits to the settlements on the Columbia.[91] British warships were on the Northwest Coast in 1847, 1848, and 1849, but none
ventured into the Columbia; the gradual extension of American authority
in Oregon Territory coincided with the withdrawal of the Hudson's Bay
Company. At no time during this transfer of influence were British interests endangered.

[87] These became points of dispute later. John S. Galbraith, *The Hudson's Bay Company as an Imperial Factor, 1821-1869* (Berkeley and Los Angeles, 1957), 253-55,
260-61, and 271.
[88] Frank E. Ross, "The Retreat of the Hudson's Bay Company in the Pacific Northwest," *Canadian Historical Review*, XVIII (September 1937), 262-80.
[89] Company agents at Honolulu had advised Seymour of the great necessity "to leave
one of HM Ships at the River until everything was finally settled." Reported in
Pelly and Allan to Gov., H.B.C., 1 October 1846, A. 11/62, fols. 139, 139d,
H.B.C.A.
[90] Seymour to Ward, 27 September 1847, Y 174, Adm. 1/5578.
[91] This advice was forwarded to the next Commander-in-Chief, Pacific. W. A. B.
Hamilton to Rear-Admiral T. Phipps Hornby, 10 December 1847, instructions,
PHT/3/5, N.M.M.

X

The Oregon Crisis, 1844-1846

The Royal Navy played a dual role throughout the Oregon crisis. In the first place, ships on the Northwest Coast acted in various capacities — upholding the Hudson's Bay Company, maintaining law and order and acting as deterrents to any possible American filibuster. According to the Directors of the Company, the *Modeste*'s presence, for example, helped prevent a "collision between the inhabitants of British origin, that would have led to most serious difficulties with the parent states."[92] Six ships were stationed on the coast during 1845-1846 and others were ready to act in support of British interests if needed. Hudson's Bay Company officials were accordingly grateful for such overwhelming protection. As Chief Factor James Douglas remarked, the British government had indeed shown "an extraordinary degree of solicitude and taken most active measures for the protection of British rights in this Country."[93]

In the second aspect of its dual role, the very fact of the Royal Navy's predominance in the world — if not always in the Pacific as Seymour and Ellenborough knew — proved instrumental in keeping the peace.[94] There is little reason to doubt that the Oregon compromise, as two notable scholars of American sea power have shown, "saved the United States from a repetition of disasters" characteristic of the War of 1812.[95] The overall fact of British supremacy at sea, the operations of British warships at points of stress such as Oregon, and artful British diplomacy in European and American affairs enabled Great Britain to accomplish its objectives — to protect colonial territories of her worldwide empire and to provide security for the homeland and for growing seaborne trade. As a result of this strength Polk's "bluster" proved to be exactly that.

[92] Directors of H.B.C. at Ft. Vancouver to Capt. Baillie, 1 May 1847, extract, in Seymour to Ward, 27 September 1847, Y174, Adm. 1/5578.
[93] Douglas to Governor and Committee, Hudson's Bay Company, 28 July 1846, extract, encl. in Pelly to Earl Grey, 11 December 1846, C.O. 305/1 (original in B. 223/b/34, fol. 34, H.B.C.A.).
[94] Statistics on the relative strength of British, American and French warships, both sail and steam, are given in Merk, *Oregon Question*, 348.
[95] Harold and Margaret Sprout, *The Rise of American Naval Power, 1776-1918* (Princeton, 1939), 132.

XI

FORESTS AND SEA POWER:
A VANCOUVER ISLAND ECONOMY, 1778–1875

In the age of fighting sail, long before the introduction of the iron ship and the iron mast in the mid- and late nineteenth century, the rulers of Britain's Royal Navy constantly worried about having adequate naval timbers in quantity. The woodlands of England were insufficient to supply oak for the nation's "wooden walls," and nowhere at home were grown trees suitable as masts. Almost from the beginning of English ascendancy in naval power and more especially in the seventeenth century, the lords of the Admiralty were obliged to look overseas to secure naval stores, particularly timber, pitch, and hemp.

The search for naval timber was central to English commercial policy. Some supplies were obtained in the eastern Baltic, where Riga was the principal port of embarkation of timbers bound for British ports. In addition, under British colonial policy, agents secured abundant supplies of timber in eastern North America. Before the American Revolution, the Crown reserved timbers in both northern and southern colonies. After 1783 the Crown shifted its "broad arrow" policy (whereby suitable trees were marked and reserved for the king's use) northward to New Brunswick, Quebec, and Upper Canada, which became valued as "Great Britain's woodyard" at a time when British maritime ascendancy was challenged by French and American naval power.[1]

After 1815 and during the period of general peace known as the *Pax Britannica*, British men-of-war were seen on the distant seas of the world in the role of policemen. British ships on "foreign stations" primarily carried out British commercial and consular activities; and from time to time, when circumstances warranted, they exercised "gunboat diplomacy" against foreign powers or native leaders. British admirals and captains of vessels stationed in distant locales such as the South China Sea, the Indian Ocean, or the North Pacific were anxious about whether they would have adequate supplies of masts and spars at their disposal.

In the Pacific, where the distance from port to port could be measured in thousands of miles and the passage consume literally months on end, a ship's rigging and equipment suffered extensive wear and tear. Cape Horn was the first test for any vessel entering the Pacific from the South Atlantic, and the logs of British men-of-war in the Pacific are full of accounts of severe tests at

---

1. On Riga woods, see Robert G. Albion, *Forests and Sea Power: The Timber Problem of the Royal Navy, 1652–1862* (Cambridge, Massachusetts: Harvard University Press, 1926), p. 141. Also A. R. M. Lower, *Great Britain's Woodyard: British America and the Timber Trade, 1763–1867* (Montreal, Quebec: McGill-Queen's University Press, 1973).

Reprinted from the Journal of Forest History 32 (3), (July 1988): 117–24, published by the Forest History Society, Durham, NC; www.foresthistory.org.

2   Forests and Sea Power: A Vancouver Island Economy, 1778–1875

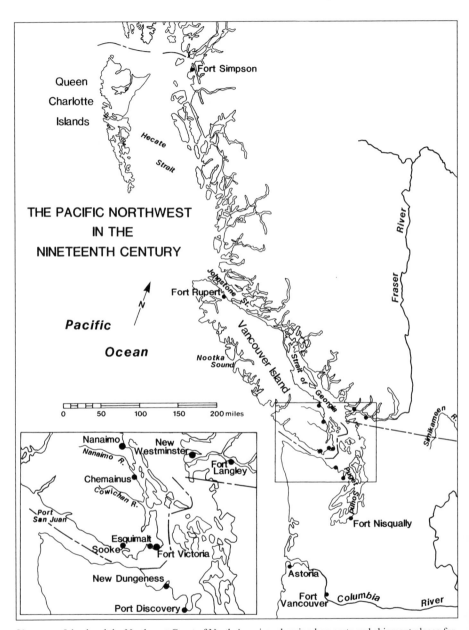

Vancouver Island and the Northwest Coast of North America, showing key ports and shipment places for spars and ship timbers. Map supplied by author.

Cartography by P. Carnochan, W.L.U. 1987.

sea, including rigging being washed overboard, makeshift repairs being made, and heroic seamanship saving ships and crew from disaster and death. The Northwest Coast of North America is one of the world's great timber areas, producing among the strongest timbers for construction purposes. The first exports of timber from the Northwest Coast included spars destined for use on British ships of war and planks, or "deals" for use in naval construction. But this never grew into a great trade. The export of spars and other ships' timbers from north-western forests remained economically marginal in the mid-nineteenth century, due principally to problems of distance from and demand by markets, the seizure or absence of shipping, the vagaries of international relations and customs regulations, and the ready availability of timbers for ships of war on station.

In the late eighteenth century, when British warships approached the Northwest Coast on expeditions of discovery and exploration, their captains found the timber of the Northwest Coast particularly useful. At Nootka Sound, Vancouver Island, in 1778, Captain James Cook replaced various masts and spars of the *Resolution* and *Discovery*. Subsequently, British naval captains George Vancouver and William Broughton also took advantage of the great local forests.

Sea-otter pelts were the primary export from the Northwest Coast in the late eighteenth and early nineteenth centuries, but a secondary cargo was sometimes in forest products. Merchant mariners such as John Meares, at Nootka Sound in 1788, began to carry loads of spars and deal to Chinese ports, where "spars of every nomination" were constantly in demand.[2] Meares, bound for China, stowed as many spars as he could. He left Vancouver Island with this lasting impression: "the woods of this part of America are capable of supplying with there [sic] valuable materials, all the navies of Europe." The number of maritime fur-trading vessels carrying timbers as part of their outward-bound cargoes is not known; however, in 1816 the ship *Mentor* left with spars for China, and in 1819 the *Arab* left with spars for Chile.[3]

Neither European nor Chinese demand for timber and wood products was at that time sufficiently strong to sustain a local export economy. Moreover the decline of the sea otter, due to overhunting, depressed the entire export

---

2. Barry M. Gough, *Distant Dominion: Britain and the Northwest Coast of North America, 1579–1809* (Vancouver: University of British Columbia Press, 1980) pp. 32–33; and John Meares, *Voyages Made in the Years 1788 and 1789, from China to the North West Coast of America* (London: Logographic Press, 1790), pp. 32, 224.

3. W. Kaye Lamb, "Early Lumbering on Vancouver Island," *British Columbia Historical Quarterly* 2 (January 1938): 31. This pioneering article provides a summary of Brotchie's activities (pp. 33–38) and a larger explanation of the lumber industry than is herein intended.

market, and between 1815 and the mid-1840s few if any cargoes of timber left the Northwest Coast. Beginning in the 1840s, however, the rapid rise of commercial activity within the Pacific rim, particularly in Oregon, California, and Hawaii, once again made Northwest Coast timbers a marketable commodity. Timber exports were also boosted by the rapid rise of shipping and international rivalry in the Pacific – particularly among Britain, France, and the United States, all of which had interests at various places within the Pacific rim, more particularly Oregon, California, Hawaii, and Tahiti. Such rivalries and interests brought ships of the Royal Navy to the Pacific in increasing numbers, and in due course the British based their naval activities on Esquimalt, Vancouver Island. That island had been established as a British colony under Hudson's Bay Company auspices in 1849.

Ships of the Royal Navy in the Pacific were far from home supplies of all sorts. Their captains were obliged to forage for new spars where they could. In 1778, for example, James Cook proceeded into Nootka Sound in need of wood and water. Officers such as Captain the Hon. John Gordon of the frigate HMS *America*, on the Northwest Coast in 1845, carried explicit instructions from the commander in chief, Rear-Admiral Sir George Frances Seymour, to examine and report on local resources in timber as well as coal suitable for supplying the Navy.[4] Gordon was also directed to learn the nature and dimensions of the available timber. He was to load spars seventy-two feet long and twenty-seven inches in diameter for the mainyard of the flagship HMS *Collingwood* and for the service of the squadron. Gordon worked from earlier suggestions, perhaps based on an 1844 report by Commander Thomas Baillie of HMS *Modeste*, as to where the best timber might be found near the Columbia River, Port Discovery, New Dungeness, Fort Victoria, and Fort Simpson.[5] When the *America* lay in Port Discovery the following summer, 1845, her ship's carpenter went ashore to cut a main mast for the *Collingwood*, at that time disabled at Valparaiso, Chile. When *America* quit the Strait of Juan de Fuca on October 1, bound for the Hawaiian Islands and

---

4. Rear-Admiral Sir G. F. Seymour to Captain the Hon. John Gordon, 13 February 1845, Seymour Letter Book 1, CR 114A/414/1; also memo to Gordon, 13 February 1845, Seymour Journal 1, CR 114A/412, Warwickshire Record Office, England (hereafter WRO).

5. Gordon to secretary of the Admiralty, 19 October 1845, Adm. 1/5564; see also Barry M. Gough, "H.M.S. *America* on the North Pacific Coast," *Oregon Historical Quarterly* 70 (December 1969): 293–311. Port Discovery is now Discovery Bay, Jefferson County. It bears the name of George Vancouver's ship. New Dungeness is now Dungeness, Clallam County. It was named by Vancouver in 1792. Barry M. Gough, *The Royal Navy and the Northwest Coast of North America, 1810–1914: A Study of British Maritime Ascendancy* (Vancouver: University of British Columbia Press, 1971), p. 66; also F. V. Longstaff and W. Kaye Lamb, "The Royal Navy on the Northwest Coast, 1813–1850; Part 1," *British Columbia Historical Quarterly* 9 (January 1945): 19.

elsewhere in the protection of British interests, she was heavily laden with spars for the *Collingwood* and other ships of the squadron.[6] Rear-Admiral Seymour acquired a particular preference for Northwest Coast spars brought him in the *America*. Though California pines made good spars, Seymour had them set aside in favor of the "very superior spars from Puget Sound" when preparing "for the great masts, etc. in the *Collingwood*."[7] Northwest Coast timbers were of very fine quality, he wrote enthusiastically to the surveyor of timber for the Royal Navy. Moreover, such spars could be obtained without expense other than their "cutting and conveyance."[8] So confident was he of their quality that Seymour had the hired English ship *Palinurus* convey a cargo of Vancouver Island spars and other timbers, including the local oak (*Quercus garryana*), to Portsmouth for testing. Vancouver Island Douglas-fir, called pine by Englishmen,[9] proved superior to standard stock obtained from Riga. "It hence appears," the Admiralty's report cautiously opined, "that in so far as strength is concerned the Pine from Vancouver's Island is a superior Wood." To this was hastily added the caution that "its durability must be decided by experience."[10]

From time to time thereafter, the quality and quantity of Northwest Coast timbers were glowingly described by ships' captains. One such, Captain G. W. C. Courtenay of HMS *Constance*, reported that in Esquimalt Harbour spars of any size could be had for the cutting.[11] Officers remained under orders to cut spars for the squadron. The navy's demands for spars persisted through the 1870s, and in some cases led to the obtaining of timber reserves for the exclusive use of the Admiralty, including 155 acres at False Creek and English Bay, now part of Vancouver, British Columbia.[12]

---

6. Lieutenant Thomas Dawes, journal of HMS *America*, JOD/42, ms. 57/005, National Maritime Museum, Greenwich, England (hereafter NMM).

7. Seymour, private diary, 19 July 1846, and appendix p. 138, CR 114A/373/23, WRO. Lieutenant Sherard Osborn, "Notes Made on a Passage to the Ports of San Blas and Mazathlan, on the Coast of America," *Nautical Magazine* 18 (March 1849): 145.

8. Seymour to Smart, 17 July 1846, Order Book 2, CR 114A/414/2, WRO.

9. Douglas-fir or Douglas-spruce (formerly *Pseudotsuga taxifolia* and now *Pseudotsuga meniesii* var. *menziesii*) is neither a true fir nor spruce. It is actually closest to hemlock: *Pseudotsuga* means "false hemlock." It, like hemlock, is in the pine family, *Pinaceal*. It stands on its own as Douglas-fir and is one of the world's great woods. It was discovered by the Scottish botanist David Douglas in 1829 and takes its common name from him. In the mid-nineteenth century it could most commonly be found in coastal locations boasting more than sixty inches of rainfall.

10. Report of officers of Portsmouth Yard, 27 December 1847, in James Meet to Rear-Admiral Sir G. F. Seymour, 10 January 1848, Admiralty Correspondence 1, Provincial Archives of British Columbia, Victoria, British Columbia (hereafter PABC).

11. Courtenay to Rear-Admiral T. Phipps Hornby, 15 November 1848, PHI/3/5, NMM.

12. See, for instance, Phipps Hornby's instructions to Captain John Shepherd of HMS *Inconstant*, 24 February 1849, PHI/1/24, NMM.

A ship could get its masts and spars on the spot, so to speak, but the Admiralty sought ways and means of bringing Northwest Coast woods home to yards and storehouses. The customary way of doing this was by contract, a practice substantially unaltered from the seventeenth century.[13] On 23 April 1844, the lords commissioners of the Admiralty made a contract with a Captain E. Swinton of 15 Arundel Street, London, to supply the navy with spars. Their lordships agreed to pay one hundred pounds for a spar measuring twenty-three inches in diameter, seventy-four feet in length, and thirteen inches in diameter at its top. They would pay forty-five pounds for a spar measuring twenty inches in diameter, sixty-two feet in length, and eleven and one-half inches in diameter at its top. They would pay other amounts for a variety of sizes in between. This contract was renegotiated on 10 June 1847 when the Hudson's Bay Company learned of Swinton's intentions. In response to inquiries addressed to the Colonial Office, the company received from the Admiralty information that the navy was prepared to receive from Swinton a cargo of Northwest Coast spars, not exceeding eighty in number, suitable for topmasts. The spars were to be delivered in England by 31 December 1849, a condition later extended to 31 December 1851.[14]

Swinton's contract was taken up by John Lidgett, an enterprising London merchant and shipping agent. Lidgett entered into an agreement with one Burlinson Sedman, owner of the 480-ton ship *Albion*, to lease this vessel for the purpose of obtaining a full cargo of spars on the Northwest Coast. The *Albion* measured 124 feet overall. Her crew was under obligation to render such assistance as the loggers required to procure timbers on shore and tow them off to the vessel. The *Albion's* master was Richard O. Hinderwell. Her supercargo, to whom all business matters were entrusted, was the energetic, enterprising, and unfortunate Captain William Brotchie, who had been a Hudson's Bay Company skipper on the Northwest Coast from 1831 to 1844.[15]

Brotchie and Hinderwell bore the strictest instructions, which indicate that this was a meticulously planned project. They were to adhere precisely to the requirements of the Admiralty contract. They were to protect, store,

---

13. Bernard Pool, *Navy Board Contracts 1660–1832: Contract Administration under the Navy Board* (London, England: Longmans, 1966).

14. R. J. Dundas, storekeeper general, to E. Swinton, 23 April 1844, in Brotchie to governor and committee, 21 March 1851, Fort Victoria, B.226/b/5b, fol. 2. Dundas to Barclay, 7 July 1847, A.8/14, fol. 234, Hudson's Bay Company Archives, Winnipeg, Manitoba (hereafter HBCA).

15. On Brotchie, John T. Walbran, *British Columbia Coast Names, 1592–1906* (Ottawa, Ontario: Government Printing Bureau, 1909), p. 64. Also "Tribute of Respect," *Victoria, British Columbia, British Colonist,* 5 March 1859.

and measure timber correctly. They were to keep the sizes and quantities secret, thereby protecting the concern from possible interlopers. They were enjoined to ensure that the wood was free of knots and sap. They were to cut timber larger than specified, and this for two reasons: wood would shrink, and dockyards customarily trimmed down their stock. They were to stow spars by size, preferring those twenty-four inches in diameter and upward. Timber procurement was an exact science, and Brotchie and Hinderwell were reminded that they served to lose or gain by the scheme.

The instructions specified that the *Albion* would sail from the Thames for Sydney, New South Wales, with freight and then proceed to the Northwest Coast. The *Albion's* owners possessed a license from the British government to obtain spars on territory other than Vancouver Island and had permission from the Hudson's Bay Company to cut spars on the colony of Vancouver Island, provided a duty of 10 percent was paid on each cargo.[16]

It was intended that Brotchie would first investigate Vancouver Island opposite Cape Flattery in the vicinity of Port San Juan. He could exchange goods with Indians for their labor but was not to undertake any fur trading, at least not on British territory. Brotchie also had authorization to purchase forests in Oregon Territory or to buy up to one hundred acres of land at the set rate of one pound per acre on Vancouver Island if in his opinion this was necessary. Lidgett's objective was to get the best possible spars, and he hoped to get as many as 120. The United States had sovereignty on the southern shore of the strait, where the best spars were known to exist, but Brotchie could obtain timber there at his discretion. If for some remote reason the scheme failed ("Your voyage will require all vigilance and energy to effect the purpose," Lidgett reminded Master Hinderwell), Brotchie was to proceed to the Chincha Islands for guano or to sail elsewhere for a cargo.

After the *Albion* left the Thames River on 23 March 1849 Lidgett dispatched the ship *Fifeshire* from Newport with a cargo of coal for sale at Panama. The *Fifeshire* was then to sail for Vancouver Island, bringing items for sale and supplies for Brotchie. She would bring away a further cargo of spars. Lidgett planned that others would follow in her wake. His long-range plan called for a series of vessels. Indeed, he evidently had an interest in the *Palinurus*, which had already taken a cargo of Vancouver Island spars to Portsmouth for testing.

16. Instructions to Captain Brotchie, 22 March 1849, and instructions to Captain Hinderwell, 23 March 1849, in Western Americana Collection no. 3, Beinecke Library, Yale University, New Haven, Connecticut (hereafter WAC). Also, charter-party agreement, 23 March 1849, register of *Albion*, and surveyor's statement, 31 March 1831, WAC.

The *Albion* entered the Strait of Juan de Fuca on 21 December 1849 with a skeleton crew, having lost most of her seamen to the Australian gold fields. She came to anchor in Port Discovery on Christmas Eve, and she remained until New Year's Day, 1850. While in port, Brotchie examined forests on both sides of the strait in a well-manned, well-armed longboat. He concluded that New Dungeness was the best site to begin operations. Though on American territory, it was at least free from Hudson's Bay Company surcharges and interference. Great trees, as correctly advertised by Captain Gordon, stood there in abundance. Port Discovery was, in fact, very close to the center of Douglas-fir distribution and was an excellent harbour.

For all these reasons, Brotchie had the *Albion* move to New Dungeness on January 5. He authorized the purchase of forest, put up two dwellings, cleared land, and took up a land claim under the laws of the Oregon Territory. He hired Indians and began putting up a stock of select spars. For three months he and his crews cut and limbed trees, hauled them to the water's edge, and loaded them into the *Albion*. He collected forty-two spars of varying lengths between sixty and ninety-six feet and measuring eighteen to twenty-six inches square at the butt.[17]

Brotchie's activities did not go unnoticed. Across the strait at Fort Victoria, Hudson's Bay Company officers viewed Brotchie with amused suspicion. Eden Colvile, the governor of Rupert's Land, who was then visiting Fort Victoria, thought that in the circumstances Brotchie would have difficulty loading his ship. Colvile dismissed the whole business as rather "an unprofitable speculation."[18]

Brotchie's activity also aroused the attention of the United States customs officials, who were beginning to flex their muscles in the newly acquired Washington Territory. They warned Brotchie to move himself off American soil. However, as Hudson's Bay Company Chief Factor Peter Skene Ogden somewhat smugly reported to company headquarters, Brotchie felt that he had a right to cut spars for the British government in American forests.[19] Governor Richard Blanshard of Vancouver Island held no such opinion and refused aid to Brotchie on the grounds that his business activities lay outside of the colony's and governor's jurisdiction. Whatever the legalities of the case or Brotchie's possible foolishness, U.S. revenue officers came north from Astoria at the mouth of the Columbia River and

---

17. A. Barclay to J. Douglas, 23 March 1849, WAC.
18. E. E. Rich, ed., *London Correspondence Inward from Eden Colvile, 1849–52* (London, England: Hudson's Bay Record Society, 1956), pp. 13–14.
19. P. S. Ogden to Sir George Simpson, 14 June 1850, private, B.223/b/39, fol.42, HBCA.

XI

seized, libeled, condemned, and sold the *Albion*. Some years later a commission held the United States responsible for damages of twenty thousand dollars, which the U.S. government paid to the *Albion's* owner, John Lidgett.[20]

Thus Brotchie's first attempt at cutting spars for British markets ended in disaster. He was the victim, zealous and loyalist British Columbian historians have charged, of "petty persecution" for "this trifling trespass."[21] Captain Hinderwell was dreadfully disheartened: "I am afraid all this business will be broken up," he wrote to Lidgett in London on 23 May 1850.[22] But Brotchie persevered. He determined to go first to Port San Juan, Vancouver Island, and to persuade Chief Factor James Douglas at Fort Victoria, who was also governor of Vancouver Island, in succession to Richard Blanshard, to purchase the *Fifeshire's* cargo upon her arrival.[23]

After deciding against Port San Juan for reasons unknown, Brotchie sailed instead in HMS *Daedalus* to Fort Rupert, near the northern end of Vancouver Island, where the Hudson's Bay Company was developing a coal mine. There he examined the country to determine if it could provide good masts and spars for the navy. The officer in charge of Fort Rupert, George Blenkinsop, received orders from Douglas to offer Brotchie every assistance but to give him no advances on account.[24] Brotchie found the forests near Fort Rupert completely to his liking. Yet he was unable to meet the Admiralty contract, Lidgett apparently having given up the scheme.

In March 1851 Brotchie offered to enter into a partnership with the Hudson's Bay Company. He had a handsome stock on hand: forty spars that lay ready at Fort Rupert's Beaver Harbour met the conditions of the contract, and there were thirty-two others of differing dimensions.[25] The company voiced interest in his offer, but they were cautious. They empowered Douglas to purchase spars from Brotchie. Brotchie offered the whole lot of spars,

20. Hinderwell to the Hon. William Strong, judge, Oregon District Court, 2 November 1850, inventory of cargo, undated, WAC no. 3, and particularly *Senate Exec. Doc.* 30, 31st Cong., 2d sess., 15 February 1851.

21. F. W. Howay, W. N. Sage, and H. F. Angus, *British Columbia and the United States: The North Pacific Slope from Fur Trade to Aviation* (Toronto, Ontario: Ryerson Press, 1942), pp. 135 and 134 respectively; Lamb, "Early Lumbering on Vancouver Island," pp. 33–35; *Report of Decisions of the Commission for Settlement of Claims under the Convention of February 8, 1853* (Washington D.C.: A. O. P. Nicholson, 1856), pp. 376ff; Hubert Howe Bancroft, *History of Oregon*, 2 vols. (San Francisco, California: Bancroft Book Company, 1888), 2:106ff.

22. Hinderwell to Lidgett, 23 May 1850, in *Sen. Exec. Doc.* 30.

23. Brotchie to Lidgett, 25 May 1850, in *Sen. Exec. Doc.* 30.

24. Douglas to Blenkinsop, 30 September 1850, B.226/b/3, fols. 15–15d, HBCA.

25. Brotchie to governor and committee, 21 March 1851, B.226/b/5b, fols 1–1d; also statement of spars, 22 March 1851, ibid., fols. 2–3, HBCA.

Captain Augustus L. Kuper of HMS *Thetis* was one of several British naval officers who advertized the value of Vancouver Island spars at Fort Rupert, Vancouver Island. In 1852 he supported the energetic but unfortunate activities of the spar merchant William Brotchie.

Provincial Archives of British Columbia photograph no. B-778.

ranging from 60 to 116 feet in length, at the extraordinarily low price of six pounds per piece, delivered alongside the ship. He proposed that he would receive one-third of the profits from the scheme. Douglas, still trying to adapt to being a timber merchant, did not know the price of the spars. He noted that any ship sent to Vancouver Island to receive these spars should have bow and stern ports, but in the immediate absence of such transport he was unable to purchase the spars.[26]

Despite these initial setbacks, Brotchie experienced considerable success in cutting and preparing spars and other nonsawn timbers for shipping. The forests were abundant, as numerous visitors remarked, and Indians eager to work as laborers were equally plentiful. Brotchie also apparently enjoyed the cooperation of the officers of the Hudson's Bay Company.[27] His license with the company, obtained in London, now proved very useful to him. From time to time Brotchie would write to mariners and officers of naval ships visiting Beaver Harbour and advise them of the spars awaiting shipment. In July 1852, for instance, Brotchie offered spars to Captain Augustus L. Kuper of HMS *Thetis*. Kuper, with the *Thetis's* master, personally investigated the spars and reported very favorably on them to his superiors. Kuper said Brotchie deserved great credit for the patient and persevering manner in which he had

---

26. Douglas to Brotchie, 16 February 1852, B.226/b/4, fols. 46–46d., and Douglas to governor and committee, 18 March 1852, A.11/120, fol. 66d., HBCA.

27. Regrettably, the Fort Rupert post journals are not extant for the years after 1850. They would have provided useful insights on Brotchie and the spar trade. I have therefore been obliged to rely on other documents for this section.

taught the local Indians, the Kwakiutl, to square and trim very large spars. Kuper much regretted, he wrote to his commander in chief, Rear-Admiral Fairfax Moresby, that Brotchie had exhausted all his finances and had not been able to ship the spars to England to meet the Admiralty contract. In Moresby's opinion, the introduction of spars from Vancouver Island for the purposes of the British navy would be most desirable.[28] Indeed, HMS *Thetis* took away some immense spars from Vancouver Island, though not from Fort Rupert.[29]

Toward the end of 1852 Brotchie, under the arrangement with the Hudson's Bay Company, was able to ship his first cargo of spars in the company vessel *Norman Morison*. The company paid five or six pounds each for spars measuring seventy to ninety feet delivered alongside the receiving ship. George Blenkinsop, officer in charge of the fort, was under strict instructions from James Douglas to collect the 10 percent export duty.[30]

Though the prospects of the spar trade were marvelous, Douglas tried in vain to persuade the company into major adventures in spar export. Coal mining had failed at Fort Rupert, and Douglas was anxious to provide a new economic base of activity. The answer lay in spars, he said. "The place," he wrote to company governor Sir George Simpson, "produces the finest spars perhaps in the world, and might be made to pay handsomely, if the Company would enter into the spar trade, about which I have addressed them repeatedly without success." What was needed, Douglas suggested, was a ship of six hundred tons cut with special ports, two at the bow and one at the stern, through which the great trees could be passed.[31]

Perhaps encouraged by the *Norman Morison* shipment, Brotchie plodded on. When Commander James C. Prevost of HMS *Virago* visited Beaver Harbour in May 1853 he found that Brotchie had nearly one hundred spars varying from sixty to one hundred feet in length ready at high-water mark. Indians, who supplied the only labor, were preparing another fifty spars in the woods. Prevost measured one tree and found it 116 feet to the first branch, without a knot. Felled and trimmed it could provide a magnificent spar

28. Captain Augustus L. Kuper to Rear-Admiral Fairfax Moresby, 20 July 1852, San Francisco, in "Four Letters Relating to the Cruise of the 'Thetis,' 1852–53," W. Kaye Lamb, ed., *British Columbia Historical Quarterly* 6 (July 1942): 197.

29. They were sold in San Francisco "for the benefit of the ship's fund . . . and a goodly sum they brought, for the city was mainly one of wood in those days, and timber precious"–John Moresby, *Two Admirals* (London: John Murray, 1909), p. 137.

30. James Douglas to A. Barclay, 7 December 1852, B.226/b/6, fol. 151, and Douglas to G. Blenkinsop, 16 December 1852, B.226/b/7, fol. 56, HBCA.

31. Douglas to Simpson, 17 March 1853, B.226/b/6, fols. 195–96, HBCA.

tapering from thirty inches square at the foot to twenty inches square at the head. Prevost noted that a Liverpool company was to send a ship in February 1854 "to offer [the spars] to the Government." And Brotchie was making active preparations to cut spars at nearby Cormorant Island where he found timber equal to that near Fort Rupert. In Prevost's view all that awaited was shipping.[32]

Meanwhile in England the storekeeper general of the navy waited patiently for the contracted Vancouver Island spars, advising Rear-Admiral Moresby of this on 6 March 1852. On 24 October 1854, under pressure to meet the needs of naval yards during the Crimean War, he asked Moresby's successor as commander in chief to the Pacific, Rear-Admiral David Price, to report on the extent of spars for top masts and on the best means (with attendant costs) of shipping them to England. The storekeeper general appended a list of spars that Brotchie had been unable to convey to England, including 107 spars still lying at Fort Rupert.[33] On 24 October 1855 a similar request went forth to Price's successor, Rear-Admiral Henry William Bruce, who instructed Commander A. J. Curtis of HMS *Brisk* to investigate the matter in full detail.[34]

Commander Curtis undertook a systematic survey. He consulted Governor James Douglas and Chief Factor Roderick Finlayson. Not least, he obtained the opinion of John Muir of Sooke. Some years earlier Muir had abandoned coal mining for the more successful prospects of sawn timber exports. From Sooke he had loaded fourteen vessels with spars for San Francisco, Valparaiso, and China markets. Muir recommended Sooke as the best harbour for shipping spars, and he offered to supply good quality spars and planks "at reasonable rates afloat in Sooke Harbour."[35] Finlayson, by contrast, pressed for Fort Rupert, where Brotchie's spars lay near tidewater and in the woods. Finlayson misrepresented the facts when he told Curtis that the spars had not been shipped because of "want of capital."[36] Curtis's report stressed the accessibility and safety of Sooke over Beaver Harbour. Muir could meet a four-month contract. As for Brotchie, ever optimistic, he promised three cargoes a year, at ten pounds per spar, and he claimed that spars at the north end of the island were superior to those of the south.

32. Commander James C. Prevost to Moresby, 7 June 1853, Esquimalt, Admiralty Correspondence, Adm. 1/5630, Y73, Public Record Office, Kerr, Richmond, Surrey, England (hereafter PRO).

33. Dundas to Moresby, 6 March 1852, Admiralty Correspondence, vol. 1, PABC.

34. Dundas to Rear-Admiral David Price, 24 October 1854, Adm. Corr., vol. 1, PABC. See Bruce Journal, 14 July, 6 and 9 August, and 5 September 1855, Adm. 50/308, PRO.

35. John Muir to Commander A. J. Curtis, 30 July 1855, Adm. Corr., vol. 1, PABC.

36. Roderick Finlayson to Curtis, 31 July 1855, Adm. Corr., vol. 1, PABC.

All of these matters were detailed to the storekeeper general by Rear-Admiral Bruce on 5 September 1855. Bruce was of the opinion that he could enter into an advantageous contract for a regular supply of spars, if the navy wished to proceed. He noted that the spar trade would be "of great benefit to the young colony, where capital is so much needed for the development of its resources." But in an about-face, though an explainable one owing to the end of the Crimean War and reduced demands for construction materials, the Admiralty advised Bruce on 28 February 1857 that no spars were needed from Vancouver Island.[37] This crushed Brotchie's hopes for shipping spars from Fort Rupert, or from anywhere else for that matter.

Why did the navy never undertake to establish its own timber reserves on Vancouver Island? And why did the navy not undertake its own system of harvesting the forests on a systematic basis? To answer these questions, one must understand that independent supply operations were not a usual practice in the Royal Navy at this time. The navy acquired most of its supplies and stores by the time-honored contract system, which seemed to meet the needs of the day. But the Vancouver Island forests never entered the navy storekeeper's records as a regular source for Admiralty contracts. In time of peace Baltic sources were preferred; and even in time of war, 1854–56, Vancouver Island timbers did not account for much of the navy's consumption.

The failure of the export market was largely a result of market forces. In the first place, Vancouver Island timbers were not the only competitive timbers available to the navy. Australia and New Zealand possessed seemingly "inexhaustible supplies," according to the colonial land and emigration commissioners in a report to the Colonial Office in 1859. Because of this it was "scarcely conceivable," the commissioners said, that the Admiralty should make a timber reserve on Vancouver Island. Small quantities could be obtained by ships on station as required. Timber licenses in New Brunswick as well as in Upper and Lower Canada had proved "vexations" and "unnecessary," the commissioners observed, and should certainly not be used at Vancouver Island or British Columbia.[38]

Still the lords commissioners of the Admiralty remained interested in Vancouver Island spars as late as the 1870s. There was a constant demand for good spars in British naval yards. Eastern Canadian and New Zealand supplies were dwindling. Spars cut near Chemainus, Vancouver Island, were

---

37. Bruce to Osborne, 5 September 1855, Adm. 1/5656, Y111, PRO, and Admiralty to Bruce, 28 February 1857, Admiralty Correspondence, vol. 1, PABC.

38. Colonial Land and Emigration Commissioners to H. Merivale, 18 April 1859, enclosure in Colonial Office to Admiralty, 10 May 1859, Adm. 1/5721, PRO.

cheaper than those available at Valparaiso.[39] In consequence, the superintendent of contracts in Britain continued to offer to purchase such spars as might arrive from Vancouver Island at competitive prices. In 1875, for instance, the Admiralty promised to purchase eighty Douglas-firs of large size.[40] And about the same time the Admiralty instructed the commander in chief of the Pacific to get the naval storekeeper at Esquimalt to report on spar stocks and the ability to meet a contract.[41]

In his reply the storekeeper pointed out the nagging problems relating to shipping. Ships could not be chartered at Esquimalt or mainland ports to convey spars. Moreover, such ships as were needed for such a contract – of eight hundred to one thousand tons – were specifically chartered before arrival at Esquimalt. If such ships were available, the storekeeper could meet the terms of the contract, he said, though he noted that spars between 98 and 102 feet long with appropriate diameters were not plentiful and, when found, were difficult to fell without breaking. He regarded Vancouver Island spars as "tough" in comparison to the "brittle" spars of the mainland.[42]

But market conditions forced the Admiralty to decide to purchase selected spars on European spar markets. Of late, they noted in 1874, these markets "have afforded a wider choice than heretofore."[43] Besides, the cost of freight for spars, the cost of insurance, and the difficulties of selection (which would have required the cost of a timber surveyor), priced Vancouver Island spars out of the market.

By and large the Royal Navy's use and purchase of Vancouver Island timbers for spars and masts was never more than a casual trade. Ship captains foraged for timbers where and when they could. Despite Brotchie's energy

---

39. The prices were twenty-five pounds for a Chemainus spar versus four hundred pounds for a similar one at Valparaiso. How long Chemainus (formerly Horseshoe) Bay was used by the navy for spars is not known. In 1873 HMS *Reindeer* took a cargo of 214 "remarkably fine spars" from there. See Rear-Admiral J. Hillyar to secretary of the Admiralty, 11 August 1873, Adm. 1/6263, Y91, and Hillyar to secretary of the Admiralty, 26 August 1873, Adm. 1/6263, Y124, PRO. Also Captain W. R. K. Kennedy, *Sporting Adventures in the Pacific Whilst in Command of the "Reindeer"* (London, England: S. Low, Marston, Searle and Rivington, 1876), pp. 194–95. On spars from Australia to New Zealand, see Albion, *Forests and Sea Power,* pp. 364, 400, and M. M. Roche, "Forest Conservation for Royal Navy Timber Supplies in New Zealand, 1840–41," *The Mariner's Minor,* 73 (August 1987): 261–64.

40. Department of the Superintendent of Contracts to Admiralty, 20 Nov. 1873, draft, Adm. 1/6263, Y124, PRO.

41. Admiralty to Rear-Admiral A. A. L. P. Cochrane, 19 November 1873, Esquimalt Naval Establishment Records (hereafter ENER), vol. 2, Maritime Museum of British Columbia, Victoria (hereafter MMBC).

42. James H. Innes to senior naval officer, Esquimalt, 19 August 1874, enclosure in Commander Richard Hare to Cochrane, 24 August 1874, ENER, vol. 2, MMBC.

43. Robert Hall (Admiralty) to Cochrane, 31 December 1874, ENER, vol. 2, MMBC.

and the ready availability of spars, he probably sold very few to ships of the navy on station. Until government regulations reserved all timber to Crown control, little prevented a shore party from cutting "a proper stick," to use James Cook's term. Thus the Royal Navy met its needs on the spot.

Despite the quality and quantity of wood suitable for masts, spars, decking, and other purposes, Vancouver Island was simply too distant from the markets, which themselves offered variable demand. The export market was also constrained by the scarcity of suitable transport ships and a lack of cooperation by government and private officials. Brotchie got embroiled in United States customs regulations, and he never enjoyed the full cooperation of the Hudson's Bay Company, which ignored James Douglas's urgings to embrace the timber trade and thereby failed to realize one of the greater economic promises of the Northwest Coast. As for Brotchie, his later years were spent in more profitable occupations – selling and shipping ice to San Francisco from northern inlets and serving as harbour master of Victoria.[44]

---

44. He seems to have quit Fort Rupert in 1855. He died in 1859 after considerable illness. See Walbran, *British Columbia Coast Names*, pp. 64–65.

XII

Possessing Meares Island

How did Meares Island, British Columbia, come to be possessed by the historical record? And what were the circumstances that led it to be transferred, in historical memory, from Native occupancy and fur-trading realm to Indian Reserves and Timber License 44? How did the land claim bring all of these issues together, and leave as legacy a different perception of Meares Island, as a place saved from forest exploitation by the alliance of Native voices and environmental groups? These themes are explored in this essay, which concludes that it is crisis that gives uniqueness to the history of otherwise unknown locales.

Comment est-ce que Meares Island, en Colombie britannique, a réussi à être dévorée par le registre historique? Quelles furent les circonstances qui l'ont amenée à être transferrée, de mémoire historique, d'occupation autochtone et du domaine du commerce de la fourrure, en Réserves indiennes et permis de coupe 44? Comment est-ce que la revendication territoriale a réuni toutes ces questions, et a légué une perception différente de Meares Island, en tant que région sauvée de l'exploitation forestière par l'alliance des voix autochtones et des groupes environnementaux? Cet article explore ces thèmes, et conclut que ce sont les crises qui apportent une certaine originalité à l'histoire d'endroits autrement inconnus.

I have in my study an old steamer trunk, which in an earlier age sheltered goods in transit from London to Vancouver, and nowadays is my treasure trove of Meares Island history. I doubt if there is such a cache of materials on this subject elsewhere, for the various items included are fragments of memory and politics brought together, conveniently, and at considerable cost, under legal instructions to leave no stone unturned in my research.

In that trunk are legal files, statements of claim, legal responses, lists of documents, injunctions and notes of all sorts gathered from near and far. These materials contain some Spanish references, traces of the first Europeans to voyage to Vancouver Island's shores. Some American trading voyage papers are also to be found in the trunk. Most of the documentation, as could be expected, is British and colonial. Given the English fetish for keeping records for legal purposes, the short colonial period of Vancouver Island history suffers from no shortage of documentation. The successor governments – British Columbia (BC) and Canada – continued the tradition, and the modern practice of photocopying means that literary fragments of Meares Island history are now scattered globally.

It was not always so. Only two decades ago, Meares Island was *terra incognita* to the outside world. Like many another place on this earth, it was possessed and comprehended solely by local inhabitants. In the centuries before that, first occupants had come from the Asian periphery, crossed Beringia (or coasted the shore), and taken preliminary possession in and around the place we now call Meares Island.[1]

Nowadays, and in the relatively recent past, we have come to possess Meares Island in another way, or ways: as Native homeland, forest preserve lying dormant, Native ecological park, and even battleground in a great court fight. Plucked from virtual oblivion within the larger political affairs of British Columbia, Meares Island attained importance and notoriety far out of proportion to its geographical size. It was "put on the map," so to speak.

Where is this island of history and politics? Today, if going by the customary route, you would drive by car to the village of Tofino on Pacific saltwater shores, just north of magnificent Long Beach and what Parks Canada calls Pacific Rim National Park. You are just about on the 49th parallel and about 130 miles west of Vancouver. You are there on the rim of the world. Tofino, they say, is life on the western edge. Named for a Spanish hydrographer, Don Vincent Tofino, the place acquired military distinction as an air station during the Second World War, and now boasts a fine small landing strip. Before the age of air travel – indeed, before a road was punched through by logging companies and the BC Highways Department about 50 years ago – the place was accessible only by sea, and then only seasonally. The life of the missionary in those days was one of lonely seclusion; the Native peoples called the site home.

Meares Island lies just north and east of Tofino, and from Tofino you can on most days see it clearly, for its horizon is dominated by a large cone-shaped mountain, now shown on maps as Lone Cone (2,470 feet). The Ahousat Native people know Meares Island as "We go by the Mountain" (*Hilhoogis* is the closest rendering in English phonetics; *Hithuugis, ipa* is the transliterated spelling), and Lone Cone is *wanachs*. The meaning of Meares Island, explained to me by Peter Webster, an Ahousat elder (conversation 18 April 1989), is "People who go, or steer, by the Mountain" – that is, are guided by it.[2] It is easy to see why this is so, for the cone is an aid to navigation, distinct from the other hills or mountains of the neighbourhood, including the more easterly Mount Colnett, which is not so dramatic in shape. Given the blue-grey hues of the landscape, such variations as these in the terrain can tell all to a mariner approaching from a distance.

It is one of the ironies of history that Meares Island is named for a person known generally as a scallywag. Seldom is a place-name associated with a person of questionable veracity – honour usually triumphs in such things – but Meares Island carries the name of a person who claimed all sorts of geographical discoveries that were subsequently shown to be false. Commander John Meares, RN, was born about the time the French and British were concluding their desperate struggle for Louisbourg and Quebec. Promoted lieutenant in the navy the same year James Cook made his remarkable voyage to Nootka Sound and Alaska (1778) and put Friendly Cove, or Yuquot ("Where the winds blow"), on charts for all time, Meares took to merchant voyaging after the American Revolutionary War. We subsequently find him in Calcutta forming a company to exploit the Northwest America trade in sea otter, then the ermine of Asia.

Meares (and his backers) had read James Cook's *Voyages* and comprehended the vast profits that could be realized if sea otter skins, said to be the most beautiful of all animal skins, could be sold either through Russian access to Peking or through the difficult arrangements near Canton. It is worth remembering that the modern as well as prehistoric history of Canada's West Coast began in Asia, not

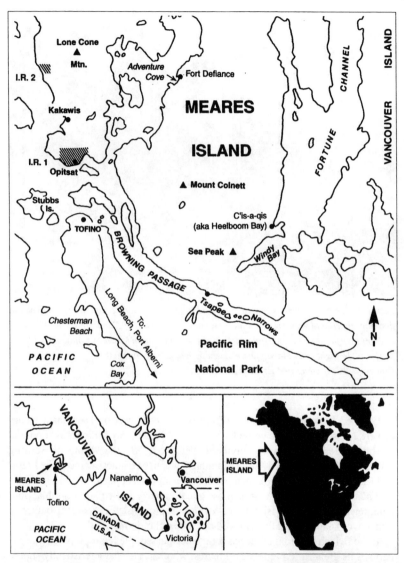

Figure 1: Indian Reserve I.R. 1 is known as Opitsat and was dedicated in 1890 as a Clayoquot Indian reserve. I.R. 2 is known as Cloolthpich and was dedicated in 1890 as a Kelsemat Indian reserve. Cartographer: Gary Brannen

Figure 2: The North West America, *built and launched at Nootka Sound (1788), was the first non-aboriginal vessel built on the west coast of what is now Canada. Northwest Coast timber made possible this coastal vessel, constructed for John Meares's syndicate. Chinese artificers, brought from Macao and elsewhere, helped in construction.*
Courtesy: BC Archives and Records Service.

in Europe.[3] Indeed, a 1794 chart of the Northwest Coast by Lieutenant Henry Robert, RN, shows the area immediately north of present-day Whistler as "Foosang of the Chinese Navigators about the Year 453." So the "Land of Shining Mountains," later renamed "Gold Mountain" when the Chinese came to the Fraser and Cariboo goldfields, took on a poetic, even stylized appelation.

The reigning queen, Victoria, chose to call the terrain British Columbia. Sub-components Vancouver Island and Meares Island, which is really tributary to Vancouver Island, naturally followed the imperial ordering.

If the British imperial order has long since passed, the hydrographic record is perhaps its greatest living legacy. Meares, who had the characteristically superb techniques of the mariner, was a fine draughtsman and surveyor. His noted *Voyages to the North-West Coast of America*, published in London in 1790, told of his travels in the ship *Nootka* in 1786 from Bengal, one of the first commercial voyages to that part of the world. Meares's book contains coastal views – elevations, more correctly – of the coastline in and about Nootka Sound. "Views of the Land in 49.3N°" show the sugar cone, lone sentinel like that at Rio de Janeiro, differentiating Meares Island from all the rest. Meares also left a fine plan of the

Figure 3: Captain John Meares, after whom Meares Island is named, noted early British trader to Nootka, Clayoquot and Canton in the sea otter business. He also carried in his ship the first known export cargo of Northwest Coast timber.
Courtesy: BC Archives and Record Service.

harbour entitled "A Sketch of Port Cox in the District of Wicananish" (facing p. 133); on it you will see Lone Cone lying horizontally this time on the page, and the various inlets of this maze of rock and water and forest.

June of 1788 found Meares exploring the coast south of Nootka Sound, and on the 12th he "saw an high mountain over the entrance of Wicananish." The weather changed, becoming squally and violent, and they even had to close-reef their topsails; they stood off from the shore in the evening gale. At daybreak on the 13th, "the remarkable hill above Wicananish appeared very plain in the form of a sugar loaf.... As we stood in for the shore, several canoes came off to us from a cluster of islands ... in most of which there were upwards of 20 men, of a pleasing appearance and brawny form, chiefly clothed in otter skins of great beauty." Meares marvelled at the great speed of the canoes and the fact that the Native peoples had no fear of coming aboard the trading vessel. There were two chiefs in the cluster of canoes, Hanna and Detootche, both extremely handsome, the former about 40 "and carrying in his looks all the exterior marks of pleasantry and good humour," the latter young, beautiful, graceful and posessed of fine qualities of the mind. Then, as now, the local Native peoples were hospitable, friendly: "They appeared to be perfectly at ease in our society, shook every person on board by the hand, and gave us very friendly invitations to receive the hospitality of their territory. They were extremely pressing that the ship should go in among the islands."

Meares, driven by commerce, wanted to find the great chief, the fabled Wicananish and his residence. Accordingly, he shaped a course for the islands, which appeared to be a maze of rock and water with, from several miles off-shore, no discernible channel. The two chiefs, given trinkets, paddled away while Meares pursued his course. About noon, Wicananish arrived in another small fleet of canoes and undertook to pilot the ship into his harbour. It was now an easy sail; the vessel entered and came to anchor in a roadstead Meares thought wild in appearance. Nearby was a village (shown on Meares's plan) where, upon invitation, the English mariners feasted. Meares was dumbfounded by what he saw: heaps of fish, seal skins filled with oil and a great vat for the making of whale-flesh stew or broth, "that delicious beverage." The house was magnificent, the roof propped up by trees that would make dwarf the mast of a first-rate line of battle ship – such a lovely imperial comparison.[4] They entered through a decorated door of a huge image. Inside were raised platforms and uniformly arranged human skulls festooning this royal apartment. Wicananish made every attempt to make Meares happy, and he was successful, for these two headmen made a compact that the one would collect skins and the other would return in the next trading season to take in the prize cargo, in one of the first-noted trading contracts of the Northwest Coast.

Then, as now, particular chiefs were anxious to defend their pre-eminence in the face of rivals. James Cook faced this situation at Nootka Sound; similarly, Wicananish insisted that neither Hanna nor Detootch trade directly (nor even visit) with Meares – all must come through Wicananish. Meares gave Wicananish many presents: six brass-hilted swords, a pair of pistols, and a musket and powder. In return, he procured 150 fine otter skins. And so the trading proceeded.

Soon it was time to sail – to continue trading, to reach Canton in time. Thus Meares concludes his record for that year. As James Cook and others observed, the Northwest Coast Indians were people of property. Everything, even a blade of grass, was accounted for; Cook, exasperated, complained that everything had value to the Native peoples.[5] Meares even says that he was probably duped by the trading practices of Wicananish – he does not say *cheated* only *duped* by their cunning, that is, outsmarted. As to the people of Wicananish, Meares thought them superior in industry and activity to those of Nootka Sound.

Thus this little-known place became written into the record as something different from Yuquot and Nootka Sound – a place apart, less well travelled and dominated by cunning traders. Meares had no trouble with them. Others had different experiences.

If the British came to trade, it was the Americans who first set up a permanent, or semi-permanent, base of operations. Most dramatic in the record of Meares Island history is the visit, in September 1791, by the famous Boston ship *Columbia*, celebrated for first carrying the Stars and Stripes around the world and for exploring the great river of the west that bears its name. The *Columbia* was commanded by Robert Gray, one of those hard breed of men in that toughest of trades around Cape Horn. The Bostonians sought a winter haven, and even brought bricks for the purpose of making a hearth. At a snug place they called Adventure Cove, on Lemmens Inlet, Meares Island, they moored the ships to the trees and erected a post they dubbed Fort Defiance. At Adventure Cove they completed the sloop *Adventure*, brought out in frame from Boston. Long before Meares Island became a place of legal dispute, archaeologists and students of American maritime history, including the great admiral and professor Samuel Eliot Morison, arrived at Lemmens Inlet to find the fort, recover the bricks and take soundings. Eventually Ken Gibson of Tofino located the precise spot.

In the written record, however, we have one of those explosions of data that we are not sure how to evaluate. A young officer says that the Americans put the torch to a nearby village, Opitsat, for the Native peoples had become too heavily armed, too dangerous for the visitors. Thus was consumed "the work of ages."⁶ The Native peoples rebuilt, and on subsequent visits mariners found the villagers at Opitsat in residence, as they are today, although on territory called Indian Reserve Number One. Before we leave this phase of history, it is important to note that Meares acknowledged the warlike nature of these people – warfare was indeed for them a way of life.

I entered the story of Meares Island when I received a telephone call from lawyers representing the Nuu-chah-nulth Tribal Council, a federation of some dozen band councils of which the Clayoquot, Ahousat and Kelsemat (all claimants to Meares Island) are constituent members. "We understand you know something about the colonial history of Vancouver Island," ran the line of reasoning. "You have been recommended by an anthropologist to do the legal history of Meares Island. You would leave no stone unturned in reporting on the details of the encounter between outsiders and the Native peoples. You would have about three years to complete your work. Would you be interested?" Law and constitutional rights drive history unlike no other force: besides being paid for services rendered, my disciplinary obligation is to get the facts right, which R.L. Stevenson said was the most important part of narrative anyway. Without prejudice to the claim, or the counterclaim, I was given free reign to prepare a report, with ancillary documents, concerning everything that related to 8,500 hectares of land. Anthropologists, genealogists, tree-use experts and others were part of the team; my job was to deal with the written record. In the end, as we went to court to support the case of *Moses Martin et al. v. H.M. the Queen et al.* (British Columbia Supreme Court, Vancouver Registry, Action No. C8459340, 1984), we found ourselves in opposition to the world's biggest logging company, MacMillan Bloedel, the Crown in the right of the Province of British Columbia, and the Crown in the right of the Government of Canada – a formidable opposition. Our lawyers, Jack Woodward, David Rosenberg and Paul Rosenberg, were artful and resourceful, new kids on the block, so to speak, but highly reputed in British Columbia. Tom Berger, the distinguished jurist and historian, came in to state eloquently the claim.

At stake was Tree License 44, held by MacMillan Bloedel, which gave the corporation rights of logging. To initiate the challenge, the Native band councils, assisted by the Friends of Clayoquot Sound and, backed by the Western Canada Wilderness Committee and the Sierra Club, had brought a successful court injunction – extended to this day – to halt the cutting of the trees of Meares Island. Meanwhile, archaeologist and tree experts had discovered numerous Native heritage sites. Huge trees were discovered standing that had seen human use hundreds of years ago, for stripping bark and even for cutting out a canoe. All the enthusiasm of ecoheritage was brought forward in that fight. Somehow, saving the

XII

forests got added on to the agenda of historical record and Native rights, and alliances of convenience were forged.

As the trial progressed and the evidence came forward, the Province of British Columbia made final admission that aboriginal title, so long denied, would be acknowledged. Thus the province and the Dominion both recognized the principle for which the Aboriginal peoples had so long argued. The case never concluded. Backroom talk became the order of the day, and then in 1995 the court extended the injunction, mentioned above, that in effect ended modern-day forestry in that area. A battle was, eventually, won over Meares Island. But soon the conflict was transferred to the Clayoquot Sound river valley, to the Stein Valley east of Vancouver and elsewhere. And so it continues.

Meares Island's history would be relatively unknown to outsiders had it not been for the forest crisis. You can find snippets of the island's history in the records of John Meares, Robert Gray, the Oblate missionary Brabant (who built an industrial school for Native peoples on the island), BC Hydro, and various Indian commissions looking into the welfare or, more accurately, the patrimony of the Native bands. If not for the timber-cutting crisis, all of this would have remained uncovered, gathering dust. Now the history of Meares Island is also the history of the land claim. And it has taken on gigantic, even mythical proportions.

The Native peoples of the area have come to repossess Meares Island. What do we do with these scraps of documentation? In my steamer trunk is the making of another book, and perhaps a book within the book – not only the dry record for court but the crisis over control of Meares Island.

How many other "possessions" of places thereabouts will be revealed in the course of time?[7] History is essentially about politics and politics about systems of control and management. Temagami is one variant of what I am trying to conceptualize here; the Lubicon people would be another – and examples need not involve a place. The specifics of the story in themselves count for little, for there is a grander scale to the events: who cares, who fights, who wins, who loses. For most Canadians, or others who interest themselves in such things, Meares Island is scantily known – a mirage on the horizon, with Lone Cone rising up through the clouds over the salal and the conifers damp and mossy. I suspect it will revert to a more benign place in our annals of historical matters. It may return to the land of legend, the haven of the kayakers, even, though not unimportantly, the focus of eighteenth-century coastal history.

The struggle for the forest is a struggle unlike any other. It brings forth all manner of emotions that are far more powerful than the scientific reasoning of graduates from forestry schools. A scenic diversion sets the mood here. On the way west from Port Alberni to Tofino and Meares Island, you cross the spine of Vancouver Island, and near Cameron Lake you come to a spot that used to be called Cathedral Grove. It is now called MacMillan, named for the chief forester of British Columbia, who magically put in place the tree license system and then, even more magically, left the civil service to head up the great company that bears his name. I always stop there enroute to Tofino and Meares Island, which I visit every other year or so. The giant

184

hemlock, Douglas fir and cedars still stand there some 300 feet high. It is better to go that way and to tread the path among those giants than to fly over Vancouver Island enroute to some First Nation band council meeting or vacation hideaway, for the flight will only break your heart: there is very little forest to fight for and no inhabitants to resist, only outside support from non-residents. Having been born on Vancouver Island and camped through most of its available locations, I naturally feel an enormous sadness over this ecological tragedy.

Writing history, Lord Acton said with insight, is really the art of comparison. And so it is with Meares Island. Meares Island could be "saved," so to speak, because it was an island, with a known perimeter and definable beaches. It became symbolic in a special way that a watershed cannot. Sooner or later watersheds, as in the case of Clayoquot Sound, can be subdivided – some for tree huggers, other parts for backpackers, and tenters and tree harvesters. But an island has definition; I wish we had more islands.

NOTES

1. The island was named Meares by Captain George Henry Richards of the Royal Navy in 1862. Richards, a noted hydrographic surveyor, was then in command of H.M.S. *Hecate*. In 1864 he was appointed hydrographer of the admiralty (John T. Walbran, *British Columbia Coast Names, 1592-1906* [Ottawa: Government Printing Bureau, 1909, and numerous reprints] 334, 422). On John Meares, see J. Richard Nokes, *Almost a Hero: The Voyages of John Meares, R.N., to China, Hawaii and the Northwest Coast* (Pullman: Washington State University Press, 1998).

2. For added details of Webster's record of time and memory, see his *As Far As I Know: Reminiscences of an Ahousat Elder*, illustrated by Kwayatsapalth (Campbell River: Campbell River Museum and Archives, 1983).

3. Barry Gough, *The Northwest Coast: British Navigation, Trade and Discoveries to 1812* (Vancouver: University of British Columbia Press, 1992) chaps. 4-6.

4. On the export of timber and forest products initiated with John Meares, see Barry Gough, "Forest and Sea Power: A Vancouver Island Economy, 1778-1875," *Journal of Forest History* 32.3 (July 1988): 117-24. Meares, who shipped the first cargo, marketed it in China.

5. John C. Beaglehole, ed., *The Journals of Captain James Cook ... 1776-1789*, 2 pts. (Cambridge: Hakluyt Society, 1967) 306. Cook's view were shared by James King (Beaglehole, 1407).

6. The story of Opitsat, and of Fort Defiance, may be traced in the following: F.W. Howay ed., *Voyages of the "Columbia" to the Northwest Coast 1787-1790 and 1790-1793* (1941; Portland: Oregon Historical Society, 1990) 247-48, 304, 381-82, 390-91; and Donald H. Mitchell, "The Investigation of Fort Defiance: Verifications of the Site," *BC Studies* 4 (Spring 1970): 3-20.

7. For another case in point, see Greg Dening, "Possessing Tahiti," *Archaeology Oceania* 21 (1986): 103-18.

XIII

SEA POWER AND SOUTH AMERICA:
THE "BRAZILS" OR SOUTH AMERICAN STATION OF
THE ROYAL NAVY 1808–1837

During that celebrated period of British overseas influence in the nineteenth century known as the *Pax Britannica*, the government of the United Kingdom maintained ships-of-war on several "foreign" stations. They did so with a view to securing "British interests" on and over the seas. Each station had an area or zone to patrol, a squadron of ships, and a headquarters or base of operations. Each station also had a Commander-in-Chief who wore his pennant in a flagship. To the Commander-in-Chiefs and to the Lords Commissioners of the Admiralty in London all men and vessels of the Royal Navy "on station" were responsible and answerable for fulfilling the standing regulations of the Service and for following any special instructions sent from Their Lordships. In the annals of British naval history the West African, East Indies, and Mediterranean stations are rather highly regarded, perhaps owing to the heightened appreciation of scholars in the history of anti-slavery and anti-piracy works in Africa and China waters respectively, and of naval-diplomatic pressures exercised by the British fleet in the Mediterranean. The Cape of Good Hope, the Australian and the Pacific stations are less well known. Of all British "foreign" naval stations, the South American or Brazils station ranks as the least well known.[1] Despite this neglect by historians, the South American station constituted a significant command of the Royal Navy on foreign service. A full account and analysis of naval operations by British warships on this station is not offered here, but rather an outline of the administrative structures and obligations of that particular command.

The Spanish and Portuguese empires in Latin America had been built on grand scales, but they were prone to administrative difficulties, illicit trade and contraband, and, not least, the perils of international relations. Napoleon's invasion of the Iberian Peninsula precipitated the revolutions of Spanish

---

1. Some of the East Indies and Pacific station boundaries are recorded in Gerald S. Graham, *Great Britain in the Indian Ocean, 1810–1850* (Oxford: Clarendon Press, 1967), pp. 455–59, Barry M. Gough, *The Royal Navy and the Northwest Coast of North America, 1810–1914: A Study of British Maritime Ascendancy* (Vancouver: University of British Columbia Press, 1971), pp. 243–46. I gratefully acknowledge the assistance, rendered over many years, by John Bach, who first guided me through the perils of reading Admiralty correspondence and whose pioneering research has been published as *The Australia Station: A History of The Royal Navy in the South West Pacific, 1821–1913* (Kensington, N.S.W.: New South Wales University Press, 1986). For their assistance and in reading an earlier version of this essay I also wish to thank C.R. Boxer, A.C.F. David, Ronald Newton and David Higgs.

America. "The nationalist monarchist movement in Spain," wrote the distinguished English historian of these matters, R.A. Humphreys, "was paralleled by a semi-nationalist, semi-monarchist movement in America. It began ostensibly as an assertion of freedom from French control. It ended as a war of independence against Spain." At the local level colonial conditions and aspirations led to a variety of overlapping and sometimes competing political and administrative responses that British naval officers could only be amazed at, or more likely, puzzled and even befuddled by. Commenting on why the war became a revolutionary one against Spain, Professor Humphreys explained that this was "due partly to the action of the Spanish, partly to that of the colonial authorities, partly to deeper colonial conditions and aspirations. Like the earlier revolution in North America that in Latin America was not merely a struggle for home rule; it was also a contest as to who should rule at home." The fulfilment by the Spanish Americans themselves, not least the inspired activities of their great leaders Bolívar and San Martín, remains "a legitimate source of pride to a people whose past has been too little understood and whose successes have been too little appreciated."[2] And during the period that the South America station had to concern itself so heavily with such radical political transformations the map of the Western Hemisphere was being transformed and reordered.

British commerce in South America made steady, if slow, gains during the late eighteenth and early nineteenth centuries. Such activity required official protection from interference and piracy. The presence of a British sloop-of-war lying in the roadstead near a trading port was always a salutary sight to British merchants and commission agents as well as to those of other nations: similarly, it was a cautionary message to any insurgents or pirates who might consider tampering with a British or European cargo vessel or warehouse. Moreover, during that protracted period of insurgency, revolution, civil war, and feared repression from the imperial powers who dominated the affairs of South America before the independence achievements of the 1820's, the Royal Navy's vessels "on station" provided a constant reminder of British policies. These policies were to foster the cause of peace for the purpose of profit, and to promote the health and trade of states in South America. To a certain degree, the pursuit of those objectives meant preventing the former imperial powers, Spain and Portugal, from reasserting their old dominance. Equally, the Royal Navy watched the threatened rivalry of the two other nations which had

---

2. R.A. Humphreys, ed., *British Consular Reports on the Trade and Politics of Latin America, 1824–1826* (London: The Camden Society, 1940), pp. viii–ix. For further particulars on British policy for promoting trade, see D.C.M. Platt, *Finance, Trade, and Politics in British Foreign Policy, 1815–1914* (Oxford: Clarendon Press, 1968), pp. 322–23.

extensive, indeed growing commercial and diplomatic interests in South America, France and the United States. In the words of the liberator Simon Bolívar, "Only England, mistress of the seas, can protect us against the united force of European reaction." [3] As the pioneering and distinguished British historian of South American diplomatic history, Sir Charles K. Webster, so aptly put it, "by two main agencies – her trade and her fleet," Britain was able to establish a very strong role in Latin American affairs.[4] This was a view fully appreciated by nationalists and revolutionaries seeking to establish states free from the dominance and potential interference of the Old World.

A second duty of the Royal Navy on the coasts of South America was to attempt to check the slave trade. This was an onerous duty, for the places of disembarkation were numerous and invariably out of the way, and for that reason the Navy's squadrons on the western and eastern coasts of Africa attempted to stop the trade "at its source," so to speak. From time to time a British sloop-of-war such as the *Frolic* might drive a slaver ashore on the coast of Brazil or capture a slave-carrier and bring her to a port where an Admiralty court might condemn the ship and free the captives. The British government was unable in the 1820s and 1830s to enforce the abolition of the Brazilian slave trade. Despite the signing of a strengthened anti-slave trade treaty in 1826, which made Brazilian involvement after 1830 the equivalent of piracy, the trade continued. The abolition, which was always a British demand as a price of international recognition of Brazil's independence and stature among nations, was unpopular in certain local quarters and led to the abdication of Dom Pedro in 1831. Pressure from Lord Palmerston, the Foreign Secretary, did not have much effect, and it was not until Parliament passed Lord Aberdeen's 1845 Act, whereby Britain unilaterally assumed powers to suppress the Brazilian trade, that matters changed. Under this measure, coercive naval action was employed by the Royal Navy in Brazilian waters. Final abolition depended on Brazilian governmental will and ability to enforce, and on influential Brazilian opinion. But the student of these matters, Leslie Bethell, states that this Act and the naval work of the squadron was "the main factor leading to the effective ending of the trade almost immediately."[5]

---

3. Quoted in Dexter Perkins, *The Monroe Doctrine, 1823–26* (Cambridge, Mass.: Harvard University Press, p. 32), p. 154.

4. Sir Charles K. Webster, *Britain and the Independence of Latin America* (2 vols.; London: Oxford University Press, 1938), 1:11.

5. George Francis Dow, *Slave Ships and Slaving* (Salem, Mass.: Marine Research Society, 1927), p. 250. Graham, *Great Britain in the Indian Ocean*, p. 110 ff. Leslie Bethell, *The Abolition of the Brazilian Slave Trade: Britain, Brazil and the Slave Trade Question* (Cambridge: Cambridge University Press, 1970). Also, Bethell, *Cambridge History of Latin America, Volume III: From Independence to c. 1780* (Cambridge: Cambridge University Press, 1985), p. 224.

The headquarters of the South American station was Río de Janeiro. From the mid-eighteenth century, British and European merchant vessels had made Río a frequent port of call. The imposing entrance to the great haven, dominated by the Sugar Loaf, Pão de Açúar, always afforded a welcome sight for mariners as they approached this safe port after usually a lengthy voyage. As they drew nearer, they could see two three-decker stone forts, one on either side of the entrance. Shore and island batteries lay within the entrance. A large citadel and a monastery dominated the town's skyline. This magnificent harbor, perhaps the best in South America, offered a safe refuge, a good place for refit and repair if necessary, and a beautiful locale for obtaining drinking water, provisions, especially fresh fruit, and wood. From thence, ships of war would proceed outward bound, and round the Cape of Good Hope or Cape Horn on voyages of discovery, of consular duty, or of war. And from Río they would proceed also on more specific missions, especially hydrographic surveying duties. By 1777 Río had become unofficial headquarters for British warships operating in South Atlantic or even Pacific waters.[6]

From the Brazilian perspective, having British warships call at Río benefitted local business. But in the eighteenth century not always did the Portuguese governor at Río respond to the arrival of a British warship without a good degree of fear and concern, understandably suspicious as he was of foreign intentions and possible interference. For instance, when Captain James Cook, R.N., the celebrated surveyor and explorer, called at Río in 1768 outward bound to the South Pacific, he was enjoined by the Portuguese governor against reporting any particulars of Río's coastal defenses, an injunction which he subsequently ignored but which went undetected by the local authorities. When H.M.S *Providence*, William R. Broughton commanding, called there in 1795, Portuguese officials announced their policy that they would not let a British officer land unless attended by a Portuguese officer of equal rank. Despite these anxieties and tensions, the British and the Brazilian authorities maintained a nominally cordial relationship. They did so before, during, and after the establishment of an independent Empire of Brazil under Dom Pedro I, acclaimed as Emperor in 1822. The continuing association of British diplomacy and Portuguese needs on both sides of the Atlantic was constantly sustained by the Royal Navy. Thus, when the Portuguese royal

6. Rudy Bauss, "Río de Janeiro: Strategic Base for the Global Designs of the British Royal Navy, 1777–1815," in Craig L. Symonds et al., *New Aspects of Naval History* (Annapolis, Md.: Naval Institute Press, 1981), pp. 75–89. For numerous charts, plans, elevations and other views of Río and the Coast of Brazil, 1768, see Andrew David, ed., *The Charts and Coastal Views of Captain Cook's Voyages: The Voyage of the "Endeavour" 1768–1771* (London: The Hakluyt Society, 1988), pp. 8–45.

family sailed from the Tagus to Brazil in 1807 to escape Napoleon's dominance at home, it was a small British squadron which afforded security to the Portuguese fleet. The Royal Party arrived in March 1808, and Río became the new capital of the Portuguese Empire.[7]

In 1808, the state of British interests in South America was sufficiently demanding of the Navy's attention that the Brazil station was established. Heretofore, British warships cruising South American waters would have been sent on "detached," that is, special service from England, or from the North American and West Indies Station, or even from the West African or Cape of Good Hope stations. However, by November 1807, in consequence of the impending removal of the Portuguese crown from Portugal to some secure spot in Brazil, the requirements to have an adequate British naval presence on the Brazilian coast were sufficiently strong that a new administrative unit, or station, was mandatory. In consequence, on 25 January 1808, Rear-Admiral Sir William Sidney Smith, appointed first Commander-in-Chief of the squadron to be stationed off the Brazilian coast, received instructions to give "permanent protection" to "the coasts of the Portuguese dominions."[8] The object was to afford security to the Prince Regent's government, and the whole scheme, including preparing a large enough naval force of eight ships-of-the-line, was done in consequence of the decision and direction of cabinet and particularly of George Canning, Secretary of State at the Foreign Office. That fleet, which arrived at Río on 17 May 1808, became the basis of the squadron which served permanently on the coasts of South America.

The establishment of the "Brazils station" was commensurate with British diplomatic initiatives as regards Latin America. In that same year, 1808, Lord Strangford was sent as the envoy-extraordinary to the Portuguese Court in Río de Janeiro. Río's position as key port and city for the South Atlantic, eastern South America, and even trade and communications beyond Cape Horn gave Strangford an advantageous location from which to communicate with the key cities and provinces of Spanish-held South America.[9] At Río, Strangford pursued several sensitive matters with the local government.

---

7. Between 1816 and 1822 "Portuguese" forces and "Brazilian" forces fought campaigns in various parts of Brazil for control. The origins and success of the Brazil fleet, with no official support from the United Kingdom in these wars, is the subject of an article by Brian Vale, "The Creation of the Imperial Brazilian Navy," *The Mariner's Mirror*, 57,1 (January 1971): 63–88.

8. The South American station included within its limits the coasts and waters of South America south of the equator and west of the 30th meridian of west longitude. It also included within its boundaries the entire eastern Pacific (approximately demarked by what is now the International Dateline). Admiralty Minute, 18 December 1816, Adm. 3/88, Public Record Office, Kew, England.

9. Instructions, William Wellesley-Pole to Rear-Admiral Sir William Sidney Smith, 25 January 1808, Adm 2/1365; also, Canning to Admiralty, 25 December 1807, secret, Adm. 1/4206.

XIII

These included the attempted suppression of the Portuguese-Brazilian slave trade, and the attempted checking of Portuguese aggrandizement on the southwestern frontiers of Brazil, especially in the Banda Oriental, to which a force of military occupation had been sent in 1811. Strangford did not succeed in ending the slave trade. Nor did he succeed in keeping Brazilian forces out of the region, which became eventually the Republic of Uruguay in 1828. However, he did keep Great Britain on friendly terms with the government in Río.

Cordial relations with the local government were advanced by successive British diplomats, including Lord John Ponsonby. In Río, as in Montevideo, Buenos Aires, Valparaiso and elsewhere, British policy was peace for the purpose of profit. Thus diplomats such as Strangford, Ponsonby or Woodbine Parish in Buenos Aires and the captains of British warships visiting these principal ports sought to maintain a strict neutrality. As one captain's instructions ran in 1831: "to give countenance and protection to this extensive commerce, and to support the influence of British interests in these countries is the first and indispensible duty of the squadron placed under your command." He was also reminded that the British had £10,000,000 invested in the South American states, and that the civil state of none of these states was tranquil.[10] Moreover, France, the United States and Portugal also competed strongly for commercial ascendancy in various ports of South America, more especially in the Río de la Plata. In this region the Portuguese had a settlement at Colonia. In addition, Montevideo and Buenos Aires were rivals in the hide and beef export trades and also kept ambitiously watchful eyes on the interior provinces to the north drained by the Paraná River.

In these circumstances, commanding officers of British warships had to be exceedingly careful so as not to be seen as agents of British commercial bullyness. Moreover, they certainly could not take the side of the insurgents and the revolutionaries against the local legitimate government. This was the case even though the Foreign Office might have come to the conclusion that the independence of the South American states constituted the preferable course of action if British commercial and political interests were to be sustained and enhanced. To send an armed party from a warship to secure a limited objective on shore afforded a tempting response for any frustrated commanding officer who saw British property and lives at risk. In 1831, for instance, British and French naval commanders combined forces, and landed seamen and marines to protect nationals at Río. The Admiralty denounce the practice as "inexpedient and unsafe," and stated in the clearest language

10. Rear-Admiral Baker to Captain Waldergrave, [?] April 1831, Adm. 1/35.

possible: "Remonstrance with the civil authorities on shore is the duty of the British resident."[11] "It took adroit diplomacy," wrote Rear-Admiral Sir Manley Dixon in praise of Commodore William Bowles on completion of his tour of duty in the Río de la Plata, "for the maintenance of friendly relations with the heads of the contending parties on each bank of the river; a relationship not very easy to maintain without having had a due observance to that system of neutrality, which has been so strongly recommended [by government] and so successfully adhered to." Bowles himself was well aware of the difficulties that he had had to face. Some years after leaving his duties, in 1838, he wrote to the First Lord of the Admiralty complaining that other persons of his rank in the Navy had been appointed Companions of the Order of the Bath but that he had been overlooked on what was then the Honors List. Believing it his duty to bring the Lords of the Admiralty the details of his 42 years' service, he included these particulars about his subsequent work on the South America station, 1816–1820: ". . . having been entrusted with the command of a squadron stationed in South America for the protection of British interests and commerce under circumstances of peculiar difficulty and delicacy, at a period when hostilities were actively carried on between Spain and her Colonies in that country, and when every duty, diplomatic and consular, as well as Naval, devolved upon me, not a single British subject sustained injury, or even serious molestation, within the limits of my command." He went on to point out that during that time the British government was never once involved in any dispute or unpleasant discussion with either of the contending parties. Surely these, Bowles concluded, were meritorious contributions deserving of recognition at the national level.[12]

In keeping with national policies, the Royal Navy in South American waters, apart from the unauthorized, abortive 1806–1807 expedition of Commodore Sir Home Riggs Popham, R.N., to occupy the Río de la Plata,[13] harbored no territorial designs on South America. On only the most desperate of occasions would a British naval captain send a landing party ashore – to secure a bank's assets, to dissuade the patriots from making a forced levy on

11. Rear-Admiral Baker to Secretary of the Admiralty, 14 June 1831, and Admiralty Minute of 16 August 1831, Adm. 1/36; also, Bach, *Australia Station*, pp. 16–17.

12. Rear-Admiral Sir Manley Dixon to J. W. Croker, 20 April 1814, No. 156. Adm. 1/22; also Commodore W. Bowles to Dixon, 11 April 1814, encl. in Dixon to Croker, 16 April 1814, No. 152, ibid. Bowles to C. Wood, 27 July 1838, Adm. 1/1568, Cap B 174.

13. Sir John W. Fortescue, *A History of the British Army, vol. 5 (1893–1807)* (London: Macmillan, 1910), pp. 310–18 and 369–487. I am also indebted to the unpublished, anonymous paper "An Account of the British Expedition to the River Plate in 1806 and 1807" [1978] with Addendum [1983] deposited in the Scott Polar Research Institute, Cambridge. Here I also exclude the ancient British colonial interests in Guiana, or Orinoco River region.

British merchants, or to protect a customs house against interference. In those rare instances when extreme cases of "gunboat diplomacy" were employed the Foreign Office appreciated even more fully the foolishness of intervention. Every time the British attempted armed coercion of local governments they tended to get their hands burned – as Lord Aberdeen, the Secretary of State for Foreign Affairs, learned to his regret in the Río de la Plata affair of 1845, when seeking to assist Montevideo's independence and to safeguard British trade in the face of "senseless and barbarous" interference from the Argentine leader, General Juan Manuel de Rosas.[14] Customarily, the Navy's duties were confined to doing what it could effectively do: "to check piracy, protect trade, prevent the abuse of the right of blockade and keep any acquistive European power from intervening."[15] Altogether the Service's task constituted a large one. Yet as long as Britain held command of the sea, real or imagined, during the wars of liberation of Spanish-held South America, Spain had no good chance of reasserting her former authority. Meanwhile, provided local governments were in agreement, the whole continent lay open to commercial penetration by British and other European traders.

Securing the sealanes and promoting the maritime ascendancy of the United Kingdom were root causes of British policy to reoccupy the Falkland Islands or Malvinas in 1832 and 1833. The islands had long been claimed by England, and at one time France and Spain had settlers and agents there. In 1820 the United Provinces of South America, otherwise Argentina, established a settlement on a spot long since abandoned by the other powers. This state of affairs continued until 1831 when, in order to protect American sealing vessels that had been interfered with, the United States corvette *Lexington*, Silas Duncan commanding, laid waste to the Argentine base Puerto Soledad, as the settlement was called, and evicted the Argentine residents and entrepreneurs who were engaged in cattle-raising, sealing, and supply whaling and sealing ships that came for refreshment and repair. The British subsequently intervened on the grounds that they never had lost their claims to sovereignty and that the Argentines were interlopers. To reassert British influence, the sloop-of-war *Clio*, mounting 10 guns and commanded by John James Onslow, R.N., was sent from Río "for the purposes of

14. Platt, *Finance, Trade and Politics*, pp. 322–23. Also, John F. Cady, *Foreign Interventions in the Río de la Plata, 1838–50: A Study of French, British and American Policy in Relation to the Dictator Juan Manuel Rosas* (Philadelphia: University of Pennsylvania Press, 1929). On Anglo-Argentine relations, see Henry S. Ferns, *Britain and Argentina in the Nineteenth Century* (Oxford: Clarendon Press, 1960).

15. G.S. Graham and R.A. Humphreys, eds., *The Navy and South America* (London: Navy Records Society, 1962), p. xxxiv.

exercising the rights of sovereignty there, and of acting at the said Islands as in a possession belonging to the Crown of Great Britain." Onslow carried out his responsibilities with cold directness. The captain of the Argentine armed schooner *Sarandí,* José Pinedo, was obliged to retire in the face of overwhelming British forces, including seamen and marines landed from the *Clio.* The Union Flag was run up, and for a number of years thereafter before a British colony proper was established, Britain's lonely imperial outpost in the South Atlantic was run as "a stone frigate," that is, on-the-books of the Commander-in-Chief, South America. Argentine's aggrieved response to this British intervention fell on deaf ears: the foreign secretary, Lord Palmerston, told the Argentine minister in London, Manuel Moreno, that not only was Captain Onslow's repossession authorized but that British rights were incontestable. Further particulars on this episode and its legacies are subjects of historical inquiry elsewhere.[16]

Based on Río, the Brazils squadron also kept up an extremely important function as freighters of bullion, specie, bank notes, and bills of exchange. This little known function of the Navy is the subject of another contribution to the understanding of the peaceful benefits of the *Pax Britannica* published elsewhere.[17] Suffice it to say, the conveyance of specie or "freight" was authorized by government and controlled by regulation. In an era of periodic anarchy in Latin American affairs, H.M. warships were a symbol of security to nervous merchants and anxious creditors. The Navy was the Securicor or Wells Fargo of that age, and it suffered no "hold-ups." One British treasure-carrying vessel was lost; on occasion fraudulent practices occurred (one shipper fooled a captain by shipping lead instead of silver); and naval officers were not immune from corruption. By and large, however, the service carried on the business to its credit. Ships took on "freights" from west coast ports as far north as Guaymas and San Blas, Mexico, and from Panama, Guayaquil, Callao, Valparaiso, Buenos Aires, Montevideo and, of course, Río. The last-mentioned was the collection point for periodic shipments to Portsmouth and thence the Bank of England. Almost every man-of-war returning from Río upon completion of a three or four year commission on the South American station took home a handsome "freight."

To safeguard shipping, whether British or foreign, ranked among the principal duties of ships of the Royal Navy on this and other stations. To this

16. Barry M. Gough, "The British Reoccupation and Colonization of the Falkland Islands, or Malvinas, 1832–1843," *Albion,* 22, 2 (Summer, 1990): 261–287. This also represents part of a book, in progress, *The Struggle for Empire in the South Atlantic.*

17. Barry M. Gough, "Specie Conveyance from the West Coast of Mexico in British Warships, 1820–1870: An Aspect of the *Pax Britannica,*" *The Mariner's Mirror,* 69, 4 (November, 1983): 419–33.

end, besides policing the seas, the Navy undertook to survey them, and thus to make the waters safer for navigation and trade. Captains and navigating officers were required to keep "Remark Books." In these they were instructed to record hydrographic information, and these volumes they had to render to the Hydrographer to the Admiralty on completion of their commission. Inshore water, high seas, coasts, islands, rocks – all were the subjects of concern of the Hydrographer. Commensurate with the increase of sea-going commerce in Latin American waters, the Admiralty published charts of the coasts and the entrances and anchorages of such key places of commercial exchanges such as Río or Valparaiso. Nonetheless, the eastern shore of South America from Trinidad to the Río de la Plata was, the British hydrographer reported in 1814, "erroneously laid down in charts and maps . . . and therefore wants rectifying."[18] For this reason, Their Lordships ordered a general survey to be undertaken. In 1825 the Admiralty directed Captain Phillip Parker King of H.M.S. *Adventure*, accompanied by the *Beagle*, commanded by Pringle Stokes, to survey the southern coasts of South America. This famous survey, 1826–36, in which Captain Robert FitzRoy made a celebrated contribution (in succession to Pringle Stokes), resulted in the preparation of new charts and sailing directions, or pilots. These aids to navigation were a further stimulus to seaborne commerce.[19] Other specific contributions were made by individual surveyors, that of B.J. Sulivan in the Falkland Islands and the Paraná-Plata system being particularly exemplary. Other surveys were conducted by Mayne in the *Nassau* and Nares in the *Alert*. The contribution of Admiralty charts and sailing directions to safe passage of vessels in South American waters cannot be quantified. However, it is a generally understood fact that hydrography was the harbinger of commerce, and that all seaborne commerce, irrespective of nationality, benefited from this work.

Specifically, as regards the Admiralty charts of such ports as Río or Valparaiso, these documents were based on information provided from sources other than their own. The Admiralty were not going to send a British survey vessel uninvited to survey a major port of a sovereign foreign country. Thus the 1839 Admiralty chart of Río was based on a Portuguese manuscript dated 1823, and that of Valparaiso on a Spanish survey of 1790. The British

18. Thomas Hurd, Hydrographer, Memo on the State of Hydrography, of May 1814, in Vice-Admiral Archibald Day, *The Admiralty Hydrographic Service, 1795–1919* (London: H.M.S.O, 1967), p. 28.

19. Rear-Admiral G. S. Ritchie, *The Admiralty Chart: British Naval Hydrography in the Nineteenth Century* (London: Hollis and Carter, 1967), chs. 12 and 14. Maps to illustrate the surveys of Magellan Straits, 1826–35, and the South American surveys, 1826–35, are on pp. 172 and 222 respectively. See also, George Basalla, "The Voyage of the *Beagle* without Darwin," *The Mariner's Mirror*, 49 (1963): 42–48.

government were circumspect about surveying foreign coasts, and would undertake such hydrographical inquiries provided local governments made no objections or if consent was provided.[20]

The requirements of the station always exceeded the resources available to the Commander-in-Chief. This was as true on the South American station as it was in other waters. As a learned and astute commentator in the London-based *United Service Journal and Naval and Military Magazine* put it in 1833:

> So far from a reduction taking place in the naval force of this country, there is every reason to expect an augmentation: for a moment's reflection will satisfy the most skeptical, that the Mediterranean, Portugal, Spain, and the East and West Indies are far from being in a tranquil state, and where so much British property is at stake, it behoves the Government to afford every protection. In South America the very extent of the command must always cause a respectable naval armament to be employed there.[21]

What was the "naval armament" of the South America station? In that year, one which is typical, the Commander-in-Chief, Rear-Admiral Sir Michael Seymour Bart., K.C.B., wore his flag in the *Spartiate*, a two-decker, ship-of-the line carrying 76 guns, at Río. The Pacific division had its own Senior Naval Officer, Commodore the Rt. Hon. Lord J. Townshend, who wore his pennant in the frigate *Dublin*, 50 guns. A corvette or two and a couple of sloops, each mounting say 28 guns and 18 guns respectively, worked the coasts and islands on either side of Cape Horn, while a couple of brigs or schooners each mounting ten or six guns would engage in duties requiring the threat of more modest armament. In 1833 the squadron numbered eleven ships mounting a total of 374 guns.[22] The resources available to a Commander-in-Chief were always stretched to their limits by the constant demands of "showing the flag." Rear-Admiral Baker held the opinion that the new republics respected "nothing but actual force of arms," and he was often tempted to employ force in contradiction to the Foreign Office's strictures not to get entangled in messy matters ashore. Baker complained to the Lords of the Admiralty that he had so many requests for support that all he could do with his limited resources was to direct commanding officers to make fast cruises up and down the coast looking in at these places for a day or two at a time and passing on as quickly as possible to the next place of need.[23] In short, meagre resources were taxed to maximum limits on the South American station.

---

20. Robert FitzRoy and P. Parker King, *Narrative of the Surveying Voyages of His Majesty Ships Adventure and Beagle* (4 vols.; London, 1839), 2:32.

21. *United Service Journal and Naval and Military Magazine*, December 1833, p. 531.

22. Baker to Admiralty, 20 June 1831, Adm. 1/36.

23. *Ibid*.

XIII

The maintenance of ships on this station, as on others, depended on supplies and stores sent regularly from England, as well as on whatever local sources were available and could be purchased at acceptable prices. Two storeships reached Río from England each year, one in January, the other in July. Until 1832, one of these vessels would sail from Río round the Horn to Valparaiso and there unload supplies directly into H.M. ships waiting to receive them. After 1832, supplies and stores were sent by private freight to the British consul at the Chilean port, who would supervise their distribution. At Valparaiso after 1843 a need existed for a permanent storehouse. However, for many years a storeship, the *Nereus*, lay at anchor there, though Chilean governments protested to the Foreign Office of the existence of this "foreign" base and did their best to get rid of it. At Callao, the port of Lima, the Navy also kept stores, especially after 1847, when the old British warship *Naiad* became a coal hulk for the Service. Meanwhile, Río continued as the main stores and supply base of H.M. ships in South Atlantic waters.[24]

Increasingly, the duties of the squadron beyond Cape Horn began to take their own order of precedence. For years ships based on Río had used Valparaiso as their western base of operations. Ships of the squadron on three-year tours of duty would range up the western coasts as far north as Mexico; or Alta, California and occasionally even to the Northwest Coast of North America. This was an extensive station: as one Commander-in-Chief gasped, in a moment of dismay, even Bering Strait was included in his command.[25] These ships would also visit the key archipelagos of the Pacific, the Society, Marquesas and Hawaiian Islands being the most common. Here French and American rivalry, commercial, religious and political, seemed in the ascendant. By 1837 these new demands meant that a new command, the Pacific, had to be established, responsible for waters west of Cape Horn. The boundaries of the South American station were adjusted accordingly, and its duties more immediately confined to attending to the protection of British interests in Brazil and the other South American republics on the Atlantic side of the continent.[26]

The period after 1837 does not belong within the present context of analysis. Nonetheless, it may be instructive to mention that well into the late nineteenth century the British continued to base ships on Río for the protection of British interests in South America. As steam propulsion became more universally adopted in the Royal Navy after the Crimean War, the

24. John Bach, "The Maintenance of Royal Navy Vessels in the Pacific Ocean, 1825–1875," *The Mariner's Mirror*, 56, 3 (August 1970): 262–63.

25. Journal of Sir Graham Eden Hamond, 16 September 1834, HAM/125, p. 7, National Maritime Museum, Greenwich.

26. Gough, *Royal Navy and the Northwest Coast*, pp. 243–44.

Falkland Islands acquired a new strategic value, and Río, Valparaiso, and Esquimalt, British Columbia, gained enhanced status as bases of supply. The boundaries of the South American station shifted, too, and did so according to administrative and political demands at home as well as changing geopolitical needs abroad. The types of vessels, furthermore, continued to be those for consular and police duties, and were not at all valuable for modern warfare. Gradually the British phased out their South America station, and this was partly owing to the ascendancy of the United States Navy in the Western Hemisphere. And as Britain built new capital ships – *Dreadnought* class battleships and *Invincible* class battle cruisers – so did the Lords of the Admiralty see it as less in the national and imperial interest to station smaller ships in such distant waters. In 1905 the South Atlantic station (incorporating the east coast of South America) was closed. An end had come to the old order of things, of keeping British ships on "foreign stations."[27] Nonetheless, South American waters remained vital to British trade and security, because on the east coast of the continent lay waters which formed part of the strategically significant South Atlantic Corridor, through which substantial volumes of high-valued cargoes passed. The geographical position of Río de Janeiro in relationship to the wider waters of the world had never really diminished. "There is no station that occupies so central and commanding a position as Río," lamented a senior clerk of the Admiralty in 1892, who hoped for the station's reestablishment. He explained: "cruisers could be dispatched from thence, at a moment's notice, to the Pacific, China and Australia, as well as to the Cape, the east coast of Africa, India, and the Strait Settlements by cable from Whitehall with as much secrecy as dispatch."[28] Consequently, the history of the Brazils station forms one chapter in the larger chronicle of the history of Britain's relations with Latin America and more especially the naval-diplomatic influence of the world's preeminent naval service during the early years of Brazil's national history and of those of her neighbors.

---

27. A. E. Ekoko, "British Naval Policy in the South Atlantic," *The Mariner's Mirror*, 66 (1980): 209–23, esp. 214 ff.

28. Sir John Henry Briggs, *Naval Administration 1827 to 1892: The Experience of 65 Years* (London: Sampson Low, Marston, 1897), p. 175.

XIV

SPECIE CONVEYANCE FROM THE WEST COAST OF MEXICO IN BRITISH WARSHIPS
c. 1820–1870:
An Aspect of the *Pax Britannica**

THE carriage of specie, that is, bullion or coin in gold and silver, by British ships of war had been authorized 'for centuries' according to Admiral Sir Cyprian Bridge, but by the early nineteenth century the practice was virtually confined to the west coast of America, especially to Mexico which boasted half of the world's silver. It was the only method whereby Mexico and other Pacific states of the Americas, then emerging from the blanket of Spanish authority, could safely effect trade with Europe and conduct commerce with foreign powers. The shipping of 'freight', as specie was called, was theoretically illegal in Mexico after independence in 1821 but the practice was regular and understood.[1] Exporting specie in British warships reduced piracy; thus, as in the later stages of prohibition in the United States, only a facade of authority was needed to maintain a profitable and necessary practice.

So far as H.M. ships were concerned, specie conveyance was recognized and approved. Various Admiralty regulations of the early nineteenth century controlled the amounts that admirals and ships' captains would receive for the conveyance of freight. The 'gratuity' for the transport of treasure served as an inducement to officers, flag-officers and post captains, to carry freight in their ships. Freight at this time was of two kinds, public or state-owned and privately-owned. Only gold, silver and jewels were to be shipped. Officers received no gratuity for 'public treasure' in 1801 but in 1807 convinced the Admiralty that ½% should be given for the conveyance of 'public treasure.'[2] Privately-owned treasure was variously regulated and the percentage of gratuity is not known. The return of peace in 1815 brought a reassessment of regulations. By 59 *Geo.* III (1819), cap. 25, 'An Act to enable His Majesty to fix a Rate, and direct the Disposal of Freight Money, for the Conveyance of Specie and Jewels on board His Majesty's Ships and Vessels'; commissions were set by proclamation for carriage as follows: from

*I acknowledge, with thanks, the assistance of four scholars of Latin America in the preparation of this work: Michael Mathes, J. C. M. Ogelsby, Christon Archer and Peter Smith.

England beyond the Capes, 1% of the 'public treasure' in time of war or peace, $2\frac{1}{2}$% of 'private treasure' in time of peace, and 3% of 'private treasure' in time of war. Of the commission, one-quarter went to the admiral on station, one-half to the ship's captain, and one-quarter to Greenwich Hospital for Seamen.[3] In 1831, because of the continuance of peace and the decline of risk attendant with the carriage of specie, the government steeply reduced these percentages to 1% of the 'public treasure' for conveyance in time of peace or war, $1\frac{1}{2}$% of 'private treasure' in time of peace, and 2% of 'private treasure' in time of war.[4] These regulations were printed regularly in *The Navy List* and thus found their way into the hands of every naval officer and agent conducting Navy business.

In the 1830's government modified these regulations to reflect the risk attendant in the conveyance of specie over longer distances: the longer the voyage the higher the gratuity. Thus commissions of $1\frac{1}{2}$% were given for freight conveyed within the South Pacific or the South Atlantic; 2% from the North to the South Pacific, from the west coast of South America to Rio de Janeiro, or from Rio to England; and $2\frac{1}{2}$% from the Pacific to England.[5] For this reason, among others as we shall see, the Pacific station was a much prized command for admirals and captains. In these circumstances, numerous disputes among officers occurred over the regulations and station boundaries. As far as the responsibility of a ship's captain was concerned, it began only when the freight was alongside his ship and ceased at the moment it was landed at its port of destination. This defined his responsibilities and protected him against legal action by interested private parties. By the late Victorian age conveyance of specie was no longer a hazardous undertaking. Thus in 1881 the percentages were again reduced to 1% for both state and private treasure carried anywhere, and in 1914 the system of 'gratuities' was eliminated altogether.[6]

By the early years of the nineteenth century, ships on the South American station took specie from major east coast ports of Latin America, particularly Rio de Janeiro and Montevideo.[7] Ships captains also began to expand the practice to the Pacific side of the Americas, first at Valparaiso, Chile, then farther north at Callao, Peru, Guayaquil, Ecuador, and by 1882 at west coast Mexican ports. From time to time the Commander-in-Chief of the South American or 'Brazils' station would detach a ship for this assignment, as well as for the necessary purpose of 'showing the flag' in support of British commercial and diplomatic interests. Internal problems in Latin American states, particularly Chile which gained independence in 1823, forced naval captains to be wary of any involvement in domestic affairs, but it was a risky business nonetheless. The first major shipment of specie from this coast appears to have occurred in 1820 when the frigate *Hyperion* (42), Captain Thomas Searle, took at least $1,500,000 from Callao to Spithead.[8]

Farther north, in Mexico, merchants at Guadalajara and Tepic were anxious to establish, for the first time, a direct commercial intercourse with England. On 28 March 1822, the frigate *Conway*, Captain Basil Hall commanding, reached San Blas, the port for Tepic. The merchants told Hall that the arrival of a British warship had been long anticipated and that they hoped to remit a considerable quantity of specie to England in the *Conway*, for which returns were to be made in English goods. The Mexican government, under the belief that national wealth could not leave the country, had to give permission before the treasure could be exported. Hall wrote that the Mexican commoners were ill-informed about government policy and the change from Spanish mercantilism to national capitalism: in his opinion they

> had not yet learned to separate the idea of wealth and power from the mere possession of gold and silver; not seeing that it was solely by the process of exchanging them for goods and services which they stood in need of, that either wealth or power could arise from the precious metals, of which they had more than they wanted.

The new, independent Mexican government, only some six months old, granted permission. However, the general public in the port towns looked on the Royal Navy, in taking gold and silver from their shores, as 'pirates'. Ultimately more than half a million dollars were shipped, bound for London; some by Spanish merchants, a small quantity by Mexicans, but the whole was intended for the purchase of British goods. In these circumstances this was a practice that British governments were obliged to support. Already specie was being shipped in private vessels, but the risk involved meant high insurance premiums on the shipments and speculation on bills of lading sent to Europe by other routes.[9] The Navy gave these merchants the security they long had been seeking.

In the 1820's British interests in the Pacific were as yet not sufficiently important to warrant the establishment of a station separate from the South American Station. British warships were sent to the Pacific for a variety of reasons but as of yet no regular ports of call for warships were established and the Pacific Station was not constituted as a separate command until 1837. In the meantime, whatever British warships were on the coast were instructed by the Commander-in-Chief or the Admiralty or cajolled by local merchants into conveying freight and, in some cases, their captains solicited business.[10]

Another example of early British willingness to take on specie is shown in the case of H.M.S. *Blossom* (26), Captain Frederick William Beechey. Enroute from the Bering Sea, where she had been co-operating with the search for the Northwest Passage being undertaken by Captain William Edward Parry and Captain John Franklin, the *Blossom* called at San Blas on 20 December 1827. Beechey received an appeal from Eustace Barron, the British vice-consul, to delay his departure (after putting in primarily for naval stores, provisions and refit), until specie could be shipped. Beechey agreed and remained on the coast for over three winter months and did not quit San Blas for Valparaiso (where he also took on specie) and Spithead until 8 March 1828.[11]

Beechey, like Hall before him, found that lawlessness remained a real danger to local merchants and to producers of Mexican silver and gold. Loads of specie, in the forms of bars, plate or coin, were carried to ports on donkeys, provided bandidos and guerrillas did not interfere. The *Blossom's* first lieutenant, George Peard, recorded in his journal some of the details of the transactions between these merchants and the Mexican government:

> The duties [for export of specie] are so extremely oppressive that even the most respectable Merchants do not scruple [sic] either to evade them altogether or to modify them in a certain degree by bribing the Officers appointed to collect them. The pay of the Commissionary General of a Province is 4000 dollars, that of the Collector 2000, and I was informed by a Gentleman whose veracity I can depend on that the presents made by him within the last two years to the Collector of the customs at Mazatlán amounted to 40,000 dollars, besides minor sums to the next officer or Contador, and that notwithstanding the lenity [sic] he had experienced in consequence, the duties he had actually paid to government in the same time were near 200,000 dollars.[12]

Peard noted that silver or *plata piña* was boxed in bars and that for the casting of the metal into bars the government received 5%. If the bars were then made into coin, the fee would be an additional 5%. The licence for the export of coin, called by the British 'dollars', and the Mexicans 'pesos', the only shape in which silver could be legally sent out of the country, was $3\frac{1}{2}$% more.[13] Bar silver and gold, however, seems regularly to have been exported because Mexican officials failed to enforce that regulation. In all, it was a transaction beneficial to merchants, governments and the Navy. The value of specie shipped to England in the *Blossom* is not known, but an entry in Peard's journal for 11 and 12 January 1828 notes that the ship received from the Mazatlán customhouse 82 boxes of 'bar silver, *piña* and dollars.'[14]

From time to time British warships would visit west coast Mexican ports but the demands on the small material resources of the squadron throughout the eastern Pacific did not allow for a regular visit. In 1835,

H.M.S. *Conway* was again on the coast, and the British consul advised her captain that the amount of treasure transported in the *Conway* should be proof of the need of a naval vessel there at all times. If a ship was permanently there, Barron said, British merchants would secure on the coast 'an annual remittance to England of at least twice as much as we now do.'[15] The *Conway* received $1,900,000, of which $100,000 was to be landed at Rio de Janeiro.[16]

The growing size of specie shipments from Mexican and other ports confirmed Barron's reports that Britain should give this special cargo appropriate attention. In 1837 H.M.S. *Blonde* took $1,200,000 to England.[17] In 1838, H.M.S. *Cleopatra* conveyed $1,586,000[18] and this actively prompted the first Commander-in-Chief, Pacific, Rear-Admiral Charles Ross, to begin to refer to the 'annual freight' from Mexico.[19] As of yet, however, no warship remained on the coast. In 1839 H.M.S. *Imogene* left San Blas with $1,641,158. Her commander, Captain H. W. Bruce, advised Admiral Ross

> that for the proper accomplishment of this service, a ship of war is required to be constantly on the coast, and to leave it every six months – periodically – when she would convey away, at the most moderate computation, to the amount of one million and a half Dollars; one of her objects should be to receive Deposits, which would be put on board as opportunity serves at the ports of Guaymas, Mazatlán, and San Blas; while her presence on the station would be of immense advantage, giving confidence and security to commerce.[20]

In Bruce's view, local merchants should be assured of a regular visit of a warship because ships were weak and bullion could not be left on shore owing to revolution and plunder.

> England being the receptacle of almost all of this treasure, [Bruce advised] the mode of its conveyance cannot but be of importance to her, and the inference is obvious, that this Mexican coast with its progressively improving state of commerce, demands the serious attention of our Government.[21]

Throughout the 1840's pressures for naval protection of British interests in Mexico as well as California and Central America continued to increase. In 1844 the vice-consul in Central America, Frederick Chatfield, complained of the navy's 'total neglect'. In reply to this charge the Commander-in-Chief advised the Admiralty that the Foreign Office should point out to the anxious consul that fourteen warships had visited Central America since 1834.[22] In Mexico, merchants came under pressure in 1844 from the French agent Duflot de Mofras, acting under the pretence of a scientist, to ship specie in French frigates promised annually.[23] In 1843 these same pressures had forced Commander R. F. Gambier of H.M.S. *Satellite* to take freight from the smaller vessel

H.M.S. *Champion* to England, thereby inviting the animosity of the *Champion's* captain, the displeasure of the Commander-in-Chief, Rear-Admiral Richard Thomas, and the censure of the Admiralty.[24] Farther north again, in California, British subjects in California complained that H.M. cruisers visited Mexican ports but not ports in California.[25]

Irregularities in specie conveyance continued and in 1844 De Mofras charged in his *Oregon, California and Vermillion Sea* that according to information given to him during his visit to Mexico, British commanders were exciting Mexican merchants to smuggle. The British consul at Tepic, Barron, informed his superior in Mexico City that this was a fabrication, adding that many persons try to 'propagate reports injurious to the legitimate merchants, and derogatory to the honour of British Officers'. Nonetheless, this episode resulted in Lord Aberdeen, the Foreign Secretary, laying down explicit instructions.

> H.M.'s Govt. [he wrote] consider it in every respect expedient that H.M.'s Naval Officers should hold themselves entirely aloof from even the appearance of engaging in, or countenancing in any way, any smuggling transaction with respect to the shipment of Specie in Mexican ports; and should any officer be implicated in any such transaction, he would incur the serious displeasure of H.M.'s Govt.

In every case, he warned, officers could not 'bring off specie in their own boats.' They must possess a custom's house certificate to show the duty paid on the specie. The Mexican government, he noted, had responsibility for certifying that the duty was paid. He advised the British Minister in Mexico that the great duties levied were the cause of the contraband and all the difficulties arising out of it. In his opinion, Mexico should reduce the duties to stop the smuggling because the profits from the specie transactions would go to the Mexican treasury rather than to the smugglers. Aberdeen, fearing violence, also ordered the Commander-in-Chief, Pacific, to inform his captains that boats were not to go to shore with armed crews unless absolutely necessary.[26]

The vagaries of specie conveyance did not diminish during the 1840's. Merchants continued to appeal for more security for their trade on shore and for the safe conveyance of specie to England. French and American warships visiting the coast intensified international rivalry. But still the British naval presence was maintained, if in a not altogether systematic way. At least once a year a frigate, corvette or sloop-of-war would call at west coast American ports, and the conveyance of specie remained an important consideration for the interested parties in the Royal Navy, particularly the Commander-in-Chief and the captain of the vessel fortunate enough to be assigned to convey home freight towards the end of his commission. Rear-Admiral Sir George Francis Seymour,

XIV

who became Commander-in-Chief in 1844, took pains to detail the commissions from freight received by Greenwich Hospital (the equivalent of his share as Commander-in-Chief) in the years 1839 to 1843. His figures show that by no means was the Pacific the most lucrative command of all 'foreign stations' but, with the North American and West Indies and East Indies stations, it was among the best.[27] In setting forth to the Pacific in H.M.S. *Collingwood* Seymour could anticipate coming home a rich man. If the years 1839–1843 were an indication of what could be anticipated, he would receive about £2,500 annually from specie conveyance.

By the mid-1840's a command in the Pacific had become a particularly attractive admiral's appointment. Such an appointment was also the sought-after goal of post-captains. The Mediterranean offered much sun and the Pacific offered the chance of money, a clerk of the Navy Office recorded, and appointments in command of larger ships destined for these stations were much prized. The frigates, Sir John Henry Briggs recalled, 'were commanded almost exclusively by captains who were noblemen or members of noble families: the former station being one of pleasure; the latter more lucrative, as their ships invariably brought home heavy freights.'[28]

In one instance the possibilities of gain made questionable the proceedings of one ship's captain and endangered British interests on the Northwest Coast of North America at a critical time in Anglo-American relations. In 1843, the Lords of the Admiralty directed the Commander-in-Chief, Pacific, to send a warship in support of British interests in Oregon, where the Hudson's Bay Company was the nominal authority. Sovereignty over the Pacific cordillera from Russian America to California was contested by Britain and the United States, as American settlers and missionaries were making major inroads into the Columbia and Willamette river valleys. In 1844 the sloop of war *Modeste* visited the Columbia River in support of British interests and in the following year the frigate *America* (50) entered the Strait of Juan de Fuca and Puget Sound for the same purpose.[29]

The *America's* Captain was the Honorable John Gordon. He had entered the Navy in 1805 and had risen to captain's rank in thirteen years.[30] On half pay for 27 years, he was appointed to the *America* owing to his 'interest', his eldest brother being Lord Aberdeen and another, the Hon. William Gordon, M.P., a Lord of the Admiralty. Seymour, before his appointment to the Pacific Station, also had been a Lord of the Admiralty. These connections were apparently important in bringing Gordon into active service.

Gordon's instructions from Seymour required him to remain on station in support of British interests in Oregon, California, the Hawaiian Islands and elsewhere. Instead, he left the station contrary to orders after having displaced the sloop *Daphne* (18), Captain John Onslow, which was to have conveyed the freight home at the end of her commission. Gordon knew that American insterests were in the ascendant in California and Oregon. Yet he was indifferent to the protection of British interests there. He seems to have come under pressure from Mazatlán merchants who doubted the security that the smaller *Daphne* could afford and urged that the specie be conveyed in the *America*. In the circumstances Gordon saw it as his responsibility to convey the treasure, worth $2,000,000 by his estimate, to England.[31]

Meanwhile his commander-in-chief, Rear-Admiral Seymour, was making repeated requests on the Admiralty to send more ships, including two more line-of-battleships, to the Pacific in support of British interests. He later learned that the *America* had sailed for England 'without orders, with money'. 'Gordon's ill-judged Decision might have turned the fate of war with the U.S. against us,' Seymour noted in his diary, 'taking off the station the only strong ship except the *Collingwood* when he was aware I considered war most probable.'[32] To the Admiralty Seymour expressed his entire disapproval of Gordon's actions.[33] Captain Henry Byam Martin of the frigate *Grampus* recorded his astonishment 'that a man of family should so disgrace himself for a little money.'[34]

When the *America* reached home the Admiralty had decided that Gordon's conduct was 'so reprehensible' as to require a court martial.[35] The charge of leaving station contrary to orders was fully proved. Gordon was severely reprimanded. But he was acquitted of motives of personal gain and remained in command of the *America*, if but for a short time. Gordon resigned 10 October 1846 to take advantage of the newly-instituted retirement scheme. He claims to have given over his commission of $10,000 for freight conveyance to Captain Onslow of the *Daphne* but this has not been substantiated.[36] Ironically, had he remained on station it is likely, as his court martial defence argued, he might have returned home later with a larger freight.[37] In any event, Gordon's case sparked wide interest in Britain and served to cause Boards of Admiralty and Commanders-in-Chief, Pacific, to watch more closely the movements of warships with respect to freight conveyance.

After the Oregon crisis international disturbances on the Pacific side of the Americas continued to affect the conveyance of specie. The American invasion of Mexico in 1847, resulting in the definition of the boundary between the United States and Mexico in the Treaty of

Guadelupe Hidalgo of 2 February 1848, served to complicate the conveyance of specie during the late 1840's. The U.S. Navy blockaded Mexican ports. Mexican merchants pressured Captain Henry Byam Martin of the *Grampus* to break the blockade at Guatulco and take on board a large quantity of silver bars and cochineal, a valuable red dyestuff. An agent for these merchants told Martin that the freight would be so great that there would be no difficulty in persuading him or the captain of H.M.S. *Juno*, also on the coast, to break the blockade.

> If I catch the fellow, [Martin wrote angrily in his diary about the agent] I'll keel haul him; and I wrote to Mr Forbes [the British Consul in Tepic] to . . . inform this gentleman that such a proposal and such a letter is highly unbecoming. I suppose one will have one's nose frequently rubbed with filth before this dollar hunting cruise is over.[38]

In another way specie transmission became further complicated. The United States government first of all, under General Winfield Scott's declaration, prohibited specie exports and then increased the duties previously reduced by Mexico on export.[39] This would be injurious to Mexican merchants, Martin feared. However at San Blas he embarked more dollars than he had expected, about $700,000 at that port alone.[40]

During his months on the Mexican coast, Martin had an opportunity to observe details of the specie conveyance, and his journal entries provide good evidence on mining, transportation and commercial transactions. Specie arrived at San Blas in a ship or 'conducta', amounting to nearly $500,000. The conductor in charge was a bold fellow who had already lost an arm in defending his charge from bandits. The specie was carried on mules, each bearing $4000–$6000. As the long file of mules reached shore, each mule was unloaded. The bags were laid upon the sand, counted and delivered to Martin. The ship's boats were waiting for the bags and took them to the ship. To stop smuggling and fraud the dollars were counted, an improvement over earlier guesswork when major mistakes were sometimes made as in 1821 when the *Superb* unknowingly took lead from Lima (the fraud was discovered in England, and her captain was held liable, lost the entitled freight and was put in jail). Thus every bar of silver, every coin was examined and counted. The counters, usually five in number, were paid $2.00 per thousand and this gratuity aided, in the case of H.M.S. *Brisk*, the ship's 'paint fund' (normally paid by the first lieutenant out of his pocket) and liquidated the mess debt. The specie was boxed in crates made by the ship's carpenter. The captain bought Vancouver Island deal plank and sold it to the carpenter. For fashioning the boxes the carpenter received £200, his two mates £30 and three others of the carpenter's crew £20.

XIV

These are large sums indeed and show that specie conveyance was also highly remunerative to certain members of the crew. Boat parties, against Admiralty regulation, also were rewarded for the risks taken in bringing specie off from the shore.[41] The necessity of rewarding crew for hard work in these circumstances is obvious and the benefits of specie conveyance were spread throughout the ship.

When the laborious task of counting, boxing and stowing species was completed, a bill of lading for the precise amount of treasure was prepared. To keep the process strictly legal the captain had to exercise close surveillance. But even then he would come under pressure from Mexican merchants to engage in clandestine operations. Captain Martin of the *Grampus*, for instance, agreed to ship $30,000 in silver in order to save it from capture by Americans. With Veracruz and Tampico on the Gulf coast in the hands of 'Los Yankes', Martin wrote, more gold and silver was being sent to Pacific ports. 'And this ends this little dollar hunting excursion', he wrote in his journal, 'which has been far more profitable than I expected'.[42]

All told the *Grampus* shipped specie worth $2,628,900 bound for the Bank of England. Slight adjustments, involving lawyers for the interested parties, had to be made because a small portion was disembarked in Rio de Janeiro. Martin expected to receive, as his commission, £5351-1-6. He advised Rear-Admiral Seymour that the flag's share was about £2675-6-9.[43] A similar sum would go to Greenwich hospital. In actuality a dispute developed between Rear-Admiral Seymour and his successor, Rear-Admiral Sir Thomas Phipps Hornby who entered Pacific Station limits on 14 March 1848 and immediately wrote to Seymour in measured tones that he was 'desirous of partaking in the advantages arising out of the conveyance of Treasury'.[44] The Admiralty ruled that Seymour was not entitled to receive a share to any specie shipped in the *Grampus* after he had quit the station even though at the time he may not have been beyond the station limits.[45] Subsequently outgoing and incoming commanders-in-chief disputed their shares, and on one occasion a newly-appointed one threatened resignation because his predecessor lingered on station.[46] Similarly, disputes arose between ships' captains as to specie entitlement.[47] In all, as Admiral John Moresby rightly observed, specie conveyance 'certainly was not to the moral advantage of any who were concerned in this particular form of privateering'.[48]

What clandestine operations were carried on by naval officers cannot be accurately documented. Some, like the principled Captain Henry Byam Martin, would 'never be a party to any transaction that will not bear daylight'.[49] There were others, like Captain George Wellesley of the *Daedalus*, who exposed frauds.[50] But it was general practice to take advantage where there was no surveillance. Thus, to cite one example, the captain of the *Thetis*, Augustus Kuper, 'as upright a man as any', resolved to smuggle 'as all his predecessors had done before him' and to employ the ship's resources to obtain all he could.[51] Only a small portion of specie was duty paid, according to Sir Cyprian Bridge when he was in H.M.S. *Brisk* on the Mexican coast in 1856.[52] The smuggling was known to captains and customs officers alike and in view of its benefits to both parties was carried on despite regulations to the contrary.

During the 1850's specie conveyance remained a rewarding business. The frigate *Thetis* in 1853 took $3,000,000 or £600,000 from Mexico.[53] Two years later H.M.S. *Brisk* carried $2,700,000 or £540,000.[54] In 1858, to give still further examples, H.M.S. *Alert* shipped $584,351 and H.M.S. *Havannah* $740,789.[55] At this time, by one calculation, a three-year admiral's command would bring 'the comfortable sum' of £10,000.[56] While the size of treasure continued large, the Admiralty sought to tighten the regulations against smuggling. Orders were issued that required documents of transfer to be retained in the ship until the vessel reached England, where the cargo was to be checked against the bills of lading.[57] As late as 1872 the Admiralty learned that treasure was being shipped illegally on board H.M. ships, and captains were reminded that all transactions had to have custom clearance at the port where shipment was made.[58]

Commanders-in-chief, Pacific, continued to remind ships' captains that any officer implicated in smuggling specie would incur the serious displeasure of government. The strictures set down by Lord Aberdeen remains as policy until the near abolition of specie commissions in 1881.[59] Nonetheless the legitimate conveyance of specie and the illegitimate process of smuggling 'happily now by Order-in-Council virtually abrogated', Moresby wrote, 'brought into active operation the worst weaknesses of poor human nature'.[60] The British Vice-Consul Barron was of a similar opinion:

> No one knows better than I do the disinterestedness of British Naval Officers . . . yet it is not to be expected of human nature that a Commander would be desirous of receiving on board what would subject him to immense risk and trouble, without any advantage to counter-balance it.[61]

Gradually the practice of shipping specie by H.M. ships diminished. The introduction of commercial steam navigation in the Pacific allowed merchants to ship treasure on Pacific Mail Company steamers to Panama where it was transhipped across the isthmus and sent by steamer to England. Even then Royal Navy officers and men were placed on board mail steamers to give security to the vessel and cargo. The rise of San Francisco as a commercial centre for the Pacific after the discovery of gold there in 1848 led merchants to send large remittances of silver to California to be exchanged for gold and then to remit this gold to England or the United States where it yielded a better return than specie sent direct. After the Mexican War, ships of the United States Navy made inroads into the specie conveyance work of the Royal Navy.[62] Yet throughout the 1850's, as has been demonstrated, H.M. ships continued to take specie via Cape Horn to England and they often conveyed Mexican specie to Panama and San Francisco. The growing productivity of Mexican mines continued to afford attraction for admirals and ships' captains. However, H.M.S. *Tribune*, sent from the Pacific to China waters in 1857 in response to the *Lorcha Arrow* incident, did not benefit from specie conveyance. '. . . the China station with prospects of active service and promotion', Commander F. M. Norman wrote, 'was much more attractive than our present one, though to be sure our captain lost his chance of freight – one of the little pickings of the Pacific'.[63]

For all its faults, the conveyance of specie in British warships was conducted over a fifty-year period with credit to the service. The temptations were high and the cases of abuse are known. Nonetheless, British warships afforded security to merchants during precarious times of revolution and national emergence in Latin America. No Mexican shipments were lost.[64] In these circumstances it is not surprising that Mexican merchants continued to rely on ships of the Royal Navy to convey specie, their main source of income and credit, to England. The *Pax Britannica* was progress underscored by peace, a peace reinforced by the might of the Royal Navy. Of course this might was often more apparent than real on the Mexican coast. Yet it sufficed to provide enough security for British and Mexican merchants to carry on their operations, clandestine and otherwise.

NOTES

1 Admiral Sir Cyprian Bridge, *Some Recollections* (London, 1918), pp. 127–30. Officials took the position, dating from the Habsburg Monarchy, *se obedece pero no se* (I obey but do not enforce) in order to conduct business.
2 Michael Lewis, *The Navy in Transition, 1814–1864: A Social History* (London, 1965), pp. 242–5. See also, Michael A. Lewis, ed., *A Narrative of my Professional Adventures (1790–1839) by Sir William Henry Dillon* (2 vols.; London: Navy Records Society (hereinafter 'N.R.S.'), vols. 93, 97; 1953, 1956), I, 75 and II, 270–3.

3 Great Britain, Statutes at Large, 59 *Geo.* III (1819), cap. 25. An order-in-council of 12 July 1819 implemented this statute.
4 By Proclamation of William IV, 8 June 1831. *Navy Lists.* See also changes effected 23 Apr. 1831 in [Admiralty] *Orders in Council,* III (London, 1856).
5 See Public Record Office (hereafter P.R.O.), Colchester Papers, P.R.O. 30/9, 6, part II/10, for details.
6 Lewis, *Navy in Transition,* p. 245.
7 Gerald S. Graham and R. A. Humphreys, eds., *The Navy in South America, 1807–1823: Correspondence of the Commanders-in-Chief on the South American Station.* (London, N.R.S., vol. CIV, 1962), *passim.* One of these ships, the *Thetis,* sunk off the Brazilian coast with £160,000 of which £157,000 was found. W. Senior, 'The Treasure Frigate "Thetis"', *The Mariner's Mirror,* 2 (Feb. 1912), 33–7.
8 Searle to Hardy, 8 Nov. 1820, encl. in Hardy to Croker, 12 Dec. 1820, Admiralty Papers, 1/26, P.R.O. (hereafter Adm.).
9 Captain Basil Hall, R.N., *Extracts from a Journal, written on the Coasts of Chili, Peru, and Mexico in the Years 1820, 1821, 1822* (2nd ed., 2 vols.; Edinburgh, 1824), II, 183, 185, 190–1, 226–8, and 257–8.
10 John P. S. Bach, 'The Royal Navy in the South Pacific, 1826–1876', Ph.D. thesis, University of New South Wales, 1964, ch. 2; Barry M. Gough, *The Royal Navy and the Northwest Coast of North America, 1810–1914: A Study of British Maritime Ascendancy* (Vancouver: University of British Columbia Press, 1971), App. A.
11 Beechey to Croker, 8 Dec. 1827, Adm. 1/1576, Cap B 42.
12 Lieut. George Peard, 'Journal of H.M.S. *Blossom,* 1825–1828', Add. MSS. 35,141, ff. 101–102, British Library, London (Hereafter B.L.); also, Barry M. Gough, ed., *To the Arctic and Pacific With Beechey: The Journal of Lieutenant George Peard of H.M.S. 'Blossom', 1825–1828* (Cambridge: Hakluyt Society, 2d ser., no. 143, 1973), p. 251.
13 Ibid.
14 Ibid.
15 Barron to Mason, 20 Apr. 1835, Adm. 1/44.
16 Hamond to Wood, 24 Aug. 1835, ibid.
17 Hamond to Wood, 23 Aug. 1837, Adm. 1/48.
18 Ross to Wood, 12 Aug. 1838, Adm. 1/51.
19 Ross to Wood, 1 Oct. 1838, Adm. 1/52.
20 Bruce to Ross, 10 May 1839, San Blas; extract in Bruce to Wood, 12 May 1839, Adm. 1/1587, Cap B 100.
21 Ibid. Bruce noted the respective value of shipments in 1838 from Guaymas ($900,000–$1,000,000 in gold and silver bullion), Mazatlán ($1,910,000 of which ¼ was coin, ⅛ gold and ⅜ silver), and San Blas ($800,000–$1,000,000, all in half dollars).
22 Chatfield to Commander-in-Chief, Pacific, 27 July 1844, encl. in Thomas to Admiralty, 18 Nov. 1844, Adm. 1/5550, Y119.
23 Russell to Thomas, 28 Mar. 1842, in Thomas to Herbert, 2 May 1842, Adm. 1/5512. H.M.S. *Actaeon,* Captain Robert Russell, took $1,381,000 from Mexico in that year. (Ibid.) At this time, Britain and other powers established consulates in Mexico and California. See A. P. Nasatir, 'International Rivalry and the Establishment of the British Consulate', *California Historical Society Quarterly,* XLVI, 1 (Mar. 1967), 53–70.
24 Thomas to Herbert, 2 Oct. 1843, and Adm. minute, 10 Jan. 1844, Qa10, Adm. 1/5538.
25 Glyndwr Williams, ed., *London Correspondence Inward from Sir George Simpson, 1841–42* (London, Hudson's Bay Record Society, vol. 29, 1973), pp. 130, 152.
26 Barron to Bankhead, 10 Jan. 1846, encl. in Barron to Aberdeen, 17 Jan. 1846, No. 1, F.O. 50/203, and Aberdeen to Bankhead, draft, 31 Aug. 1844 (copy to Adm. this date), No. 27, Foreign Office Papers, P.R.O. (hereafter F.O.), 50/172.

432   CONVEYANCE OF MEXICAN SPECIE 1820–1870

27

Year	No. American & West Indies £	East Indies £	Pacific £	Brazil £	Med. £	Cape £
1839	4121	1121	1067	1867	545	446
1840	6636	955	4163	1135	645	23
1841	5554	781	3209	1237	215	162
1842	3730	1383	1272	1381	32	160
1943	1666	4494	2921	1376	113	14

'An Account of Freight or Treasure in £s received by Greenwich Hospital from the following stations . . .,' Private Diary of Sir George Francis Seymour 1844, CR 114A/374/21, p. 110, Warwickshire Record Office. I acknowledge with thanks the permission of the Marquess of Hertford, great-great-grandson of Admiral Sir George Francis Seymour, to publish statements from the Seymour of Ragley Collection in the W.R.O.

28 Sir John Henry Briggs, *Naval Administrations, 1827 to 1892* (London, 1897), pp. 29–30.

29 Gough, *Royal Navy and the Northwest Coast*, ch. 3.

30 For a fuller report on this and related matters, see Barry M. Gough, 'H.M.S. *America* on the North Pacific Coast', *Oregon Historical Quarterly*, LXX, 4 (Dec. 1969), 292–311.

31 Mazatlán Merchants to Barron, 13 Jan. 1846, encl. in Gordon to Sec. of Admiralty, 19 Aug. 1846, Adm. 1/5562. Also, *United Service Gazette*, 29 Aug. 1846, and *The Times*, 27 Aug. 1846.

32 Seymour, Private Diary, 14 Aug. 1846, and appendix, p. 129, Cr 114A/374/23, W.R.O.

33 Seymour to Sec. of the Admiralty, 2 Sept. 1846, copy in Official Letter Book I, Cr114A/416/1, W.R.O.

34 *Grampus* Journal, 14 Aug. 1846, Martin Papers, Add. MSS 41,472, B.L.

35 Corry to Gordon, 8 July 1846, Adm. 2/1696.

36 John Moresby, a midshipman in the *America*, claims that Captain Onlow of the *Daphne* 'received no compensation whatever for his loss of several thousand pounds'. Of Captain Gordon, he wrote: 'I need hardly say that the type of naval officer I have here described is rare indeed. I recall few other such in naval records'. John Moresby, *Two Admirals* rev. ed. (London 1913), pp. 50–1 and 59–60.

37 See Gough, 'H.M.S. *America*', pp. 309–311.

38 *Grampus* Journal, 9 Dec. 1847, Martin Papers, Add. MSS 41,472, B.L.

39 To 7% on bar silver, 5% on gold and 6% on silver coin. Martin to Seymour, 5 Jan. 1848, Martin Papers, Add. MSS. 41,469, fol. 51, B.L.

40 Ibid.

41 Bridge, *Some Recollections*, pp. 129–30. On the payment of boats' crew, Captain Martin of the *Grampus* was annoyed that Mazatlán merchants were not giving a gratuity to boat crew. 'I am fully aware that all charges whatever beyond the amount of freight, fixed by Order-in-Council, are illegal, – and this I have invariably expressed to you and to all whom I have conversed with on the subject; – but I certainly would not have sent my boats out of sight of the Ship, but for a direct and unsolicited promise, that their crews should be liberally rewarded. . . . I shall know better in my future dealings with the gentlemen of Mazatlán'. Martin to Consul Forbes (Tepic), 29 Feb. 1848, confidential, Martin Papers, Add. MSS 41,469, fols. 56–7, B.L.

42 *Grampus* Journal, entries for 4 Jan., 20 and 23 Mar., 12 Apr. 1848, Add. MSS. 41,472, B.L.

43 Martin to Seymour, 8 Nov. 1848, copy, Martin Papers, Add. MSS 41,469, B.L. Journal of Rear-Admiral Sir Thomas Phipps Hornby, Commander-in-Chief Pacific, 1847–51, PHI/1, 10 July 1848, National Maritime Museum, Greenwich (hereinafter N.M.M.). Martin to Seymour, 8 Nov. 1848, Martin Papers, Add. MSS 41,469, B.L.

44 Hornby to Seymour, 14 Mar. 1848, PHL/1, N.M.M.
45 W. A. B. Hamilton to Martin, 22 Nov. 1848, Martin Papers, Add. MSS 41,469.
46 See, for instance, Baynes to Sec. of the Admiralty, 31 Feb. 1858, and Adm. Minute of 13 Apr. 1858, Adm. 1/5694, Y57. Also Maitland to Sec. of the Admiralty, 14 Jan. 1861, and Adm. Minute of 4 Mar. 1861, Adm. 1/5761, Y51.
47 See the case of the captains of H.M.S. *Pylades* and *Amethyst* in Baynes to Sec. of the Admiralty, 4 Apr. 1860, Adm. 1/5736, Pt. 1, Y94.
48 Moresby, *Two Admirals*, p. 118.
49 Martin to Forbes, 7 Jan. 1848, Martin Papers, Add. MSS 41,469, fol. 52, B.L.
50 Moresby, *Two Admirals*, p. 116.
51 Ibid., p. 117.
52 Bridge, *Some Recollections*, p. 128.
53 Moresby, *Two Admirals*, p. 117. In the 1909 edition of this work Moresby equates the $3,000,000 to £600,000.
54 Bridge, *Some Recollections*, p. 129.
55 Baynes to Sec. of the Admiralty, 27 Feb. and 27 July 1858, Adm. 1/5694, Y62 and 152 respectively.
56 Bridge, *Some Recollections*, p. 129.
57 Special Instructions to Captains ... Pacific, 27 Jan. 1858, Adm. 1/5694, Y192.
58 Revised station orders to Rear-Admiral Hillyar, 13 Sept. 1872, Adm. 1/6236, pt. 2.
59 See, for instance, Special Instructions to Captains ... Pacific, 27 Jan. 1858, Adm. 1/5694, Y192, and *Station Regulations ... Pacific* (Victoria, V.I., 1863), p. 3; copy in Adm. 13/184/12.
60 Moresby, *Two Admirals*, p. 115.
61 Barron to Bankhead, 10 Jan. 1846, encl. in Barron to Aberdeen, 17 Jan. 1846, No. 1, F.O. 50/203.
62 Hornby to Moresby, 12 Feb. 1851, PHI/2/2. pp. 242–3, N.M.M. On U.S. conveyance, see Hornby to Ward, 29 June 1849, PHI/2/1, p. 154, N.M.M.
63 Cdr. F. M. Norman, '*Martello Tower*' in China and the Pacific in H.M.S. Tribune, *1856–60* (London, 1902), p. 59.
64 After the loss of the *Thetis* in 1830 (see footnote 7, above) care was taken to ensure that 'In all cases of taking up Freight, the vessel is to be examined previous to the conclusion of the Charter Party, as to her state of sea worthiness, equipment and sufficiency of her officers and crew'. Baynes to Commanders, 13 May 1858, Adm. 1/5694, Y191.

XV

THE RECORDS OF THE ROYAL NAVY'S PACIFIC STATION

The rapid growth of Pacific studies in recent years has led to the discovery of many pertinent manuscripts. The records of the Royal Navy on the Pacific Station contain an immense, and still largely untapped, body of information for scholars. The following guide seeks to define the area of jurisdiction of the Commander-in-Chief, Pacific, and the documents at present known, both official and private.

During the nineteenth century British warships were the instrument of Britain's commercial and political policies for the Pacific, a new frontier of maritime enterprise. Early in the century the Admiralty sent ships to the west side of the Americas to guard British commerce and whalers. The creation of a separate station for the Pacific in 1837 was further recognition of British political influence and maritime activity in those seas.[1] This command evolved from and assumed the duties west of Cape Horn of the old South American Station.[2] In the early years the principal tasks were protecting British mercantile interests in Pacific South America during an era of revolution, acting as amphibious diplomatic agents, and shipping specie or merchant moneys from ports as far north as the Gulf of California to England.[3] Warships also went to the Pacific Islands with increasing frequency during the 1830s and 1840s when Britain found her colonial and mercantile aspirations to be in competition with those of France, Russia, and the United States.

This extension of the Royal Navy's influence west of Cape Horn paralleled that in the seas east of the Cape of Good Hope. After the Napoleonic Wars, the Indian Ocean, China Seas, and waters of the Antipodes were visited more often by British naval vessels. The task of ensuring that British traders, missionaries, and consular agents would be free from hostile attack or interference in these vast tracts of water rested with the East Indies and China Station.[4] After 1820 that command extended to the meridian 170°W longitude where it met the western

---

[1] Although Rear-Admiral Charles B. H. Ross was appointed to the command on 4 Sept. 1837, he did not assume 'Command of Her Majesty's Ships and Vessels employed on the Western Coast of America, and in the Pacific', until he entered the station limits in early Mar. 1838: Ross to Wood, 19 Mar. 1838, Adm.1/51. The genesis of the station is explained in John Bach, 'The Royal Navy in the South Pacific, 1826-1876', Ph.D. thesis, University of New South Wales (Sydney, 1964), ch. 2.

[2] Established in 1808.

[3] See Gerald S. Graham and R. A. Humphreys (eds.), The Navy and South America, 1807-1823: Correspondence of the Commanders-in-Chief on the South American Station (London, Navy Records Society, 1962), vol. CIV.

[4] For the boundaries of this and the Cape of Good Hope command, see Gerald S. Graham, Great Britain in the Indian Ocean: A Study of Maritime Enterprise, 1810-1850 (Oxford, 1967), Appendix, 455-9.

extremity of the South American Station. Several subdivisions of the East Indies and China Station followed but, by 1859, the increasing importance of Australia, New Zealand, and the islands of the western Pacific led to the creation of an independent command, the Australian Station.[5] Five years later the China Station became a separate entity charged with halting piracy and protecting British trade and colonial dependencies in those seas. Thus by 1864 the waters within the Pacific rim had been divided into three naval districts: the Pacific, the Australian, and the China stations.

Britain's largest naval station was the Pacific, bounded on the north by Bering Strait, on the south by the Antarctic Circle, on the east by the longitude of Cape Horn, and on the west by 170°W longitude.[6] As such, this command encompassed all the American shores west of the Horn, and all the islands westward to Samoa. The Navy gave special attention to the Galapagos, Hawaiian, Marquesas, Society, and Cook Islands. Pitcairn Island, the landing place of the *Bounty* mutineers in 1790, was closely watched. So, too, were the guano-clad Chincha Islands off the Peruvian coast where the horrors of coolie labour never ceased to shock naval commanders who called to guard British ships engaged in transporting this potent fertilizer. At other places along the coasts of the Americas, as developments warranted, the Pacific command undertook various tasks: encouraging Spanish colonies to win their independence; watching British spheres of influence and communications in Central America; guarding British fur traders on the North Pacific Coast; securing the British colonies there from Indians, American gold seekers, and Britain's two North Pacific rivals, Russia and the United States; and protecting Canadian schooners engaged in sealing in northern waters from American interference.

As for the Pacific Islands, the western limit of the Station receded with the expanding influence in Pacific affairs of the Antipodes and, after 1878, the Western Pacific High Commission. From 1837 until 1866 the meridian of 170°W longitude was the western boundary; then the Admiralty redefined it as 'On the west by the Meridian of 160° West Longitude to 12° North Latitude thence along that parallel to the Meridian of 170° West Longitude and along that Meridian Northward to Behring Strait'.[7] This change established that the Phoenix, Samoan, and Friendly Islands were clearly under the control of the Australian Station. A further limitation of the Pacific Station, along with a subsequent expansion of its Australian counterpart, occurred in 1894 whereby all major groups, exclusive of the Hawaiian, Tuamotu, and Marquesas Islands, were to be served by the Australian Station. Consequently, the intricate western periphery of the Pacific Station became 'the meridian of 149° 30' west longitude [Tahiti], from the Antarctic circle to the equator; thence along that line west to the meridian of 160° west longitude; thence on that meridian northward to 12° north latitude, along that parallel to the meridian of 180°; thence on that meridian north to the shores of Asia'.[8] Such was the bewildering western limit that faced the commander-in-chief until closure of this station in 1905!

[5] Admiralty minute of 25 Mar. 1859, Adm.1/5716.
[6] Herbert to Seymour, 25 July 1844, Adm.172/4.
[7] Reported in Revised Standing Orders to Hillyar, 13 Sept. 1872, Adm.1/6236, pt. 2.
[8] Station Orders, Pacific Station, 1898, p. 7; in Y53, Adm.1/7374.

As the imperial interests of Great Britain expanded from the South Pacific to include the North Pacific as the nineteenth century advanced, the Admiralty looked for a suitable site for a new headquarters of the squadron. From 1843 to 1873 the Navy maintained storeships and sheds at Valparaiso, Chile, and from 1847 to 1865 at Callao, Peru. Because of severe winds, Valparaiso had to be abandoned for Coquimbo. But none of these South American ports, where revolutions were common, could offer a sufficient degree of security as the station headquarters. The Royal Navy, therefore, investigated the Falklands, the Galapagos, Panama, and various positions on the Mexican and Californian coasts.

The solution was found on the southwestern tip of Vancouver Island which had become a British Crown colony in 1849. Although too distant from the South Pacific yet too close to the United States, Esquimalt with its sheltered harbour, its proximity to ample supplies of coal, spars and provisions, and its moderate climate, gave promise of a better naval base than elsewhere available in the eastern Pacific. The Navy used Esquimalt with increasing regularity after 1848.

From 1862 until 1905, when the Royal Navy withdrew to home waters, Esquimalt was for all practical purposes the British naval base of ships on the Pacific Station although the Commander-in-Chief was compelled to leave it for South American waters in the 1860s and 1870s when disputes arose between Chile and Peru.

The source materials dealing with the Pacific Station contain a vast body of information of political, geographical, economic, and sociological importance.[9] Those listed below are held in various repositories in Great Britain and Canada. The Official Pacific Station Records were placed at one time or another in three state repositories: the Public Record Office (London), the Public Archives of Canada (Ottawa), and the Provincial Archives of British Columbia (Victoria, BC). Initially most of these records, accumulated by commanders-in-chief, Pacific, remained at Esquimalt for some years after the transfer of that base in 1910 to Canada, who had assumed responsibility for defending her Pacific shores. In 1923 the largest body of official records of the Pacific Station, numbering thirty-nine volumes (exclusive of the index to the first twenty-two volumes) were deposited by the Admiralty in the Public Archives of Canada direct from Esquimalt.[10] In 1937

[9] The forthcoming *Guide to Manuscripts in the British Isles relating to Australia, New Zealand and the Pacific Islands*, sponsored by the Australian National University and the National Library of Australia, *ed.* P. Mander-Jones, will list Admiralty records dealing with the area 'from the coast of Western Australia to Easter Island and from a curve embracing the Marianas and Hawaiian Islands to the Antarctic'. P. Mander-Jones, 'A guide to manuscripts in the British Isles relating to Australia, New Zealand and the Pacific Islands', *The Journal of Pacific History*, II (1967), 190.

[10] In 1914 the government of British Columbia sought the custody of the records that remained at Esquimalt, but Sir Arthur Doughty, the Dominion Archivist, tried to secure some of them for the Public Archives in Ottawa. At the suggestion of the Admiralty, an arbitrator was chosen to decide the issue between the provincial and federal authorities. Sir Joseph Pope, who had been appointed by the Governor-General, the Duke of Devonshire, ruled in favour of the Public Archives of Canada because the British North America Act, Section 91, gave the Parliament of Canada exclusive jurisdiction in matters relating to 'naval service; defence; navigation and shipping; marine hospitals; quarantine; beacons; buoys; lighthouses; and generally all matters germane thereto'. Quoted in Memorandum of B. Wilson, Public Archives of Canada, to P. Mander-Jones, 5 Mar. 1968, encl. in W. Kaye Lamb to P. Mander-Jones, 7 Mar. 1968, copies in writer's possession.

six volumes of correspondence, which had been returned to the Admiralty in 1914, were divided, three going to the Public Record Office forming Adm. 172/1-3 and three to the Provincial Archives of British Columbia 'on permanent loan'. In 1959 a volume indexing records 1893-1903 (i.e. records in the first twenty-two volumes, now rebound as twenty, at Ottawa) was placed in the Public Record Office forming Adm. 155/1.

Other collections given in the following list include the Esquimalt Naval Establishment Records, maintained by the naval storekeeper and now in the Maritime Museum of British Columbia (Victoria, BC); the private papers of three commanders-in-chief, Pacific—Seymour, Phipps Hornby, and Baynes;[11] and the 'Admiralty Correspondence' as well as the Ships' Letters (correspondence between the administrations of the colonies of Vancouver Island and later British Columbia with naval authorities) in the Provincial Archives of British Columbia.

The list which follows in no way attempts to include all documents relevant to the Royal Navy's Pacific Station. Only the main collections and significant records have been listed. Researchers may unearth further manuscripts dealing with the Pacific Station that could be classified as Station Records. It should also be added that the term 'official' can only be applied to some of the documents listed below. These are divided into the 'Official Records Filed on the Station' and 'Other Official Records', i.e. correspondence and journals sent from the station as well as the Admiralty's copies of out-letters and so forth. A third classification, 'Private Papers', comprises only the major records known to the writer.

The following list is compiled from information kindly supplied by Miss Phyllis Mander-Jones, Director, Guide to Manuscripts Relating to Australia and the Pacific Islands; Dr W. Kaye Lamb, Dominion Archivist, Public Archives of Canada; Mr Willard E. Ireland, Provincial Librarian and Archivist, Provincial Archives, Victoria, BC; Mr A. W. H. Pearsall, Custodian of Manuscripts, National Maritime Museum, Greenwich; and Mr M. W. Farr, County Archivist, County Record Office, Warwick. The writer is especially grateful for the assistance of Miss Phyllis Mander-Jones.

OFFICIAL RECORDS FILED ON THE STATION

Public Record Office, London

Adm. 172/1. 1843-58, contains correspondence and reports concerning the Contract Mail Service (Panama, South America and Great Britain).[12]
Adm. 172/2. 1845-58, contains hydrographical information. It has a list of contents and many reports relate to the Pacific Islands.
Adm. 172/3. 1845-57, relates to the Samoa, Tonga and Fiji groups, and consists of correspondence and reports, with a list of contents.[13]

---

[11] These three collections are the only accessible papers of Commanders-in-Chief, Pacific, known to exist; according to the National Register of Archives, London, the letter-books of Vice-Admiral Sir Arthur Farquhar (Commander-in-Chief, Pacific, 1869-72) are still with the family and are not accessible.
[12] Descriptions *verbatim* from P. Mander-Jones, 'Admiralty Station manuscripts on the Pacific in the Public Record Office, London', *The Journal of Pacific History*, II (1967), 170-1.
[13] Adm. 172/1-3 have been microfilmed for the Australian Joint Copying Project.

Adm. 155/1 [Index 24475]. 1893-1903. An index to the first twenty-two vols[14] (now reorganized as twenty vols) of general correspondence, 1893-1903, held in the Public Archives of Canada.[15]

Public Archives of Canada, Ottawa, Ontario

R.G. 8, III B, Admiralty Pacific Station Records, 1858-1903, 39 vols 7 ft.

Vols. 1-20	General Correspondence, 1893-1903.[16]
Vols. 21-22	Esquimalt Correspondence, 1889-93, 1896-1900.
Vols. 23-32	Bering Sea Correspondence, 1890-99 (includes vols of published correspondence).
Vol. 33	Rough contemporary table of contents relating to vols 1-32.
Vol. 34	Copies of letters relating to Russian territory, 1858-73.
Vol. 35	Copies of letters relating to international subjects, 1859-65.
Vol. 36	First Report of the Royal Commission appointed to enquire into the Defence of British Possessions and Commerce Abroad, together with the Minutes of Evidence and Appendix, Confidential, 1881. (Sir John A. Macdonald represented Canada before the Commission.)
Vol. 36	Third and Final Report of the Royal Commissioners appointed to enquire into the Defence of British Possessions and Commerce Abroad with the Appendix, Minutes of Evidence and Digest of Evidence. Confidential, 1882. (Incomplete.)
Vols. 37-39	Correspondence and reports relating to San Juan Island, 1859-72.

Provincial Archives of British Columbia, Victoria, BC

Great Britain—Admiralty Correspondence. These volumes relate almost solely to the maritime history of the Northwest Coast of America.

2 vols of 'Admiralty Correspondence', covering 1848-59. These records probably were deposited here soon after the closure of the station and are not to be confused with the block of three vols transferred to this repository in 1937 that are listed below.

Vol. I. 'Vancouvers and Queen Charlottes Islands vol. 1'. This contains correspondence from Oct. 1848 to Feb. 1857, comprising dockets 1 to 11. Indexed.

Vol. II. 'Vancouvers and Queen Charlottes Islands vol. 2'. The manuscript title page, however, reads 'Vancouver Island and British Columbia Vol. II'. This contains correspondence from June 1858 to Oct. 1859, comprising dockets 12 to 32. Indexed.

3 vols of Admiralty Correspondence covering 1866-98.[17] These were transferred to this repository in 1937 and are classified as *British Columbia—Records of the Senior Naval Officer stationed at Esquimalt, 1866-1879*. In vols I and II there is a discrepancy between dates of general contents of each vol. and actual inclusions.

Vol. I. 1866-79. Nos 1-54, 8 Feb. 1866-26 Aug. 1881. Indexed.

Vol. II. 1874-81. Nos 55-62. 16 Apr. 1874 only, then 30 Aug. 1877-19 Apr. 1881. Indexed.

Vol. III. 1880-98. 28 Aug. 1889-10 Apr. 1890; only one letter after 1889 included. Rough index.

Maritime Museum of British Columbia, Victoria, BC

Esquimalt Naval Establishment Records, 1861-81. 3 vols. Relating almost solely to the operation of the naval base (victualling yard, magazines, property, coal sheds, etc.).

14 The records of Admirals Stephenson, Palliser and Bickford.
15 The Public Archives of Canada has a microfilm of this index.
16 From the Public Archives of Canada, Manuscripts Division, *Preliminary Inventory: Record Group 8, British Military and Naval Records, 1954* (Ottawa; Queen's Printer, 1955), 25.
17 The Public Archives of Canada has a microfilm copy of these records.

XV

151

OTHER OFFICIAL RECORDS

Public Record Office, London

Adm. 1. (Secretary's In-Letters) for the South America and Pacific Stations.
Adm. 2. (Secretary's Out-Letters).
Adm. 6/70. 1830-44. Papers relating to commissions, appointments and services of the South America and Pacific Stations.
Adm. 12. (Indexes), IND. 4761. Contains brief notes on correspondence and ship movements for the early period of the Pacific Station.
Adm. 50/308-314 and 357-360. Admirals' Journals from the Pacific Station, 1855-1903. Details of correspondence received and sent.
Many other classes contain relevant material such as Logs, Pay Books, Musters, and records of Material and Medical Departments. Entries in the Digests and Indexes, Adm. 10, 11 and 12, supply items of information that have unfortunately been 'weeded'.

National Maritime Museum, Greenwich, SE10

Some Admiralty Records are placed here, notably correspondence of the Navy Board and Victualling Board.

Provincial Archives of British Columbia, Victoria, BC

Letter-book of Governor James Douglas containing copies of letters to naval commanders. This is titled 'Vancouver Island Naval Letters Commencing 6th July 1863 Ending 15th February 1864'. It consists of letters to Rear-Admiral John Kingcome and Commander Hardinge, Senior Naval Officer, plus one letter signed William A. G. Young (the Governor's secretary) addressed to the Hon. H. D. Lascelles, Senior Naval Officer in Command. This volume, while classified as one of six under the series 'Great Britain—Admiralty Correspondence' is suspected to be in fact a 'colonial government' record.[18]
Ships' Letters. Arranged alphabetically by ship. Correspondence between Ships' commanders and the colonial administrations of Vancouver Island and British Columbia relative to the affairs of the Northwest Coast.

PRIVATE PAPERS

Public Record Office, London

Adm. 172/4. In-letters of Rear-Admiral Sir George Francis Seymour, 1844-45, including instructions relating to Consul Pritchard, Queen Pomare and the French Protectorate over Tahiti.[19] This is probably a collection of private correspondence which deals with official business but has been catalogued in the Public Record Office, London, as a volume of Pacific Station Records.

National Maritime Museum, Greenwich[20]

Rear-Admiral Sir Thomas Phipps Hornby, Commander-in-Chief, Pacific, 1847-51.
1. Journal.
PHI/1 Admiral's Journal, 1847-49.
2. Letter & Order Book.
PHI/2/1 Letters to the Admiralty, Sept. 1847-May 1851.

[18] The Report of the Provincial Archivist for 1910, p. N11, uses this term in reference to 'Douglas, James (Governor). Correspondence with Naval Officers'.
[19] Adm.172/4 has been microfilmed for the Australian Joint Copying Project.
[20] Much of what follows is from the lists of the National Maritime Museum.

PHI/2/2   Squadron letters, Nov. 1847-Mar. 1851. Out-letter book kept by Hornby on HMS *Asia*, mainly at Valparaiso.

PHI/2/3   Miscellaneous letters, ministers and consuls, Apr. 1848-Feb. 1851.

3. Loose Papers—Original Letters Received

PHI/3/1   Papers relating generally to British claims on Salvador and Honduras, 1849-50.

PHI/3/2   Papers from Mr Chatfield respecting British claims on Salvador and Honduras and Central America generally, 1848-50.

PHI/3/3   Papers relating to Tigre Island, Central America, 1849-50.

PHI/3/4   Mr Chatfield's suggestions for the occupation of three principal islands in the Gulf of Fonseca (otherwise Bay of the Union). Views of HM Government thereon, 1849.

PHI/3/5   Question of Hudson's Bay Company interests on the Northwest Coast. California—(future after the Mexican war finished), 1848. Reports on Vancouver Island—number of Indian tribes and population, 1848.

PHI/3/6   Sandwich and Society Island and Captain Fanshawe's last report relative to Pitcairn's Island. Honolulu, 1848—despatches sent to Palmerston, 1847-48, documents relative to Sandwich and Society Islands, 1848, sent out from Flag Officer for information of Hornby. Pitcairn's Island, 1850—copies of despatches of 1848-49.

PHI/3/7   Valparaiso—Storeship *Nereus* and hired stores and provisions supplied by contract, 1849-51.

PHI/3/8   Wages of Merchant Seamen entering HM Service, 1849-51.

PHI/3/9   Miscellaneous letters on various subjects—conveyance of Chilean subjects from California to Valparaiso, Aug. 1849. Postal arrangements across Panama. Plan to construct a railway, June 1850. Extent of scurvy at Valparaiso, Nov. 1850.

PHI/3/10   Case of Lt James King, HMS *Inconstant*, 1849.

PHI/3/11   Case of Lt George Brine, HMS *Champion*, 1850.

PHI/3/12   Valparaiso Sick Quarters, 1849-50.

PHI/3/13   HMS *Gorgon*—defective state on leaving England, 1850.

PHI/3/14   Military Revolution in Guayaquil, 1850.

PHI/3/15   Letters from the Admiralty. Includes orders for HMS *Enterprise* to look for Franklin, 1850, in the Arctic. Flag Officer's ruling re the Galapagos Islands, 1848. Case in relations with French Squadron, 1848.
Letter from Moresby (Rear Admiral).

PHI/3/16   Alterations to HMS *Swift*, 1850.
Report in French on navigation and information re islands etc. in Pacific signed Barazer, 1851.
Letter from Admiral Seymour on relinquishing command to Hornby, 1848.
Correspondence re building of a railway across the Isthmus of Panama.

PHI/4, MS 58/097. Press cuttings etc. relating to the period of Sir Phipps Hornby arranged by Cdr W. Phipps Hornby, 1958. 1 folder.

Rear-Admiral Sir Robert Lambert Baynes, Commander-in-Chief, Pacific, 1857-60.

BAY/1   Service Career. 1810-65. Commissions, certificates, decorations, also an autobiographical note on his career, 1810-57.

BAY/2   Official Papers. 1821-57. Letters, orders and some ships' records. Ten folders, one folio book and two small notebooks, one of which gives much detail on ships and their movements.

BAY/3   Personal Papers. 1832-50. Personal papers including some invitations to Court Balls. One envelope.

153

Captain Sir F.G.D. Bedford

BED/5 Diary of HMS *Shah*, 1877, containing an account of the action with the Peruvian ironclad *Huascar*.

BED/6 Diary of HMS *Triumph*, 1869.

British Museum, London

Letter-book of Sir Henry Byam Martin containing copies of his official letters while in command of HMS *Grampus*, 17 Nov. 1845-16 Oct. 1847. Martin Papers, Vol. CXXV, Add. MSS 41470.

Journal of HMS *Grampus*, Sir Henry Byam Martin, 17 Nov. 1845-20 Oct. 1848. Martin Papers, Vol. CXVII, Add. MSS 41472.

County Record Office, Shire Hall, Warwick[21]

The Seymour of Ragley Collection includes the papers of Rear-Admiral Sir George Francis Seymour, Commander-in-Chief, Pacific, 1844-47. These contain much material relating to a most important period of Pacific history. At this time the rivalries with France and the United States for influence in the Society Islands, the Hawaiian Islands, Oregon and California commanded the attention of the Royal Navy.

CR114A/412/1, 2. Journal as Commander-in-Chief. 1844-47. Two vols.

CR114A/413. Signal log of HMS *Collingwood, Modeste, Salamander* and other ships on the station. List of names and armaments of foreign vessels sighted at end. 1844-48.

CR114A/414/1, 2. Special order books: registers to ships on the station. May 1844-Jan. 1848. Indexed. Two vols.

CR114A/415/1, 2. Squadron letter-books: registers of orders. [415/2 also labelled 'Special Order Book']. Dec. 1844-July 1848. Part indexed. Two vols.

CR114A/416/1, 2. Official letter-books: registers of letters to the Board of Admiralty. May 1844-Apr. 1849. Indexed. Two vols.

CR114A/417/1, 2. Miscellaneous letter-books: registers of letters mainly to Consuls, Governor-Generals and other British officials (including naval) on the station. July 1844-July 1848. Indexed. Two vols.

CR114A/418/1-4. Private letter-books: registers of unofficial letters relating to naval matters and policy, also personal business correspondence. Sept. 1844-Nov. 1850.

CR114A/419. Rough notebook. Autograph. 1844-46.

CR114A/420. Miscellaneous memoranda for letters and orders. *c*. 1837-47. One bundle.

CR114A/421. Accounts and notes of visits to places in the Pacific Station and on the east coast of South America e.g. Guayaquil, Chatham Is., Panama, Rio de Janeiro. 1845-48. One bundle. Autograph.

CR114A/422A. 'Memorandum on difficulties which occurred relative to the appropriation of the ships under my command during the first six months after my arrival in the Pacific. A detail of temporary perplexities only . . .' N.d., *c*. 1846. Autograph.

CR114A/422B. Chart: 'Track of Sir G. F. Seymour to and from N America in 1840 and of HMS *Collingwood* bearing his flag to and from the South Seas in 1844 and 1848.' N.d., after 1848.

---

21 From the lists of the County Record Office, Warwick.

XVI

Canada and the North Pacific, 1871–1914: Problems of a Lion's Cub in an Open Den

In the years between 1871 and 1914, several nations—notably Russia, France, Germany, and Great Britain—exercised a growing influence in the Pacific and along its rim. Canada, possessing in British Columbia "the Empire's Pacific frontier,"[1] had a vested interest in the affairs and future of that great ocean. However, even though Canadian commercial and missionary activity in the Pacific and Asia was increasing during this period, Canada did not mount anything resembling a national presence in the Pacific. Thus, prior to 1914 Canadians did not establish a navy capable of patrolling the coast of British Columbia. Moreover, successive Canadian governments in this era avoided commitments with Australia and New Zealand for Pacific naval cooperation. Instead, they placed their faith in railways, cables, and steamships, in British naval power, in cordial Anglo-American relations, and in the Anglo-Japanese alliance, signed in 1902 and extended in 1911. In this way, it may be argued, they were pursuing a national point of view evidenced as early as 1862 during the debate over the Canadian Militia Bill. According to one authority, "the explanation of the country's apparent

1. Commentary by A. J. Dawson on F. B. Vrooman, *British Columbia and Her Imperial Outlook* (Paper read before the Royal Colonial Institute, 19 March 1912), Duke University Pamphlet Collection, Durham, N.C., p. 17.

XVI

Canada and the North Pacific

apathy . . . was neither lukewarmness towards the British connexion . . . nor a spiritless reluctance to make sacrifices for the preservation of the province's national existence. It was first, a lack of conviction of the serious probability of war, and, secondly, a failure to appreciate the gravity of Canada's situation in the event of war occurring."[2]

Yet it would be wrong to deny the importance of the Pacific in Canadian attitudes and development during the period under review. It will be shown here that the Pacific and its potential markets lured Canadians westward to its shores, that that vast ocean developed as a path of national and imperial communications by steamship and submarine cable, that it provided the nascent nation with new fields of commercial opportunity, and that its strategic problems contributed to British Columbia's confederation with Canada in 1871. It will also be shown that territorial complications in Alaska and Hawaii were of significance to Canadians as were pelagic sealing and freedom of navigation in the Bering Sea. In all these ways it can be demonstrated that during this time the Pacific was not exactly a backwater to Canadian strategic interests. More generally, this study may provide further evidence that the Pacific has offered Canadians opportunities and problems.[3] It may also give further indication as to why in time of peace successive Canadian governments sought to avoid military commitments in their own behalf or that of the British Empire, but instead concentrated on resolving border or trade problems with the United States, and, at the same time, developed railway and telegraphic communications to encourage transcontinental and interoceanic bonds with sister nations in the emerging British Empire-Commonwealth.

For four centuries beginning with the fifteenth, the Pacific was a determinant in Canadian history. Its riches drew men to it from

2. C. P. Stacey, *Canada and the British Army, 1846–1871* (rev. ed., Toronto, 1963), pp. 135–36.
3. Each generation Canadians seemingly rediscover the Pacific and the Orient. Pierre Elliott Trudeau's *Foreign Policy for Canadians* (Ottawa, 1970) is an example of this. For another, see Lorne J. Kavic, "Canada and Asia: Evolving Awareness and Deepening Links," *Pacific Affairs*, 45 (Fall 1972), 521–34. For earlier views, the following are noteworthy: C. P. Woodsworth, *Canada and the Orient* (Toronto, 1941), A. R. M. Lower, *Canada and the Far East—1940* (New York, 1940), and N. A. M. Mackenzie, "Canada and the Changing Balance of Power in the Pacific," in *The Empire and the League* (Toronto, 1936).

Europe and America; its hazards necessitated maritime technological development; its shores were conquered by numerous nation-states. It was, in general, a place of invasion by the Western whites "who, with their accompanying diseases, animals, plants, institutions, and ideologies created a vast panorama of moving frontiers which produced some of the greatest changes of physical and cultural landscape that mankind has witnessed."[4] However, no nation was strong enough to claim the Pacific as its own. The sheer vastness of the Pacific Ocean is sufficient in itself to explain the frailty of British maritime authority during the nineteenth century.

But the British came as close as any nation to maintaining a hegemony: even the shrinking dimensions of the *Pax Britannica* allowed Britain and her outlying dominions great influence within the Pacific littoral in the nineteenth century, but only as long as British naval strength—divided into three widely dispersed squadrons—was maintained at its minimum level. In 1874, when stringent Gladstonian economies prevailed, the China station, then the largest squadron in the British fleet, had 20 ships and 2,428 men, the Australian station had 9 ships and 1499 men, and the Pacific station 9 ships and 924 men.[5] These ships and the men who manned them were really the illusion of power, capable of being reinforced when necessary from the great sea base of Great Britain and the several naval bases acquired in various quarters of the world before or during the Napoleonic Wars. In the Pacific, as elsewhere at this time, the white ensign on Her Majesty's ships symbolized orderly commerce, protection from piracy in certain areas, free trade, and charting of the seas. No European rival would dare interfere with British naval predominance.

British naval protection was accorded automatically and at no cost to Canada as a self-governing dominion, and to the two emerging imperial partners in the South Pacific, New Zealand, and Australia. This protection was also given to Singapore and the Malay States, adjacent to coveted trade channels of the eastern seas; to Hong Kong, the entrepôt of trade at one end of the long chain of bases and ports stretching from the Cape of Good Hope to the China Seas; to

4. Archibald Grenfell Price, *The Western Invasion of the Pacific and Its Continents: A Study of Moving Frontiers and Changing Landscapes 1513–1958* (Oxford, 1963), p. v.
5. Great Britain, *Parliamentary Papers*, 1876 (225), XLV, 522–23.

Weihaiwei, the British bastion on the Yellow Sea after 1898; and to the Falkland Islands, at the southeastern entrance of the Pacific. Farther north, British protection extended to British informal empires in such places as Peru, Chile, and Ecuador. Still farther north, at the Isthmus of Panama, the British Empire had territorial claims dating from Elizabethan times and by treaty with the United States in 1850 the rights to joint development of a transisthmian canal, rights which she would release at the end of the century to the United States. The British had a small naval base at Tobago on the Pacific side of the isthmus. West of Latin America, at various dots across the Pacific, the imperial presence was being exercised: for instance, at Pitcairn Island, Norfolk Island, and Fiji, the last two added to the British Empire for strategic reasons.

But from the Canadian perspective, British Columbia was the most important part of the Empire fronting on the Pacific. Developed in the late eighteenth century as the focal point of a lucrative but short-lived British trade in sea-otter pelts, it came under Canadian commercial control through North West Company auspices in the early nineteenth century. This company initiated Canadian west-coast trade with China, using furs from Athabaska and New Caledonia. This initiative led Sir Alexander MacKenzie and other Canadian promoters of empire to envision a corridor of trade across the North-west to Pacific shores and thence to Asia. The trade was a marginal success and was taken over by the Hudson's Bay Company upon merger with the Nor'westers in 1821. From that time forward to the 1870's, it became diversified: company agents sold Fraser River salmon, packed in barrels, in San Francisco, Hawaii, and Tahiti. They marketed Northwest Coast spars, deals, and other timber in Canton. The company's agricultural subsidiaries sold produce to Russians on the northern Northwest Coast from 1839 to 1867. Thus furs, salmon, timber, and agricultural produce were established as exports of the British Columbia economy in the Pacific rim by the late 1850's.

After the discovery of coal on Vancouver Island in 1850 and of gold in British Columbia in 1857, exports in these products developed rapidly. Coal in particular added to the strategic value of British Columbia. Steam navigation and railways aided the process by which British Columbia built up an extensive export trade in products of the forest, farm, mountains, and sea. Gold and silver, lead and copper, pulp and paper, fish and timber were the commodities that brought profits for Canada's Pacific province. In 1901, in metalliferous mining alone, production totalled $20,080,780, almost six times that of a decade earlier.[6]

In these circumstances, British Columbia's entrepreneurs, promoters, and politicians knew very well that seaborne trade on the North Pacific coast and across the Pacific was the source of their wealth and their hope for the future. Yokohama, Hong Kong, Shanghai, Brisbane, Sydney, and Auckland were considerably closer to the new port of Vancouver than they were to London. Small wonder Vancouver's promoters applied to it such appellations as the new "Constantinople of the Pacific," the "Terminal City," the "City of Imperial Destiny." They regarded its harbor entrance, "Lion's Gate," as the Britannic access to the Pacific, the Canadian counterpart to San Francisco's "Golden Gate." Moreover, they looked on the completion of the Panama Canal to reduce the routes from Europe to British Columbia by some nine thousand miles. They looked, too, for interimperial preferential trade duties that would further stimulate trans-Pacific trade between Canada and the Antipodes.[7]

Meanwhile, the British and Canadian presence in the North Pacific was dramatically changed by British and Canadian constitutional and political decisions to outflank what their respective parliaments regarded as "Manifest Destiny." The British government granted a charter to the Hudson's Bay Company in 1849 to counter the possibility of an American squatter settlement at Vancouver Island. In 1858 the same government brought British Columbia into existence as a colony proper in order to forestall any projected American filibuster. In 1866, these colonies were united, and not least among the reasons for their doing so was Governor Frederick Seymour's desire that "British authority, British influence, and British power in the Pacific" be increased.[8] And in 1871 British

6. See, for instance, A. R. Colquhoun, *The Mastery of the Pacific* (London, 1904), pp. 217–18; R. E. Gosnell, *The Year Book of British Columbia and Manual of Provincial Information* [for 1903] (Victoria, B.C., 1903), p. 138.

7. The CPR promoted this idea. One of its publications, *The Imperial Highway* (1912), by A. N. Homer, F.R.G.S., put it this way: "Without question it may be said of Vancouver that her position, geographically, is Imperial to a degree, that her possibilities are enormous, and that with but a feeble stretch of the imagination those possibilities might wisely be deemed certainties" (p. 84). See also Margaret A. Ormsby, *British Columbia: A History* (Toronto, 1971), pp. 298–300.

8. Governor F. Seymour to E. Cardwell (Secretary of State for the Colonies), 17 Feb. 1866, Confidential Print, C.O. 880/5, No. 37, p. 38.

Columbia became part of the recently developed Canadian confederation for reasons of increasing security with respect to the United
States, which in 1867 had acquired Alaska, and of increasing the
prosperity of the province.

Two strategic considerations were involved in British Columbia's
union with Canada. The first was naval. Esquimalt became Pacific
fleet headquarters in 1862 as the result of the Admiralty's recognition
of the growth of British interests in British Columbia. The Gladstone
ministry urged retrenchment in naval expenditure and so in 1869 the
fleet headquarters was withdrawn to Valparaiso, Chile. Two years
later, however, British Columbian politicians exacted a promise from
the Canadians that pressure would be exerted on the British government to maintain Esquimalt as a naval base: this decision was subsequently made, and Esquimalt was restored to its former importance.
The British Columbians also wanted a graving dock, a view also held
by a succession of British admirals on Pacific station since the
mid-1850's. But costs remained an important consideration. Finally
in 1887 a graving dock was opened at Esquimalt. It was capable of
holding the largest of British warships in the Pacific. Now the Royal
Navy was independent of American or Chilean drydocks for normal
repairs. And Esquimalt's importance in imperial defense greatly increased, though, of course, it also presented problems of defense,
especially during the Penjdeh or Afghanistan crisis of 1885, when
war with Russia was a near reality. The contribution of the dock to
the growth of Canadian and imperial mercantile shipping in the
Pacific is also notable, especially with regard to the Canadian Pacific
Railway's trans-Pacific steamship line which began in the same year,
1887, with regular service to Japan and extensions to other Asian
ports.[9] We will return to the strategic implications of this service
later.

The second strategic consideration involving British Columbia's
confederation with Canada was the promise of a railroad to be completed within ten years and to run from the St. Lawrence to Esquimalt, in 1873 designated as the Pacific terminus. The Canadian
Pacific Railway lay uncompleted until 1886 for reasons of finance

---

9. Barry M. Gough, *The Royal Navy and the Northwest Coast of North America,
1810–1914: A Study of British Maritime Ascendancy* (Vancouver, 1971), pp. 169–96,
223–27.

and geography, but the point here is that it completed the Canadian imperial design. It fulfilled a resolution of the House of Commons in 1879 "That the Pacific Railway would form an Imperial Highway across the Continent of America entirely on British soil, and would form a new and important route from England to Australia, to India and to all the dependencies of Great Britain in the Pacific, as also to China and Japan."[10] Also in this scheme of things the Canadian west would be peopled, trade would advance, and the nation made more secure from American expansion. For some Canadians, British Columbia took on a new significance. George Parkin, a pro-Empire Canadian, put it this way:

British Columbia, insignificant in population, was significant enough in position and some of its resources. It fronted on the Pacific; it had splendid harbours and abundant coal; it supplied a new base of sea power and commercial influence; it suggested a new and short pathway to the Orient and Australasia. The statesmen at Ottawa who in 1867 began to look over the Rockies to continents beyond the Pacific were not wanting in imagination; many claimed that their imagination outran their reason; but in the rapid course of events their dreams have already been more than justified.[11]

Sir John A. Macdonald, the prime minister, was of a similar mind about the larger implications of the railway. As one historian has stated, he was more concerned with the railway as "a strategic measure for external defence" than as a means of binding the nation together.[12] The reason for this seems clear: Canada had a vested interest in imperial defense, and a Canadian interoceanic railway would assist Canada in her own security.

This position, adopted by the government, was well stated by Canadian delegates to the Colonial Conference of 1887. They argued that "The Queen's Highway," paid for by Canadians, enabled Britain to supply the Pacific squadron at Esquimalt with munitions, provisions, and men, and allowed the War Office to transport troops and stores through the Queen's North American territories to Pacific

10. Quoted in James C. Bonar, *British Columbia and the Highway to the Far East* (n.p., n.d. 1945 [?]), p. 3.
11. George Parkin, *The Great Dominion: Studies of Canada* (London, 1895), p. 159.
12. Richard A. Preston, "Defending the Undefended Border," (MS in the process of publication), ch. 2. I am obliged to the author for allowing me to see this manuscript in advance of publication.

XVI

shores and beyond. Urgent and perishable stores could be sent from Halifax to Esquimalt in seven days in contrast to the three months or more via Cape Horn or the six weeks via the Isthmus of Panama. Mails and telegrams could be sent across imperial rather than American territory, thus eliminating a potentially dangerous situation in the event of an Anglo-American war.[13]

Above all, the new Canadian railway gave the Empire a certain war route to the Pacific for conveying troops and foodstuffs. The availability of such a route was significant because by the 1880's ministers in Whitehall had come to realize that the Suez Canal could be blocked by a belligerent by "a mere turn of the helm" and the route by way of the Cape of Good Hope might in certain circumstances be endangered. This view was particularly strong at the time of the Penjdeh crisis of 1885 when British strategists quickly became aware of the Russian desire to develop her North Pacific ports across the Pacific from Vancouver Island, which now took on added importance. In 1886 the Intelligence Department of the War Office sent Captain Leonard Darwin, R.E., to appraise the military capabilities of the Canadian Pacific Railway. He reported that its steamships and railways could transport troops from Liverpool to Port Moody, at Pacific tidewater, in 14 days in summer and 14½ in winter. This was the quickest route to the east if Suez was closed. He noted, however, that the CPR was vulnerable to American attack, a fact well recognized in Canada.[14]

With regard to the trans-Pacific steamship service, Canadian and British strategists regarded it as an essential extension of the railway. The initiative came from Ottawa, but the project's military potential appealed to both governments. Studies were initiated as to its effectiveness and the results justified the expectations of the railway promoters. Initially, the CPR chartered sailing ships, which dodged

---

13. Ibid., ch. 4, citing _The Canadian Militia Gazette_, 3 (3 Nov. 1887), p. 142 and reply in ibid., No. 10, 1887, p. 149. See also views of General Selby Smith, in _Militia Report_ (1879); Maurice Ollivier (comp.), _The Colonial and Imperial Conferences from 1837 to 1887_ (3 vols; Ottawa, 1954), I, 42–44, 52–53; II, 92–93, 96, 120–21, 124, 128, 144; John E. Kendle, _The Colonial and Imperial Conferences, 1887–1911: A Study in Imperial Organization_ (London, 1967), pp. 7–13.

14. Memorandum by Major-General Sir A. Clarke, Inspector-General of Fortifications, in "Report of the Committee . . . on the Canadian Pacific Railway for . . . a Line of Steamers . . . ," June 1886, Confidential Print, C.O. 88019, vol. 116, pp. 20–22. Memorandum on the Canadian Pacific Railway from an Imperial Point of View . . . by Captain R.L. Darwin, R. E., March 1886, F.O. 881/5207.

Chinese pirates and brought teas to Canada. They made the return trip with Canadian staples. Later, the route was taken over by three steamers, and, beginning in 1891, by the three Empresses—*India*, *China*, and *Japan*. These coal-burning vessels were not large, with gross tonnage under 6000 tons each, but they were designed as crack auxiliary cruisers according to Admiralty specifications. They could mount eight 4.7-inch guns in wartime, as one of them did, steam at an average of 16 knots, and be used as troopships. They carried Empire mails under a £60,000 annual subsidy from the imperial government. Their fortnightly sailings between Vancouver and Tokyo and Yokohama symbolized both Canadian commercial aspirations in the Pacific and imperial desires to be ready for war in an ocean which might be difficult to reinforce quickly with naval power. In 1893, an Australian line instituted a Vancouver to Brisbane and Sydney run under subsidies from the Canadian and certain Australian colonial governments. The Pacific passage of 19½ days made this the quickest route from England to Australia.[15]

The emergence of the services of these steamships was not unrelated to promotions simultaneously undertaken by Canadians and other citizens of the British Empire for a trans-Pacific cable. The project particularly attracted Canadians, but Australians and, to a lesser degree, New Zealanders who sought commercial expansion and military security were similarly interested. But with the British government content with existing telegraphic links to Australasia via the Eastern Extension Telegraph Company and that company's lowering its rates in order to forestall the Canadian proposal at the Colonial Conference of 1887, the Pacific cable was slow to win the approval of the British treasury.[16] Sandford Fleming, CPR investor, engineer, and promoter *extraordinaire*, championed the idea. "Canadians," he said, "may fairly claim that they have some right to press the matter of cable extension in the Pacific from a national point of view, since such an extension would be the natural complement of what they have done towards British consolidation. The great enterprise by which the Dominion has been spanned by a transcontinental railway and telegraph system has not only opened up new and immense fields

15. W. Kaye Lamb, "Empress to the Orient," 2 pts. *British Columbia Historical Review*, 4 (Jan., Apr. 1940), 29–47, 79–110. James Croil, *Steam Navigation and Its Relation to the Commerce of Canada and the United States* (Toronto, 1898), p. 164.
16. Kendle, *Colonial and Imperial Conferences*, p. 11.

XVI

for national growth but has made great changes in the strategic relations of the empire."[17] Fleming, who as early as the 1860's had toyed with the idea of a cable across to Asia by way of the Aleutian and Kurile Islands, became in the late 1880's the moving spirit behind laying a cable from Bamfield, British Columbia, to Brisbane, Queensland.

Along the path of this particular "all-red route" lay Oahu and other Hawaiian islands, where the Americans had made substantial inroads as missionaries, planters, traders, and advisors to governments. Fleming and Macdonald seem to have considered extending Canadian trade with Honolulu in the 1880's, but they were also motivated by strategic reasons. The United States government and its consuls watched CPR agents with some concern, noting their "aggressive plans to secure Pacific commerce and to gain political and commercial influence" in the Hawaiian Islands. They regarded the cable project as no "idle dream" and John L. Stevens, the U.S. minister in Hawaii, warned the State Department that American interests should be safeguarded by annexing Hawaii. A further indication of American concern that the British were about to preempt the Americans at Honolulu is the recent historical discovery that a telegram sent by the British consul in San Francisco to the British admiral at Esquimalt asking that a gunboat be dispatched to Honolulu to protect Empire interests was delayed in the Western Union telegraph office, doubtless at United States government instructions.[18] The delay gave the Americans time enough to get their own naval vessels to Honolulu ahead of the British.

In these moves and countermoves, the Canadians seem to have been no less devious than the Americans. Fleming, anxious that the Dominions and Britain build an all-British, state-owned Pacific cable and secure a mid-Pacific island as a way station, engaged in his own imperialistic venture. He hired a retired naval officer living in Ontario and sent him to Hawaii to raise the Union Jack over nearby Necker Island, an unclaimed islet not far distant from the islands of

---

17. Canada, *Sessional Papers*, 1893, no. 35, pp. 6–7.
18. John L. Stevens to John W. Foster (Secretary of State), 20 Nov. 1892, quoted in W. J. Illerbrun, "A Selective Survey of Canadian-Hawaiian Relations," *Pacific Northwest Quarterly*, 63 (July 1972), 95: Barry Rigby, "The Grant Administration and the Pacific Islands, 1869–1877," (M.A. Thesis in History, University of Hawaii, 1972), pp. 188–89.

the Hawaiian Kingdom. The whole plot, however, was abortive. The Hawaiian Kingdom, fearing a Canadian filibuster, sent a minister of government and a gunboat to Necker Island to extend Hawaiian sovereignty. There they fortunately avoided the British protected cruiser *Champion* from Esquimalt that happened to be engaged in gun practice nearby.[19] Britain was displeased because the event upset the Foreign Office's own plan to negotiate with the Hawaiian Kingdom for the island. As for Fleming, his design had been exposed. However, his project lived on, if in a different form. The Dominions and British governments, who agreed at the 1894 Colonial Conference that a cable be laid via a neutral mid-Pacific point, found an alternative route—via Fanning instead of Necker Island. In 1902, the cable was laid, thus completing an important all-red route across the Pacific, in peace and war, and British, Canadian, Australian, and New Zealand governments contributed to its cost.

As far as Hawaii is concerned, MacDonald and the Canadian cabinet had favored an extension of trade in the 1880's and the idea of reciprocity of tariffs. They listened to Hawaiian proposals for closer ties. However, they never acted to solidify them by trade treaty, probably because American interests in the Islands were substantial and growing, and the political chaos within the Kingdom was not something in which the growing Dominion wished to be involved.[20] By 1898, the United States annexation of Hawaii was completed, and the Canadians seemingly had all they wanted in the way of the then projected cable.

With regard to certain other places in the North Pacific, the Canadians and their government were not so demure. Three events brought tensions involving strategic questions in Canadian-British-American relations. The North Atlantic triangular relationship often involved North Pacific problems. These were, in turn, the gold rush in the Yukon, the Alaska boundary dispute, and the Bering Sea question.

Maritime access to the Yukon territory, the Eldorado of the late 1890's, was by way of sea-lanes stretching from Seattle, San Fran-

19. Illerbrun, "Canadian-Hawaiian Relations," p. 99. For a version sympathetic to Fleming, see Lawrence Burpee, *Sandford Fleming: Empire Builder* (London, 1915).
20. W. H. Ellis, Managing Editor of the Victoria *Daily Colonist*, was keenly aware of the relationship of British Columbia to the Pacific. Ottawa was not of the same view. Merze Tate, "Canada's Interest is the Trade and Sovereignty of Hawaii," *Canadian Historical Review*, 44 (March 1963), 34–42, passim.

cisco, and Vancouver to the mouths of the Stikine, Yukon, and Porcupine Rivers. Canadians nominally possessed rights of navigation on these rivers under the Treaty of Washington, 1871. However, United States customs officials and justices often imposed restrictions to the benefit of American shipping interests and at the expense of their Canadian counterparts. The Canadian government sought to secure alternate sea-routes to the Yukon territory, and negotiated with the United States for a port on Lynn Canal. They also sought a redefinition of the Anglo-Russian Treaty of 1825.

They succeeded in neither, and in the end the differences between the diplomatic positions of the United States and Canada served to heighten the Canadian response with respect to the second matter under consideration, the Alaska Boundary question.[21] The Canadian diplomatic position was based on uncertain claims inherited from Britain as a result of the treaty of 1825. With President Theodore Roosevelt of the United States threatening to send troops and gunboats and, if necessary, to "run the line on his own hook," Canadian and British governments were forced to submit to an arbitration of claims. This did not uphold the Canadian position. The bitterness of the Canadian commissioners and press regarding the ill success of their case in 1903 is an example of colonial nationalism emerging at a time of imperial aims for Anglo-American *rapprochement*.

While Canadian failure in this quarter of the North Pacific littoral left a deep impression on the Canadian conscience, the Bering Sea case had quite a different outcome. Here Canadian and British positions with respect to freedom of the seas and compensation for commercial loss were successful. In the late 1880's, pelagic sealing in the Bering Sea became a contentious issue in Canadian-American relations. This industry occupied an important position in the maritime economy of British Columbia, especially in Victoria. In 1901, for instance, British Columbian sealers took 24,442 skins, and of these almost half were from the Bering Sea. The United States State Department, however, claimed the Bering Sea as *mare clausum*, because it was, so they claimed, related to United States territorial claims in Alaska.[22] According to this American diplomatic stance,

21. We now know about Canadian ambitions and rhetoric with respect to this dispute. See Norman Penlington, *The Alaska Boundary Dispute: A Critical Reappraisal* (Toronto and New York, 1972).

22. Gosnell, *Yearbook* [for 1903], p. 235; Robert Craig Brown, *Canada's National*

waters adjacent to the American-owned Pribilof Islands, the main rookery of seals, came within United States jurisdiction. The British and Canadian position was just the opposite: that freedom of the seas existed and that the United States did not have control over pelagic sealing in the Bering Sea. At one point in the dispute, in 1886, United States revenue cutters captured Canadian sealers and condemned them for taking seals, contrary to the laws of the United States, in waters over which that country claimed jurisdiction. The British government protested this act as unjustifiable, and the British admiral on the Pacific station was about to seize the United States cutters in turn and free the Canadian ships as they sailed south through Canadian waters. The Foreign Office, however, now brought somewhat closer to Her Majesty's warships by telegraphic communications, cancelled his orders.[23] The British pursued the matter in diplomacy, both nations agreed to arbitration, and in 1903 a Paris tribunal upheld the British and Canadian case, and Canadian sealing interests were compensated for damages. Meanwhile, from the 1880's to 1903, the Royal Navy kept two or three vessels on patrol in this portion of the North Pacific protecting Canadian interests.

In each of four imbroglios then—Hawaii, the Yukon, the Alaska boundary, and Bering Sea—the interests of Canada and the Empire had been involved. Territorial claims, commercial benefits, or Canadian claims to sovereignty or trade were root causes of Canadian involvement. The Pacific and its littoral, especially that portion contiguous to Canadian soil, were bringing the fledgling nation into touch with the diplomatic thrusts of the United States in Hawaii, in Alaska, in the Bering Sea, and the process was painful and not always rewarding.

During this same era the Canadian position on these specific issues generally was somewhat compromised or made more uncertain by what might be called the shrinking dimensions of the *Pax Britannica*. It seems not surprising that the Canadians were least successful where the British were least powerful—in the North Pacific. In that ocean the British could no longer claim a semblance of a maritime hegemony, the illusory nature of which we have al-

Policy 1883–1900: A Study in Canadian-American Relations (Princeton, N.J., Princeton University Press, 1964), pp. 7, 42–54.

23. The correspondence between Rear-Admiral C. F. Heneage and the Admiralty dealing with this "near run thing" is in Adm. 1/6914.

XVI

ready noted. By 1890 the United States Navy was superior to the
Royal Navy squadron in the eastern Pacific. For this reason in 1901
and again in 1902, Rear Admiral A. K. Bickford, the commander-
in-chief on the Pacific station, warned the Admiralty of the "danger-
ously weak state" of the squadron under his command. His squadron
had ten ships of all sorts, including two torpedo boats and a sail-
powered survey ship, against his United States counterpart of nine-
teen warships of all classes. Their Lordships, however, could do
nothing except chide him for his complaints and disrespect. In truth,
the need for warships in European waters and China seas meant that
the fleet operating out of Esquimalt had necessarily to be less than
adequate to protect British interests. As Admiral Bickford well knew,
in a possible diplomatic crisis over the Alaska boundary or the interoceanic canal across Panama, the Pacific squadron would be unable to support British diplomacy and would reluctantly have to acquiesce to American demands. The Admiralty acknowledged that it
could no longer be paramount in every ocean.[24] No doubt this fact
accounts for the growing desires in Britain for *rapprochement* with
the United States and peaceful resolution of conflicting claims in
Alaska, Venezuela, and Panama.

   Because of these momentous changes, Canadian national interests
in the North Pacific were beyond her control: the British were seeking an end to their commitments in defending the British dominions,
and the rise of rival naval powers was directly affecting Canada's
involvement in the North Pacific. Sir John A. Macdonald's prediction
of 1871 that once the British ceased to have naval supremacy the
coast of British Columbia would be "at the mercy of the American
fleet" had come true.[25] Moreover, Japan's growth as a modern industrial and military power, so obvious as a result of the Sino-
Japanese War of 1894–95 and the Russo-Japanese War of 1904–5,
Russia's construction of the Trans-Siberian Railway to Vladivostok,
and Germany's inroads in Samoa and Kaiochow, altered the balance
of international relations in the western Pacific. No longer could

   24. Gilbert N. Tucker, *The Naval Service of Canada: Its Official History* (2 vols.;
Ottawa, 1952), I, 84; Minute of Admiral Walter T. Kerr, 14 Oct. 1901, Adm. 1/7513.
   25. Sir John A. Macdonald to Charles Tupper, n.d. [1871?], Macdonald Papers,
Madonald-Tupper Correspondence, II, 165ff, Public Archives of Canada, Ottawa;
quoted in Goldwin Smith, "Notes on the Problems of San Juan," *Pacific Northwest
Quarterly*, 31 (1940), 185.

British naval power preserve the Chinese Empire from the Great
Powers. In these unsettling circumstances, Britain signed an alliance
with Japan in 1902 to offset her growing inferiority in sea power in
the Pacific. This alliance was, at the bottom, an insurance policy for
the British, and was aimed initially at the Russians. After the Russo-
Japanese War of 1904–5, the alliance was probably directed against
Germany.[26]

But Canadians, especially British Columbians, did not like it, tied
as it seemingly was to the immigration of Asiatics. There were nearly
5,000 Japanese in Canada in 1902, but increased immigration led to
riots in Nanaimo in 1913 and Vancouver in 1907. The provincial
government of British Columbia persistently sought to restrict Asiatic
immigration, employment, and political rights. Chinese were subject
to a "head tax." The Japanese, regarded in Canada as a more serious
threat because of their nation's enhanced stature following the
Russo-Japanese War and their entrenched commercial positions in
southern Manchuria and Korea, were regarded as a potential fifth
column. The Canadian government sent its minister of labour,
Rudolphe Lemieux, to Tokyo in 1907 and by the "Gentleman's
Agreement" of January 1908, Japanese immigration was limited to
400 per year. In each of the years 1911 through 1915, this number
was exceeded.[27]

This record tended to give added evidence to those who did not
regard the Gentleman's Agreement as a sufficient deterrent. Across
the Pacific they envisioned a growing Mongolian colossus, one which
might engulf the Empire in British Columbia and elsewhere. "We in
British Columbia," one of them told an anxious audience at the
Royal Colonial Institute in London in 1912, "have determined that so
far as we can accomplish it the Pacific Ocean must be a white man's
ocean. The Western Hemisphere must be a white man's hemi-

26. Ian H. Nish, *The Anglo-Japanese Alliance: The Diplomacy of Two Island Empires, 1894–1907* (London, 1966).

27. The 1911 census revealed 19,565 Chinese, 8,587 Japanese, and 2,291 East Indians in a total population of 392,480. In 1881 there had been 4,350 Chinese out of 50,000 inhabitants. Robert A. Huttenback, "No Strangers Within the Gates: Attitudes and Policies towards the Non-White Residents of the British Empire of Settlement," *Journal of Imperial and Commonwealth History*, 1 (1972–73), 295. Lower, *Canada and the Far East*, pp. 69–70; Woodsworth, *Canada and the Orient*, p. 63; and Peter Lowe, "The British Empire and the Anglo-Japanese Alliance, 1911–1915," *Historical Journal*, 54, no. 181 (June 1969), pp. 216–17.

XVI

sphere.'' Caught between Japan's expansion and Britain's withdrawal, British Columbia was like a finger trapped in a door jamb, he
warned. The remedy, one of his attentive listeners advised, was to
follow Rudyard Kipling's panacea for the British Columbia situation:
''Pump in the Whites.''[28] Sir Wilfrid Laurier's government in 1911
and Sir Robert Borden's, which followed, would denounce indiscriminate Japanese immigration on strategic grounds. However, they
acknowledged that the Anglo-Japanese alliance, in the words of their
contemporary Philip Kerr, ''allowed [England] to concentrate her
resources against the menace of the German fleet, . . . guaranteed the
peace of the Far East, and the safety of the Indian frontiers, and
protected the Empire against the hostility of Japan.''[29] Better to have
Japan an ally than a foe. As Laurier realized, in 1908, the day might
come when the Anglo-Japanese alliance would safeguard the Dominion. For this reason, in 1911 Laurier and his fellow prime ministers
from Australia, New Zealand, and South Africa supported the British
renewal of the alliance.[30] Though to varying degrees each dominion
feared Japanese power and Asiatic immigration, in the last analysis
imperial defense was their common cause.

Canadian concerns about the future of the Pacific had been
heightened by the withdrawal of the British fleet from Esquimalt on
March 1, 1905, as part of the Admiralty's general fleet reorganization plan to provide a margin of safety in the face of a formidable and
growing naval rival across the North Sea. Now Canadian west coast
defense lay in two sloops and a survey ship the Admiralty kept there
(a marked decrease in naval power from a decade before) and whatever warships Japan could provide should the Anglo-Japanese Alliance become operative. In addition, the naval base at Esquimalt
came into Canadian hands in 1911—a place of repair for Britain's
warships, in emergency or wartime, and headquarters of the Pacific
fleet of Canada's ''tin pot'' navy (with one gunboat in the Pacific
and another in the Atlantic) created by the Naval Service Act of 1910.

The Anglo-American agreement of 1902 for American development of a Panama canal acknowledged American naval paramountcy

28. Vrooman, *British Columbia*, pp. 11, 13, 18. He went on to explain that British
Columbia and the United Kingdom should work together to ''Pump in the Britons.''
29. *The Round Table*, 1 (Feb. 1911), pp. 122–123.
30. Woodsworth, *Canada and the Orient*, p. 162; Lowe, ''British Empire and the
Anglo-Japanese Alliance,'' passim.

in the Western Hemisphere. It was not unrelated to the general policy advocated by the War Office, the Admiralty, and the Committee of Imperial Defence for a withdrawal of the British military presence from Bermuda, Jamaica, St. Lucia, Halifax, and Esquimalt. So far as Earl Selborne, the First Lord of the Admiralty, was concerned, the First Sea Lord, "Jackie" Fisher, had made up his mind that Britain could not possibly "escape an overwhelming and humiliating defeat by the United States and therefore he would leave Canada to her fate and no matter what the cause of the quarrel or merits of the case he would not spend one man or one pound in the defence of Canada." Fisher never changed his opinion on this point, and three years later he told King Edward that the principles of imperial defense did not extend to the Western Hemisphere, for the United States could annex Canada whenever she wished.[31] In these circumstances, the general British fleet revision, the British withdrawal from Esquimalt (not liked in British Columbia), and Laurier's admission that the Monroe Doctrine was Canada's security for the future were not unnatural concomitants.

When the British withdrew from the North Pacific, their position was not filled by Canadian military interests. The Canadians, perhaps because of their long border with the United States, their racial division, their protection under the Monroe Doctrine and Anglo-Japanese Alliance, and their dependence on the Royal Navy, did not immediately seek to build a large fleet for even so much as coastal defense. Ottawa, not London, possessed the control over naval policy. Perhaps this is what mattered most to the majority of Canadian politicians and statesmen. Thus, when the guns went off in August 1914, it was the Japanese cruisers *Idzuma* and *Asama* which provided British Columbia with coastal defense and probably diverted the German squadron of Admiral Von Spee south of the track of the Canadian Pacific Railway's Empress liners. It is one of the ironies of history that British Columbia, so long concerned with the "yellow peril," was in 1914–18 made secure by it.

In sum, then, the period 1871–1914 witnessed the growth of Canadian commercial interests and seaborne trade in the Pacific rim,

31. Lord Selborne to A. Balfour, 26 Dec. 1904, Balfour Papers, British Museum, London; quoted in Samuel F. Wells, Jr., "British Strategic Withdrawal from the Western Hemisphere, 1904–1906," *Canadian Historical Review*, 49 (Dec. 1968), 348, 349.

XVI

Canada and the North Pacific

especially from British Columbia. Canadian desires for trans-Pacific
steamships and a cable were fulfilled. With the CPR, a Northwest
Passage to the East had been developed. This constituted, Canadian
governments argued, the nascent Common's contribution to defense
of the Empire. Concurrently, however, the Pacific and its littoral
posed problems for Canada—in Hawaii, the Yukon, Alaska, and the
Bering Sea. The Alaska boundary award, apparently in favor of the
United States, forced some Canadians, expecting perhaps some returns for Canada's support for the British position during the Anglo-
Boer War, to turn inwards and consequently away from the benefits
of the Empire.

Canadians were witnessing the crosscurrents of changing power
relationships in Europe, the Far East, and the Pacific. They looked
for stability but they did little to defend themselves. As long as allies
afforded them free naval defense, as Britain, the United States, or
Japan did at one time or another, taxpayers and politicians were
content. British strategists such as Field Marshal Earl Roberts might
warn that the world's focus was shifting to the Pacific. But Ottawa
was largely indifferent to its possibilities, as one historian has written, and, related to this fact, incapable of mounting a presence on the
world stage. In 1909–14, Canada would not assume, with Australia
and New Zealand, responsibility for a cooperative system of Pacific
naval defense.[32] This lion's cub was unwilling to roam in a den
which its mother could not dominate. Situated adjacent to the two
great northern oceans—the Atlantic and the Pacific—with coasts
flanking the direct routes between North America and northern Asia
and Europe, Canadians had by the end of the century a vested interest
in the question of who would rule the waves. But as a thinly populated, North American nation, *realpolitik* was beyond them and con-
sciously or unconsciously Canadians were essentially bystanders to
the great changes that brought them war in 1914.

---

32. Donald C. Gordon, *The Dominion Partnership in Imperial Defense, 1870–1914*
(Baltimore, The Johns Hopkins Press, 1965), pp. 240, 249. See also Richard A.
Preston, *Canada and "Imperial Defense": A Study of the Origins of the British
Commonwealth's Defense Organization, 1867–1919* (Durham, Duke University Press,
1967), pp. 391–94, which points out the absurdity of Admiralty proposals for a Cana-
dian fleet unit for the Pacific.

XVII

THE ROYAL NAVY
AND CANADIAN DOMINION

W E are here within a mile of the great river of empire. The Thames waterway, Joseph Conrad wrote in the evocative, brilliant images in the opening pages of *Heart of Darkness*, leads 'to the uttermost ends of the earth'. 'The tidal current', he continued, 'runs to and fro in its unceasing service, crowded with memories of men and ships it had borne to the rest of home or to the battles of the sea. It has known and served all the men of whom the nation is proud, from Sir Francis Drake to Sir John Franklin, knights all, titled and untitled. . . .' And the great ships had known the river too: the *Golden Hind,* returning with her 'flanks full of treasure,' and the *Erebus* and *Terror,* that never returned. To all seas the river had given men and ships. 'Hunters for gold and pursuers of fame, they all had gone out on that stream, bearing the sword, and often the torch, messengers of the might within the land, bearers of a spark from the sacred fire. What greatness had not floated on the ebb of that river into the mystery of an unknown earth! . . . . The dreams of men, the seed of commonwealths, the germs of empire.'

Often it has been said, and not without exaggeration, that the British Empire owed its existence to the sea. The outlying ramparts of British influence and obligation were established by the use and control of the sea. Whether it was trade or colonization, the British imperial ethos was a seaborne matter. This was as true in the early gropings for overseas influence dating from Tudor times as it was in the latter days of shrinking commitments, of which we are yet to see the sundown. And it was as true of the eighteenth century and the great wars for empire as it was of the nineteenth century, more correctly the years 1815 to 1914, that peculiar period of almost universal peace, the *Pax Britannica.*

These four centuries of British ascendancy, in maritime enterprise and naval pre-eminence, are precisely commensurate with the founding, growth and maturity of the British North American colonies. They may be marked by the activities of Martin Frobisher at the beginning and by the new order of naval realities exhibited in the person of Jackie Fisher at the end of this

XVII

era. Leaving aside the internal development of the constituent parts of what came to be known as the Dominion (later the Government) of Canada, it may be stated that Canada's history before 1914 was not a little dependent on the Royal Navy, which was after all the seaborne arm of British authority and influence.

I

The hallowed names of English adventurers by sea are integral to early Canadian history. For the Tudor age: John and Sebastian Cabot, pioneers to the Atlantic and Arctic flanks of the continent, the High Admiral Sir Martin Frobisher, thrice a voyager in pursuit of a passage to Cathay and India; Sir Francis Drake, Elizabethan claimant to the west coast of North America, Nova Albion; and John Davis, master hydrographer and scientific navigator, who in his arctic discoveries lighted Henry Hudson into his strait and William Baffin into his bay. All showed the way – 'Beyond this flood a frozen Continent lies dark and wild, beat with perpetual storms' – and cast light on that raging dark of Milton's *Paradise Lost*. For the early Stuart age: Hudson himself, explorer of his icy bay and his great river, presaging the founding of the Hudson's Bay Company and New York City, and Thomas James whose crew feared they were damned to starvation on a piece of ice. For the Hanoverian age: James Cook, who charted Newfoundland, surveyed Louisbourg harbour and the St Lawrence preparatory to the triumph of British arms, and initiated British trade and discovery in that distant dominion, Vancouver Island, in 1778; also George Vancouver, Nathaniel Portlock, George Dixon, William Broughton, even William Bligh, pioneers of surveying and discovery on the Northwest Coast. And for the Victorian age, the last, the professional sailors as explorers: Sir Frederick William Beechey in the far western arctic, Sir Francis Leopold McClintock in the eastern arctic, Sir James Clark Ross of terrestrial magnetism fame, and Back, Crozier, Kellett, Collinson, Pullen, Osborn, McClure, Belcher, Maguire – *among others*. Not least is that promoter of arctic exploration for science, for empire, and employment of his fellow officers, Sir John Franklin, who had fought under Nelson at Trafalgar and who made three expeditions beginning in 1819 to explore the arctic coast of Canada, his last in 1845 in the *Erebus* and *Terror* leading to the death of himself and his men, and to the discovery of the celebrated passage. The fifty expeditions by land and sea that searched for the Franklin expedition survivors added greatly to scientific knowledge of the Canadian arctic and of the Inuit and Indian inhabitants. This great barren land, whose outline was fixed by the actions of these knights-errant of sea and ice in Britain's northernmost empire, was transferred to Canadian sovereignty by Westminster in 1880.

For the River St Lawrence and for the Great Lakes two figures predominate in the history of hydrography, that science so fundamentally important to the extension of political power and commercial ascendancy: William Fitzwilliam Owen and Henry Wolsey Bayfield, both of whom reached flag rank and both of whom died in British North America, in New Brunswick and Prince Edward Island respectively. Owen, not to be confused with his older brother Commodore Edward Owen, under whose command he was placed in May 1815, was entrusted with the military survey of the Great Lakes, more particularly the securing of the boundaries of Canada with the United States, the surveying of the still largely unknown Great Lakes, especially Ontario, Erie and Huron, and the delineation of the connecting waterways and harbours of that vulnerable western frontier. Owen was a particularly hard worker. His successor of 1817, Bayfield, who with Vidal, Becher and Harris, had toiled for the unmerciful Owen (whose energies found ample vent in East African waters), kept a more equal regimen but never lost his admiration for Owen. What Owen began Bayfield finished. By the time he had retired in 1856 he had completed surveys of Lakes Erie, Huron and Superior, the River and Gulf of St Lawrence, Belle Isle and the Islands of Anticosti, Prince Edward and Cape Breton, and the Coasts of Labrador and Newfoundland. He had written sailing directions for the St Lawrence, for Newfoundland, Labrador, Nova Scotia and New Brunswick. And he had added significantly to the charting of the great ports – Halifax and Montreal – and to the navigating in safety of that long arm of the sea that led to mid-continent, at least for ships of limited size. Gifted and zealous, Bayfield ranks as the pre-eminent naval surveyor in Canadian waters. And yet it is not perhaps without importance to note that in 1842, his mentor Owen returned to British possessions in North America to undertake a survey of the great tidal basin, Bay of Fundy. And more eccentric than ever before, the Passamaquoddy Hermit, as he was known to the locals, secured control of Campobello Island and lived there in quiet isolation for the last years of his life.

The western ocean flank also became firmly delineated in consequence of the Navy's presence. Wood, Kellett, Mayne, Pender and others filled in the spaces. But none did it so well as George Henry Richards, who from 1856 to 1863 superintended the drawing of 36 principal Admiralty charts and the preparation of sailing directions for Vancouver Island, British Columbia and Queen Charlotte Islands. His reward came in being named Hydrographer of the Admiralty in succession to Admiral Washington in 1863, a position he held until 1874. Another Hydrographer of the Navy, Sir John Franklin Parry, served on the British Columbia coast in the early twentieth century in H.M.S. *Egeria*. His surveys constitute the final chapter in the Admiralty's work in making western Canadian seas safe for seamen. And he also left for us pioneering histories of the Pacific Station and of the hydrographical service on the British Columbia coast.

XVII

II

Even though the history of Canada is inextricably linked with English exploration and British naval surveying it is in larger matters of policy that the Navy is most to be remembered in the Dominion's history. The exploration of Canada was undertaken not for amusement but for strategic and commercial purposes. That exploration may have begun with a search for a short cut to eastern seas. But it certainly had ended with a political commitment to the northern half of the North American continent, the removal of great rivals for sovereignty in that area, and the possession of two naval bases as anchors at either end of the Dominion.

In the era of early English ventures towards North America, Spain held the sceptre of the seas in the North Atlantic and its great western annex, the Caribbean. Keeping a colonial establishment on the western verge of the ocean, as the French and Dutch also were to learn to their distress, depended on the colonizing power's ability to maintain communication with its over-. seas plantations. Elizabethans might well 'singe the King of Spain's beard' in a bold privateering expedition. But maintaining even self-sufficient colonists overseas against rival raids on the spot and diplomatic manoeuvres in Europe depended on possessing a merchant marine and a navy of suitable size and competence to maintain the sea communications with the colony.

Towards the close of the sixteenth century, the possession of portions of North America became an issue in the struggles of European states. And in regards to Canada, European mariners came to exploit the cod fishing of the Grand Banks and, to a lesser extent, the seal and whale fishery of the Gulf of St Lawrence. Gradually beaver and the Indian trade drew the newcomers up the great river and into the continental interior. Newfoundland and Cape Breton, the great island markers to the St Lawrence's entrance, were strategically as well as economically important. And there, in turn, were established the English 'nursery of seamen' and the French bastion of power, Louisbourg. France made the river kingdom its North American base for a century and a half after Champlain founded his colony at the river narrows, Quebec, in 1608. Meanwhile, English statesmen and non-conformists were drawn south, to Virginia and Massachusetts, respectively. Until that great contest for empire, the so-called second hundred years war began in the late seventeenth century, a war for North America was not an object. By the close of that century, national power based on seaborne trade, colonial possessions, and armed force at sea became the statesman's distinct object. Thus the War of the Spanish Succession, which ended in the Utrecht Peace of 1713, brought a rearrangement of colonial boundaries: Spain withdrawing claims to Newfoundland, Britain establishing sole control of Hudson Bay territories and gaining Acadia save for Cape Breton, and France finding itself with contracted possessions and facing the reality of an ascendant England. And yet the English had failed to secure the great river, and the ignominy of Rear-Admiral Sir Hovenden Walker's wrecked fleet on Egg Island, River St Lawrence, remained. And French predominant control continued until Brigadier General James Wolfe and Vice-Admiral Sir Charles Saunders brought not only the men and material but the knowledge and technique to secure Canada to British sovereignty.

Make no mistake, this was a great amphibious expedition, whose destination lay a thousand miles from the open Atlantic, and which involved 277 ships. Wolfe may be the symbol of British triumphant occupation, but it was Saunders and the careful, silent workings of James Cook surveying the river narrows that brought the Highlanders and the Royal Sussex Regiment among others to that extraordinary encounter whereby under cover of darkness, upstream to a back-door access to the fields of farmer Abraham, the British army assembled to fight a battle for a continent in which both commanders died. Now France fell to British arms, and British bayonets were seen among Quebeçois or Canadiens for fully five years before civil rule was restored. The long contest for empire in northern North America ended in a military occupation which left an indelible imprint on the political culture of Quebec and modern Canada.

But on the other side of the Atlantic the final naval battle of the war, and for the command of Canada, was soon to be fought between British and French. This was Quiberon Bay. The object of British strategy was to contain the enemy in Europe on land and sea. The 'Western Squadron', as it was called, carried instructions to hold Brest and other western ports sealed. The blockade would trap the French warships and merchant vessels in their ports. If the enemy ventured to sea, the 'Western Squadron' would fall on the enemy and thereby prevent any invasion of England or Ireland or any supplies reaching the new world. In the fading afternoon of 20 November 1759 Admiral Hawke swept down on the fleet of the French admiral Marshal de Conflans which had gone to sea, and destroyed and scattered it, and with it French naval power for the duration of the war. Quiberon Bay secured Quebec for British arms, for it meant that the French king's ships could not intervene where Wolfe's army had been so precariously perched. By making the Bay of Biscay an English sea (allowing English sailors to cultivate cabbage on its islands) the fate of New France was sealed. Montreal surrendered to British arms in the Spring of 1760.

To expand British interests and check future French encroachments in a still little known quarter, James Cook was instructed to make accurate surveys of the waters of Newfoundland and Labrador. The Treaty of Paris, 1763, had confirmed British sovereignty to Newfoundland, but St Pierre and Miquelon besides the 'French Shore' from Point Riche to Cape Bonavista remained outposts for the rival nation's fishermen. Cook's work, of national economic advantage, allowed for a further exploitation of the marine resources of this fabulous ocean quarter: his *Newfoundland Pilot,*

XVII

published in 1769, and his charts, printed in a collection by Thomas Jefferys in 1769–70, were models of their kind. They established Cook's reputation preparatory to his first Pacific voyage. Coupled with his 1778 Nootka Sound reconaissance they earned him the broad claim, as evidenced in his Pall Mall statue beside Admiralty Arch, London, to have 'traversed the ocean gates of Canada'.

But to return to British America in 1763. Now, for a brief moment of time, a peculiar interlude in the history of the western continent, British supremacy held firm from the Arctic Ocean to the Mexican gulf, and from the mouths of the Hudson and St Lawrence to the flanks of the Mississippi and Missouri. Colonial American continental ambitions and principles of liberty, born in an earlier era of non-conformist rejection, meant that Englishmen in America would have to be ruled by the sword – tantamount to a civil war – and that the Royal Navy would be obliged to fight its first war against a continental power of almost inexhaustible domestic resources: in food, in manpower, and in material. Such a mission was impossible, and the more so if Britain were to face, as she did, a hostile alliance of European nations – France, Holland and Denmark – in support of the young Americans. The Navy was ill-fitted for war, and suffered an astonishing collapse. American privateers swept the seas of British transports and trading vessels. 'We have no friend or ally to assist us,' complained the First Lord of the Admiralty, Lord Sandwich (who in time was to receive much blame for the poor state of the British fleet). 'On the contrary,' he continued, 'all those who ought to be our allies except Portugal act against us in supplying our enemies with the means of equipping their fleets.' Isolated from traditional sources of supplies, the Royal Navy's ships were 'in a wretched state of feebleness and decay', and some were scarcely able to get home at the end of an exhausting five years of war.

The Battle of Yorktown sealed the fate of the earliest British Empire in North America. It fractured that magical union, and at the same time created two polities: the United States of America and British North America. The latter afforded a new home, especially in New Brunswick and Upper Canada, for displaced persons who sought the security of the crown and who were determined to establish constitutional jurisdictions that would in no way mirror their American counterparts but would form a buttress for King and Country against rampant, dangerous republicanism.

American merchants were also extending their activities by sea, and by the year 1800 Yankee brigs and schooners were frequently seen in the trading entrepôts of eastern seas. The United States government put little value on a naval force, however, and actually liquidated the fleet of the Revolution. But by 1812, a new navy had been ordered, and a competent one too, nicely capable of damaging British convoys sailing to garrisons in Jamaica and Halifax and thus a fine complement to the land-based objective of Mr

Madison's war: to secure Canada, especially its western frontiers, for the United States. George Washington had prophesied that the continental United States would never be secure as long as the enemy, Britain, held Canada. The War of 1812 was fought in part to end that threat.

In other words, the War of 1812 brought into armed conjunction two empires – one European, the other North American; the one an entirely seaborne creature, the other a continental centaur who had as work-mate a leviathan. The War of 1812 was a curious affair, and it ended largely as it had begun – with an increased Anglo-American antipathy, a secure British North America, and a balance of power established in North America between the United States and the British-held North American provinces. This delicate balance of power, made possible only by British naval authority and to some degree by American forbearance, allowed for the continuance of the British Empire's interests on the northern continent until such time as the Anglo-American antagonism, born in the horrors of revolution over a century before, had been eased in the face of larger, more sinister external threats. In the interim, the Navy accorded Canada security from American expansion, the threat of which was more real than imaginary and which certainly cannot be sustained as an 'undefended frontier', now regarded as mythical.

British command of the sea was early established in the war, though United States Navy successes in several single-ship encounters gave witness to the value of heavily-gunned ships with well-trained crews. But Captain Sir Philip Bowes Vere Broke, Bt., in command of the *Shannon*, a fine 38-gun frigate sailing out of Halifax, was one example of the officer who challenged American danger to British security on the high seas, more particularly British merchant shipping losses, which were appalling and numbered more than 1000 vessels. His brilliant capture of the USS *Chesapeake* was made possible by his adroit tactics, fearless courage, and readied ship and crew. Broke's success, coupled with the gradual extension of British naval influence in a blockade which came to dominate from the St Lawrence to the Mississippi, showed how a seaborne power could do much to damage a continental power such as the United States already was. And it again revealed, in the Battle of New Orleans, that amphibious expeditions were extremely hazardous. Yet in other locales the blockade had searing effect. Along the entire seaboard of the United States, in creek mouths and harbours, British boat crews made raids.

The Royal Navy moved into the Potomac and scorched Washington in retaliation for the American burning of the Upper Canada capital York; they also pressed up the Chesapeake near Baltimore doing damage to civilian establishments. 'A war falling on women and children is horrible,' complained Lieutenant Henry Edward Napier of H.M.S. *Nymphe*, 'but perhaps necessary to work its own ruin, the Americans having commenced this

XVII

species of warfare in the Canadas, attended with the most aggravating circumstances.' Another contribution had been made to Canadian–American antipathies, but revenge never again overtly exhibited itself among the policy makers – at least in regards to Canada. And with the close of the War of 1812 and the coming of peace through the Ghent Treaty a new era of continental balance was entered into, one not without difficulties and uncertainties including several threats of war. To a certain degree an equilibrium had been struck between the land-based power of the United States and the ocean-based influence of Britain and the British Empire of which British North America was the general beneficiary.

The War of 1812, and the wars fought by Britain against the France of revolution and Napoleon, brought Canada into its own as a place for naval stores, especially timber in deal (or pieces), masts, and square timber. Cut off from traditional Baltic supplies, the government looked to the British North American colonies for stores which were the material foundation of naval power. The government put in place preferential duties and administrative regulations to make Canada's forests 'Great Britain's woodyard'. British North America had acquired, the Duke of Wellington admitted, a role which was central to the maintenance of Britain and her empire. The few arpents of snow as so disparaged by Voltaire were demonstrating their military utility, and any Little Englander's views of liquidating British imperial obligations in Canada were quickly dispelled. In this last phase of the age of fighting sail, British North America acquired a strategic value for Britannia's trident.

Newfoundland, too, developed in an ancillary way to the mother country's naval needs. Regarded as a 'nursery of seamen', the key to world power said the elder Pitt, its sole function was to serve the fleet, to the neglect of colonial settlement and good government. Each spring several English warships would take up station in Newfoundland waters, protecting the British fishing and maintaining order. A floating 'Governor and Commander-in-Chief in and over' (the first of whom was Captain Thomas Graves, 1763) was the constitutional designation accorded by the Admiralty. Under this scheme Newfoundland was merely 'a fief of the Admiralty', as a member of parliament complained in 1830. At St John's the Navy's presence brought a constant infusion of money and investment. But elsewhere the ownership of private property in land was discouraged and indeed made illegal under royal instructions, the object being to deter a resident colony which would dominate the fishery for local as opposed to metropolitan advantage. Not until 1832 did 'the great ship' moored near the Grand Banks come to have its own form of representative government.

III

Nonetheless, colonial reform did come there and elsewhere in British

XVII

North America and with it new British views towards colonial self-defence. The British were never entirely successful (if at all) in persuading the colonies to shoulder the burden of their own defence. In regards to British North America the Colonial Office became the 'fixer' in establishing the Canadian confederation in 1867, which provided a means for establishing a Canadian militia. But even then Canadian commitment to self-defence was unthinkable, even unnecessary, given the seeming pre-eminence of the British lion, which appeared strong enough to deal with any threat from the testy American eagle. The British pursued a policy of 'recalling the legions' from the garrison towns – Halifax, Quebec and Kingston. But the American Civil War found that policy momentarily reversed.

Gradually as tensions eased between Britain and the United States after the Fenian raid scares of the late 1860s, British statesmen again looked for means of making the Canadians self-sufficient in their own naval defence. After all, had they not announced that self-government carried with it the obligation of self-defence? The Canadian provinces had been the beneficiaries of British security; now the Canadians must look after themselves. Yet it was not such an easy issue, as Charles Stacey in his description of the 1868–69 gunboat controversy has explained. Canada objected to paying for the whole expense, that is for ships, working expenses and fighting crews. And although the Colonial Office and the Canadian Governor General, Lord Monck, attempted a revolution in responsibility in 1868, the Canadian parliament balked, and the old system continued. The next year the Admiralty wanted to have Canada replace the three gunboats on the Great Lakes. Their Lordships even graciously offered to let Canada decide what force was required. That might have been acceptable to the canny Canadians, but paying for ships was another matter. Again they rejected London's generous plans for autonomy in self-defence. The imperial government's response was to let the gunboats, such as that at Fort Wellington on the upper St Lawrence, lay at harbour, having withdrawn their fighting personnel. The Canadian Minister of Militia 'obstinately refused either to commission a gunboat on the river or to call out volunteers to support or relieve the garrison'. The consequence of this was that the British withdrew and left the border seemingly undefended, the Canadians became vexed, charged the British with timidity and now selected the necessary course to pursue: avoiding any further obligations in defence responsibilities.

On the Pacific coast the story had close parallels. Since the 1840s, British warships had been visiting the Northwest Coast in support of British interests, mainly the Hudson's Bay Company, whose chief factors liked the security afforded by the White Ensign when American, Russian or Indian raids threatened. As British trade and settlement in British Columbia and the North Pacific grew, the Lords of the Admiralty soon found that they were obliged to establish a Pacific station headquarters at Esquimalt, Vancouver

XVII

Island, in 1862, and there to keep a dozen ships or so for coastal duties and for work throughout the eastern Pacific, including Hawaii, Tahiti, Pitcairn, Easter Island and the coast of the Americas from Bering Sea to Cape Horn. A large shore establishment with hospital and dock came into existence. Local spars and coal were beneficial to the Navy and to colonial development. And the British obligation grew despite the rise of a new province and Canadian dominion on that western window after 1871.

On the Atlantic shore another similar case developed. Halifax, founded in 1749, became the North America and West Indies fleet headquarters. The Atlantic admiral would winter in Bermuda rather than his Pacific counterpart's Hawaii. Otherwise, the duty was the same: to keep a close watch over British interests, especially the fisheries, in the face of American pressures. Here the establishment and fleet were much larger – 35 ships in all at the height of the American Civil War. The Navy was Halifax's biggest business, and the social influence of the service on this Nova Scotian community was profound.

But, as in Esquimalt, the British presence at Halifax could not continue indefinitely. Retrenchment, reorganization and reform came dramatically towards the close of the nineteenth century, and under Admiral John Fisher, who had been Commander-in-Chief on the North America and West Indies station for 1897–9, naval efficiency and readiness became the watchword of the fleet in an age of technological advancements and diplomatic revolutions. Fisher, as a sea lord, put his reforms in place: among other things, the concentration of the main fighting strength of the Navy in the North Sea, the ruthless abolition of small ships of little fighting value, and the closing down of various small foreign dockyards. Halifax, Esquimalt, Trincomalee, and Jamaica were shut down or transferred to local authority; Ascension and Bermuda were reduced; and 150 of the older ships, including many Canadian service veterans, were with one stroke of the pen struck off the Navy List. The 'all big gun', fast ship was but the final development of the Fisher reforms.

What made Fisher's revolution possible, at least as regards Canadian defence, was the rise of the United States in the 1890s as an imperial and naval power. In 1902 the dominion prime minister, Sir Wilfrid Laurier, acknowledged the Monroe Doctrine of continental security to be the fundamental guarantee of Canadian defence. Britain's strategic withdrawal from the defence of the western hemisphere was made possible by the friendly posture of the new, if reluctant ally, the United States. Canada now found herself proud possessor of two great naval dockyards. The Anglo-German naval race led to Canada founding her own Naval Service, the Royal Canadian Navy, in 1910. Two training cruisers constituted no fleet; the Canadian navy had one ship for each ocean. Yet the beginnings of a navy had been established, if tentatively, by a nation which understood that security from enemy attack – Russian, Japanese or German – would have to come through a well-nurtured alliance with the United States, the defence of the Empire also resting with the Royal Navy, the senior, mother service of the RCN to this day.

In the twentieth century the North Atlantic Triangle, previously so important in the effect that the tensions between Britain and the United States had on Canada, now took on a new shape. In the words of Winston Churchill, Canada came to be 'the linch pin' of the allied effort in the Second World War. Canada's resources and manpower were brought to bear when imbalances of power and tyranny had reared themselves in Europe as they did twice in the first half of this century. And with the close of the second great war, Canada came to tie itself even more closely through a military alliance to the United Kingdom and to Europe from whence had come its men and resources, its ships and its fighting seamen that had played such distinctive and influential roles in the making of modern Canada.

XVIII

SEA POWER AND BRITISH NORTH AMERICA: THE MARITIME FOUNDATIONS OF THE CANADIAN STATE

When pressed to reply to the question, 'What is the most important date in the history of Canada?' an innocent instructor, even a seasoned scholar, is tempted to blurt out, '1867—the founding of the Dominion of Canada!' On second thought he might say, '1759—Wolfe's conquest at Quebec'. Then he might be tempted to remark, '1931—the Statute of Westminster', or, if a modernist and sufficiently adventuresome along the same line, '17 April 1982—the new Canadian Constitution'. Admittedly such answers would reflect the all too common 'whiggish' interpretation of Canadian history prevalent for much of the first half of the twentieth century, that is, history as a servant of state progress. They would also reflect an even more recent and ongoing Canadian preoccupation with constitutional status, to many a dreadfully boring tendency now happily confined to the least accessible shelves of our research libraries.

Nonetheless, preoccupation with matters constitutional is eminently understandable. Canada's constituent parts formed some of England's earliest colonies overseas. The first 'alien' overseas European peoples in the Empire, the Irish excepted, were the French in Acadia. Colonial self-government (so-called) was first achieved in British America, by Nova Scotia after 1846. And the first federal experiment within the Empire came into being in 1867 under terms of the British North America Act, which established the new dominion of Canada. In all these developments the connection between the British government and the British American colonial entities which formed the new federal state offered to the historian a very attractive and satisfactory theme. Canada's constitutional story possessed a compelling theme. 'Imperial' scholars could point to landmarks in constitutional achievement, and

32

'Canadian' scholars could indicate with pride all those little gains in colonial self-government—especially the control of the civil-list, which came to be known as 'the winning of responsible government'. It can now be fairly said that so-called 'responsible government' was a sham—the real question being who controlled appointments to office—and it has hoodwinked so many students of Canadian history, and many others of Commonwealth history besides. Moreover, the British American colonies really never enjoyed 'self-government' except in the very limited influence of the legislative assembly which could always be overridden by the governor, the executive council and, if necessary, the Colonial Office and the 'law lords'. Nor was such government really 'responsible'. Colonial elites such as the Chateau Clique or the Family Compact and trans-Atlantic business connections in the form of bankers, fur traders, shipping interests and others continued very much along the same lines. The rebellions of 1837–8 and the 'triumph' of responsible government in 1846 really made little difference. The British Empire continued largely unchanged in British North America, though the techniques of management had changed. The continuities of the Anglo-Canadian relationship are indeed much more powerful and all-pervasive than the few departures which politically conscious historians have endeavoured to foist on us as being the significant dates in Canadian history.

What then is the most important date in Canadian history? Let me put in a plea, and an explanation, for 19 October 1781. On that date General Lord Cornwallis commanding British forces at Yorktown, Virginia, was obliged to capitulate with 7,000 men to American and French arms. The British Army subsequently evacuated Charleston and Savannah and the land operations by the British during the American war were virtually over. American independence was now practically assured. The Battle of Yorktown sealed the fate of the earliest British Empire in North America. It fractured that union which for that brief moment in time, that peculiar interlude in the history of the western continent, British supremacy had held firm from the Arctic Ocean to the Mexican gulf, and from the off-shore islands and mouths of the Hudson and the St. Lawrence to the flanks of the Mississippi and the Missouri. At Yorktown dreams of a British Empire dominating all of North America disappeared. Now two polities were created: one was the infant United States of America; the other was that curious, ungainly and ununified assemblage, British North America. Put differently, the American War of Independence yielded not one new state in North America but two. From the ashes of one empire rose another. British North America and later Canada, legatee of the old British American empire, came to wear the mantle of Britain in the new world.

What had brought about this collapse of the old British Empire in America? Leaving aside, as historical causes, the irrepressible

XVIII

SEA POWER AND BRITISH NORTH AMERICA 33

aspirations of independence of the Americans on the one hand or the conflict between a continental-based empire and a maritime one on the other, it can be fairly said that the British were unable to secure their military aims and objectives because they were unable to sustain Lord Cornwallis in his hour of need. The collapse of British sea power and its replacement, even temporarily, by French command of the sea sealed the fate of the British Army in the Chesapeake. In that war Britain had been obliged to face the combined weight of European nations—France, Spain and Holland—in support of the young Americans. Ill-fitted for war, the Royal Navy suffered an astonishing collapse. American privateers swept the seas of many British transports and trading vessels. The combination was deadly. 'We have no friend or ally to assist us', complained the First Lord of the Admiralty, Lord Sandwich. 'On the contrary', he continued, 'all those who ought to be our allies except Portugal act against us in supplying our enemies with the means of equipping their fleets'.[1] The British sea lords and politicians who had neglected the condition of the fleet now were obliged to restore the Navy to its former fighting condition. But in the interim the British had lost America, a main prop of their old empire, and in doing so had become reawakened to the essential fact that the continued possession of an empire in North America, even the tattered remnant, Canada, lay in Britain's armed power at sea.

From Yorktown in 1781 to the abrogation of the Anglo-Japanese Alliance in 1922 Canada's defence rested with that of the British Empire, and its arm of influence the Royal Navy. From the time that American forces established a continental preponderance at Yorktown to the time that Canada acknowledged by international diplomacy that her security rested with United States dominance on land and sea, Canada's independence from any American aggression, real or imagined, rested in the Anglo-Canadian alliance. That link had its foundation in British sea power. Indeed it was the only cement which held together the alliance. Without the Royal Navy's intervention British America would have fallen to United States arms in the subsequent conflict, the War of 1812.

The corollary of this is also noteworthy. The Empire in North America sustained the home islands. Once Napoleon's armies and fleets had come to dominate the Baltic world they cut off Britain's traditional supply of naval stores. Consequently, the British government looked to its new source, British America, to find the strategically necessary goods, especially red pine and red spruce, for masts and other ship's timber.[2] And in the subsequent period of peace the technique of the British government for fostering the exports of 'Great Britain's woodyard' was the imposition of a massive tariff on foreign timber, a measure that served to shelter colonial timber for naval necessities and ordinary business. 'This staple trade in wood', its historian, A.R.M. Lower, has written, was 'created by war and nourished by mercantilism'.[3] Similarly, the timber tariff continued but only as long as it was in the fiscal interests of the Empire, and it was lifted as part of the general easing of the laws of navigation and trade that came to its ultimate conclusion, repeal, in 1849. Thus the forcing integration of a war fought against France beginning in 1793 and against the United States beginning in 1812 provided a new economic value for British America. Thus, too, that clear-thinking man of arms the Duke of Wellington quickly appreciated the role Canada could play in keeping the Americans preoccupied on their northern flank.

The War of 1812 also showed very clearly how a balance of power could be established in North America by two empires—one predominantly maritime, the other essentially continental. The Americans might very well win certain aspects of a *guerre de course*, or cruiser war, and even control the Great Lakes and other interior waters. However, if command of the North Atlantic could be acquired by the British, as it was by 1813, a coastwise blockade of American ports could be established which in turn would secure the Empire's interests by limiting the enemy's actions on the seas, and allowing the British to raid the enemy's coasts at will. As regards the specific defence of Canada, Montreal and Kingston were by their very positions and intrinsic advantages the key points for the communication which linked the empire of the St. Lawrence with the sea power of Great Britain. In consequence, as British strategists argued, the command of the sea in that or indeed in any future war would be the essential means of securing these western anchors of empire. Even in the Great Lakes, as Wellington advised the ministers of state repeatedly, 'a naval superiority on the Lakes is a *sine qua non* of success in war on the frontier of Canada, even if our object should be solely defensive'.[4]

Nonetheless, a delicate and precarious balance of power existed in northern North America, especially in the early decades after Waterloo, and it exhibited itself at times of Anglo-American crisis, which were frequent. This balance of power was made possible only by British naval authority and to some degree by American forebearance. It benefitted the Empire in at least two ways. It allowed for the continuance of British interests on the northern continent and for the profitable commercial intercourse between Britain and the United States after 1815. Not least, it gave protection to the still nascent colonies of British America and this too at a time when American presidents and their secretaries of state were defining their own hemispheric policies, policies which did not look particularly kindly on foreign, that is any further non-United States territorial possessions in the Americas. The Monroe Doctrine, a specific statement of this policy, did not seek to reverse Britain's sovereignty over Canada; but it clearly forecast what might happen if European powers should undertake any further territorial acquisitions, especially in northwestern North America where Britain and Russia were rivals.

That Great Britain and the United States fully realized the importance of a balance of power in North America is reflected in the diplomatic accords reached in 1814, 1817 and 1818 between the two. The War of 1812 had registered the fact that the defence or conquest of Canada depended on naval control of the Lakes.[5] In consequence the Rush-Bagot Agreement of 1817 was designed to prevent a naval preponderance on the Great Lakes by either of the powers.

The agreement was an early attempt at military parity, but not complete disarmament[6] unannounced to the other. And by its terms a set tonnage and number of war ships was accepted as the maximum by each contracting party. The signatories did not always adhere to the terms, and numerous infractions led to fears of a rearming of the Great Lakes and even of a war. Yet the agreement recognized the great inland seas as a mutual sphere of operation. The Peace of Ghent, 1814, also led to the Convention of 1818, and this brought forth a new western boundary designed to resolve the territorial differences of the two powers in the continental interior. The war had been prosecuted on the British side to keep Canada secure and to protect her Indian allies.[7] Similarly, the new boundary along the 49th parallel of latitude westwards to the Rocky Mountains was an attempt to bring peace to the rival fur trading interests and their Indian allies in the continental hinterland. Even in the far west, the Old Oregon country, the agreement of peace acknowledged a condominium for joint economic exploitation without in any way prejudicing the claims to sovereignty of either signatory. And in that region too, British sea power was instrumental in securing national political and commercial objectives, during and after the War of 1812.[8]

In these several ways was the basis established for a lasting peace between Great Britain and the United States. By war and diplomatic means the new terms of reference for sharing the northern half of the continent had been achieved. That having been said this did not mean that there were no further threats of war between the two powers over the western territory, as indeed there was in the Oregon crisis of 1844–46 and its residual problem, the San Juan Island Boundary crisis of 1859. Nor did this mean that the two powers would neglect their Great Lakes armaments, or cease to eye each other with suspicion.[9] Moreover, this did not mean that Great Britain could afford to become unwatchful and to allow Upper and Lower Canada and the Maritime Provinces to remain relatively undefended. Quite the contrary. Throughout and after the first half of the hundred years following 1815, Britain continued to keep a very sharp eye out for any threatening actions by the restive American republic, one which was to undergo a major civil war and thereby reinforce British fears.

This theme of military protection can be seen in two ways that are in fact not mutually exclusive. As for the armed defences and garrisons of Canada, it may be noted that Britain garrisoned various

XVIII

36

points—Kingston, Montreal and Halifax[10]—and promoted the size and efficiency of a Canadian militia. It may also be noted that Britain constructed new fortifications at the Quebec citadel, erected several other emplacements and a few Martello towers, and designed and built a military canal, linking the Ottawa River with Kingston on Lake Ontario to provide a conduit for supplies and troop movements at a distance from any threatening American invaders.

As for the defences of Canada at sea, Britain developed or enlarged the defensive establishment and support capabilities at two great harbours. Each of these lay at or near to the extremities of the future dominion and adjacent to the main lanes of oceanic commerce. In the northwestern Atlantic stood Halifax, Nova Scotia, 'warden of the north' as its historian has called it.[11] Founded in 1749 to counter French influence at Louisbourg, Cape Breton Island; Halifax grew during the wars against the French and the Americans into the key base of operations for a sizeable squadron whose ships patrolled Newfoundland, the St. Lawrence and Caribbean waters. On the other side of the continent beside the great circle route of the north Pacific stood Esquimalt, Vancouver Island, termed 'the key to the Pacific', among other clichés. Named as a naval store establishment in 1862 and as headquarters of the Royal Navy's ships in the Pacific, Esquimalt, like Halifax, grew as a base (but not during the wars mentioned) in consequence of the Russian-American-British rivalries in western North America and the North Pacific Ocean during the Crimean War and the Civil War. Its fleet was also there to afford protection to besieged British interests—Hudson's Bay Company traders, colonial governors of Vancouver Island and British Columbia, and missionaries and justices of the peace in need of a gunboat to enforce the authority of the Crown and to put in place, on this extremely remote and distant maritime frontier, a system of law and order.[12]

These two naval bases, these two squadrons, afforded not only security to the extremities of the future dominion,[13] they supplied the means of British influence and diplomacy throughout the waters of the western hemisphere. From Halifax a sloop-of-war might police the slave trade or put down a slave rising in Jamaica. From Esquimalt a steam frigate might be intimidating recalcitrant natives somewhere along the Northwest Coast, even in Alaska or Washington Territory, or be bolstering the position of a beseiged British consul in El Salvador or Panama who might be facing the unwelcome prospect of an American filibustering expedition or a seemingly periodic insurrection, revolution or civil war. Put differently, the British navy in Canadian waters may have had the specifically useful task of safeguarding British Americans from an American assault, or one might add a Fenian raid from Boston or San Francisco. But British sea power operating from Canadian waters also had the additional role of sustaining all those various techniques of the *Pax Britannica* in the western hemisphere, a form of naval service which by the close of the nineteenth century came to earn the Royal Navy the title of a floating world police force. As for the specific defences of Canada it is clear that British and Canadian politicians shared a concern during the American Civil War for the defence of British North America. The British garrisons were not withdrawn in keeping with the introduction by Britain of free trade and self-government. They were, in fact, increased in size. The same is true of harbour defences, which were strengthened. The two fleets based on Halifax and Esquimalt were similarly enhanced in number of vessels. As for locally-raised Canadian contributions they too were considerable in the establishment of militias, regular and reserve. That Canadian politicians put great weight on the degree of the crisis is evidenced in an exchange of views during the Civil War. Canadian representatives to the pre-confederation conference of 1865 put the following to the British ministers, as given in their report:

> ... The result arrived at was, that if the people of Canada undertook the works of defence at and west of Montreal, and agreed to expend in training their Militia, until the Union of all Provinces was determined, a sum not less than is now expended annually for that service, Her Majesty's Government would complete the fortifications at Quebec, provide the whole armament for all the works, guarantee a loan for the sum necessary to construct the works undertaken by Canada, and in the event of war undertake the defence of every portion of Canada with all the resources of the Empire.[14]

In reply to these assurances the British ministers were prepared to restate the imperial guarantee. In the words of their own report:

> On the last point, it seemed sufficient that Her Majesty's Government should accept the assurances given by the Canadian Ministers on the part of Canada, that the Province is ready to devote all her resources both in men and money to the maintenance of her connexion with the Mother Country, and should assure them in return that the Imperial Government fully acknowledged the reciprocal obligation of defending every portion of the Empire with all the resources at its command.[15]

But the British guarantee never exonerated the dominion from taking a share in its own naval defence. The Colonial Office view was eminently clear on that.[16] Canada, however, tended to drag her feet in assuming control for British gunboats stationed in Canadian waters. Coast guard and fisheries protection vessels were another matter, and by the end of the century Canada would boast a sizeable 'fleet' of such ships, which some might regard as a precursor for the Naval Service born in 1910. Canada's defence preparations thus tended towards the enhancement of the means of commercial benefit, leaving largely to the British, save perhaps in the development of a permanent Canadian Militia Force in 1883, to provide for its sea defences.

All of this would have been unprofitable and ineffective save for the balance of power established by Britain and the United States in North America. While the new republic consolidated its continental regions, even purchasing Alaska, it pursued a policy of 'studied isolation'.[17] The Royal Navy was not only aiding the protection of Canada; it was affording support for the United States in South American and other waters, and this allowed the United States to remain an isolationist and non-naval power almost until the 1890s.[18] Far from holding Canada hostage, the United States's policy of isolation rested on good relations with Great Britain. 'While Great Britain is undoubtedly one of the most formidable of our possible enemies', wrote Captain A.T. Mahan in 1890, 'it must be added that a cordial understanding with that country is one of the first of our external interests'. An Anglo-American accord was a prerequisite to the security of either nation. 'Formal alliance between the two is out of the question', Mahan added, 'but a cordial recognition of the similarity of character and ideas will facilitate a co-operation beneficial to both; for if sentimentality is weak, sentiment is strong.'[19]

By 1890 it may have been clear to Mahan that war between Britain and the United States was unlikely. But until Canadians could be assured that their neighbour would not make a northern incursion again, as in 1775 and 1812, Canadian politicians were very anxious to keep the armed support of the mother country on hand. That is why they had resisted strongly (though not altogether successfully) the withdrawal, by 1871, of the British Army from garrison duty in all places except Halifax. That is also why they continued to press Canadian governments, both national and provincial, to induce London to maintain naval squadrons of sufficient size to meet their extensive requirements in the North Atlantic and Pacific oceans. That is why, too, they employed sundry stratagems to get London's fiscal backing, including the guaranteeing of bonds at preferred rates, in order that all the improvements and technological advances of that age could be put in place to maintain and enhance the commerce and the influence of the British Empire in North America. In this connection, the following features, characteristic of an imperial infrastructure, come to mind: dry and floating docks, harbour improvements, canals and bridges, transcontinental railways, trans-oceanic steamship services, improved postal systems, and submarine cables. Many of these advances were made with a view to securing British imperial interests and of defending Canada in the late nineteenth century. These were essentially one and the same thing from the perspective of policy-makers in Ottawa and London.

But try as they might, British politicians and especially the Colonial Office and War Office achieved very little in the way of success in persuading Canada to undertake sufficient measures for her own defence. As regards the army, Canada did put in place a Militia Act and did establish the Royal Military College in Kingston for the education of officers. Canada also periodically undertook military appraisals of its own defences. But Canada never kept a sizeable force in arms, though as in the Boer War and First World War it had little trouble in raising sizeable numbers of enlistments. As regards naval defences, Canadians could see no value in establishing much more than a fleet of coastal surveillance and fisheries patrol vessels. The Fisheries Protection Service may have provided the nucleus of a Canadian naval service,[20] but wooden-hulled and lightly-armed vessels were a poor substitute for even the beginnings of a fleet in the early twentieth century. On the personnel side, the Canadian government was more active. Ottawa passed a bill constituting the Naval Militia of Canada in 1904, and there were other early moves to establish a naval reserve, all of these preparatory to the establishing a regular naval service.

In actuality, Canadian politicians remained on the face of things reluctant, some would say woefully so, to establish their own naval service. Three chief reasons account for this. The first is that Canada as a part of the British Empire benefitted by being shielded by the world's pre-eminent naval power. What reason was there for another fleet, even for local, inshore purposes? The second reason, equally valid, is that Canada was making her own specific contribution to the defence of the nation and the Empire by the construction of the Canadian Pacific Railway and other railroads. In turn, prime ministers Macdonald and Laurier pressed home that point with monotonous regularity in their discussions with colleagues at colonial and imperial conferences. In London the Canadian view was not widely appreciated, but as Captain J.C.R. Colomb, the influential strategist, could rightly say in 1886, 'The Empire's answer to a "blocked" Suez Canal has been given by Canada. The influence which the "Canadian Pacific" can exercise on a naval and military position in the far East is immense.'[21]

The third reason, perhaps the most fundamental of all, as to why Ottawa was insufficiently willing to take steps to put in place a naval service was simply that Canada's leaders could see no immediate prospect of war. Even a conflict with the United States, an unlikely contingency, would find Mother Britain coming in support, perhaps with the aid of colonial forces. There might be the odd crisis—an unknown fleet (usually of Russian provenance) lingering off the foggy west coast, or a seized sealing or fishing vessel sailing out of a Canadian or Newfoundland port, or a boisterous American president threatening to establish his own border between Alaska and the Yukon if Canada and Britain would not acquiesce. But in actuality the United States and the United Kingdom were reaching a modus vivendi which constituted a revolution in their foreign relations. This may be regarded as the natural extension of the North American continental balance of power achieved in the late eighteenth and early nineteenth centuries, and made especially clear in consequence by the

40

Union victory in the Civil War: that American land power could not be contained. By the Hay-Pauncefote Treaty of 1901 a new period of Anglo-American *rapprochement* had begun, with hemispheric and intercontinental ramifications.[22] The Panama Canal could be built by the Americans. Hawaii could be organized as a United States Territory, and the Caribbean could now be regarded as an American sea. The British could now safely withdraw their naval and military forces from the Western Hemisphere. And from the Canadian perspective the Monroe Doctrine had successfully reached a new plateau: as Prime Minister Laurier admitted in 1902, 'the Monroe Doctrine protected Canada against every aggression'.[23]

If the geographical proximity of Canada to the United States offered the principal cause for Anglo-American friction in the nineteenth century and obliged the British to maintain two fleets based in Canadian waters at virtually no cost to Canadian taxpayers, by the end of that century and virtually commensurate with the closing years of the *Pax Britannica*, the several outstanding problems which had been a constant form of cross-border irritation were coming to an end. They were doing so because larger interests beyond the seas of North America were obliging Britain and the United States to resolve the relatively petty disputes of the two powers in the Western Hemisphere, and to deal with more pressing realities attendant to the shifting balances of power in Western Europe and East Asia. By the Boundary Waters Treaty of 1909 Canada and the United States became signatory to an ongoing standing commission to deal with matters arising between two states inseparably conjoined and sharing the same continent. Under the treaty the International Joint Commission was created, and its purpose was 'to prevent disputes regarding the use of boundary waters and to settle all questions which are now pending between the United States and the Dominion of Canada involving the rights, obligations or interests of either in relation to the other or to the inhabitants of the other, along their common frontier, and to make provision for the adjustment and settlement of all such questions as may hereafter arise . . . ' Gunboats were no longer needed to guard against attack. Garrisons and shore defences were now of secondary importance. Northern North America had become a land of no major international conflicts. 'Fortress America', with Canada a client beneficiary, was now at hand.

The eyes of London and Washington, indeed of Ottawa, were now cast outwards to the new realities, to the potential threats which presented themselves. In Asian waters, the collapse and dismemberment of the Chinese Empire, the rise of German, British and Russian spheres of influence and naval bases, and the emergence of a victorious Imperial Japanese Navy altered appreciably the balance of power in the western Pacific. These events had profound effects on Canadian, American, British and other national interests. In European waters, the rise of the German Empire, and its armed strength on land and sea, posed the major challenge to a European balance of power. Britain's response, which immediately affected her naval commitments in North American waters, was to build new battleship and battle cruiser fleets, to scale down or eliminate altogether her warships on 'foreign' stations, and to transfer authority of her naval bases to local authority wherever possible. Thus in 1905 Canada's British or imperial naval protection was reduced dramatically by the withdrawal of the Pacific and North Atlantic squadrons. Similarly, in 1910, Canada came into unenthusiastic possession of two sizeable naval shore establishments at Esquimalt and Halifax. These changes did not mean that Canada was without naval protection from the Royal Navy, but they were a clear representation of new realities as understood by the Admiralty and the Foreign Office. And they underscored this fact as acknowledged by Sir Wilfrid Laurier and Sir Robert Borden: Canadian defences at sea needed not only the Royal Navy but the United States Navy as well, especially the Pacific fleet based in Bremerton, Washington State. Beyond this, they acknowledged, though reluctantly, that Britain's alliance with Japan was an uneasy necessity, at least for the time being. However, by the Treaty of Washington 1922 was ended the formal alliance of the two great island empires, and this reflected Canada's desire, one shared by the United States, that an Anglo-American accord was the predominant need for the defence of Canada and the Western Hemisphere.[24] Around Canada's defences had pivoted that still little-appreciated change in world affairs in which the *Pax Britannica* was being succeeded by the *Pax Americana*, or perhaps more cautiously British dominance on and over the seas, actual or imagined, was being succeeded but not totally by that of the United States.[25]

It has been said that in August 1941 by the Atlantic Charter the centre of gravity of the British Empire shifted itself across the Atlantic from London to Washington. During the war effort Canada, in Churchill's words, became the 'linch-pin' of the three-sided trans-Atlantic alliance. But in the years after Yorktown many of the causes of anxiety were not European or Asian in origin but North American. The defence of Upper Canada or of Vancouver Island against any possible American aggression may now seem of miniscule importance to the student of history so preoccupied with the study of total war in this century. From our own times in which Canadian-American continental defence and the N.A.T.O. alliance are almost taken for granted it may seem well nigh implausible that Anglo-American tensions were the prevailing cause of concern to those persons preoccupied with the successful defence of British North America. Yet British predominance at sea played a profound role in the history of Canada in the age of the *Pax Britannica*. It was the counterweight to American land-based power. Moreover, British sea power in Canadian waters was conducive to

XVIII

42

imperial interests in the seas adjacent to the Americas. By the close of the nineteenth century, however, new tensions in international affairs were bringing the dominion into a new North American alliance, one so dramatically different from the sometimes precarious balance of power that had dominated British North America's defence needs for the century or more after Cornwallis's capitulation at Yorktown.

ENDNOTES

1.	'If we had had a superior fleet in America, Lord Cornwallis would have been saved', said Lord Sandwich. Quoted in Gerald S. Graham, *The Royal Navy in the War of American Independence* (London, H.M.S.O., for the National Maritime Museum, 1976), p. 22. On the importance of Chesapeake Bay to American history, Samuel E. Morison says that without the loss of British command of the sea Washington, not Cornwallis, would have been obliged to capitulate. For a review of this battle, see Jacques Mordal, *Twenty-Five Centuries of Sea Warfare*, translated by Len Ortzen (London, Futura, 1976), pp. 131–152.

2.	The British Empire's North American stores for naval sources had long been known but not developed owing to lack of necessity. Bernard Pool, *Navy Board Contracts 1660–1832: Contract Administration under the Navy Board* (London, Longmans, 1966), pp. 100–101. See also Robert G. Albion, *Forests and Sea Power: The Timber Problem of the Royal Navy 1652–1862* (Cambridge, Mass., Harvard University Press, 1926). Also, Nathaniel Gould, 'On the Pines of Canada', *Nautical Magazine*, 2, 11 (January 1833), pp. 22–28.

3.	A.R.M. Lower, *Great Britain's Woodyard: British America and the Timber Trade, 1763–1867* (Montreal, McGill-Queen's University Press, 1973), p. xii.

4.	The Duke of Wellington to Sir George Murray, 22 December 1814. *Wellington Depatches*, edited by Gurwood, vol. XII, p. 224; A.T. Mahan, *Sea Power in its Relations to the War of 1812*, 2 vols. (Boston, Little, Brown & Co., 1905), I, 305.

5.	Kenneth Bourne, *Britain and the Balance of Power in North America, 1815–1908* (London, Longmans, Green & Co., 1967).

6.	See the views of the distinguished proponent of disarmament, C.H. Levermore, *The Anglo-American Agreement of 1817 for Disarmament on the Great Lakes* (Boston, World Peace Foundation, 1914). See also the retrospective Robert Wild, 'The Rush-Bagot Convention', in *Report of the Proceedings of the Meeting of the State Bar Association of Wisconsin for the Year 1915* (Milwaukee, 1916), pp. 100–111.

7. Norman Gash, *Lord Liverpool: the Life and Political Career of Robert Banks Jenkinson, Second Earl of Liverpool* (London, Weidenfeld and Nicolson, 1984), p. 111.

8. Barry M. Gough, *The Royal Navy and the Northwest Coast, 1810–1914: a Study of British Maritime Ascendancy* (Vancouver, University of British Columbia Press, 1971), chs. 2, 3 and 7; cf. Frederick Merk, *The Oregon Question: Essays in Anglo-American Diplomacy and Politics* (Cambridge, Mass., Belknap Press, 1967), ch. 12.

9. In 1815 the British decided to keep a larger garrison in Canada than in 1812, and kept it up for a few years. For an examination of the idea that the border was not demilitarized after 1815 see Charles F. Stacey, 'The Myth of the Unguarded Frontier, 1815–1871', *American Historical Review*, 46 (1950), pp. 1–18. For a very different view, see Edgar W. McInnis, *The Unguarded Frontier: a History of American-Canadian Relations* (New York, 1942). Stacey is right, of course, but the myth could be extended to include the years to 1910.

10. See Charles P. Stacey, *Canada and the British Army, 1846–1871*. Rev. ed. (Toronto, University of Toronto Press, 1963). Just as there was a reappraisal of garrisons overseas so was there a review of naval squadrons. See C.J. Bartlett, 'The Mid-Victorian Reappraisal of Naval Policy', in K. Bourne and D.C. Watt, eds., *Studies in International History: Essays Presented to W. Norton Medlicott* (Hamden, Conn., Archon Books, 1967), pp. 189–208.

11. Thomas H. Raddall, *Halifax, Warden of the North* (London and Toronto, Dent, 1950).

12. Barry M. Gough, *Royal Navy and the Northwest Coast*, and by the same author, *Gunboat Frontier: British Maritime Authority and Northwest Coast Indians, 1846–1890* (Vancouver, University of British Columbia Press, 1984).

13. I have left aside the influence of the Royal Navy and the British and colonial governments (an influence continued by the Royal Canadian Navy and Ottawa after 1910) on the rise of communities and urban complexes at Halifax and Esquimalt (and Victoria) respectively. For an introduction to this theme see Donald S. Sutherland, 'The Merchants of Halifax, 1815–1850: a Commercial Class in Pursuit of Metropolitan Status' (unpublished Ph.D. dissertation, University of Toronto, 1975).

14. *Accounts and Papers, Colonies and British Possessions*, Vol. 48: Correspondence respecting the proposed union of the B.N.A. Provinces, no. 16254.

15. *Ibid.*

16. *Cambridge History of the British Empire*, vol. 6 (Cambridge, Cambridge University Press, 1930), p. 717.

17. H.C. Allen, *Great Britain and the United States: A History of Anglo-American Relations (1738–1952)*, (New York, St. Martin's Press, 1955), p. 202.

XVIII

44

18. Harold and Margaret Sprout, *The Rise of American Naval Power, 1776–1914)*, (Princeton, Princeton University Press, 1939). There are later editions.

19. A.T. Mahan, *The Interest of America in Sea Power*, p. 27; quoted in *ibid.*, p. 126.

20. Nigel D. Brodeur, 'L.P. Brodeur and the Origins of the Royal Canadian Navy' in James A. Boutilier, *The RCN in Retrospect, 1910–1968* (Vancouver, University of British Columbia Press, 1982), pp. 16–17.

21. J.C.R. Colomb, 'Imperial Federation—Naval and Military', *Journal of the Royal United Service Institution*, 30, no. 136 (1886), p. 857.

22. The Hay-Paucefote Treaty 'committed Great Britain to naval inferiority in American waters and therefore to friendship with the United States'. Bourne, *Britain and the Balance of Power*, quoted in *American Historical Review*, 74 (1968), p. 172.

23. John B. Brebner, *The North Atlantic Triangle* (New Haven, Yale University Press, 1945), p. 271; also S.F. Bemis, *Diplomatic History of the United States* (New York, 1942), pp. 793–794.

24. On the promotion of Anglo-American conciliation, see M.G. Fry, *Illusions of Security: North Atlantic Diplomacy 1918–1922* (Toronto, University of Toronto Press, 1972). On Canada's specific relationship to Britain on the matter of naval defence, see Barry D. Hunt, 'The Road to Washington: Canada and empire Naval Defence, 1918–1921', in Boutilier, ed., *RCN in Retrospect*, pp. 44–61.

25. Lord Beloff presses on me to think of the *Pax Britannica* closing later than 1914, perhaps as late as the fall of Singapore or even the Suez crisis (letter of 10 November 1985). Elsewhere he argues cogently that American power never replaced that of the declining European empires, partly owing to American anti-British enthusiasms, a legacy of American history. Lord Beloff, 'The Consequences in US/British Relations of the Dissolution of the British Empire and the Assumption of World-wide Commitments by the United States—A British View' (Paper for a Ditchley Foundation—Woodrow Wilson Center Conference, March 1985). See also, William Roger Louis, 'American Anti-Colonialism and the Dissolution of the British Empire', *International Affairs*, 61 (1985), pp. 395–420.

PAX BRITANNICA: PEACE, FORCE AND WORLD POWER

PAX BRITANNICA, according to the Oxford English Dictionary, means the peace imposed by British rule. Put differently, the *Pax* was a system of force from which, it was argued by its practitioners and propagandists, devolved the benefits of peace. Peace for the purpose of profit was one such benefit, and hastened the free-trade movement. Humanitarian advancements, the attempted elimination of piracy and slavery and the propagation of Christianity and education, also derived from the *Pax*. This essay advances the argument that with world leadership comes the need and even the propensity to intervene physically, where diplomacy fails, to meet the pronounced need of the state. The British Empire of the nineteenth century was based as much on the official use of violence as it was on seaborne trade or industrial leadership. The high-minded aspirations of colonial secretaries, governors and consuls for sustaining the *Pax*, or of increasing its influence, were only as good as the forces readily available and the willing cooperation of native rulers and allied states.

In strictest terms of international law, peace constitutes the normal state of relations in international society, and to the student of the history of the British Empire this may well appear to be a curious definition. For as Sir John Seeley explained in his *Expansion of England* (1883), the eighteenth century additions to British dominions were acquisitions by conquest. By 1815 the UK possessed a world-wide empire based on certain communication points, some of them of obvious commercial advantage. Most of these 'keys', according to the Secretary of State for Foreign Relations, Lord Castlereagh, gave their possessor military advantages and had been kept at the peace of 1815 in order to insure British pre-eminence in such outlying spots and beyond. Thus when Britain entered upon a remarkably long era of general European peace, marred only by the not inconsiderable Crimean War which she fought in concert with France and the Ottoman Empire, statesmen and politicians became increasingly interested in the longevity of this state of affairs and trusted to its continuance. Only later did they perceive the *Pax* as a British favour or obligation that they could give to or

XIX

PAX BRITANNICA: PEACE, FORCE AND WORLD POWER

enforce upon the world and its 'lesser breeds without the law', to employ Kipling's wellworn phrase.

The term *Pax Britannica* was first uttered publicly on 12 July 1886 by the Rt Hon Sir George Bowen during a protracted discussion of defence matters at the Royal United Service Institute in Whitehall, London. The occasion was an address by Captain J. C. R. Colomb, a retired officer in the Royal Marine Artillery, who at the time was standing for election to parliament in the Conservative interest (successfully as it turned out). Colomb, known as an author of a work on naval protection of commerce, had offered to the Institute a critique of imperial defence under the heading 'Imperial Federation—Naval and Military'.[1] Colomb, Bowen and 20 other commentators were concerned whether Great Britain could face the challenges being raised to her by rivals. The rhetoric was not 'for war'. It was for protecting the state and its responsibilities on and over the seas. And among those duties were securing sovereign territories, protecting seaborne trade, and fulfilling the various obligations of the British people.

In the 1880s Britain stood alone, in what some have called 'splendid isolation'. Yet Britain's world power depended on a number of axiomatic truths: the crimson ties of kinship among the self-governing colonies and dominions, a skilfully nurtured European continental balance of power (coupled with artful diplomacy and consular services), and a largely agreeable *modus vivendi* with the USA. Britain's power also rested on alliances with certain new states. British influence in the early nineteenth century had secured Greek independence from the Ottoman Empire, and afforded security to the new nation states of Latin America from external intervention by the old power Spain. Even then British pre-eminence was never universal, for it did not prevent France or Austria from asserting a presence in the affairs of the Americas nor did it control Russia in her Alaskan holdings. The British were reminded daily of their limitations of authority and of their inabilities to intervene in every circumstance. In addition, the Suez Canal had modified British strategic thinking in remarkable ways, led to further territorial obligations and commercial dealings in the Near East, and resulted in increased British commitments on the Asia subcontinent, in the Indian Ocean and in the China Seas. Furthermore, railway construction—across Canada, the USA, Siberia, Eastern Europe and elsewhere—was altering the character and speed of troop deployment, and challenging, even subverting, the seaborne pre-eminence upon which British influence and defence has rested for so long.

Sir George Ferguson Bowen KCMG, DCL (Oxon), embodied that link between the classical world and the late-Victorian age.[2] Irish born, and educated at Trinity College Dublin, Brasenose College, Oxford, and Lincoln's Inn, he had entered the colonial service at Corfu, Ionian Islands. He also served as Corfu University's president, and devoted his spare time to classical studies. To him the British Empire and the Hellenic tradition had much in common. Like many a colonial governor he was schooled in Greek and Latin and ancient history, and he was educated in a public school that was in its own way a cradle of empire. He had 30 years of colonial service behind him when he was invalided home in 1885, in time to take part in the last phase of the Carnarvon Commission's review of the defence of British possessions overseas. In the 1880s, Bowen

168

PAX BRITANNICA: PEACE, FORCE AND WORLD POWER

ranked as the special authority on colonial questions, and the belief held by his peers that Bowen had ended the protracted Maori wars through his special breed of tact, discretion, strength, and firmness was a matter for their particular admiration. This colonial veteran would have been listened to when he commented on Captain Colomb's paper. Bowen voiced concerns about the Empire's security. Local naval forces were needed for local defence, he said, while imperial naval forces were required to guard the high seas. To his way of thinking, self-governing colonies ought to have a voice in the making of the Empire's foreign policy: the Mother Country and the Daughter Dominions would be linked by responsibility. Then he said, in terms reminiscent of a *Pax Romana*: 'So we should see *Pax Britannica* far transcend what Pliny called the *"immensa Romana Pacis Majestas"*'. He hoped to view not only an imperial union but even a conjunction with the English-speaking American Republic. The larger association would afford, he said, 'a guarantee of the peace and prosperity of the whole world'.[3]

From Bowen's first utterance grew the currency of the term *Pax Britannica*. Joseph Chamberlain, MP, employed it in a speech in 1893 to illustrate the beneficient results of British rule in India. Proconsuls Curzon, Cromer and Milner enunciated it, and Rudyard Kipling kept the inspiration alive. The Poet Laureate Alfred Austin wrote verse under that rubric in 1896, and in his *Songs of England* (1900) talked of England's 'long-armed sceptre', and of England's boast that 'the fettered must be free'. As Rome's power was built by the heroics of her sons carrying out the traditions of her peoples, with the divine decree determining, wrote Austin, so too with Britain. A universal peace and empire constituted the highest object of the new Romans.

The *Pax*: historiographical considerations

What is the relevance of the *Pax Britannica* to historical studies and contemporary international affairs? This question ranks as one of fundamental importance, more especially to those students of the history of international relations who continue to attempt to compare that era of Great Britain's pre-eminence, or moment of power, with that of the USA's leadership of the western world.[4] Of late, there have been two strains in the literature on the subject that merit mention. One line of argument is found in the analysis of the history of Anglo–American relations in the twentieth century by Lord Beloff. His thesis is that 'What we are witnessing—not merely instability but deprivation, famine, civil and tribal war and genocide—are the direct result of what we might style the catastrophe of decolonization'. Far from blaming the Soviets for their malevolence, Beloff argues that the failure of the Americans to fill a void created by a faltering British empire has led to the present, presumably chaotic state of international affairs. 'Despite its enormous economic and military potential the United States has not been able to find a way of bringing this time of troubles to an end', concludes Beloff. To this he adds, 'The *Pax Britannica* has disappeared; the *Pax Americana* has yet to be made manifest'.[5] But is this so? Can the collapse of the *Pax Britannica* account for the disorder of our times? Professor William Roger Louis, on the basis of his examination of selected key documents of the special Anglo–American relationship, has demonstrated that American presidents and statesmen made no covert attempts to subvert British leadership and thereby hasten the process of decolonization. Rather, as he has explained, the Americans in their moment of power find themselves in circumstances quite unlike those of the British in the era of their world primacy. More than that, the very rhetoric of the eighteenth century American revolutionaries continues to dominate White House and State Department thinking, and it tends to favour the rights of subject peoples to rule themselves. 'Americans did not admire British imperialism', concludes Louis. In fact, they made this patently clear in regard to the independence of India in 1947 and of Libya in 1951. Also, at the time of the Suez crisis in 1956, they demonstrated by their newly won world leadership that they possessed no desire to supplant the British or to provide an alternate means of regional security.[6] Whether Beloff or Louis command the day, it is doubtless true that the historiography of international relations, or of international history, heavily concerns itself with the legacies of the *Pax Britannica*.[7]

The second line of historical discussion is that of what we might call 'the fear-of-failure school'. This has been announced (though in different ways) by Correlli Barnett and John Darwin. Barnett, in two deliberately provocative books, has argued that Britain lacked the material means to undertake a job of world leadership and maintain a costly empire, and more, Britain lacked the economic and industrial capacity to advance that leadership in peace and war in the twentieth century.[8] Dr Darwin, in a recent essay, has written of 'the fear of falling' that pervaded informed opinion in Whitehall, Westminster and Fleet Street in the early twentieth century. This fear persisted in the minds of British politicians in the twentieth century and is demonstrated in the various books and articles written about the collapse, decline or fall of the British Empire.[9] But even if a collapse of power occurred, there were enduring legacies of empire and authority. Professor D. A. Low's *Contraction of England*, as his 1984 inaugural lecture at Cambridge University is entitled, calls not only for an understanding of both the complexities of the modern Commonwealth and its history, but further for an appreciation of the valued residues of language, education and institutions which were in their several ways distillates of Empire and the enduring legacies of a transient British hegemony.[10]

The *Pax* as historical fact

In the classic era of its existence, 1815 to 1914, the *Pax Britannica* was a seaborne operation. The British Empire owed its existence and wellbeing to the sea; so too did its security rest on the force of the Royal Navy whose duties were many and various, not the least of which were to maintain garrisons overseas and to protect regimental transports during their marine passages. The Britannic peace also was predicated on a European equilibrium, on skilfully nurtured alliances, and with a British realization after the rise of Bismarck and the Schleswig-Holstein crisis that Britain could no longer, as she had in the days of Marlborough or Wellington, unilaterally land an army on continental shores to redress an imbalance. The failure to maintain that equilibrium in the years immediately leading up to 1914 lay beyond British control, and signalled the end of the old order. This early collapse of British power and influence announced the end of the *Pax* and indicated the commencement of its long if unsteady decline.[11]

In 1815, at the outset of the *Pax*, the Navy ranked as the world's pre-eminent naval service, and possessed, theoretically at least, sufficient size and strength to protect Britain's interests on and over the seas. The Navy's duties were global. In the generation after Waterloo it faced some of its greatest difficulties 'at home', owing to trenchant reforms at which the Treasury was the centre.[12] Despite severe fiscal restraints, the armed services of the UK were obliged to maintain and secure British possessions, to show the flag, to defend colonial outposts, to supply garrisons, and to secure the seas for legitimate commerce, besides undertaking a number of duties under the general heading of 'humanitarian obligations'.

The security afforded by the victory over France in 1815 and the satisfactory resolution of difficulties with the USA, generally known as the War of 1812, did not allow for a diminution of naval duties. Rather the reverse. The French were in the ascendant in the Indian Ocean, obliging the Royal Navy and the Bombay Marine to take even more active measures to secure pre-eminence in those seas. The French were similarly active in the Near East and took an independent foreign policy during the Mehemet Ali crisis of 1840, one which might have led to a war in Europe. Britain's line of argument was initially pacific. As the Secretary of State for Foreign Affairs, Lord Palmerston, said, the commerce of Britain was best maintained by peace '. . . because without that, it is vain to hope for a prosperous commerce; and not only must that peace be maintained for England, but also for other countries'.[13] Eventually, however, diplomacy backed by force was employed. Admiral Sir Robert Stopford was sent to demand the restoration of Turkish ships, and this ultimatum delivered to Mehemet Ali, rebellious subject of the Ottoman Sultan. This British operation was conducted with celerity and vigour, and it led to the occupation of Sidon and Beirut and to the bombardment of Acre. In consequence, Mehemet Ali was obliged to evacuate Syria, and France abandoned her threatening attitude. In this case, as Palmerston argued, paramount sea power had brought untold commercial advantages and kept a European rival at bay.

Not everywhere was British sea mastery effective. Land frontiers created special, intractable problems for British authority. For instance, Russian activities towards Afghanistan heightened London's fears of interference with the border tribes of the North-West Frontier. This obliged the British to mount a preventive campaign, otherwise known as the First Afghan War, 1839–42, but with disastrous consequences to British arms. A second Afghan war followed and still others. Thus, by force of arms, and not always successfully, the British maintained a presence in the Punjab and on the North-West Frontier against hostile tribes and Russian intrigues.[14] More often than not, native troops showed the Union Jack, and in the tribal areas British agents sought ways of propping up leaders whom they believed might control turbulence within and check Russian advances without.

Along another border, that with the USA, the British Empire in North America was seldom secure from threats of aggression during the nineteenth century, and in the New Brunswick–Maine boundary dispute tempers flared and sabres rattled until the business was patched up in the Webster–Ashburton

Treaty. Tensions in Anglo–American relations shifted to the western continental fringe during the Oregon crisis, 1844–46, then to the San Juan Islands, 1858–59, and eventually to the Alaska Boundary, 1898. These crises and others—in the Pacific Islands, where in the 1840s the French were hotly contesting British influence in the Hawaiian Islands and Tahiti, orr in the Falkland Islands, where Argentina and American sea harvesters obliged the British to intervene in 1832 to secure the sealanes to the Southern Ocean—were making constant demands on British naval and military resources.

Indeed, in keeping with Lord Castlereagh's maxim that Britain needed the maritime keys to lock up the world, British foreign policy aimed at ensuring that her great rivals, France, Russia and the USA, did not acquire new naval bases, or spread their influence to economically and strategically advantageous areas where in consequence Britain would suffer a disadvantage. The Navy was the diplomatic tool for this, directly answerable to the Foreign Office, from which censure or acclaim might radiate to other offices of government, depending on how successfully operations were carried out.

Securing Britons, Europeans and Christians

First among British duties of the *Pax* was to protect British and in certain cases other European citizens around the world. The Royal Navy was 'on call' especially, in Professor C. J. Bartlett's words, in 'those parts of the world where respect for a British citizen and his property were not automatic, where conceptions of justice differed from those of western Europe, or were not reinforced with sufficient regularity or thoroughness'. The early years of the *Pax* 'witnessed a great expansion in such duties by the navy, sometimes to the embarrassment of the naval and more purely political objectives of the fleet'.[15]

From the earliest years of the *Pax* the British undertook to free European captives, English or other, who for one reason or other had found themselves hostages or slaves to non-European, ally or client powers. An early example of this dates from 1816 when the Dey of Algiers refused to abolish slavery and insulted Admiral Edward Pellew, Viscount Exmouth, the Royal Navy's Commander-in-Chief in the Mediterranean. Lord Exmouth possessed orders to obtain a satisfactory outcome, by intimidation or by actual violence as was required. The object was to obtain reparation for the massacre of fishermen at Bona, and to exact for the future an unconditional abolition of Christian slavery, and to treat Christian captives as prisoners of war. After battle was fully engaged and the outcome clearly realized Exmouth offered terms of peace which were submitted to by the Dey. The Exmouth–Algerian episode provides a microcosm of British policy-making for this age: if British interests, economic, humanitarian or otherwise were endangered, forces (either threatened or used) was to be employed to bring the circumstance to a conclusion satisfactory to the British. The outcome was regarded in Spain, the Netherlands, and the Vatican as a *Christian* rather than *English* victory. But Exmouth did not eradicate piracy, and in 1824 England again had to send a fleet to Algiers, and France finally solved the problem by annexing the place in 1830.[16]

The same was the case in the Don Pacifico affair. British citizenship,

PAX BRITANNICA: PEACE, FORCE AND WORLD POWER

Palmerston said in 1850, had its roots in the Roman pattern. In Romana's time as in Britannica's the same held true, he stated: 'As a Roman, in days of old, held himself free from indignity, when he could say *civis Romanus sum*; so also a British subject, in whatever land he might be, shall feel confident that the watchful eye and strong arm of England will protect him against injustice and wrong'.[17] Thus he defended his use of the British fleet commanded by Admiral Sir William Parker in establishing a blockade of Piraeus in order to get satisfaction for the claims of two persons—Dr George Finlay and David Pacifico—against the Greek government. In fact, Don Pacifico was not British, Finlay settled out of court, and Pacifico got a portion of his claim from an independent tribunal. It is a telling fact that Palmerston believed in the efficacy of a naval blockade. And on numerous occasions throughout this period, and after—the Rio de la Plata in 1845, Greece in 1850, and Mexico in 1861—naval force was employed to protect the rights of British and European subjects.

However, many critics came forward to challenge Palmerston's narrow assumptions. Gladstone, the champion of the opponents, had a vision of Europe as a community of Christian peoples possessing equal rights and subject to a code of public law divinely inspired. Gladstone attacked Palmerston's arrogant claim about British rights in the Don Pacifico affair. The British should not be privileged: there were no privileged castes or nations in contemporary Europe, he proclaimed. All men and all nations were subject to the same rule of law, and if any distinctions were to be allowed, they should be associated with the respect due to feeble nations and to the infancy of free institutions. Sir Robert Peel said that Palmerston's policy was not consistent with the dignity or the honour of England. Like Gladstone, he held that law and the rule of nations enabling peace was the means of according a good name to Britain in Europe.[18] In these circumstances, Britain was to be a moral force in Europe, and it served to reason that she would be a moral force everywhere the British flag flew and everywhere a British consul, gunboat or garrison was situated. At least, that was the intention, from which practice frequently departed.

Anti-piracy

In addition to protecting the rights of British and European citizens, the policing of piracy was a specifically designated duty of the navy during the *Pax* and was the other side of the coin of protecting legitimate seaborne trade. It was a worldwide task, conducted against Barbary pirates, against certain offending tribes off the British Columbia coast, and against Brazilian privateers in the Rio de la Plata. It also was conducted against pirates in Malay straits, Chinese seas, and Pacific waters. In some of these places piracy could be stamped out. In others, such as the China seas in the 1860s, it 'persisted undiminished and unintimidated'.[19] In the suppression of piracy, more often than not aggressive diplomacy had to be matched with naval intimidation. Rooting out pirates nests was an ongoing duty of the *Pax* now largely forgotten.[20]

In the Persian Gulf, pirates, both Arab and European, had infested its waters, falling upon legitimate traders and peaceful native states. The Bombay Marine took up the cause on behalf of the East India Company and the Bombay government after 1809. However, the principal indigenous pirates, the Wahabis and

Jawasimi, were uncontrollable until a decade later, when a fleet based on Bombay took the Jawasimi base at Ras al Khaima, razed the forts to the ground, and burnt or captured upwards of a hundred vessels of the pirates. A general peace treaty followed on 8 January 1820, and British vessels remained there and for a time at Basidu, Qishm Island, to preserve order in the Persian Gulf. The British occupied Aden in 1839, ostensibly to check the piratical activities of the locals, but the added benefit was to get a coaling base adjacent to the newly established Suez-Bombay mail steamship service.[21] Meanwhile, native acceptance of the stipulations of the treaty (by which each principal sheik was required to sign a preliminary agreement) did not come immediately. Indeed, it took years to establish a maritime protectorate of the Persian Gulf and to enforce a *Pax Britannica* even in this confined area of the sea. More often than not, quarrels between rival Arab chieftains could be blamed for the continuance of piracy. Thus in 1835 the British negotiated a general Maritime Truce. This grew, but only by consent of the Gulf-state rulers, into the Treaty of Peace in Perpetuity of May 1853. This great document went beyond its precursors in the especial way: it gave the British final authority, in its words 'that the "perfect maritime peace" now established for evermore should be watched over and enforced by the British government, that, in fact, in the event of aggression on any one of the parties by sea, the injured tribe should not itself retaliate, but refer the matter to the British authorities in the Gulf'.[22]

In the Persian Gulf and Red Sea, as in most waters where 'British interests' required succour, Britain's maritime forces, including armed merchantmen, attempted to sweep clean the seas of such corsairs. Here as elsewhere, the object of British naval captains was to keep free the world's waters for legitimate commerce. Freedom of the seas was the end; intervention by the Navy was the means. In the case of the Persian Gulf, all nations were believed by British authorities to be the beneficiaries. Doubtless British actions initiated some cases of local unemployment among the pirates, but the maritime peace achieved by 1850 afforded great benefit to indigenous and Indian traders and shipowners.[23]

If British attempts to control piracy achieved specific gains and had various general benefits, they also disclosed some of the worst practices of British nationals abroad. Take the case of China in the 1860s. There, the historian of this subject, Grace Fox, tells us, 'British merchants armed the pirate fleets against which they expected the protection of the Queen's ships; British officials licensed convoys to protect Chinese traders which used the cover of the English flag to plunder the cargoes that they were paid to protect; British and other Westerners joined the crews of pirate junks. The generous rewards offered to British seamen for the capture of pirates at times caused the destruction of the lives and property of innocent men'.[24] And against the Japanese at Kagosima, British men-of-war exacted fearful punishment: the object was nothing less than forcing open the gates to free, that is, British trade.[25] The official uses of violence were also extensive in South China seas.[26]

Anti-slavery work

The Navy was also under Foreign Office instructions to check the trade in slaves. The slave trade was abolished by Parliament in 1807, but was carried on illegally within the empire and legally by other states for a good many years. The work of the Royal Navy's West Africa squadron was a heroic and hazardous one, perilous for officers and crew. The East African or Indian Ocean command had an equally heroic though less well-known work to that of its West African partner. Dhow-chasing was not always brought to a successful conclusion, and there as well fever and pestilence exacted a fatal price, the price of Admiralty, to end inhuman practices. In the West Indies and along the Brazilian coast, warships under the command of the North American and West Indies and the South American stations respectively attempted to police the traffic adjacent to the markets.

As in the case of the anti-piracy patrol, the suppression of slavery was only as good as the assistance of the headmen, chiefs and sub heads. Take the case of the Haida, Tsimshian and Tlingit of the northern British Columbia coast. They had no desire to give up their marauding, slave-taking and booty-yielding ways, at least until such time as rival chiefs would agree to do so. In 1860, Captain George Richards RN, backed by three ships, extracted mutual promises of good behaviour. By that single diplomatic stroke they virtually though not totally obliterated a mode of behaviour which was for these people a way of life.[27] Indigenous slavery could not be immediately abolished there, and the similarity of this area to the East African coast is rather striking. Elsewhere there were limits to British anti-slavery policy. The British did not attempt to abolish slavery among Mohammedan societies, for slavery was legally recognized by the Koran. Checking the export trade in slaves was an altogether different matter. Muscat and Sur, which received ships bearing slaves from Zanzibar or the Red Sea, and bought and shipped slaves to Turkey, Persia, Sind, the Arab states and even western British India, as a British officer confessed in 1856, were places of special attention from the Navy.[28] As with the anti-piracy agreements, so with slavery suppression. The first treaty with the Sultan, Sayyid Said of Muscat in 1822, forbade the sale of slaves to Christian nations by the Sultan's subjects and made punishable the buying of slaves for sale to Christians. It also empowered the British to place an agent in the Sultan's dominions to watch the trade, and to seize Omani vessels found carrying slaves to Christian countries.[29] Agreements followed, with Trucial Oman in 1838–39 and 1847, with Bahrain in 1861, and with Teheran in 1848 (prohibiting importation of African slaves, and giving British warships right of search of incoming vessels). Treaties were not enough: pressure had to be placed continually on old allies such as Sayyid. The Sultan asked for England's consideration for financial compensation for loss of the trade. However, Palmerston at the Foreign Office insisted, as he put it, that his man-on-the-spot, Captain Atkins Hamerton, 'should take every opportunity of impressing upon these Arabs that the nations of Europe are destined to put an end to the African S[lave] T[rade], and that Great Britain is the main instrument in the Hands of Providence for the accomplishment of this purpose'.[30] Palmerston hoped that legal commerce would arise when the slave trade was abolished and this, he reasoned, would more than make up for the loss.

Despite these measures the African slave traffic continued and even increased. Parliament grew restless and struck a commission of inquiry in 1871. In the following year the government sent Sir Bartle Frere to Zanzibar to arrange a treaty with the Sultan to end the slave trade from the East African mainland. The Sultan eventually decreed slavery's end there in 1890. Meanwhile the trade continued, despite increased but not always constant naval and military actions and diplomatic initiative. As wise admirals and captains knew all too well slavery and the slave trade could only be checked in the continental interior and when trading chiefs and sultans received adequate compensation for loss of business.[31] In 1902 the British Political Agent at Muscat could report distressingly that the importation of African slaves to Sur remained in 'a flourishing condition'.[32] Even as late as 1928, Sir Arnold Wilson who knew the area intimately, could write that though the methods to end the slave trade had become more effective, the task was not yet completed.[33] Perhaps it is not to this day. Yet it is indisputable that the attempts at clearing the Persian Gulf and east African waters constituted a gain to aid the cause of personal freedom as cherished by the British, who held no monopoly of enlightenment but who possessed a crusading zeal to try to convince others that slavery was immoral and therefore ought to be illegal.

The improving instinct and the extension of obligations

There are no end of contemporary statements in the era of *Pax Britannica* that the British were bringing the benefits of civilization to the dark, distant quarters of the world. Nor are there shortages of references to the high-mindedness of missionaries and mission societies who were establishing another, altogether different British presence overseas than that of the trader. The *Pax* had its own strident rhetoric. Yorkshire-born William Duncan of Metlakatla, British Columbia, believed that the pride and pomp of 'rule Britannia' would not please God. 'Rule Britannia', he said, was inconsistent with Britain's position as the pre-eminent nation.[34] The good of the governed was what mattered. The Empire was one of trust. The British, under the peace established by their power, had a special obligation to pursue God's work among their subject peoples.

Under the aegis of the British Empire missionaries such as Duncan might have had half a chance of success if the locales and peoples that were the subjects of this work had been free from several difficulties. In some locales, as in British Colubia, indigenous slavery existed. In others, such as Melanesia, cannibalistic practices persisted. In West Africa indigenous liquor production and foreign importations flourished. Moreover, traders and trading commodities were subverting and modifying native economies, displacing locally used produce with crops for metropolitan advantage. They introduced new material goods which bred dependency and required on-going supply. They escalated native desires for wealth and they supplanted old commercial networks. The biggest struggle was that over the native domain. The gunboat or the regiment could be a useful source of persuasion when the peaceful intervention of the governor or consular agent would not suffice. Law and order was to be preserved within the zones of British influence. The British held as a tenet of their system that one of the primary functions of government was to provide a system of law and order. The object was to prevent anarchy, chaos, and violence in the territorial jurisdiction, for lack of order leading to violence has only one unfortunate outcome— victimization of the subject peoples. Progress, the Victorians held, could not occur without order. And to enforce law the state had to have the authority to exercise judicial influence—through courts, magistrates, justices of the peace, sheriffs and constables.

Some Britons saw it as their mission to extend their authority to the 'savage' and to the 'uncivilized'. British servants of empire, whether in Whitehall or the wilderness, were married to the concept of law and order, or, to use the time-honoured phrase, 'peace, order and good government'. The 1837 House of Commons Committee on Aborigines considered it a national duty 'to carry civilization and humanity, peace and good government, and, above all the knowledge of the true God, to the uttermost ends of the earth'.[35] The high-minded Colonial Secretary Lord Glenelg shared this view. Another Secretary of State for the Colonies, the third Earl Grey, held in 1852 that the extermination of less civilized peoples could be averted by the 'enforcement of order'. Rather than let the natives be exterminated, the imperial mission of civilization and Christianity was in Grey's words, 'a high and noble object well worthy of considerable sacrifice on the part of the British people'.[36] The Colonial Office left matters of order to colonial officials on-the-spot. Whitehall's arm was neither long enough nor strong enough to control such distant zones of influence where, in any case, new settler populatons had their own views of how land should be used. Yet the unbridled principles of law and improvement remained in high places. 'The true strength of imperialism', the Earl of Carnarvon, then Disraeli's Colonial Secretary, said in 1878, lay in building a powerful and munificent English community and in restoring order, law and liberty in 'backward societies'. This, Carnarvon said, would create systems 'where the light of morality and religion can penetrate into darkest dwelling places'.[37] To the Glenelgs, the Greys and the Carnarvons of that age, law, civilization and Christianity went hand in hand. This was a persistent and growing theme of the nineteenth century *Pax*, and it continued to add to Britain's burdens.

Many British tended to speak disdainfully of lawlessness among the 'uncivilized'. Indeed native peoples were perceived as 'uncivilized' because they were peoples beyond the rule of European law and influence. The Colonial Office understood better than any other department of government (yet the view was also held by certain parliamentarians who could not be dismissed as mere philanthropists or high-minded proponents of native rights) that British nationals on distant, unorganized frontiers would act in lawless fashion. Traders, whalers and beachcombers, settlers, missionaries and sailors were everywhere pressing outwards from the home islands. The acquisitive habits of these persons on the borderlands of civilization, Lord Glenelg wrote in 1837, 'compelled the strong to encroach on the weak, and the powerful and unprincipled to wrest by force or fraud, from the comparably feeble and defenceless, wealth or property or dominion, richer pastures, more numerous herds, and a wider range of territory'.[38] In such trying circumstances, the British attempted to stabilize their frontiers by showing the flag, by manning a garrison, by sending a regiment, or even by annexing a territory or making a colony to prevent turbulence on or adjacent to the existing frontiers. Thus they had to control indiscriminate, lawless behaviour by whites not only against non-whites, but by whites against whites. To give but one example, Britain created the

PAX BRITANNICA: PEACE, FORCE AND WORLD POWER

colony of British Columbia in 1858 not to secure the gold in the ground, but to forestall California vigilantes from the chance of a revolution, one that would have led to a repetition of violence that was to the Colonial Office an all too obvious occurrence on the adjacent American frontier.

Precisely this sort of problem of turbulence led to British expansion of formal empire. When faced with the dilemma of letting those frontiersmen police themselves, or of intervening through means of authority, both civil and military, almost invariably the British chose to intervene. 'If colonists of European descent', Earl Grey argued in 1852, 'are to be left, unsupported by the power of the mother country, to rely solely on themselves for protection from fierce barbarians with whom they are placed in immediate contact, they must also be left to the unchecked exercise of those severe measures of self-defence which a position of so much danger will naturally dictate. Experience shows that in such circumstances measures of self-defence will degenerate into indiscriminate vengeance, and will lead to the gradual extermination of the less civilized race'.[34] In other words, the extension of law and order was inseparable from native trusteeship. And frequently—despite efforts to the contrary—it led to an extension of territorial jurisdiction. Thus, far from being acquired in a fit of absentmindedness as Seeley jested the British Empire grew for a variety of reasons, not least because it had to protect British interests from less desirable alternatives.

But what were to be the limits of such expansion? A Pacific or West Indian island was one thing, defined by its very beaches. An Asian continent was an altogether different matter. Witness the case of Assam, in northeast India. There it was virtually impossible to define the northeastern border of British authority. Tensions and turbulence existed among the various tribesmen of hill and valley. Officers such as Lieutenant Stewart, based on Chittagong, could find their heads as trophies to Poi insurgents in the Lushai area. In such circumstances, a retaliatory force would be obliged to strike hard to sustain the British presence. Stewart's murder in 1888 also led to that all too customary phenomenon: a new definition of extended boundaries. This meant establishing a new district, in Captain (later Commissioner) W. M. Kennedy's words, in order 'to stop raids and crimes along the borders of the Naga Hills and Sibsagar districts, which, of course, had an unsettling effect on those tribes directly under our rule, as well as to impose a barrier between our settled districts and the wild tribes beyond'. Kennedy went on to note that in the enlarged zone officers were not to interfere in local native affairs; rather they were only to punish cases of murder or to settle inter-village disputes. They could not even protect the villagers within their zone from raids by independent tribes beyond the boundary of British control. As he put it, 'it is laid down that "protection must depend on proximity and convenience"'.[40] Which is to say that when defined areas were established or re-established there were always ill-defined border areas or zones beyond. To cite another case, Upper Burma was 'pacified', that is invaded in 1885, and this was done, the chief commissioner of Burma explained, to bring orderly government with peace and security.[41] Southwest Persia offers a third case in point. In the early twentieth century the British sent military agents and railroad reconnaissance personnel to work with the local Persian traders and tribes. Chief among the objects was to carve out a sphere of influence in an oil-rich area fundamental to an Empire whose fleet would soon operate on diesel rather than coal.[42] A 'sphere of influence' might thereby be carved out to ensure British interests and keep German or French but especially Russian interests at bay. This might be accomplished peacefully. Invariably it was backed by force.

The peace by force

The *Pax Britannica* was never absolute or all-embracing. More and more we are beginning to realize that the late Victorian Empire existed by the consent of the governed. Much depended on the co-opting of elites, by keeping native princes in place wherever possible, by establishing empires within empires.[43] This was not necessary only to solve problems of doling out patronage in order to keep the system going, but of maintaining security, of keeping indigenous land holding systems, and of limiting metropolitan influences. A 'dual mandate' was a fiscal necessity as well as a shared human benefit in British East Africa and elsewhere. Then there is that little analysed pattern of empire of how the white dominions, so-called, consolidated power in their own hands, assumed control when and where the British left off, and extended their sway over possessions in some cases thousands of miles from their own capitals. Leaders in decolonization, they were also empire builders in the Canadian Arctic archipelago, among the Pacific islands, or even in the barren islands and continental wastes of Antarctica. These ex-colonies and neo-colonial states pronounced their own forms of *Pax*, the characteristics of which were born in the metropolis but nurtured and matured on the spot. Nonetheless, empires are based upon power, and through the state or official use of violence derives order, or an absence of anarchy.

This lengthy state of peace was actually a long era of colonial wars, some not so very 'small' as writers of this genre are wont to call them. These were the 'bush wars' of the Veldt, of the West African coastal zones, of the Canadian prairies, and of the New Zealand hills. By one count there were some 230 of these wars during Queen Victoria's reign. This tally is exclusive of all those countless gunboat actions which were an ongoing feature of Britannia's influence on distant coasts and among faraway islands. The *Pax* may have constituted a unique system of global influence, even dominance. However, this peace of empire was maintained, when the preliminary diplomacy of *lex talionis*, the law of retaliation, failed, by the violence of 'Queen Victoria's Little Wars'.

These 'savage wars of peace' in the British Empire constantly embarrassed Secretaries of State for War and the Colonies, more especially during the 1830s and 1840s when humanitarian tendencies among certain parliamentarians could make for the asking of uncomfortable questions in Lords and Commons. In southern Africa and in New Zealand cross-racial warfare persisted undiminished. Lord Glenelg, perhaps the most high-minded of the Colonial Secretaries of the early nineteenth century, noted in 1838 that colonial peace unavoidably meant colonial war. In an office memorandum, he explained at considerable length that most of these small wars were the product of British expansion, of the strong encroaching on the weak, and of the settler interfering

179

XIX

with the native. Paradoxically, he explained, though Britain was expected to take commerce and Christianity to the ends of the earth, the nation by its actions only invited the censure of the oppressed and the ridicule of British pioneers who at their own risk and largely at their own cost had gone outwards from the home islands to settle the Earth's theoretically unpopulated frontiers. 'The great principles of morality are of immutable and universal obligation', he wrote in his characteristically high-minded form, adding with a touch of sadness, 'and from them are deduced the laws of war. Whether we contend with a civilized or barbarous enemy, the gratuitious aggravation of the horrors of war on the plea of vengeance or retribution, or on any similar grounds is alike indefensible'.[44] By the very character of empire, the 'gratuitous aggravations' of which Glenelg complained were the consequence of frontier expansion. The Maoris of New Zealand, the Aborigines of Australia, the Bantu in southern Afria, the Plains and Pacific Coast Indians of Canada and British Columbia—all these peoples and others besides were the subject of British concerns and British guns, though in different ways according to geographical circumstance, to local trading practices and, not least, to ethnological characteristics.

In these wars of empire, these wars of peace, advances in technology (in which the British were frequent leaders) gave the imperial rulers the lead. When diplomacy failed not always was the field gun or the gunboat enough. 'Savage warfare' in British Columbia, southern Africa and New Zealand, to cite but three cases, could press the Crown's forces to frustrating limits and not always to successful conclusions. The effectiveness of well-drilled landing parties and gun crews on board a warship had limits. Native resistance was often strong and competent, and possessed the added advantage of local knowledge of terrain and conditions. Native techniques in war were surprising and puzzling; their means of communication with the enemy, unique and perplexing.[45] The influence of one of Her Majesty's ships spread no farther inland from salt water or river fairway than the range of shot, shell or rocket. Such armed authority penetrated no deeper than the endurance of footsore landing parties slogging through wet bush or fever-infested and swampy terrain. Nonetheless, a gun-carrying steamer constituted 'a powerful "political persuader", carrying fearful instruments of speech, in an age of progress!'.[46] A colonial gunboat also enhanced a governor's prestige and increased a colony's revenue. All other things being equal, steam power and rifled guns gave their possessors a keen edge of advantage. Not just in terms of arbitrary finality ought such instruments of war be discussed. The imbalance of weaponry, professional skill and finance, maintenance and logistical ability to deploy them at great distances between European forces and their Asian or African adversaries cannot be discounted.[47] A steam-powered warship could reach farther upriver or inshore than a sailing ship. It could attempt to check illicit whisky traffic or slave taking. It could assist missionary enterprise or some new native settlement scheme. Such 'tools of empire',[48] far from being mere symbols or means of dominance, spelled change. The use of such tools gratified the Victorians of that age into believing that they were 'improving' the non-European peoples when and wherever they settled or traded among them.

In almost every circumstance, law, that underpinning of the Empire of the *Pax*, was ineffective in itself. It had to be backed by force. This was as true in

PAX BRITANNICA: PEACE, FORCE AND WORLD POWER

the largest continental dominion—Canada—as it was in the smallest island colony or protectorate—Pitcairn.[49] Colonial and foreign office documents are riddled with the rhetoric of authority. 'It will, I think be conceded', the Western Pacific High Commissioner reported to his superior in London in 1911, 'that one of the cardinal principles upon which the administration of a new country should be based is that the Pax Britannica must be enforced. It is useless to endeavour to educate a savage people in order to lift them to a higher plane of civilization unless it is demonstrated that the Government can and will make the King's peace respected'.[50]

The enforcement of law so often brought the brutality of British imperial pre-eminence of which we have often heard so much. It was distasteful to the prac-titioners of the law at the time. Gunboat commanders could be high-handed, and they could also be high-minded. They did their duty and they did not always enjoy their work. They were miscast by Sir William Harcourt, jurist and parlia-mentarian, as 'the warlike classes', the armed agents of empire who bullied their way in scrapes with natives and extended British domains in distant places. They were, with few exceptions, Victorians of conscience. Some experienced naval officers such as the anti-pirate and anti-slavery patrol veterans Fairfax Moresby and Joseph Denman could be ruthlessly tough against indigenous peoples. At the same time they would regret the necessity of their military actions. 'These wretched creatures', a Royal Navy captain wrote plaintively of his punitive expedition in the Pacific Islands, 'have been hunted and worried till it will be long before they settle again. . . . I regret that my whole voyage in these islands has been one of apparently ruthless destruction, but no other course has been possible'.[51] A second officer, writing some years after an expedition against some British Columbia Indians, confessed that the excitement of the punitive raid to him as a young gunnery lieutenant served to suppress any twinge of conscience. Later he reflected on the meaning of the barbarities that he was undertaking for queen and country. The expedition, he wrote in a memoir, formed 'one of the myriad tragedies of the red man's collision with civilization'. Such was merely another instance when 'force was the last resort'.[52]

News of the armed peace of empire came back to the motherlands to haunt ministers of the Crown and to fuel the fires of complaint. Members and secre-taries of the Aborigines' Protection Society would address impassioned letters to the Colonial Office and to the British press calling for fair practices against Maoris, Aborigines or Bantus. Trusteeship was becoming a political issue for every informed reader, every church attender. Imperialism in which the Pax was at the centre was by the 1880s a political creed of thousands.[53]

At the pecuniary level, British parliamentarians worried about the costs of enforcing the Pax. Penny-pinching Chancellors of the Exchequer called for reductions in the cost of colonial government, especially self defence. They called, too, for controls on the costs of policing the seas and keeping garrisons in distant lands. Everywhere around the world 'claims of humanity' required the British to yield assistance. Continuous demands for 'showing the flag', putting down rebellions, or intimidating natives meant continual drains on the Treasury, despite parliamentary objections. It would be possible to calculate the fiscal cost of this police work. The navy estimates, voted by year, and tallied for the century beginning 1815 and deducting special armaments, particularly that

PAX BRITANNICA: PEACE, FORCE AND WORLD POWER

of the Crimean War, would give an approximate sum. In the 1820s and 1830s the naval defence of kingdom and empire was a bargain at an annual cost off 5–8 million pounds, less than half that of the army. The annual cost grew with the century. In the 1880s and 1890s large increases were being voted in parliament, but were even more mammoth in the next decade. Much of the cost was for police work, maintaining the *Pax*. In 1871, for instance, half of the naval expenditure went for policing the seas. If economies were to be effected, said Mr G. J. Goschen, MP, First Lord of the Admiralty during Gladstone's 1868 administration, overseas squadrons would have to be reduced and fewer duties undertaken for humanity in every corner of the earth. 'The fact is', he complained, 'that half of our expenditure is not for war service in the strict sense, but keeping the policy of the seas and protecting semi-barbarous and barbarous men against kidnapping and various forms of outrage. Philanthropy decidedly costs money'.[54] Gladstone would have preferred well-defined and approved purposes of actual service. This did not happen. The time had arrived, Lord Rosebery, the Foreign Secretary, said in 1893, when Britain could not 'afford to be the Knight Errant of the World, careering about to redress grievances and help the weak'.[55] In actuality, despite the trenchant reforms of the First Sea Lord, Sir John Fisher, the British were obliged to practise the arts of gunboat diplomacy as long as the Empire continued or treaty obligations persisted.[56] World power continued to draw the world's leading maritime state into innumerable problems, many of them not of their own making. These were, like the gratuitous aggravations of empire, the costly price of Admiralty.

The audit of peace

In poet laureate Austin's age those wise enough to look back on the previous century could see the essential paradox of the *Pax Britannica*. Winston Churchill seems content to have emphasized the benefits of a worldwide naval ascendancy, 'unchallengeable and unfeared'. The ascendancy lasting since the close of the Napoleonic and American war 'had not been misused', Churchill emphasized. In his words, 'As policeman of the oceans, the Royal Navy extirpated piracy, suppressed the slave trade, and offered to the men of all the lands a safe, free passage across the broad waters on their lawful occupations'.[57] Fair enough, but such influence was not effected without costs borne at home and abroad. And even if the foreign squadrons of the Royal Navy were as successful as Churchill would have us believe they were not without limits of effectiveness.

From the perspectives of our own times we must seek to see the British imperial ethos in the classic years of *Pax Britannica*, 1815 to 1914, less in terms of the absolutes of 'good' or 'evil'. It is high time we had an honest look at this process, this creation, this moment in time. When we have taken pains to re-examine that peculiar period of peace when Britain not only 'ruled the waves' but, when expediency dictated, 'waived the rules', when, too, we have examined the processes of power in all their influences, and when we have understood that Britain was not alone in this mission, one shared by France and the USA especially, we will be less critical of those persons and those ministries who in the search for law and order, for an end to anarchy, piracy, slavery, cannabalism and heathenism, made exertions and sacrifices to bring peace, justice and the rule of law, and in doing so wrote some of the most fascinatingly paradoxical pages in the history of humankind. As Lord Bauer pointed out in *The Times* of 24 April 1985, history has not served the western world very well, and many of those who ought to have understood the imperial process better, both on the giving and receiving ends, should stop seeing the imperial process as unequivocably exploitative.

Since the year 1945 and the close of the Second World War there has existed a general state of international relations devoid of world-wide conflict, though this is one generally characterized by regional conflict and bipolar ideological warfare. It is tempting to call this era the *Pax Americana*.[58] More correctly, and even then not with sufficient precision, it ought to be called a *Pax Atlantica*, an appellation given in 1951 by the celebrated student of, and propagandist for, air power James Monoly Spaight CB, CBE.[59] At the same time, it is well to remember that such a state of international peace among superpowers is commensurate with an existing balance of power between the North Atlantic Treaty Organization and the Warsaw Pact. Thus if and when we talk of a *Pax Americana* we cannot assume a general state of international peace marked by absence of overt hostilities between states. Moreover, we cannot rightly claim this to be owing to US power in its own right, no matter how significant that may be. For such preeminence depends considerably on the aid and consultation of allies and even on the stability of client states. It also depends on the prospects of frequent interference to that normal state of peace by a state of war. In eras of great power dominance 'small wars' are likely to continue. Struggles for control of distant, apparently invaluable islands and frozen wastelands or deserts are likely to persist. Piracy, hostage taking, and terrorism will likely occur. In the era of *Pax Americana* as in that of *Pax Britannica* the gunboat or its equivalent, the marine landing party, the airborne brigade, and the diplomatic agent and native collaborator continued to shape the direction of international affairs. In future much will depend on the toughness of heads of state, secretaries of state, agents and consuls, and on the character of the domestic political will that they represent, to maintain a world 'pax'.

Notes and references

1   *Journal of the Royal United Service Institution*, Vol XXX, No 146, 1886, pp 837–861.

2   He enjoyed a wide-ranging service as governor in Queensland, New Zealand, the Colony of Victoria, Mauritius and Hong Kong. Stanley Lane-Poole, ed, *Thirty Years of Colonial Government From the Despatches and Letters of the Rt Hon Sir G. F. Bowen*, 2 vols, London, 1889. Also *Dictionary of National Biography, Supplement*, Volume 1, pp 241–242. Bowen, *The Federation of the British Empire*, London, 1886, 2nd ed, 1889. Bowen was the author of numerous works, including *Ithaca*, 1850.

3   *Journal of the Royal United Service Institution*, May 1886, p 865. Bowen was a visionary, and shared with Captain Colomb, F. P. de Labilliere, William Edward Forster, J. Denistoun Wood, and others the idea of an imperial federation. His scheme was impractical owing to political realities, both in the home islands and the self-governing colonies. Trevor Reese, *History of the Royal Common-*

XIX

PAX BRITANNICA: PEACE, FORCE AND WORLD POWER

wealth Society, 1868–1968, Oxford University Press, London, 1969, pp 66–70. It was precisely his perspectives on dominion contributions to the Royal Navy which led zealously independent Canadian and Australian politicians to establish their own naval services in 1910 and 1912 respectively.

4   On the characteristics of British and US imperialism, on the forces shaping the interrelated histories of these global powers, and on the possible choices facing foreign policy makers of these states, see the introductory work, Tony Smith, *The Pattern of Imperialism: The United States, Great Britain, and the Late-Industrializing World Since 1815*, Cambridge University Press, Cambridge, 1981.

5   Lord Beloff, 'The consequences in US/British relations of the dissolution of the British Empire and the assumption of world-wide commitments by the United States—a British view', paper for the conference on *Issues in the Third World: the End of Empire, North-South Relations, and World Stability*, organized jointly by the Ditchley Foundation and the Woodrow Wilson International Center for Scholars at the Wilson Center, Washington, DC, March 1985, p 1.

6   William Roger Louis, 'American anti-colonialism and the dissolution of the British Empire', *International Affairs*, Vol 61, No 3, Summer 1985, pp 395–420. And when addressing the question of the health of the Commonwealth, Lord Beloff remarked: 'It was a noble ideal—the Commonwealth—a pity it failed'. M. Beloff, 'The Commonwealth as history', *Journal of Imperial and Commonwealth History*, Vol 1, No 1, 1972, p 111.

7   John B. Hattendort and Robert S. Jordan, eds, *Maritime Strategy and the Balance of Power: Britain and America in the Twentieth Century*, St Martin's Press, New York, 1989, and, for an earlier and still irreplaceable study, Harold and Margaret Sprout, *Toward a New Order of Sea Power: American Naval Policy and the World Scene, 1918–1922*, 1943 ed, Greenwood Press, New York, 1969, chs 1 and 2.

8   Correlli Barnett, *The Collapse of British Power*, reprint, Allan Sutton, London, 1987; and, by the same author, *The Audit of War: The Illusion and Reality of Britain as a Great Nation*, Macmillan, London, 1986.

9   J. G. Darwin, 'The fear of falling: British politics and imperial decline since 1900', *Transactions of the Royal Historical Society*, 5th series, Vol 36, 1986, pp 27–43. 'Certainly when it comes to dealing with empires, historians betray a fascination with decay that is almost pathological—and often not simply with the nature and causes of decline but with the exact moment when it began—a somewhat futile enterprise in an enjoyable parlour game', *ibid*, p 27.

10 Cambridge University Press, 1985. These two fields of historiography tend to push aside two others well known to imperial/colonial historians. The first is the discussion of 'informal empire', initiated by C. R. Fay, codified by Robinson and Gallagher, challenged by D. C. M. Platt among others, and explained in its peripheral connotations by Professor D. K. Fieldhouse. This discussion of the relations of economics, diplomacy and territorial expansion relegated to a minor position C. A. Bodelsen and R. Schuyler's studies of mid-Victorian imperialism. The second is the work of scholars on the study of decolonization (or, on the other side, nation-formation) of which the history of Canada, Australia, New Zealand and even South Africa in the first phase, so to speak, bears not a little in common with India, Ghana, Nigeria or Jamaica in the second, ·and more recently Zambia, Barbados or Tonga in the third.

11 Lord Beloff advises me that the *Pax* was kept up long after 1914, and perhaps to as late as the fall of Singapore, the sinking of the *Prince of Wales* and *Repulse*, and even Suez. But I remain convinced that 1914 is the most decisive date and marks the end of the British Empire and the beginning of the Commonwealth. And it could be that the air age, despite Britain's designs to maximize air power's

XIX

PAX BRITANNICA: PEACE, FORCE AND WORLD POWER

military effectiveness and authoritative benefits, spelled an end to the old regime.

12   C. J. Bartlett, *Great Britain and Sea Power, 1815–1853*, Clarendon Press, Oxford, 1963. Gerald S. Graham, *The Politics of Naval Supremacy: Studies in British Maritime Ascendancy*, Cambridge University Press, Cambridge, 1965, pp 108–110.

13   G. H. Francis, *Opinions and Policy of Lord Palmerston*, London, 1852, p 413.

14   Viceroy Curzon devised a strategy to let the mountain tribes govern themselves, and to withdraw British forces to advanced positions, leaving tribal militias, commanded by Europeans, to keep the peace! This was 'setting the poacher to act as game keeper', in the words of Sir Evelyn Howell, resident of Wazinistan. Victoria Schofield, *Every Rock, Every Hill: The Plain Tale of the North-East Frontier and Afghanistan*, Buchan and Enright, London, 1984, p 150.

15   Bartlett, *Great Britain and Sea Power,* pp x–xi.

16   C. Northcote Parkinson, *Edward Pellew, Viscount Exmouth, Admiral of the Red*, Methuen, London, 1934, pp 419–472.

17   *Hansard*, 3d series, CXII, 25 June 1850. For a discussion of this debate, see A. P. Thornton, *The Imperial Idea and its Enemies: A Study in British Power*, 2nd ed, Macmillan, London, 1985, pp 2–4.

18   John Morley, *Life of Gladstone*, 3 vols, Macmillan, London, 1904, Vol 1, pp 368–370; also, Philip Magnus, *Gladstone, A Biography*, John Murray, London, 1954, p 95.

19   Grace Fox, *British Admirals and Chinese Pirates, 1832–1869*, Kegan Paul, Trench, Trubner and Co, London, 1940, p 147; also G. A. Wood, 'Pax Britannica: The Royal Navy around 1860', in *W. P. Morrell, A Tribute*, University of Otago Press, Dunedin, 1978.

20   For an example of this, see Sherard Osborn, *Quedah*; or *Stray Leaves from a Journal in Malayan Waters*, London, 1857, new ed, 1865.

21   Correspondence relating to Aden, *Parliamentary Papers*, 1839, Vol XL, No 37. Robert J. Gavin, *Palmerston's Policy Towards East and West Africa, 1830–1865*, PhD thesis, Cambridge University, 1959, pp 83–86.

22   C. U. Aitchison, *A Collection of Treaties, Engagements and Sanads relating to India and Neighbouring Countries*, Vol XII, No 909, gives the agreements with native chiefs; also, G. S. Graham, *Great Britain and the Indian Ocean, 1810–1850*, Clarendon Press, Oxford, 1967; J. B. Kelly, *Britain and the Persian Gulf, 1795–1880*, Clarendon Press, Oxford, 1968; Lt-Col Sir Arnold T. Wilson, *The Persian Gulf. . .* , Clarendon Press, Oxford, 1928, ch 13; and T. J. Bennett, 'The past and present connection of England with the Persian Gulf', *Journal Society of the Arts*, June 1902. Also C. J. Low, *History of the Indian Navy (1613–1863)*, 2 vols, London, 1877.

23   Frank Broeze, 'The shipowner of Asia since 1815', paper read at the National Maritime Museum, September 1984, p 3. Principal beneficiary of the Britannic peace was Sayyid Said, Sultan of Muscat (after 1832 he resided in Zanzibar). He kept a large fleet of armed vessels of predominantly western design, and extended his trading throughout the Indian Ocean and China Seas.

24   Fox, *British Admirals and Chinese Pirates*, p 190.

25   D. F. Rennie, *British Arms in North China and Japan: Peking 1860, Kagosima*, London, 1864. Also, Grace E. Fox, *Britain and Japan, 1858–83*, Clarendon Press, Oxford, 1969.

26   L. R. Wright, *British Policy in the South China Sea Area, 1860–1900, with Special Reference to Sarawak, Brunea and North Borneo*, PhD thesis, University of London, 1963.

27   Barry M. Gough, *Gunboat Frontier: British Maritime Authority and North-west Coast Indians, 1846–1890*, University of North Columbia Press, Vancouver,

185

PAX BRITANNICA: PEACE, FORCE AND WORLD POWER

1984, pp 85–94.
28 Lieutenant A. B. Kemball, *Extracts from the Records of the Residency at Bashire*, Bombay Selection, No XXIV, 1956; quoted in Wilson, *Persian Gulf*, pp 215–216.
29 Wilson, *Persian Gulf*, p 216.
30 Memorandum by Palmerston, 6 December 1846, FO 84/647; also, Kelly, *Britain and the Persian Gulf*, p 583.
31 Philip H. Colomb, *Slave Catching in the Indian Ocean*, London, 1873. Raymond Howell, *The Royal Navy and the Slave Trade*, St Martin's Press, New York, 1987.
32 Quoted, Wilson, *Persian Gulf*, p 223.
33 *Ibid*, p 230.
34 Jean Usher, *William Duncan of Metlakatla: A Victorian Missionary in British Columbia*, National Museums of Canada Publications in History, Ottawa, No 5, 1974, p 9. On the Navy's unofficial support for missionaries, see my *Gunboat Frontier*, ch 12.
35 Report from the Select Committee on Aborigines (British Settlements), *Parliamentary Papers*, 1837, Vol VII, No 425, p 76.
36 Grey to Cathcart, 2 February 1852, 'Correspondence relative to the state of the Kaffir tribes, and to the recent outbreak on the eastern frontier of the colony', *Parliamentary Papers*, 1852, Vol XXXIII, No 1428, p 259; W. Ross Johnston, *Sovereignty and Protection: A Study of British Jurisdictional Imperialism in the late Nineteenth Century*, Duke University Press, Durham, NC, 1973, p 10.
37 Quoted in C. C. Eldridge, *England's Mission: The Imperial Idea in the Age of Gladstone and Disraeli, 1868–1880*, Macmillan, London, 1973, pp xv–xvi.
38 Quoted in Johnston, *Sovereignty and Protection*, p 15.
39 Quoted in Johnston, *Sovereignty and Protection*, p 15.
40 Major General D. K. Palit, *Sentinels of the North-East: The Assam Rifles*, Palit and Palit, New Delhi, 1984, p 47.
41 Sir Charles Crosthwaite, *The Pacification of Burma*, Edward Arnold, London, 1912, preface.
42 Sir Arnold Wilson, *S. W. Persia: A Political Officer's Diary, 1907–1914*, Oxford University Press, London, 1941.
43 See D. A. Low, *Lion Rampant: Essays in the Study of British Imperialism*, Frank Cass, London, 1973, chs 1 and 3.
44 Quoted in James Morris, *Heaven's Command: An Imperial Progress*, Harcourt Brace Jovanovich, New York, 1973, p 86.
45 Capt L. F. Rennie, 'Savage warfare', *Journal of the Royal United Service Institution*, Vol L, No 346, December 1906, pp 1531–1533.
46 Col W. F. B. Laurie, *Our Burma Wars and Relations with Burma*, London, 1880, p 109.
47 Michael Howard, 'War and technology', *Journal of the Royal United Services Institute for Defence Studies*, Vol 132, No 4, December 1987, p 20.
48 Daniel R. Headrick, *The Tools of Empire: Technology and European Imperialism in the Nineteenth Century*, Oxford University Press, New York, 1982; also, his *The Tentacles of Progress: Technology Transfer in the Age of Imperialism*, Oxford University Press, New York, 1988.
49 The *Pax* even obtained among the mutineer residents of Pitcairn Island. Captain W. H. Bruce of HMS *Imogene* left there this salutary reminder, a Proclamation of 9 December 1837: 'Captain Bruce recommends to the inhabitants of this Island, and particularly to the three Europeans residing on it, to follow the religious and moral course of life and conduct in which the natives have been instructed and which the world of God points out in the Bible.
Captain Bruce will represent to his Superiors the necessity of a person of character and ability being sent from England to preside over the interests of

PAX BRITANNICA: PEACE, FORCE AND WORLD POWER

the island, but should his recommendation not be successful the inhabitants may be assured that a ship of war will be ordered to the island to enquire into all complaints, and should any crimes be committed to punish all offenders'. (Bruce to Commodore Sullivan, 2 January 1838, Adm 1/1586, Cap B159, PRO.)

50   Commissioner May to L. V. Harcourt, 8 December 1911, Western Pacific High Commission IC 2161/1911, quoted in James Boutilier, 'Killing the government: imperial policy and the pacification of Malaita', in Margaret Rodman and Matthew Cooper, eds, *The Pacification of Melanesia*, University of Michigan Press, Ann Arbor, 1979, p 44.

51   Quoted in Anthony Preston and John Major, *Send a Gunboat! A Study of the Gunboat and its Role in British Policy, 1854–1904*, Longmans, London, 1971, p 8.

52   Admiral John Moresby, *Two Admirals: Sir Fairfax Moresby and John Moresby, A Record of a Hundred Years*, new and revised ed, Methuen, London, 1913, p 107. Apologists of empire have indeed tended to underestimate the use of force. See, however, Low, *Lion Rampant*, pp 21–24.

53   Or, in the words of A. P. Thornton, 'In the last generation of the Victorian era, many men thought they had found just such an idea. It became their faith, that it was the role of the British Empire to lead the world in the arts of civilisation, to bring light to the dark places, to teach the true political method, to nourish and to protect the liberal tradition. It was to act as trustee for the weak, and bring arrogance low. It was to represent in itself the highest aims of human society. It was to command, and deserve, a status and prestige shared by no other. It was to captivate the imagination and hold fast the allegiance of the million by the propagation of peculiar myths—one among which was the figure of Queen Victoria herself, who became depersonalised, as an idea: the idea of the Great White Queen. While encouraging and making profit from the spirit of adventure, it was nevertheless to promote the interests of peace and commerce. While it was to gain its greatest trophies in war, it was to find its main task in serving the ends of justice, law and order. It was an idea that moved, an idea that expanded, an idea that had to continue to move and to expand in order to retain its vitality and its virtue'. (*The Imperial Idea and Its Enemies.*)

54   Quoted in C. J. Bartlett, 'The mid-Victorian reappraisal of naval policy', in K. Bourne and D. C. Watt, eds, *Studies in International History: Essays Presented to W. Norton Medlicott*, Archon, Hamden, Connecticut, 1967, p 205.

55   Marquess of Crewe, *Lord Rosebery*, 2 vols, Macmillan, London, 1931, Vol 2, p 426.

56   Sometimes they called on dominion help to enforce the *Pax*. In the 1930s, to cite one case, the Royal Canadian Navy answered the Admiralty's request to police the coast of British Honduras and to land shore parties on Caribbean islands in support of the Empire's interests. In 1947, to cite another example, the display of force against recalcitrant Pacific Islanders showed that the principle was effectively the same. In this instance the Royal Navy and the Royal Australian Navy combined forces to check the progress of 'Marching Rule', a quasi-nationalist movement among Solomon Islanders which employed terrorism and theft in order to achieve its ends. With respect to treaty rights the most significant example is the *Amethyst* affair, or Yangtse Incident. Malcolm H. Murfett, 'British naval policy on the Yangtse in 1949: a case of diplomacy on the rocks', *War and Society*, Vol 6, No 1, May 1988, pp 79–92.

57   Foreword to Sir Roger Keyes, *Adventures Ashore and Afloat*, White Lion, London, 1973.

58   'Like its predecessors of Minos, Athens, Rome, Venice, Holland and Britain, the United States found itself the only surviving maritime power capable of maintaining order on the seas, enforcing international law, and leading multinational

efforts to check piracy (especially hijacking at sea and in the air) and smuggling (arms and drugs) and in promoting weather reporting and rescue at sea. By its formidable military strength at sea and in the air the United States has balanced the continental powers of Russia and China and policed the oceans of the world. Strategically then, the era can be aptly regarded as the *Pax Americana*.' Clark G. Reynolds, *Command of the Sea: The History and Strategy of Maritime Empires*, new ed, 2 vols, Krieger, Malabar, Florida, 1985, Vol 2, pp 546–547.

59   J. M. Spaight, 'Pax Atlantica', *Journal of the Royal United Service Institution*, Vol XCVI, No 583, August 1951, pp 434–439. For a list of Spaight's many works on air power including *The Sky's The Limit*, see *Who Was Who*, Vol VI, London, 1972.

INDEX